10-15-73

10-15-73

# MARX AND THE MARXISTS

# Marx and the Marxists

AN OUTLINE OF PRACTICE
AND THEORY

DAVID CHILDS

LONDON/ERNEST BENN LIMITED

NEW YORK/BARNES & NOBLE BOOKS

First published 1973 by Ernest Benn Limited
25 New Street Square, Fleet Street, London, EC4A 3JA

and Harper & Row Publishers Inc.
Barnes & Noble Import Division
10 East 53rd Street, New York 10022

Distributed in Canada by
The General Publishing Company Limited, Toronto

© David Childs 1973

Printed in Great Britain

ISBN 0 510–26260–0
ISBN 06–491121–7 (U.S.A.)

# 1773338

# *Contents*

# Preface

A S the (incomplete) bibliography at the end of this book shows, there is no shortage of books on Marx and Engels or the movements which they inspired. Yet remarkably few books have attempted to narrate how Marxian communism developed from the lofty ideals in the mind of a Jewish bourgeois Rhinelander, to the mighty empires, and diverse movements, we know today as 'Communist', 'Marxist', or 'Socialist'. Years of lecturing on the subject have convinced the writer of the need for such narration for the general reader.

Any attempt of this kind must oversimplify here and there, and neglect aspects of the subject of great interest to the specialist. The writer is well aware of the limitations of his exposition of Marxist theory. Those with a particular interest in, for instance, the young Marx, will be disappointed. And those concerned with modern Communist movements will probably feel something should have been said about that curious phenomenon the Finnish Communist movement. Perhaps too, more could have been said about the slick, sophisticated Italian Communists. Limitations of space have forced the writer to be selective. Here the aim has been to tell what Marx and Engels actually wrote, how their immediate successors interpreted this, and how the main movements claiming to represent Marxist ideas have acted up to our own time. If certain original Marxist thinkers – Roger Garaudy, György Lukács, Ernest Mandel among them – have been neglected, this is because, up to now, they have had little influence on the big battalions of Moscow, Peking, Havana, or Belgrade.

The writer has been interested in Marxism and communism for over twenty years. During that time he has visited all the European Communist states, with the single exception of Albania, getting to know the German Democratic Republic rather better than the others. He has met many leading Marxists from these and other countries, as well as even more rank-and-

7

filers. In addition, he has tried to learn from the researches of the army of authorities cited in this volume. The greatest political lesson he has learned has been, as Engels put it, that 'people who boasted that they had made a revolution have always seen the next day that they had no idea what they were doing, that the revolution *made* did not in the least resemble the one they would have liked to make'.[1] And that, therefore, as Bertrand Russell wrote, 'it is by slower and less showy methods that the new world must be built'.[2] Secondly, he is convinced, again with Russell, that those who stand out against communism must do so, 'not from love of ancient injustice, but in the name of the free spirit of Man'.[3]

I would like to express my warm appreciation to Professor Leonard Schapiro for commenting on Chapter 5, and to Professor Ghita Ionescu for reading Chapters 7 and 8, and to them both for their encouraging words on the project as a whole. In addition, I must thank Mr Roderick MacFarquhar, former editor of the *China Quarterly*, for his comments on Chapter 9, and Professor Henryk Katz, formerly of Lodz University in Poland, for giving me his views on Chapter 10. Of course, I alone must bear the responsibilities for any errors and shortcomings which remain. Finally, I would like to thank Mr Hugh McKenzie of the Derbyshire WEA, and the students on the course on Marxism held at Alfreton Hall, in the winter of 1968–69. Their keen interest led the author in the direction of writing this book.

D.C.

*University of Nottingham*
*April 1972*

NOTES

[1] Quoted R. V. Daniels, *Red October: The Bolshevik Revolution of 1917* (London, 1967).
[2] Bertrand Russell, *The Practice and Theory of Bolshevism* (London, 1951), p. 130.
[3] ibid., p. 18.

# List of Abbreviations

| | |
|---|---|
| ADAV | Allgemeine Deutsche Arbeiterverein |
| API | Acción Popular Independiente |
| AVH | Államvédelmi Hatóság |
| CCP | Chinese Communist Party |
| CFDT | Confédération française et démocratique du travail |
| CGT | Confédération générale du travail |
| CIA | Central Intelligence Agency |
| CIO | Congress of Industrial Organizations |
| CNT | Confederación Nacional del Trabajo |
| CPSU | Communist Party of the Soviet Union |
| DFU | Deutsche Friedensunion |
| DKP | Deutsche Kommunistischepartei |
| FBI | Federal Bureau of Investigation |
| GDR | German Democratic Republic |
| ILO | International Labour Office |
| IWA | International Workingmen's Association |
| JCR | Jeunesse Communiste Revolutionnaire |
| KPD | Kommunistische Partei Deutschlands |
| KVP | Kasernierte Volkspolizei |
| MAPU | Movimento de Acción Popular Unitaria |
| MAU | Mouvement d'Action Universitaire |
| NEP | New Economic Policy |
| NKVD | Narodnyi Komissariat Vnutrennikh Del |
| NLR | *New Left Review* |
| NPD | Nationaldemokratische Partei Deutschlands |
| NSDAP | Nationalsozialistische Deutsche Arbeiterpartei |
| ORI | Organizaciones Revolucionarias Integradas |
| PCI | Partito Communista Italiano |
| PLA | People's Liberation Army |
| POF | Parti Ouvrier Français |
| POUM | Partido Obrero de Unificación Marxista |
| PSI | Partito Socialista Italiano |
| PSP | Partido Socialista Popular |

9

| | |
|---|---|
| PURS | Partido Unido de la Revolución Socialista |
| SAD | Socialistische Arbeiterpartei Deutschlands |
| SDS | Sozialistischer Deutsche Studentenbund |
| SED | Sozialistische Einheitspartei Deutschlands |
| SEW | Sozialistische Einheitspartei West Berlins |
| SHB | Sozialdemokratische Hochschulbund |
| SLP | Socialist Labor Party |
| SPD | Sozialdemokratische Partei Deutschlands |
| TUC | Trades Union Congress |
| UJC (M-L) | Union des jeunesses communistes marxistes-leninistes |
| USPD | Unabhängige Sozialdemokratische Partei Deutschlands |

# I

## The Marxism of Marx and Engels

IN 1968, on the 150th anniversary of the birth of Karl Marx, official celebrations took place in his homeland, Germany. But that country is divided, the governments of the two halves not recognizing each other. Both sides appropriated Marx: in the West as a part of their heritage; in the East, as the most important part. Meanwhile, in two of the world's most powerful states, the USSR and China, celebrations were also held. The governments of both claimed to be the true heirs of Marx's ideas and each reviled the other in the most scathing terms. And they did not stop at verbal invective. The world's major self-styled Marxist powers used tommy-gun and tank, as well as chapter and verse, to reinforce their rival claims. In that same anniversary year Soviet tanks were ordered against another Marxist regime, that of Alexander Dubček in Prague. Moscow regarded the Marxists of Czechoslovakia as heretics, and was prepared to risk war to back up its own infallibility dogma. Some other Marxists, on the campuses of Berkeley, Belgrade, and West Berlin, at the Sorbonne and the London School of Economics, in the jungles of Ceylon and South America, or in dingy rooms in London's Clapham High Street, do not regard any of these regimes as Marxist. Politicians, party bosses, and bureaucrats can quote Marxist texts, but only *they* understand them!

All this is in contradiction to what ought to have happened – from the Marxist point of view. For Marx claimed to have discovered a set of scientific laws governing the development of Mankind, the 'laws of motion of modern society'.

One wonders whether Marx and Engels would have been exasperated by the noise of their self-proclaimed disciples arguing among themselves, or whether they would have been too exhilarated at the thought of hundreds of millions of people, some willingly, some unwillingly, proclaiming their doctrines to care.

Before trying to unravel the squabbles of the modern Marxists let us go back to the beginning, and attempt to outline the original doctrines, and say something, albeit briefly, about the two men behind those doctrines.

### I. WHO WERE MARX AND ENGELS?

It is wellnigh impossible to present objective and living portraits of Marx and Engels. Both men became legends in their own lifetimes and were treated as such by their friends, and largely ignored by everyone else. Both were subject to canonization after their deaths so that their devotees reinterpreted the lives of the two according to their own political, intellectual, and moral standards. Since 1917 this process has been pursued more consciously and more rigorously. And as most of the original documents relating to the two revolutionaries are under lock and key in Moscow, the process of separating the men from their legends has become more daunting than ever. The greatest difficulty of all, however, in sketching lifelike portraits of the founders of 'Scientific Socialism' has nothing to do with the lack of adequate material. It is that we inevitably know something about the theories of Marx and Engels before we read about the men who thought out those theories. We therefore tend to be prejudiced for or against them before we have ever read a line about their private lives.

Karl Marx, born in Trier in 1818, came from a long line of rabbis. His father was something of a rebel. Influenced by the ideas of Napoleonic France, father Marx broke with the family tradition, and was converted, for career reasons, to the Prussian state Church after his part of the Rhineland was put under Prussian rule. He carried on a highly successful legal practice in Trier. Karl's mother was a Dutch Jewess whose brother later set up the electrical company of Philips.

In the small town of Trier Marx's father was a respected man and the young Karl does not appear to have had any material or psychological problems.

After an indifferent school career Karl Marx led a 'gay and dissipated life'[1] at Bonn University. A year later, in October 1836, he was admitted to Berlin University where he spent some four years. It was there that he came into contact with discontented, radical intellectuals, and Hegelian ideas. Let us pause here to consider what Marx got from Hegel.

The German philosopher Georg Friedrich Wilhelm Hegel (1770–1831) believed that ideas, not things, were the true realities of our world. He saw these ideas as constantly developing as a result of dialectical debate, a process of affirmation, contradiction, and reconciliation of the opposing ideas in a higher unity. Marx was also influenced by the materialism of Ludwig Feuerbach (1804–72). He developed from the dialectical method of Hegel and the materialism of Feuerbach a world view which became known as Dialectical Materialism. Put simply Marx held 'that matter existed before mind, that in the course of its evolution it became living and subsequently, in the brains of animals, thinking'.[2] He had stood Hegel's dialectic on its head, as he put it, by relating it to things rather than ideas. As Engels later explained:

In this way . . . the revolutionary side of Hegelian philosophy was again taken up and at the same time freed from the idealist trimmings which with Hegel had prevented its consistent execution. The great basic thought that the world is not to be comprehended as a complex of ready-made *things*, but as a complex of *processes*, in which the things apparently stable no less than their mind images in our heads, the concepts, go through an uninterrupted change of coming into being and passing away, in which, in spite of all seeming accidentality and of all temporary retrogression, a progressive development asserts itself in the end – this great fundamental thought has, especially since the time of Hegel, so thoroughly permeated ordinary consciousness that in this generality it is now scarcely ever contradicted. But to acknowledge this fundamental thought in words and to apply it in reality in detail to each domain of investigation are two different things. If, however, investigation always proceeds from this standpoint, the demand for final solutions and eternal truths ceases once for all; one is always conscious of the necessary limitation of all acquired knowledge, of the fact that it is conditioned by the circumstances in which it was acquired. On the other hand, one no longer permits oneself to be imposed upon by the antitheses, insuperable for the still common old metaphysics, between true and false, good and bad, identical and different, necessary and accidental. One knows that these antitheses have only a relative validity; that that which is recognized now as true has also its latent false side which will later manifest itself, just as that which is now regarded as false has also its true side by virtue of which it could previously be regarded as true. One knows that what is maintained to be necessary is composed of sheer accidents and that the so-called accidental is the form behind which necessity hides itself – and so on.[3]

Today we accept that even cherished scientific truths are not quite as true as they once seemed, that knowledge becomes obsolete, that truth is often more complex than it seems, that abstract ideas are not eternal in that they are subject to re-interpretation by succeeding generations, and that change is a normal feature of society. In that sense we agree with Marx and Engels. However, there is a negative side to 'thinking dialectic-ally'. This is the way in which it was used, particularly by Stalin, to justify abrupt changes of policy. When Stalin agreed to the Pact with Hitler in 1939 party members had to remember that 'that which is recognized now as true has also its latent false side which will later manifest itself'.

Marx was awarded a doctorate from Jena University in April 1841, when he was twenty-three, for a dissertation on Greek philosophy. Just over two years later he was on his way to Paris, having earned a reputation as a liberal journalist. With him was Jenny von Westphalen, whom he had married a short time before. She was the girl next door, an intelligent, beautiful, aristocrat of Prussian-Scottish background, and four years older than Marx. It was her father who had first acquainted Marx with the ideas of the French socialist Saint-Simon.

In terms of his intellectual development, his years in Paris, 1843–45, were the most decisive in his life. In Paris he underwent his final intellectual transformation.[4] There he met the poet Heinrich Heine, the anarchist Bakunin, the socialist Proudhon, and the man without whom Marxism might have died in infancy, Friedrich Engels.[5]

Like Marx, Engels was the son of a wealthy family. As he was not Jewish, there was even less cause in his 'objective situation' for him to become a revolutionary. His father was a textile-mill owner in business in Barmen, near Wuppertal, and Manchester. Later Engels claimed to have been greatly influenced by what he saw of the squalid lives of the workers in his home town. After a mediocre performance at secondary school he embarked upon a commercial career; whether this was the result of his own in-clination or his father's is not clear. In 1841, at the age of twenty-one, he anticipated the draft and volunteered for a year's service in a Prussian artillery regiment. He had long been interested in things military, and his service gave him the chance of spending a year in the Prussian capital, Berlin. Like Marx before him he was infected by the ideas of the 'Young Hegelians', and, already publishing, anonymously, poems, articles, and pamphlets, he in turn influenced them. The next great influence on Engels was Moses Hess, a Rhinelander, a Jew, a visionary, and the son of a manufacturer. He wanted to 'abolish the opposition of pauperism and plutocracy'.[6] He believed in the movement of history towards this end and he criticized the Hegelian philosophy of history for not attempting to work out 'the future from the past and the present and proceeding to influence its formation'.[7] This idea was to become an intrinsic part of the Marxist system. It was Hess who made communism credible and acceptable to Engels. It was also he who convinced him that he should go to England to study the Chartists and working-class life. Once again Engels was responding to the same stimulus as Marx who had already come to admire the ideas of Hess. A fourth great influence on Engels was the writings of Heine, Eugène Sue, George Sand, Dickens, and Disraeli. Their themes 'blended at once with the indelible memories of his childhood in the industrial towns'.[8]

When Engels left Germany for England in November 1842 he had his father's blessing, for he was going to gain more insight into the world of commerce from the vantage point of his father's firm in Manchester. Engels senior did not know about his son's other interest in going to Manchester. The fruit of this first period in England, which lasted until August 1844, was the socialist classic *The Condition of the Working Class in England*.

To anyone interested in the modern world in the 1840s Manchester was a fascinating place to be. It was the showpiece of the Industrial Revolution, a modern wonder of the world. In 1840 there were perhaps a quarter of a million cotton-factory operatives in Lancashire and perhaps a hundred thousand handloom weavers.[9] Thousands of others worked in industries which depended on cotton, such as machine-building, construction, coal-mining, and transport. The first factory with looms powered by steam had opened in Manchester as recently as 1806. In addition to being the key centre of industrial revolution, Manchester looked like being the place where political revolution would break out. If England, in the sixty years after 1789, was to have a revolution like that in France, most observers of the English scene believed it would erupt in Manchester.[10] For some time Chartism appeared likely to lead such a revolution. Chartism, 'a snowball movement which gathered together local grievances and sought to give them common expression in a nation wide agitation',[11] clearly meant different things to different men. But at its most coherent, it sought to introduce political democracy – universal male adult suffrage, secret ballot, annual Parliaments, etc. – so that a Parliament which would remedy the grievances of 'the People' could be elected. In Manchester Chartist agitation developed out of the commercial depression which followed the collapse of the boom of 1836. An estimated fifty thousand workers in the Manchester area alone were unemployed or on short time by June 1837. Many of these were Irish immigrants, many were handloom weavers. For them Chartism was 'a knife-and-fork question, a bread and cheese question', as the Chartist leader J. R. Stephens (1805–79) put it. This was the world Engels set out to describe and analyse in his first major work.

The book, *The Condition of the Working Class in England*, contains vivid descriptions based on personal reconnaissance, such as the one of the writer's own home town:

> Bolton . . . is even in the finest weather a dark, unattractive hole in spite of the fact that, except for the factories, its sides are formed by low one- and two-storied houses. Here, as everywhere, the old part of the town is especially ruinous and miserable. A dark-coloured body of water, which leaves the beholder in doubt whether it is a brook or a long string of stagnant puddles, flows through the town and contributes its share to the total pollution of the air.[12]

Engels's work is also distinguished by its clever use of the many official reports. For instance, he quotes from an official report showing that the poor died younger than the upper classes. In 1840 in Liverpool, the average age at death of the 'upper classes, gentry, professional men, etc., was thirty-five'. Businessmen and better-placed handicraftsmen died on average at twenty-two. But the average age at death of the operatives, day-labourers, 'and serviceable class in general', was fifteen years.[13]

Occasionally Engels admitted that the picture was not one of unrelieved desolation,[14] but the emphasis was very much on the well-known horrors of the time. Modern economic historians contest the view, for which not only Engels was responsible, that

the conditions of the 'English industrial worker' got worse as a result of the Industrial Revolution. Before the arrival of the modern factory system, the handloom weavers, according to Engels, lived 'in silent vegetation' in a condition that was 'cosily romantic', but not worthy of human beings.[15] His point was to show that this alleged worsening was part of a historical process which would lead to social revolution. At the end of the book he concluded that there was a war of 'the poor against the rich' in England, it was 'too late' to reach a peaceful solution. The classes were divided more and more sharply, the workers' bitterness and resistance grew, 'and soon a slight impulse will suffice to set the avalanche in motion'.[16]

The point at issue was not whether conditions were bad, but whether they were worse than they had been, whether they must get worse still, and whether they could be remedied without a violent revolution. More research into pre-industrial conditions made Engels's first proposition appear doubtful, future developments proved his prognostications wrong. In the preface to the 1892 edition he was forced to admit the book 'bears the stamp of his youth'[17] and that England had 'outgrown the juvenile state of capitalist exploitation'.[18] He went on to admit that 'there was temporary improvement even for the great mass' of workers, and a 'permanent improvement' for the 'factory hands' and those in the 'great Trades' Unions': the engineers, carpenters, joiners, bricklayers, and so on.[19] The 'great mass' of workers, however, had not improved their lot, and remained 'as low as ever, if not lower'. These were those in the East End of London, and the other large towns, and 'in the smaller towns and in the agricultural districts'.[20] Clearly Engels was having difficulty in upholding the view that the conditions of the workers must inevitably get worse, yet he had to try to square this position by reference to an ill-defined 'aristocracy of labour', on the one hand, and an even vaguer 'great mass', on the other.

## II. 'THE COMMUNIST MANIFESTO' AND 'CAPITAL'

After spending twenty-one months in England Engels left for home. On the way he visited Marx in Paris. Engels spent ten days in Paris, much of it in the company of Marx. They confirmed their mutual interests and unity of outlook. It is generally agreed that their close friendship started at this time. Marx had been editing

a magazine, the *Deutsch-Französische Jahrbücher*. In the next three to four years he completed with Engels *The Holy Family*, *The German Ideology*, and, in February 1848, *The Manifesto of the Communist Party*. It will suffice to quote Robert Payne's apt comments on *The Holy Family*. Out of some 225 pages 'there are scarcely three pages which can still be read with any profit. For the most part if is a farrago of excerpts from Marx's notebooks on every conceivable subject'.[21] And regarding *The German Ideology*, an attack on other German socialists, Franz Mehring, the Marxist biographer of Karl Marx, observed: 'even when dialectical trenchancy does show itself it soon degenerates into hair-splitting and quibbling, some of it of a rather puerile character'.[22] And Engels wrote of it in 1888: 'I have once again ferreted out and looked over the old manuscript. . . . The finished portion consists of an exposition of the materialist conception of history which proves only how incomplete our knowledge of economic history still was at that time . . . it was unusable'.[23]

What was this materialist conception of history? We find few explicit statements of it. In *The German Ideology* the two authors wrote:

> The way in which men produce their means of subsistence depends first of all on the nature of the actual means they find in existence and have to reproduce. This mode of production must not be considered simply as being the reproduction of the physical existence of the individuals. Rather it is a definite form of expressing their life, a definite mode of life on their part. As individuals express their life, so they are. What they are, therefore, coincides with their production, both with what they produce and with how they produce. The nature of individuals thus depends on the material conditions determining their production.

This view would seem to reduce men to a mere product of material conditions, unable to influence events. This was certainly not the view they later took. In his *Eighteenth Brumaire of Louis Bonaparte*, published in 1852, Marx gave men a more positive role:

> Men make their own history, but they do not make it just as they please; they do not make it under circumstances chosen by themselves, but under circumstances directly found, given and

transmitted from the past. The tradition of all the dead generations weighs like an incubus on the brain of the living. And just when they seem engaged in revolutionising themselves and things, in creating something entirely new, precisely in such epochs of revolutionary crisis they anxiously conjure up the spirits of the past to their service and borrow from them names, battle slogans and costumes in order to present the new scene of world history in this time-honoured disguise and this borrowed language.

This passage, especially the first few words, was Lenin's starting-point. Later still, Engels, in a letter to J. Bloch written in 1890, explained:

According to the materialist conception of history, the *ultimately* determining element in history is the production and reproduction of real life. More than this neither Marx nor I have ever asserted. Hence if somebody twists this into saying that the economic element is the *only* determining one, he transforms that proposition into a meaningless, abstract, senseless phrase. The economic situation is the basis, but the various elements of the superstructure: political forms of the class struggle and its results, to wit: constitutions established by the victorious class after a successful battle, etc., judicial forms, and then even the reflexes of all these actual struggles in the brains of the participants, political, juristic, philosophical theories, religious views and their further development into systems of dogma, also exercise their influence upon the course of the historical struggles and in many cases preponderate in determining their *form*. . . .

We make our history ourselves, but, in the first place, under very definite assumptions and conditions. Among these the economic ones are ultimately decisive.

Thus after more consideration, Marx and Engels had moved from a more determinist conception of history to one which gave consideration to many other factors in addition to 'the production and reproduction of life'.

The *Manifesto* was the most important single work of Marx and Engels. It is their best known, and the one which contains their essential doctrines. It was written for an obscure German *émigré* organization, the Communist Workers Educational

League, which had its headquarters in London. As regards the writing of the *Manifesto*, Franz Mehring believed that 'Marx had the greater hand in shaping its final form, but, as his own draft shows, Engels was not far behind'.[24]

The *Manifesto* opened in a dramatic way with an exaggeration:

> A spectre is haunting Europe – the spectre of Communism. All the Powers of old Europe have entered into a holy alliance to exorcise this spectre.[25]

It went on quite untruthfully to claim: 'Communists of various nationalities have assembled in London, and sketched the following Manifesto'. The main thesis is: 'The history of all hitherto existing society is the history of class struggles'.

> Freeman and slave, patrician and plebeian, lord and serf, guild-master and journeyman, in a word, oppressor and oppressed, stood in constant opposition to one another, carried on an uninterrupted, now hidden, now open fight, a fight that each time ended, either in a revolutionary re-constitution of society at large, or in the common ruin of the contending classes.

This class struggle was continuing in capitalist society, a society which had 'sprouted from the ruins of feudal society'. But there was a distinctive feature of this 'epoch of the bourgeoisie'. Class antagonisms were simplified as society split up more and more into 'two great hostile camps', the bourgeoisie and the proletariat. Marx and Engels believed that the rise and fall of slave society, feudalism, and capitalism were in each case inevitable because each of these societies contained within it inner contradictions which eventually brought about its downfall. We learn little of the working of these contradictions in the *Manifesto*, merely that 'From the serfs of the Middle Ages sprang the chartered burghers of the earliest towns. From these the first elements of the bourgeoisie were developed'. The voyages of discovery and colonization created great demands for the products in the new markets which could not be satisfied within the old guild system; 'in one word, the feudal relations of property became no longer compatible with the already developed productive forces; they became so many fetters'. Thus the new manufacturing middle class with workshops based on far greater division of labour than before. Ever greater demand meant that 'even manufacture no longer sufficed. Thereupon, steam and machinery revolutionised industrial production. The place of manufacture was taken by the giant, Modern Industry, the place of the industrial middle class, by industrial millionaires, the leaders of whole industrial armies, the modern bourgeois'. With the development of the bourgeoisie in economic had gone its development in political terms until, 'The executive of the modern State is but a committee for managing the common affairs of the whole bourgeoisie'.

Marx had much to say in praise of the bourgeoisie, compared with earlier ruling classes. It had 'created more massive and more colossal productive forces than all preceding generations together'. But it was like the sorcerer no longer able to control the forces called up by his spells:

> It is enough to mention the commercial crises that by their periodical return put on its trial, each time more threateningly, the existence of the entire bourgeois society. In these crises a great part not only of the existing products, but also of the previously created productive forces, are periodically destroyed. In these crises there breaks out an epidemic that, in all earlier epochs, would have seemed an absurdity – the epidemic of over-production.

This crisis of overproduction is caused by the workers producing more than they can consume. Because of the existence of the 'reserve army of labour', the unemployed, because increasing division of labour and increasing use of machinery destroy all skill, the workman

> becomes an appendage of the machine, and it is only the most simple, most monotonous, and most easily acquired knack, that is required of him. Hence, the cost of production of a workman is restricted, almost entirely, to the means of subsistence that he requires for his maintenance, and for the propagation of his race.

Wages are also kept down by the recruits to the proletariat from the lower strata of the bourgeoisie, shopkeepers, handicraftsmen, peasants, 'who are swamped in the competition with the large capitalists'. These groups are moulded into a uniform proletariat 'in proportion as machinery obliterates all distinctions of labour, and nearly everywhere reduces wages to the same low level'. As the workers' lives become more and more precarious they begin to form trades unions against the bourgeoisie. The concentration of workers and the improved means of communication eventually lead to 'one national struggle between classes'. The bourgeoisie itself is in part responsible for this situation in that it has been forced to 'drag it [the working class] into the political arena'. It has been compelled in the past to get the help of the proletariat in its battles with the aristocracy, with the bourgeoisie of foreign countries, and with certain elements of the bourgeoisie 'whose interests have become antagonistic to the progress of industry'. In addition, a small section of the bourgeoisie 'cuts itself adrift, and joins the revolutionary class'. In particular, 'a portion of the bourgeois ideologists, who have raised themselves to the level of comprehending theoretically the historical movement as a whole'. In time the proletarian movement becomes 'the self-conscious, independent movement of the immense majority, in the interests of the immense majority'. In the first place it was called into life by the bourgeoisie. 'What the bourgeoisie, therefore, produces, above all, is its own gravediggers. Its fall and the victory of the proletariat are equally inevitable'.

In a separate chapter Marx and Engels dealt with the role of the Communists in the struggle for proletarian emancipation:

> The Communists do not form a separate party opposed to other working-class parties. They have no interests separate and apart from those of the proletariat as a whole. They do not set up any sectarian principles of their own, by which to shape and mould the proletarian movement.

And, in another much quoted passage:

> The Communists, therefore, are on the one hand, practically, the most advanced and resolute section of the working-class parties of every country, that section which pushes forward all others; on the other hand, theoretically, they have over the great mass of the proletariat the advantage of clearly understanding the line of march, the conditions, and the ultimate general results of the proletarian movement.

How did the two revolutionaries see the future under communism? They did not attempt to draw any detailed blueprint. In different countries different patterns would emerge but, in general, the first step in the revolution 'is to raise the proletariat to the position of ruling class, to win the battle of democracy'.

Then the proletariat would use its political supremacy 'to wrest by degrees, all capital from the bourgeoisie, to centralize all instruments of production in the hands of the State . . . and to increase the total of productive forces as rapidly as possible'. In the most advanced countries the following measures would have general application: abolition of property in land and use of rents for public purposes; heavy progressive income tax; abolition of inheritance rights; confiscation of rebel and emigrant property; state monopoly of credit and banking; centralization of means of communication and transport in the state; extension of state-owned productive forces, cultivation of wastelands, and a common plan for soil improvement; the duty of all to work, establishment of industrial armies, especially for agriculture; gradual abolition of differences between towns and countryside, drawing together of agriculture and manufacturing industry; free and compulsory education of all children in publicly-owned schools, such education to be combined with material production. In the course of development class distinctions would disappear and the public power would lose its oppressive nature. Then,

> In place of the old bourgeois society, with its classes and class antagonisms, we shall have an association, in which the free development of each is the condition for the free development of all.

Such were the basic arguments and forecasts of Marx and Engels as presented in the *Manifesto*. How did they correspond to actual developments? In attempting to answer this we must refer to some of Marx's other work, especially *Capital* in which he elaborated the economic side of his world outlook. Let us first of all take up a number of specific instances where their views were clearly wrong. They claimed, for instance, that 'modern industrial labour, modern subjection to capital, the same in England as in France, in America as in Germany, has stripped [the proletarian] of every trace of national character'. And again: 'The working men have no country. . . . National differences and antagonisms between peoples are daily more and more vanishing, owing to the development of the bourgeoisie, to freedom of commerce, to the world market, to uniformity in the mode of production'. This proved to be a very poor guide to action for the socialist, and later Communist, parties. As we shall see, the 1914–18 War proved the importance of patriotism for the proletariat. Later the

Nazis were able to exploit frustrated nationalism and, later still, the Communists harnessed it for their own purposes. Secondly, their view of the peasants as 'reactionary', doomed to succumb to modern capitalism, and their solution, outlined above, impeded the advance of socialist influence in the agrarian communities. Only where socialists and Communists disregarded Marx's view on the peasants did they make headway. It must be admitted, though, that *in the long run* their view that farming would more and more resemble industry appears to be correct. Thirdly, their view that 'Society as a whole is more and more splitting up into two hostile camps' greatly oversimplified what was happening to social classes. Now it is true that in the *Manifesto* and later in *Capital* reference was made to other classes – managers, foremen, and overlookers – but the emphasis was always on the two classes confronting each other. This simply confused Marxists about likely developments in society and the likely sources of support for socialism. In some countries, such as Weimar Germany, they were to pay heavily for their incorrect analysis of social classes. They also oversimplified the structure of the industrial working class which, as any trade union organizer knows, is anything but devoid of distinctions. Fourthly, one of their best-known errors, which causes controversy to this day, is their idea that 'the modern labourer, on the contrary, instead of rising with the progress of industry, sinks deeper and deeper . . . becomes a pauper, and pauperism develops more rapidly than population and wealth'. We have already seen that Engels tried to maintain this general view while admitting that it had not really happened as predicted in England up to 1892. Mehring, writing later, was forced to concede more ground on this issue.[26]

The theory of increasing misery has continued to give headaches to those preaching under the Marxist banner. Many have just ignored it, others have misleadingly taken a brief time span, such as a period of depression, to 'prove' its correctness. Another approach is to emphasize that Marx did believe, contrary to some other socialists, that trade union action could lead, at least for some time, to an increase in wages, and that he also brought habit and custom into the picture. This would vary from country to country, from time to time. The number and extent of the worker's

so-called necessary wants, as also the modes of satisfying them, are themselves the product of historical development . . . and depend therefore to a great extent on the degree of civilisation of a country, more particularly on the conditions under which, and consequently on the habits and degree of comfort in which, the class of free labourers has been formed. In contradistinction therefore to the case of other commodities, there enters into the determination of the value of labour-power a historical and moral element.[27]

In emphasizing such passages contemporary Marxists argue that through trade union action in boom conditions workers push up their real wages to a level which then contains a new, higher, 'historical and moral element'.[28] This is all very well, but is not sufficient to explain away the extreme and adamant formulations in the *Manifesto*, in *Capital*, and still, slightly modified, being preached by Engels and others after the death of Marx. Another contemporary Marxist explanation is to present the working class of the advanced nations as Marx's 'aristocracy of labour', and the masses of the development nations as the 'pauperized proletariat'. This is a point of view, but in the writer's opinion it deviates from Marx's original concept. The same Marxists argue that despite increases in absolute standards in the advanced countries, even there 'the tendency towards the increasing misery of the working class finds continuous expression in the lowering of the workers' relative share in the national income'.[29] Here we shall have to content ourselves with saying that there is much controversy on interpreting statistics relating to national income and its distribution. But, while it is certainly true to say that the wage-earners and small-salary earners have not made the great gains so optimistically written about a few years ago by apostles of the *status quo* and others, this interpretation does not, in any case, square with Marx's original words. Finally, there is the attempt to bring Marx's theory of alienation to bolster his theory of increasing misery. The theory of alienation was dealt with by Marx in what have become known as *The Economic and Philosophical Manuscripts of 1844*. These manuscripts were first published in 1932 from incomplete papers. Put simply, alienation 'is a term that has been used, to portray shortcomings in the human condition'.[30] In the case of the young Marx, the essential alienation was economic; it could only be overcome by transforming the existing economic system. What the worker produces, the product of his labour, is, under the system of private ownership of the means of production, alienated from him. It becomes a commodity over which he has lost control. The greater this product is, therefore, the more the worker himself is diminished.

> Therefore his misery increases, regardless of how high his wages are, in proportion with the volume and importance of his labour. The more wealth he produces, the poorer he becomes, whether his own wage rises or falls in the process. Higher wages do not confer human dignity upon the worker.[31]

These lines of Ernst Fischer are thought-provoking and the last sentence especially strikes the writer sympathetically, but, as Fischer later on admits, Marx did believe in 'the continuous formation of industrial reserve armies and the simultaneous declassing of layers of the proletariat. In this respect Marx has been proved wrong'.[32] It is also worth mentioning that precisely because Marx did not feel the *Manuscripts* important, he made little effort to do anything to get them published. Engels took the same view after the death of Marx,[33] and Marx did not again mention the concept of alienation as such.

History was unkind to Marx and Engels in another matter, that of crises. The writer will not apologize for not revealing the secrets of Marx's theory of economic crisis in detail. In the *Manifesto* little is said about their origin other than 'the epidemic of over-production', which in turn was caused by subsistence wages preventing the workers from consuming all they had produced. And in *Capital* Marx says:

> The last cause of all real crises always remains the poverty and restricted consumption of the masses as compared to the tendency of capitalist production to develop the productive forces in such a way, that only the absolute power of consumption of the entire society would be their limit.[34]

But *Capital*, despite its three volumes and over 2,490 pages, was not finished, and it is generally agreed by non-Marxist economists that it contains enough inconsistencies to prevent the theory emerging as a coherent whole. As Paul A. Samuelson commented: 'The "Contradictions of capitalism", which Karl Marx saw everywhere, are as nothing compared to the contradictions of Marx himself'.[35] And another eminent economist, Joseph A. Schumpeter, believed that Marx 'had no simple theory of business cycles. And none can be made to follow from his "laws" of the capitalist process'.[36] The prominent Polish Marxist economist, and later Communist minister, Oscar Lange, seems to have agreed.[37] Marx wrote as if the growth of crises under capitalism and the increasing misery of the workers were simply two aspects of the same thing. In practice this has not been so. Capitalist crisis meant misery for many workers, but the fall in their standards was not permanent. The workers soon recovered, for instance, from the effects of the crisis which broke out in 1929. In any case, the misery tended to be concentrated in certain industries and certain areas heavily dependent on those industries, rather than among workers as a whole. The standards of some workers were rising at a time when other workers' standards were falling. Again, although crisis has been, and remains, a feature of the capitalist system, that system proved far more dynamic and durable than Marx and Engels anticipated.

Another element of the Marxist system dealt with in *Capital* which has met with much opposition is the labour theory of value. Students of Marxism differ in their estimate of its importance and it is doubtful whether it has been either understood or used much by most people calling themselves Marxists. As G. D. H. Cole explains,[38] unlike most other theories of value, Marx's theory does not seek to explain prices, but explains how labour is exploited under capitalism. The Marxist theory of value was simply a modified version of the Ricardian theory which was the then prevailing orthodoxy. According to Marx,

> The wealth of those societies in which the capitalist mode of production prevails, presents itself as 'an immense accumulation of commodities', its unit being a single commodity. . . . A commodity is, in the first place, an object outside us, a thing that by its properties satisfies human wants of some sort or another. . . . The utility of a thing makes it a use-value. . . . Use-values become a reality only by use or consumption: they also constitute the substance of all wealth, whatever may be the social form of that wealth.[39]

And,

> A use-value, or useful article, therefore has value only because human labour in the abstract has been embodied or materialised in it. How, then, is the magnitude of this value to be measured? Plainly, by the quantity of the value-creating substance, the

labour, contained in the article . . . measured . . . in weeks, days, and hours. Some people might think that if the value of a commodity is determined by the quantity of labour spent on it, the more idle and unskilful the labourer, the more valuable would his commodity be. . . . The labour, however, that forms the substance of value, is homogeneous human labour, expenditure of one uniform labour-power. The total labour-power of society . . . is . . . composed . . . of innumerable individual units. Each of these units is the same as any other, so far as it has the character of the average labour-power of society, and takes effect as such; that is, so far as it requires for producing a commodity, no more time than is needed on an average, no more than is socially necessary. The labour-time socially necessary is that required to produce an article under the normal conditions of production, and with the average degree of skill and intensity prevalent at that time.[40]

The labour-power of the proletarian, too, is a commodity like any other. Its value is also determined by 'the labour-time necessary for the production, and consequently also the reproduction, of this special article'. This labour-power, this special article, exists only as the power of the living individual:

Given the individual, the production of labour-power consists in his reproduction of himself or his maintenance. For his maintenance he requires a given quantity of the means of subsistence.[41]

It is what the worker produces beyond what is required for his own subsistence which accrues to the owner of the means of production, the capitalist, in the form of surplus value or profit. For Marx then, the labour of the proletariat was the sole source of wealth, a part of which was expropriated by the capitalist. He could do this by virtue of his ownership of the means of production without which the proletarian could not exercise his labour-power. This situation is not the natural order of things:

neither is its social basis one that is common to all historical periods. It is clearly the result of a past historical development, the product of many economical revolutions, of the extinction of a whole series of older forms of social production.[42]

The surplus value expropriated by the capitalist led to crisis. The wealth created by the many was being concentrated in the hands of the few who could not consume it all. In the search for more profit the capitalist reinvests part of the surplus value and extends the means of production. In the long run this is self-defeating because it intensifies overproduction. Slumps follow, many small firms going to the wall; the means of production become concentrated into fewer hands. At the same time there develops,

on an ever extending scale, the co-operative form of the labour process, the conscious technical application of science, the methodical cultivation of the soil, the transformation of the instruments of labour into instruments of labour only usable in common, the economising of all means of production by their use as the means of production of combined, socialised labour, the entanglement of all peoples in the net of the world market, and with this, the international character of the capitalistic regime. Along with the constantly diminishing number of the magnates of capital, who usurp and monopolise all advantages of this process of transformation, grows the mass of misery, oppression, slavery, degradation, exploitation; but with this too grows the revolt of the working class, a class always increasing in numbers, and disciplined, united, organised by the very mechanism of the process of capitalist production itself. The monopoly of capital becomes a fetter upon the mode of production, which has sprung up and flourished along with, and under, it. Centralisation of the means of production and socialisation of labour at last reach a point where they become incompatible with their capitalist integument. This integument is burst asunder. The knell of capitalist private property sounds. The expropriators are expropriated.[43]

The labour theory of value and its ramifications have been subjected to many criticisms by professional economists over the last hundred years. These need not concern us here. Let us simply say that the labour theory was asserted rather than proved. Engels later seemed to reduce its importance in the Marxist system. In a letter to a German Social Democrat named Schmidt (12 March 1895) he expressed the view that the labour theory of value was a *concept*, and as such could not correspond exactly to reality. But he would not agree to relegating it to the level of a myth.[44]

Concept or myth, the labour theory of value provided the socialists of many countries with a weapon to demonstrate the exploitation of the workers. But the question of whether one agrees or disagrees with some individuals living on, or receiving, unearned income produced by others, is a moral one rather than a scientific one as Marx believed. Yet Marx was writing at a time when men believed in certainties. The ranks of the upper classes were swollen with people who believed with certainty that the *status quo* was right. Marx faced them with anger and tried not to be sentimental as he read the official reports of working and housing conditions in Britain, then the richest country in the world. He quotes Dr Julian Hunter of Newcastle upon Tyne as saying that that town, 'contains a sample of the finest tribe of our countrymen, often sunk by external circumstances of house and street into an almost savage degradation'.[45]

Three even more fundamental claims of Marx and Engels proved ill-founded. Useful though the theory of class interest is, to try to explain all recorded history in terms of class struggle is greatly, and dangerously, to oversimplify the factors which have set men against each other. The Nazi persecution of the Jews, the Sino-Soviet conflict, and the Arab-Israeli conflict, to take just three examples from recent history, cannot be explained in terms of class conflict. And to put so much emphasis on class conflict ignores the great amount of class collaboration under capitalism. Again, as the late C. Wright Mills has insisted:

> The inadequacy of Marx's notion of 'class interests' is of great moral importance. He does not consider the difference between (a) What Is to the Interests of Men according to an analysis of their position in society, and (b) What Men Are Interested In according to the men themselves. Nor does he confront fully (as we must since Lenin), the moral meaning of the political uses of this distinction. (This is the moral root of problems of leninism and of the meaning of democracy and freedom.)[46]

Secondly, modern sociologists, even opponents of the *status quo* such as Wright Mills, quarrel with Marx's conception of a 'ruling class' based on dominant economic position. As Bottomore tells us, the bourgeoisie is not a ruling class, for 'it has ceased to be a cohesive group; secondly because the complexity and differentiation of modern societies make it difficult for any single group to wield power alone; and finally, because universal suffrage ensures that political power is ultimately in the hands of the mass of the people'.[47]

The third of our ill-founded claims is that the expropriators will be expropriated by the working class. Nowhere has this happened in Marx's sense. The 'Marxist' revolutions came in backward, not mature, societies, and certainly, in Russia and eastern Europe, they were not movements of the 'immense majority'.

### III. 'AN INCOMPARABLE ALLIANCE'

Franz Mehring called the friendship between Marx and Engels an 'Incomparable Alliance'. Incomparable or not, one is led to wonder how warm and close it was. In the 'year of revolutions', 1848, Marx and Engels had attempted to play a role in Paris and then in Germany. In Cologne they set up a newspaper, *Die Neue Rheinische Zeitung*. For the most part the revolutionaries of various hues ignored them, and when the revolutions failed they had to seek refuge in England. From then on Marx was completely destitute and had to rely on Engels for the bulk of his income for the rest of his life. This fact forced Engels once again into the family business to which he returned in Manchester in November 1850.

The two revolutionaries saw little of each other for the next nineteen years, until, that is, Engels retired from the business and moved to London in September 1869. Their relationship was sustained largely by political and literary correspondence, and the sums of money Engels sent to Marx. As was only to be expected, this relationship was strained at times. Engels got sick of Marx's 'querulous temper, his carping ways, his self-pity, and his strange delusions about money'.[48]

Engels lived the life of the prosperous Manchester capitalist. In 1864 he became a partner in the firm. His relations with his parents became good, his father having become convinced from brief visits to Manchester that Friedrich had settled down. Effectively, Engels junior had become integrated into local bourgeois society. He enjoyed fox-hunting and the Christmas parties of the local notables.[49] He contributed to Territorial Army journals and the *Manchester Guardian* on military affairs. He took part in the deliberations of the Statistical Society and other intellectual clubs. His political activities were very much a sideline. And his domestic arrangements with Mary Burns, an Irish ex-factory girl, his common law wife, were carefully hidden from view.

Marx's life was very different. In December 1850 he moved to 28 Dean Street, Soho, where he remained until September 1856. It was a period of disappointment, embarrassment, tragedy, and extreme hardship. Marx was forever writing begging letters to Engels. In 1852 he wrote, on this occasion to Joseph Weydemeyer: 'My affairs have now reached the agreeable point at which I can no longer leave the house because my clothes are in pawn and can no longer eat meat because my credit is exhausted'.[50] But he did little to try to remedy the situation by seeking employment. Three of his six children died during this period.

Marx was embarrassed by the birth of a son to his domestic servant, Helene Demuth, in June 1851. Engels protected his friend by taking responsibility for the child. Marx posed as the model of Victorian propriety. He certainly loved his wife very much. Yet he enjoyed the company of other women. He had little chance to indulge himself during his early years in London, but later we find him spending an afternoon in Hyde Park with Bismarck's niece, Elisabeth von Puttkamer, whom he met on a trip to Germany, reciting poetry to the wealthy Frau Tenge, and employing his didactic skills on Frau Kugelmann.

Later when Engels's improved financial position made it possible for him to settle a regular and generous income on Marx, the Marx family lived in considerable style in the fashion of the Victorian middle class. 'Surplus value' had come in very useful.

NOTES

[1] Isaiah Berlin, *Karl Marx* (London, 1963), p. 33.
[2] John Lewis, *Marxism and Modern Idealism* (London, 1944), p. 43.
[3] Karl Marx and Frederick Engels, *Selected Works* (Moscow, 1951), II, 351: 'Ludwig Feuerbach and the End of Classical German Philosophy', by F. Engels.
[4] Berlin, op. cit., p. 81.
[5] Marx and Engels met for the first time briefly in Cologne in 1842. Their Paris meeting was the beginning of their close collaboration.
[6] Gustav Mayer, *Friedrich Engels* (New York, 1969), p. 27. This is the classic biography of Engels.
[7] ibid.
[8] ibid., p. 28.
[9] Donald Read, 'Chartism in Manchester', in *Chartist Studies*, edited by Asa Briggs (London, 1959), p. 30.

[10] ibid., p. 29.
[11] Briggs, 'The Local Background of Chartism', ibid., p. 2.
[12] Frederick Engels, *The Condition of the Working Class in England* (London, 1969). With an introduction by E. J. Hobsbawm, p. 76.
[13] ibid., p. 137.
[14] ibid., p. 64.
[15] ibid., p. 39.
[16] ibid., p. 322.
[17] ibid., p. 21.
[18] ibid., p. 24.
[19] ibid., p. 31.
[20] ibid., p. 32.
[21] Robert Payne, *Marx* (London, 1968), pp. 110–11.
[22] Franz Mehring, *Karl Marx* (London, 1951), p. 110.
[23] Marx and Engels, op. cit., II, 325.
[24] Mehring, op. cit., p. 148.
[25] The text used here is the Moscow, 1955, English translation. Also the Dietz Verlag (East Berlin, 1959) German edition.
[26] Mehring, op. cit., p. 149.
[27] Karl Marx, *Capital*, translated by Moore and Aveling (Chicago, 1919), I, 190.
[28] See, for instance, Maurice Dobb, *Wages* (Cambridge, 1948), p. 106. See also his essay 'A Lecture on Marx', in *On Economic Theory and Socialism* (London, 1955).
[29] Ernst Fischer, *Marx in his own Words* (London, 1970), p. 119. This is one of the best attempts to come to terms with Marx's theory of Increasing Misery.
[30] Michael Curtis (ed.), *Marxism* (New York, 1970), p. 129.
[31] Fischer, op. cit., p. 117.
[32] ibid., p. 123.
[33] Daniel Bell, 'A Critique of Alienation', in Curtis, op. cit., p. 139.
[34] *Capital*, III (Chicago, 1909), 568.
[35] Paul A. Samuelson, 'Marxian Economics as Economics', in Curtis, op. cit., p. 235.
[36] Joseph A. Schumpeter, *Ten Great Economists from Marx to Keynes* (London, 1951), p. 49.
[37] Oscar Lange, 'Marxian Economics and Modern Economic Theory', in Curtis, op. cit., p. 222.
[38] G. D. H. Cole, *The Meaning of Marxism* (Ann Arbor, 1964), p. 210.
[39] *Capital*, I, 41–3.
[40] ibid., I, 45–6.
[41] ibid., I, 189.
[42] ibid., I, 188.
[43] ibid., I, 836–7.
[44] Quoted John Strachey, *Contemporary Capitalism* (London, 1956), pp. 87–8.
[45] *Capital*, I, 726.
[46] C. Wright Mills, *The Marxists* (New York, 1962), p. 114.
[47] T. B. Bottomore, *Classes in Modern Society* (London, 1965), p. 28.
[48] Payne, op. cit., pp. 394–5.
[49] Mehring, op. cit., p. 232.
[50] ibid., p. 216.

# II

# Marxism Becomes a Mass Movement

## 1. MARX AND LASSALLE

ALTHOUGH Marx and Engels had for years hoped for the growth of a large Marxist party in Britain, it was in their native Germany that the first mass movement officially based on their ideas developed. But the acceptance of a Marxist programme by the German socialists came only after years of agitation and argument by the followers of the exiled prophets.

The German socialist movement burst on to the political scene on a significant scale in the early 1860s. As in other countries, this movement was one of the fruits of a great industrial revolution.[1] Again, as in other countries, urbanization went hand-in-hand with industrialization. The overcrowded housing conditions provided a common denominator of social deprivation which helped to reduce consciousness of differences of background, occupation, and rates of pay.[2] Thus for both physical and psychological reasons it became easier to organize the workers into political, as well as trade union, bodies. By 1871, the year of the proclamation of the German Empire, the majority of Germans already lived in towns.

The first sizeable German socialist organization was the General German Workers' Association (ADAV) set up at the initiative of Ferdinand Lassalle in Leipzig in May 1863. It grew out of the movement of workers' educational societies which had been fostered by the Liberals. The leaders of these societies were dissatisfied with the refusal of the Liberals to treat them as political partners.

Ferdinand Lassalle (1825–64), a Jewish lawyer and writer, regarded himself as a pupil of Marx and had tried to secure the latter's co-operation – without success. Marx and Engels harboured feelings of personal antipathy towards Lassalle. Marx's wife, Jenny, hated Lassalle because she felt he was taking on a position in the German socialist movement which rightly belonged to her husband. Lassalle, a veteran of 1848, was an ambitious, flamboyant, romantic character who enjoyed the luxuries of life, including fame as a scholar as well as a politician. He died prematurely, not as the result of poverty or prison, but in a duel for the honour of an aristocratic lady. Engels saw him as 'a real Jew from the Slav frontier' who had always been on the watch for a chance to exploit anyone for his own private purposes under party pretexts.[3] Marx agreed. Nevertheless, despite Lassalle's weaknesses, Mehring felt that the two Marxists were unjustly harsh in their assessment of the 'real Jew'.[4] Marx's low opinion of Lassalle did not prevent him from seeking the help of his compatriot to find a publisher or to borrow money.[5] It did cloud the political judgement of Marx and Engels, depriving them of contact with the ADAV, and reducing their political influence in their homeland for some time. More justified were their political differences with Lassalle.

Lassalle had written a programme for the ADAV which comprised three essential points. First, the working class must constitute itself as an independent political party. Secondly, it should demand universal, equal, and direct suffrage to enable it to change the productive system. Thirdly, the state should give generous aid to workers' production co-operatives, which would gradually replace the capitalist system.

Marx and Engels regarded this programme as full of illusions, especially about the nature of the Prussian state. They too wanted universal suffrage. Yet they believed there was no possibility in Germany of achieving working-class emancipation by peaceful means. There, only revolutionary change based on the dictatorship of the proletariat would lead to socialism. To achieve his end Lassalle tried to obtain an alliance with the Prussian Chancellor, Otto von Bismarck, against the Liberal bourgeois capitalists. Marx and Engels rejected this view. They preached that socialists should establish temporary alliances with the bourgeoisie to destroy the remnants of feudalism, after which, the conflict between the bourgeoisie and the proletariat could assume its full historical dimensions. Another point of disagreement was the role of trade unions. Lassalle, basing himself on the so-called Iron Law of Wages, held trade union activities to be futile. Marx, on the other hand, thought that the unions were part of a necessary training for the workers and that, in the short run, they could better the pay and conditions of their members. They further differed on certain aspects of foreign policy.

After Lassalle's death Johann Baptist von Schweitzer (1834–75) became President of the ADAV. At this time it numbered about five hundred members. This was a respectable number. However, especially in middle and south Germany, many workers' educational societies had resisted the call of Lassalle. In these areas the workers continued to work with the Liberals. This was because they were suspicious of Lassalle's flirtation with Bismarck and Prussianism, and because they were more firmly committed to democracy in their own organizations and in the state. These societies formed themselves into a Union of German Workers' and Educational Societies. The union, under the leadership of August Bebel and Wilhelm Liebknecht, the latter a former ADAV member, eventually became the core from which the Social Democratic Workers' Party was founded at Eisenach in 1869. The opportunity to set up the new party came after the Liberals had withdrawn from the union some months before. This withdrawal was provoked by the adoption of a resolution calling for affiliation to the First International.

## II. THE FIRST INTERNATIONAL

The details of the negotiations which led to the formation of the First International are still obscure.[6] But it is fair to say that the idea came mainly from British trade unionists and French socialists. They were inspired by the struggle for the unification of Italy, in which many working men and radicals played leading parts, the crushing of the Polish insurrection in 1863, and the American Civil War, as well as their own struggles for reform. They started to exchange ideas at the Great Exhibition in London in 1851, which no doubt revealed to them the great possibilities for human betterment.

The International Workingmen's Association (IWA) was convened in London on 28 September 1864. A meeting was held at St Martin's Hall under the chairmanship of Professor E. S. Beesly of London University. The fifty-strong committee which subsequently emerged from the meeting reflected both the development of the working-class movement and the events which had recently stirred it into action. The strong British trade union movement made up half the committee's membership. Next came the German group, among whom was Marx.

These were not very representative as the Lassallean ADAV had been excluded. France had 9 representatives, Italy 6, and Poland and Switzerland 2 each.[7]

The first paragraph of the International's statutes began with the words, 'Considering that the emancipation of the working classes must be conquered by the working classes themselves'. Yet despite this clear objective there was little idea of how the workers would liberate themselves and what role the IWA should play. There were continuous arguments about whether the groups in various countries should be subject to control from London, or from national committees, or indeed whether they should operate independently. The heterogeneous nature of the membership made it impossible to resolve such arguments. Within two years of being set up the IWA was able to claim over a hundred organizations as different from each other as British trade unions, French mutual aid societies, clockmakers from Geneva and the Jura, Belgian freethinkers, the first German Marxists, and republican and democratic bourgeois from several countries.[8] In the long run it proved impossible to unite such disparate elements into an effective international revolutionary organization, and this was one of the key facts in the decline of the International.

The First International reached its zenith between 1869 and 1871 when it had sections throughout Europe and the United States. The economic crash of 1866 had left behind a great deal of industrial unrest which produced bitter, hard-fought, strikes. The International gained prestige by hindering the importing of cheap foreign labour, and by organizing financial assistance for strikers. By attributing to its machinations strikes which had their origins elsewhere, the employing classes helped to increase the prestige of the IWA still further.

Marx played a leading role in the IWA. As Mehring tells us: 'Although Marx was plagued again and again by painful illnesses, and although he was itching to complete his scientific work, he spared neither energy nor industry in the cause of the International. . . . It soon became clear that Marx was the actual "head" of the movement'.[9] He was the only member of the Subcommittee (later called Standing Committee, and then Executive Committee) of the General Council of the IWA to serve continuously from 1864 to 1872. And apart from the General Secretary, who was paid by the IWA, he was the only member of the nine-man committee who worked full-time, in his case unpaid, to further its activities.[10] Marx therefore had a decisive hand in drafting the addresses, resolutions, and statements of the IWA. It was he who drafted its Inaugural Address which included such demands as the organization of the proletariat as an independent party; the development of factory legislation; the founding of co-operatives; ceaseless struggle against intriguing, chauvinistic diplomacy; the merger of the proletariats of all countries; the destruction of class rule; and the economic liberation of the working class. Against the opposition of the French, who were more interested in discussing social questions and oppression nearer home, Marx got the IWA to agree to 'the necessity of opposing the growing influence of Russia in European affairs by re-establishing the independence of Poland on a democratic and socialist basis'.[11] He had no difficulty with his message of congratulations to Abraham Lincoln, sent on the occasion of the latter's re-election as President of the United States. The President answered the message 'in a warm and friendly tone'.[12]

In 1868 the Russian revolutionary anarchist Michael Bakunin (1814–76) joined the Geneva section of the IWA. Bakunin already had a considerable following, especially in Italy and Spain, by this time. He had classed himself as a pupil of Marx, at the same time being strongly influenced by the anti-statism of the French anarchist Joseph Proudhon.

From this point on the International was dominated by the struggle between Marx and Bakunin. In theory Bakunin opposed Marx's idea of state ownership of the means of production, preferring some form of co-operative ownership. Further, he opposed centralized power, advocating strong provincial and municipal government. In practice the political differences of the two men were not quite so clear cut. Both thought in terms of the state's ultimate abolition, both had certain authoritarian tendencies. Whatever the ideological differences, the German and the Russian fought a bitter personal struggle. Much mud was thrown. Historians have not been able to allocate the blame with any real certainty or conviction. Mehring, however, while condemning Bakunin, as one would expect a devoted Marxist to do, did admit that Marx and Engels 'attacked [Bakunin] severely and occasionally unjustly'.[13] In his view history would give the Russian a place of honour amongst the pioneers of the international proletariat, though that place may be contested so long as there are Philistines in the world, no matter whether they conceal their long ears under the night-cap of petty-bourgeois respectability or don the lion's skin of a Marx to cloak their trembling limbs.[14]

The power struggle in the IWA ended with the expulsion of Bakunin in 1872 for participation in a secret organization whose activities were harmful to the International. This secret society was Bakunin's own, often referred to as the 'Secret Alliance' or 'Secret Alliance of Socialist Democracy'.

The First International held four successful congresses – Geneva (1866), Lausanne (1867), Brussels (1868), and Basel (1869) – before the Hague congress of 1872 which voted to expel Bakunin. The split contributed to the death of the IWA which was formally proclaimed at the Philadelphia congress of 1876. The removal of the headquarters of the International from London to New York was another nail in its coffin, making communication more difficult.


III. THE GROWTH OF SOCIAL DEMOCRACY IN GERMANY

As we have seen, the 1860s saw the formation of two working-class parties in Germany, the ADAV, the 'Lassalleans', and the German Social Democratic Workers' Party, the 'Eisenachers' or 'Marxists'. Though they were scolded by Engels for non-payment of dues, the Eisenachers supported the First International, paid lip-service to Marxism, and were more democratic in their organization than their rivals in the ADAV. Persecution, the achievement of German unity, the inspiration of the Paris Commune of 1871, and the general recognition that they were seeking the same ends gradually brought the two parties together. The resignation of Johann Schweitzer from the leadership of the ADAV in 1871 was another factor helping the cause of unity. Practical co-operation in parliament was no less a factor. At the initiative of August Bebel (1840–1913), an NCO's son and turner by trade, Eisenachers and Lassalleans had rejected, in the Reichstag, credits for Bismarck's annexationist policy after the Franco-Prussian War. This was at the height of the 'Iron Chancellor's' prestige. Bebel had courageously praised the Paris

Commune in the Reichstag. He and Liebknecht, and later in 1874 Lassalleans too, faced imprisonment for their beliefs.

At a unity congress at Gotha in March 1875 the Socialist Workers' Party of Germany (SAD) was set up. The ADAV with its 16,500 members was represented by 71 delegates, while the 9,000 Eisenachers sent 16 delegates.[15]

Marx and Engels were appalled at the terms of the unity agreement. But, 'it would be difficult to imagine a more thorough misunderstanding of the situation' than that held by them.[16] They totally underestimated the strength of the Lassalleans, whose party they regarded as a 'dying sect'. Particularly annoying for the two revolutionists was the programme of the new party. It 'astonished' them 'not a little'.[17] They felt it denied the earlier internationalism of the Eisenachers, and contained Lassalle's ideas on wages, trade unions, and state-aided co-operatives. In view of subsequent history, their most important criticism was that it enshrined Lassalle's view of the state. The programme set out the usual catalogue of advanced liberal democratic demands, many of which had been achieved already in Switzerland and the United States. Marx, in his *Critique*, attacked the 'riotous misconception that it achieves in regard to the state'. It 'treats the state rather as an independent entity'[18] than as an organ of class domination. Marx asked, 'what transformation will the state undergo in communist society?' Instead of answering the question, however, he went on to set down his much-quoted paragraph:

> Between capitalist and communist society lies the period of revolutionary transformation of the one into the other. There corresponds to this also a political transition period in which the state can be nothing but the revolutionary dictatorship of the proletariat.[19]

The programme, he continued, had nothing to say about this. We must return to this later on.

Essentially, the German socialists were thinking in terms of the capture and democratization of the existing state, Marx was thinking of its overthrow and replacement by the dictatorship of the proletariat.

The criticisms made by Marx and Engels were not put before the members of the Eisenach party. They were suppressed by Wilhelm Liebknecht (1826–1900), who was the top man on the

Eisenach side of the unity negotiations. He feared their publication would jeopardize the talks for which he had worked for so long. August Bebel too had heard of the criticisms. He had received a letter from Engels which set out most of the basic points. The criticisms first became public in 1891.

In a way Engels himself admitted a justification for the action of Liebknecht and Bebel. His letter to Bebel contained the sentence, 'As a rule, the official programme of a party is less important than what it does'.[20] Those in the front line in Germany, who had already been imprisoned for their activities, no doubt felt their deeds were more important than dotting the 'i's on a party programme. It must also have occurred to them that the two emigrants were living relatively comfortable lives, in peace, well away from the din of the real political battle.

United in one party the German socialists entered upon a period of expansion which seemed to prove the Marxian thesis of the inevitability of socialism. With the exception of one election, 1878, they increased their share of the poll at every Reichstag election held in the German Empire. Fighting as separate bodies, they had received 124,000 votes (3.2 per cent) in 1871. Still campaigning separately, they gained 351,000 (6.8 per cent) in 1874. United they received 9.1 per cent of the vote three years later. In 1887 their vote reached a new high – 763,000 (10.1 per cent). By 1898 they were over the 2 million mark (27.2 per cent), winning 56 seats in the Reichstag.[21] Their parliamentary strength did not accurately reflect their vote. This was because of the unfair allocation of seats between urban and rural constituencies.

Germany's rulers did not try to hinder the socialists merely by unfair division of seats. They took more directly repressive action. In 1876 the party was banned in Prussia, the biggest state in the Empire, under the pretext that it violated the 1850 law of associations. This forced modifications of the formal party structure. Much worse was to come. In 1878 Bismarck got an excuse for a harsher measure. In May and June attempts, apparently unconnected, were made on the life of the Kaiser. The authorities found it impossible to involve the Socialist Party, though one of the assassins had been a member for a time. In the atmosphere of hysteria which followed, Bismarck was able to secure the passage of a bill against the socialists. Known as the *Sozialistengesetz*, it empowered the state and local governments to abolish societies with Social Democratic, socialist, or Communist leanings; to dissolve meetings exhibiting such tendencies; and to prohibit the publication and distribution of socialist literature of all kinds. Fines and imprisonment were the penalties for breaking this law. For areas where the socialists were strong and 'threatened public safety', the authorities could declare a Minor State of Siege. This enabled them to expel persons they regarded as dangerous. The law also prohibited the possession, carrying, import, or selling of arms.[22] Remarkably, the law had nothing to say about socialist parliamentary activities.

The anti-socialist law was renewed in 1880 for three and a half years, again in 1885 for two years, and once more in 1888 for two years. In 1890 Bismarck failed to find a Reichstag majority for its continuation. Under the law only two out of forty-seven socialist journals managed to survive and then by changing their names and toning down their content. All party and socialist trade union organizations either dissolved themselves or were dissolved by the authorities. Thousands of socialist journalists, printers, and party and trade union workers lost their livelihoods. According to Mehring,[23] some 900 persons were ordered to leave their homes in Berlin, Hamburg, Leipzig, Frankfurt, Stettin, and Spremberg. About 1,500 persons were sentenced altogether to one thousand years imprisonment. In recalling this harsh and unjust law it must be remembered that it was very mild indeed when compared to what has been done in more recent times by totalitarian regimes, including some describing themselves as Marxist.

How did the socialists react to the measures of Bismarck? Shock and despondency were the first reactions. The great majority of the leaders and members were just ordinary, law-abiding, workingmen, who had their families to think about. Some severed their socialist connections and never renewed them, the majority wanted to try to work within the law, a minority thought in terms of an underground organization. As Mehring emphasized,[24] armed resistance would have been madness.

As it was still possible for socialists to sit in the Reichstag, and other assemblies, the parliamentarians became the only possible national leadership. It was possible, legally and openly, to form what were officially temporary electoral organizations for the support of socialist candidates. In addition secret organizations of socialists were formed in most of the socialist strongholds.

The socialists held their first congress after their organization was outlawed at Wyden Castle, Switzerland, in August 1880. It appointed the party's Reichstag group as its official representative, set up a system of collecting party contributions, called for periodic congresses, and endorsed the *Sozialdemokrat* as the official party organ. The delegates recognized that they would have to engage in some illegal activity by deleting the word 'legal' from the section of the party programme which stated the party would work with 'all legal means'.[25]

Other party congresses were held abroad at Zürich (1882), Copenhagen (1883), and St Gallen (1887).

As is well known, the stick was only one side of Bismarck's policy to rid Germany of the socialists; the carrot was the other. Between 1883 and 1891 laws were enacted covering sickness insurance, accident insurance, retirement and disability pensions. They made Germany the leading state at that time in welfare legislation.

The electoral results, set out above, show that neither the stick nor the carrot was able to break German socialism. On the contrary, the movement went from strength to strength. It was in fact the socialist upsurge at the Reichstag election of February 1890, when the socialist vote practically doubled (from 10.1 per cent to 19.7), which virtually sealed the fate of Bismarck and his anti-socialist law. Already in January 1890 the Chancellor had failed to get the law renewed because the right-wing parties, shaken by a widespread miners' strike a few months before, could not agree on a modified version.

## IV. THE DEATH OF MARX

Marx did not live to see German socialism's victory over Bismarck. He died in 1883 aged sixty-five. Engels described the end as follows: 'On the afternoon of the 14th of March at a quarter to three the greatest living thinker ceased to think. Left alone for less than two minutes, when we entered we found him sleeping peacefully in his chair – but for ever'.[26]

Frau Jenny Marx had died in December 1881 and, Engels believed, at that time Karl 'the Moor has also died'. Marx's last year was spent largely in a vain effort to survive. He was attacked by pleurisy and his search for better health took him to the Isle of Wight, Algiers, Monte Carlo, and the shores of Lake Geneva, where he stayed with his daughter Laura. He returned to London in September 1882 apparently restored. His morale was then decisively undermined by the death of his thirty-nine-year-old daughter Jenny in January 1883. In the same month he returned to London from the Isle of Wight suffering from bronchitis. A broken man, he 'fell away from day to day'. Two of his daughters survived him. Both were interested in the working-class movement. Both committed suicide. His illegitimate son became a hard-working, respectable, British workman, who played a very modest, yet active, part in the early Labour Party.

In his address Engels called his friend 'the best-hated and most-slandered man of his age'. This was giving him a unique place he did not enjoy, hated and slandered though he was. There was also an element of exaggeration in the claim that 'he died honoured, loved and mourned by millions of revolutionary workers from the Siberian mines over Europe and America to the coasts of California'. That he was already a recognized international personality is indicated by the fact that Reuters News Agency cabled the news of his death around the world. This was taken up by Associated Press in the United States, and by agencies in Germany, France, and other countries. In New York 5,000 socialists attended a memorial meeting and meetings were held in other socialist strongholds.[27]

Summing up Marx's achievement at the end, Engels said:

As Darwin discovered the law of evolution in organic nature, so Marx discovered the law of evolution in human history: the simple fact, previously hidden under ideological growths, that human beings must first of all eat, drink, shelter and clothe themselves before they can turn their attention to politics, science, art and religion; that therefore the production of the immediate material means of life and consequently the given stage of economic development of a people or of a period forms the basis on which the state institutions, the legal principles, the art and even the religious ideas of the people in question have developed and out of which they must be explained, instead of exactly the contrary, as was previously attempted.

He further claimed for his friend:

But not only this, Marx discovered the special law of development of the present-day capitalist mode of production and of the bourgeois system of society which it has produced. With the discovery of surplus-value light was suddenly shed on the darkness in which all other economists, both bourgeois and socialist, had been groping.

These claims have been made by Marxists ever since. It is unlikely that their view will prevail. On the other hand, the generous, yet non-Marxist, assessment of Marx's contribution, made by Isaiah Berlin, seems nearer the truth: 'The true father of modern economic history, and indeed, of modern sociology, in so far as any one man may claim that title, is Karl Marx'.[28] But there is the negative side of Marx's legacy. As Golo Mann has put it:

> Two elements have come down from the *Manifesto* to our day with evil results: the certainty of possessing the key to the future, the complete certainty of being right while everybody else is wrong; and the readiness to make alliances with other groups – with those who are wrong – but only to use them, to cheat them and to destroy them as quickly as possible. 'We willingly support other left-wing parties', Lenin wrote, 'but as the rope supports the hanged man'. It was Marx and Engels who brought this curse of falsity into the world.[29]

In fairness, it should be added that the Marxists have not been alone either in thinking they have the 'key' or in the 'curse of falsity'.

Perhaps Marx dimly perceived this danger. It was in his last year that he used the oft-quoted phrase that as far as he was concerned he was certainly not a Marxist.[30] He had become despondent about the (dogmatic) way his ideas were being represented by his followers. Had he been able to see the twentieth century, he would certainly have rejected many things done in his name.

Somewhat mellowed, Engels enjoyed another twelve years of good living until his own death in 1895. But he used a good deal of his considerable energy in those last years sorting out Marx's papers. Without him *Capital* would have ended at volume I. He was able to visit Germany where he was impressed by the dynamic modern nation he found, and enjoy the adulation of a rapidly developing socialist movement.

## V. THE ERFURT PROGRAMME AND
## THE REVISIONIST CONTROVERSY

Having got the better of Bismarck and forced the abandonment of the anti-socialist law, the German socialists wanted to take stock of the new situation and prepare to exploit their new opportunities. This they did at the Erfurt Congress of 1891. August Bebel, the son of a professional soldier converted to Marxism by Liebknecht, emerged as one of the party's leading figures and was elected treasurer. (A year later he was elected one of the SPD's two chairmen.) The party's name officially became the Social Democratic Party of Germany (SPD) and a new programme was adopted unanimously. This programme was to be official policy for the next thirty years. Part I, the theoretical part, was largely the work of Karl Kautsky (1854–1938), who became known as the 'Pope of German Social Democracy', and as one of the two spiritual godfathers of the Russian Marxists. Born in Prague, the son of a Czech father and a German mother, and educated at Vienna University, he spent five years in London. It was there that he met Marx and Engels, and came to enjoy the confidence of the latter. Apparently, he was one of those individuals who never have any serious doubts about their beliefs or the direction of their interests. His commitment took the form of an entirely unshakeable certainty. 'This most erudite of Marxist scholars was also the most conservative of men, if conservatism signifies a profound concordance with the ideas and values of one's environment'.[31] As editor of the party's theoretical organ, *Die Neue Zeit*, he had published Marx's criticism of the Gotha Programme. Now he gave the SPD a Marxist programme to replace it.

Kautsky's part of the programme offered a brief exposition of the classic Marxist analysis of the development of capitalism:

> The economic development of bourgeois society leads inevitably to the destruction of the small workshop [*Kleinbetrieb*], whose basis is the private ownership by the worker of his means of production. It divides the worker from his means of production and turns him into a propertyless proletarian. Consequently, the means of production become the monopoly of a relatively small number of capitalists and big landowners.[32]

The advantages of large factories with their massive development of productivity are monopolized by the capitalists and large land-owners. For the proletariat and the sinking middle groups, this meant increasing insecurity, poverty, pressure, serfdom, humiliation, and exploitation. Ever great was the number of superfluous workers, ever greater were the contradictions between exploiters and exploited, which divided society into two hostile camps, and which were the common characteristic of all industrial countries. The answer was to take over the means of production for all. This could only be achieved when the working class had got political power. The interests of the workers of all capitalist countries were the same because with the development of the world market the situation of the worker in one country depended more and more on the situation of the worker in all other countries. The Social Democrats were at one with the class-conscious workers of all countries!

As both Marxist and non-Marxist writers have agreed, Kautsky overemphasized the economic factor in political development, tending towards economic determinism. The other major criticism is the failure to relate the theoretical analysis to the practical demands of the party. Nowhere in the programme do we find any explanation of how the workers are to capture power and realize socialism. Nowhere is the dictatorship of the proletariat mentioned. The second part of the programme, for which Eduard Bernstein was mainly responsible, listed the SPD's immediate goals. These were virtually the same as those of the Gotha Programme. They could have been achieved *within* the existing monarchical-parliamentary system. The idea of a democratic republic was not mentioned. 'The genuinely revolutionary principle in the context of Germany never emerged in the Erfurt program'.[33] Engels criticized this omission and added that the democratic republic was the 'specific form for the dictatorship of the proletariat'. Bebel replied that it was not possible to raise this question, given German conditions at that time.[34]

This lack of clarity in the programme left two questions unanswered. Firstly, how did the SPD leaders envisage the working class gaining political power? By parliamentary or by revolutionary means? Secondly, how did they, and for that matter Engels, interpret the term dictatorship of the proletariat?

At Erfurt Wilhelm Liebknecht, in replying to left-wing criticisms, upheld the view that the centre of gravity of the party's activity was not the Reichstag, but outside it. The SPD had no decisive influence in parliament.

> But does it follow that, because we have not a decisive influence, we must condemn parliamentarism? Parliamentarism is simply the system of representation of the people. If so far we have not achieved results in the Reichstag, that is not the fault of parliamentarism: it is simply the consequence of our not having yet in the country, among the people, the necessary power.

And he went on to remind his comrades that 'the essence of revolutionism lies not in the means, but in the end'. G. D. H. Cole, from whose book this quote is taken, concluded from this that the SPD's leaders, 'flushed by their successful resistance under the repression and by their notable electoral achievements . . . had become parliamentarians'. They had come to believe that the Reichstag could be used as an instrument for bringing about the socialist transformation of society.[35]

This view has not gone unchallenged. It has been argued that due to their experiences before 1891, Bebel and some others, if not Liebknecht, were 'ambivalent parliamentarians'. But they were also 'ambivalent revolutionaries. Success in elections and the occasional hope of influencing legislation made it unnecessary for them to think in terms of direct revolutionary action'.[36] Certainly, whatever their exact theoretical positions, if they had any, the SPD's leaders were moving in the direction of the parliamentary road to socialism. On all the evidence, the way they treated the concept of the dictatorship of the proletariat is a further indication of this. But had not Marx and Engels made it easy to combine the concept of the dictatorship with democracy?

The term Dictatorship of the Proletariat is one of the most abused in the history of ideas. Marx and Engels used it very sparingly indeed. The first use of it by the two is by Marx in *The Class Struggles in France 1848–1850*. He also mentioned it, without elaboration, in a letter to Weydemeyer in 1852. After that, for the next twenty years 'no sign of the term appears in any writing public or private by Marx and Engels'.[37] Engels uses it twice rather indiscriminately in *The Housing Question* (1872), claiming the Chartists were for it! He therefore appears to be using it loosely in the sense of 'class domination', 'rule of the working class', etc. As we saw earlier, Marx applied the term in his criticism of the Gotha Programme of 1875. Again he said little by way of elaboration. These statements are only elaborated to the extent that Marx and Engels gave advice over the years to different working-class groups. In the *Manifesto* they stated:

> . . . the first step in the revolution by the working class, is to raise the proletariat to the position of ruling class, to win the battle of democracy.

In 1872 Marx told the International that 'there are countries like England and America . . . I might even add Holland, where the worker may attain his object by peaceful means. But not in all countries is this the case'. Engels too had thought this a possibility in Britain. There, he believed, 'democracy means the domination of the working class'.[38] That was written in 1881 at a time when not all workingmen in Britain had the vote. Engels obviously that that once all had attained the vote, there would be a permanent socialist government in Britain, a government representing the 'immense majority'. In sum, although Marx and Engels believed different countries would tread different roads to socialism, they seemed to have believed that in the advanced nations it would be a civilized, parliamentary road. Further, unlike some of their followers, they were not obsessed with the concept of the dictatorship of the proletariat. No doubt they believed its content would differ according to circumstances. On the evidence one feels that in the countries of advanced democracy they took it to mean that the workers, having gained power, would resist attempts by reactionary groups to sabotage their efforts. But it must be admitted that Engels got impatient with anti-authoritarians who seemed to think revolutionaries could rule with kid gloves. 'A revolution is the most authoritarian thing there is . . . if the victorious party does not want to have fought in vain, it must maintain this rule by means of the terror which its arms inspire in the reactionaries'. So he wrote in 1873. Yet even in the case of Germany, Engels, in his final years, came to the conclusion that it was best to try for the parliamentary road. In 1895, after gloating about the regular increase in the SPD's vote over the years, he went on:

> With this successful utilization of universal suffrage, however, an entirely new method of proletarian struggle came into operation. . . . It was found that the state institutions, in which

the rule of the bourgeoisie is organized, offer the working class still further opportunities to fight these very state institutions. . . . And it so happened that the bourgeoisie and the government came to be much more afraid of the legal than of the illegal action of the workers' party, of the results of elections than of those of rebellion.

In any case, with the development of weapons and military techniques, 'rebellion in the old style, street fighting with barricades . . . was to a considerable extent obsolete'. He had not entirely thrown out the possibility of 'street fighting' but, 'the time of surprise attacks, of revolutions carried through by small conscious minorities at the head of unconscious masses, is past'. And to the German Social Democrats he gave this specific advice:

To keep this growth [of the SPD strength] going without interruption until it of itself gets beyond the control of the prevailing governmental system . . . that is our main task. And there is only one means by which the steady rise of the socialist fighting forces in Germany could be temporarily halted, and even thrown back for some time: a clash with the military, a bloodletting like that of 1871 in Paris.[39]

And elsewhere in the same work Engels courageously admitted that in the 1848–50 period, he and Marx had been wrong. 'But history has shown us too to have been wrong, has revealed our point of view of that time to have been an illusion'.[40]

With such advice the leaders of German Social Democracy could feel that their revolutionary purity was in no way in danger as they concentrated their efforts on the parliamentary and trade union struggles. They did not need explicitly to throw out the dictatorship of the proletariat, for in as much as they thought about it at all, it was more and more becoming synonymous with democracy, and that meant rule of the majority, of the working class.

Having become a mass party, it was only to be expected that the SPD would not speak with one voice on all issues all the time. Its programme, and the theories on which it was based, would be challenged when they did not appear to accord with the factors or with the interests of the party.

The man who came to challenge official party orthodoxy most systematically and most intellectually was Eduard Bernstein

(1850–1932) – the 'father of Revisionism'. Bernstein was the son of a Berlin train driver. A 'non-Jewish' Jew, he left the grammar school at the age of sixteen to work in a bank. He joined the Eisenachers in 1872 and later worked as a party journalist in Switzerland and then in London. Like Kautsky he became closely associated with Engels who thought highly of him. It was in London that Bernstein began to have second thoughts on some aspects of Marxism. This development was aided by his contacts with the Fabian Society, among whose leading members were Bernard Shaw, Graham Wallas, and the Webbs. In 1896 his first revisionist articles appeared and his major revisionist work, *Die Voraussetzungen des Sozialismus und die Aufgaben der Sozial-demokratie* (The Preconditions of Socialism and the Tasks of Social Democracy), in 1899. His main revisionist works were published, therefore, while he was still in exile.

Which parts of Marxist thought did Bernstein want to revise? First of all, he criticized particular aspects of the Marxian view of the way capitalism was developing. Secondly, he was worried about the more fundamental question of whether Marxism was scientific – as it is supposed to be. Thirdly, his theories led him to urge revision of the SPD's practical politics. The particular aspects of Marxism he felt were in conflict with the facts included: the pauperization of the workers theory; the view that the small peasant was due to disappear; the notion that increasing concentration was taking place in the economy and thus eliminating small firms; the expectation that the middle classes would gradually be thrust down into the working class with the subsequent increase in class conflict; the awaited deepening crisis of capitalism. Further, he was not happy with the Marxian theory of value:

> the existence of surplus value is an empirical fact which can be demonstrated in experience and needs no deductive proof. Whether Marx's value theory is correct or not is of no significance whatever for the proof of the reality of surplus value. It serves, in this respect, not as a proof but as an aid to analysis, and as an illustration.[41]

Even more fundamentally, Bernstein attacked the notion that Marxism was scientific. He claimed that socialism was ethically desirable, but not something which one could prove historically inevitable. He wanted to replace the scientific determinism of

Marx by the ethic of Kant. For Bernstein the final goal was
nothing, the movement all. He rejected the idea that a nation
could arrive on the sunny banks of socialism. Rather, the
socialist movement was continuously travelling towards the
promised land without actually getting there. In other words, the
socialist movement could successfully fight to improve society,
but there would always be new problems waiting for the courage,
energy, and imagination of reformers. These theories led him to
preach that the SPD should openly admit that it was no longer a
party of revolution, but a radical, parliamentary reform party.
Clearly, such theories were bound to meet with a great deal of
opposition. They amounted to telling the faithful that Heaven
did not exist and that a great deal of blood, sweat, and tears would
be needed just to ameliorate conditions in this 'vale of tears'.
Satan would always be at work but there would be no Day of
Judgement.

If the leaders had their doubts about this or that aspect of
Marxist theory, they must have found it difficult to swallow all of
Bernstein's revisions. And, as party managers trying to hold
together a mass movement under strong pressure from its
adversaries, they must have cursed Bernstein for having unleashed the controversy about party ideology. Bebel condemned
Bernsteinism at the Stuttgart Congress of the SPD in 1898, and
again, after Bernstein's return to Germany, at the Hanover
Congress in 1899. At Dresden (1903) Bebel protested: 'I shall
remain the deadly enemy of this bourgeois society and state
system . . . undermine [it] and, if I can, destroy it'.[42] He denounced revisionism for splitting the party, holding back its
development, and forcing members to fight each other.[43]

Nevertheless, revisionism was welcomed by many prominent
in the Social Democratic movement. A measure of this was the
selection, and then election, of Bernstein to the Reichstag on the
official SPD ticket in 1902. Another was Bebel's change of mind
over Bernstein's expulsion from the party.[44] Who were the supporters of Bernstein in the SPD? There were the leaders of the
Bavarian Social Democrats, outstanding among whom was
Georg von Vollmar, who welcomed Bernstein's advocacy of
electoral pacts with the Liberals. There were the trade union
leaders Carl Legien and Theodor Leipart, who were attracted to
revisionism because it accorded their organizations a greater role
as bodies working for a step-by-step improvement in the

workers' position. There were the party officials for whom the building-up of the organization, and the great battles of words for small reforms, became everything. There were members of the SPD's parliamentary group who were either intimidated into 'respectability' by the atmosphere in the Reichstag, or who, due to daily contact, grew to respect their opponents rather than seeing them as deadly enemies. In most cases, these were ex-workers who, through the socialist movement, had now a little more to lose than just their 'chains'. They had fought hard, and in doing so had gained for themselves a foothold in society. This they did not want to put at risk by revolutionism. Bernstein justified their class position. It would be very unfair to Bernstein to imply that this had been his aim. He had needed courage to write and say the things he did. Later, he showed as much, if not more, courage, by opposing the German government in the First World War. In so doing he angered most of his erstwhile friends and foes alike.

As well as the revisionists, the leaders of the SPD had to contend with a highly articulate body of left-wing opinion before 1914. The most interesting spokesman of this trend was Rosa Luxemburg. Like Bernstein, and some other prominent intellectuals of the SPD, Rosa Luxemburg (1871–1919) was of Jewish background. Her native Poland was divided between the empires of Russia, Austria, and Germany with very limited opportunities for higher education and free discussion. Between 1889 and 1905 she distinguished herself as a student of mathematics, economics, and science at Zürich University. Her first book was a volume on the industrial development of Poland and was published in 1892. It was recognized as a work of considerable scholarship. A socialist from the age of sixteen, she married a German socialist in 1897 'to gain admission to Germany'.[45] In the SPD she was for some time associated with Kautsky in the struggle against revisionism, but later she clashed with the party leaders and Kautsky whom she regarded as 'centrists'. Her contribution to socialist theory was mainly concerned with the struggle against revisionism; the theory of the mass strike; spontaneity theory; imperialism; the national question with special reference to Poland; the critique of Lenin. Here we are concerned with her as Bernstein's opponent.

While not opposed to working for particular reforms, she wrote of the revisionists in her book *Reform or Revolution*:

Instead of the establishment of a new society they take a stand for surface modifications of the old society. If we follow the political conceptions of revisionism, we arrive at the same conclusion that is reached when we follow the economic theories of revisionism. Our program becomes not the realization of socialism, but the reform of capitalism; not the suppression of the system of wage labour, but the reform of capitalism. . . .[46]

With such arguments she was not likely to fall foul of Bebel or Kautsky. In those early years she was the ally of the platform against the Bernstein trend. Later, in the years before the First World War, the party shifted to the right and Rosa Luxemburg became increasingly isolated. An indication of this was her inability to get herself elected as a delegate to party congresses. Of the last five congresses before the war she attended only three; both in 1909 and in 1912 she failed to obtain a mandate and at Magdeburg in 1910 her credentials were challenged.[47] The Left's weakness can be explained by the growing bureaucratization of the party – by 1900 the SPD had more paid officials than the British Labour Party in 1960; the growing importance of its parliamentary wing; by prosperity and the spread of imperialist ideology. The mood of the country permeated the party.[48] On an international scale the same arguments were developing, the same trends appearing.

### VI. THE SECOND INTERNATIONAL

The 1880s saw the growth of socialist movements in a number of other countries besides Germany. The development of industry produced the industrial proletariats – the raw material of the socialist movements. The extensions of the franchise and of literacy were further conditions which aided socialist movements. Small, though not insignificant, parties were formed in Belgium, Switzerland, and Austria. There were smaller groups, which were later to be of very great significance, in Russia and Sweden. In 1887 a Czech Social Democratic Party was founded. Five years later a socialist party was established in Italy – so long an anarchist stronghold.

In America there was substantial socialist activity. The Socialist Labor Party, founded in 1877, was the main vehicle of

Marxism before the World War. Its leader was Daniel De Leon (1852–1914). Born in the Dutch West Indies and educated at the Universities of Leiden and Columbia, he was regarded as an orthodox Marxist. Although he believed in the overthrow of the capitalist system, he preached 'The ballot is the weapon of civilization'.[49] By the end of 1879 the SLP claimed 10,000 members. Yet a year later membership was down to less than 1,500, of whom perhaps 10 per cent were native Americans. The U.S. labor movement suffered from being based to a considerable extent on foreign-born socialists. They carried the quarrels of the European movement to America. Like European Marxists they neglected the farmers. Moreover, the main unions organized in the American Federation of Labor, headed by Dutch-Jewish-born Samuel Gompers, had by 1900 shed the socialist influence. In 1899 the majority of the SLP led by Morris Hillquit, a Russian immigrant, broke with De Leon. The Hillquit group joined Berger and Debbs's Social Democracy of America to establish the Socialist Party of America in 1901. The new body contained both Marxists and non-Marxists. In the 'Golden Age' of American socialism, from 1902 to 1912, the Socialist Party briefly attracted 125,826 members. In 1911, seventy-four socialist mayors or other major municipal officers were elected in the United States.[50] The year before, Austrian-born Victor Berger was elected as first socialist congressman. But the basic weaknesses of the movement remained, and the socialists now suffered from the orthodox politicians stealing their clothes. This was especially evident in the 1912 Presidential campaign. Eugene Debbs (1855–1926), former rail union organizer from Indiana, won 897,000 votes, almost six per cent of the total, against Woodrow Wilson and Teddy Roosevelt.

In Britain, still the most advanced industrial nation at that time, only small Marxist groups existed – H. M. Hyndman's Social Democratic Federation (formed in 1883 from his Democratic Federation of 1881), and William Morris's Socialist League (1884).

It was in France alone that socialist groups appeared which looked as though they might come to rival the party of Bebel and Liebknecht. There, the post-Commune White terror had ended in a general amnesty of Leftists in 1880. A Marxist socialist party, the *Parti Ouvrier Français*, was set up in 1879 with Marx's blessing. Among its noted leaders were Jules Guesde (1845–1922) and Marx's son-in-law Paul Lafargue (1842–1911). Guesde, 'a proud, honourable, bigoted man, lacking in personal charm, but with an energy, honesty, and disinterestedness that gave him strength',[51] was a journalist from a poor middle-class home. Soon, a breakaway movement led by Paul Brousse set up the *Fédération des Travailleurs Socialistes de France*. This party, which became known as the 'Possibilist' trend, was vaguely anarchist, suspicious of German control (through Marx and Engels in the first place), recognized the value of a bourgeois republic (as against a more authoritarian system), and was prepared to co-operate for limited ends with parties to its right. In all these things it contrasted with the position of the POF. There was yet another French socialist party, the *Parti Socialiste Revolutionnaire*, led by Edouard Vaillant, a follower of Blanqui. It 'combined a belief in direct revolutionary action with a belief in the importance of a small elite to lead the revolution'. And it was 'more the expression of a political temperament than of a doctrine'.[52]

The growth of all these parties, in France and elsewhere, led to a revival of interest in forming a new International of working-class organizations. The improvement in the political climate in both Germany and France made this more feasible. Obviously, the survivors of the First International were most anxious to bring this about, and many younger socialists were encouraged by the example of that body. Perhaps too, the general growth of international exchanges, trade fairs, technical and scientific congresses, even congresses of governments (Berlin in 1878, for instance), made socialist efforts in this direction seem less utopian than before.

At their congress at St Gallen in 1887 the German socialists decided to take steps to convene an international meeting of socialists. In Britain, in the same year, the Trades Union Congress accepted the idea of an international conference to campaign for an eight-hour working-day. The French Possibilists responded to the British unionists. In the following year a TUC meeting in London, attended by the Possibilists and other foreign delegates, but not by the German socialists, agreed to call an international congress in 1889. The Germans were unable to get the agreement of the British TUC and the French Possibilists to an all-embracing congress and so decided, with their international allies, to hold a rival congress. Thus two socialist congresses were held in Paris in 1889. Paris was chosen because the centenary of the

French Revolution was being celebrated there in grand style with an exhibition.

Both congresses attracted considerable support; some delegates even took the precaution of attending both! Others did not make their decision to attend one rather than the other on purely political grounds; personal rivalries and ignorance also swayed them. The Possibilists got their congress reported in *The Times*, but the Marxist congress 'could claim to be the founding congress of the new International'.[53] It was widely representative of the socialist movement throughout Europe and the United States, attended by nearly 400 delegates from twenty countries. As one would expect, the French sent the largest delegation, the Germans the second largest. These two saw members of their delegations, Edouard Vaillant and Wilhelm Liebknecht respectively, elected joint presidents. Bebel, Bernstein, and von Vollmar were also there from Germany. Three members of the Marx family helped to ensure 'the apostolic succession'[54] and to impress upon delegates that this congress was carrying on the work of the First International. Eleanor Marx, already well known in London Labour circles, was one of the British delegates, and her two brothers-in-law, Paul Lafargue and Charles Longuet, were present as French delegates. William Morris was the most distinguished British representative, Keir Hardie was to become the most influential. Engels did not put in an appearance at the congress.

The Marxist congress, like the other one for that matter, spent a considerable amount of time arguing about delegates' credentials and about procedure. Once these matters were settled, most of the remaining time was given over to hearing reports from individual parties and groups. At the end, a number of resolutions were passed without very much discussion. These were on the topics which subsequent congresses were to return to again and again: an eight-hour working-day and improved conditions of labour; extension of voting rights; war and peace; and the establishment of May Day as a day of international working-class solidarity. However, the achievement of this and later congresses was not in the resolutions passed. The congresses of the Second International provided socialists with opportunities of discussing common problems. They provided working-class politicians, some of whom were later to become important ministers in their respective countries, with an extension of their education. They helped to sustain and foster the smaller parties whose members took courage from the progress made by their stronger brother parties. It can also be fairly claimed that the Second International was in some ways a useful forerunner of the League of Nations and the United Nations. As in the case of these later bodies, the hopes of its founders were not realized. Indeed, the International had a negative side. Princes, politicians, and proletarians credited it with far more power and influence than it ever had. The International fostered the illusion that the organized masses could and would stop any attempts to plunge the world into war.

The size, influence, and financial resources of the SPD, and the lack of a united French party, meant that the Second International became increasingly prone to German influence. The anarchists, who were particularly critical of the German party, though not only of the German party, were rejected or expelled in 1891, 1893, and 1896. The strength of the Germans and the absence of the anarchists meant that a superficial Marxism pervaded the International. 'Marxist phraseology was the lingua franca of the parties of the Second International'.[55] The resolutions adopted tended to be very similar to those passed previously at SPD conferences. A notable example of this was the resolution condemning revisionism adopted at the Amsterdam Congress of 1904. This resolution, which followed an oral duel between Bebel and the French socialist leader Jean Jaurès, was virtually the same as one accepted the previous year at the SPD's Dresden conference.

It is neither possible nor necessary to discuss here all those resolutions and the debates which preceded them. Suffice it to look at the development of the International's position on the crucial issue of peace and war – the issue their orthodox Marxism was not adequate to handle, the issue which destroyed the International.

Marx and Engels were anything but pacifists. They had distinguished between 'just' and 'unjust' wars. Wars which advanced the march of history, wars for revolutionary ideals, wars of liberation, were 'just'. The war to rid Germany of Napoleon's armies was just, as was the American War of Independence. When the Franco-Prussian War broke out in 1870 they had agreed with their comrades in Germany that a war to defend the Fatherland against the French Emperor was just. However, after the French defeat at Sedan, when Germany advanced claims to

Alsace-Lorraine, Marx and Engels and Bebel condemned the war as aggressive. A system particularly hated and feared by the Left was Tsarism. Engels and Bebel had clearly indicated what socialists should do in case of war with Russia. So Bebel in 1891: 'The soil of Germany, the German fatherland belongs to us the masses as much and more than to the others. If Russia, the champion of terror and barbarism, went to attack Germany to break and destroy it . . . we are as much concerned as those who stand at the head of Germany'.[56]

What should socialists do in peacetime? How should they react to the military appropriations which were placed before them in their parliaments? The SPD had an answer.[57] The party simply rejected the appropriations right up to 1914. It could have no confidence in a reactionary officer corps serving a capitalist imperial system. However, as it could not yet change the system, and as those it claimed to represent were conscripted into the forces, it advanced reforms. This could be claimed as effective propaganda, for it indicated even to non-political soldiers that the SPD was on their side. It attacked the brutality of the officers towards their men. It even advanced the cause of the khaki uniform, against the traditional blue, claiming that this would cut down the loss of German working-class soldiers in case of war! In an age of increasing imperialist rivalry in the colonial field the SPD condemned colonial wars. Such a policy was not without its complications – was it progressive to help the German imperialist armies to save lives with khaki when they were fighting colonial wars? – but it looked like a good compromise in the circumstances.

The French socialists, or rather their greatest leader of the period, Jaurès, had given the problem of war some thought. Jaurès came out quite unequivocally in favour of defence of the existing, French, bourgeois republic should it be attacked. He of course was not a Marxist.

The Second International discussed the issue of peace and war definitively at Stuttgart in 1907 and at Copenhagen in 1910. The resolution adopted at Stuttgart was the work of a subcommittee of fourteen which included Bebel and Vollmar, Jaurès and Guesde, Victor Adler (from Austria) and Rosa Luxemburg. The results of the committee's deliberations 'contained something for everybody while committing nobody to anything'.[58] The resolution contained the standard Marxist notion that 'wars are . . . inherent in the nature of capitalism; they will only cease when capitalist economy is abolished . . .'. It then went on to urge the representatives of the working class 'in parliament . . . to fight with all their strength against naval and military armament . . .'. What was needed as 'an essential guarantee for the prevention of aggressive wars' was a 'popular militia instead of the standing army'. All this was good old Social Democratic stuff which was no doubt Bebel's contribution. There was some contradiction between the notion that wars were inherent in the system and the view of militias as an essential guarantee, but that did not matter. The next sentence also suited the SPD: 'The International is not able to lay down the exact form of working-class action against militarism at the right place and time, as this naturally differs in different countries'. In other words this left the SPD, and other parties, free to take any action they thought fit. Right at the very end came Luxemburg's contribution and one wonders how she managed to sneak it in:

> Should war break out in spite of all this, it is their duty to intercede for its speedy end, and to strive with all their power to make use of the violent economic and political crisis brought about by the war to rouse the people, and thereby to hasten the abolition of capitalist class rule.[59]

This paragraph, based on the experience of the Russian revolution of 1905, clearly committed all parties to revolutionary action.

The Congress of Copenhagen in 1910 agreed a resolution calling on all socialist parties to vote against arms appropriations, to demand compulsory arbitration, and to work for general disarmament, secret diplomacy, and the autonomy of all peoples and their defence against attack and oppression. A motion proposed by the French socialist Vaillant, and supported by the 'father of the British Labour Party', James Keir Hardie, urging a general strike in case of war, did not get very far.[60]

The war clouds gathered and finally burst, and with them burst the illusion of the International. Lenin was able to harvest the fruits of this failure. Bebel and Jaurès did not live to experience this final collapse: the former died in 1913, the latter was assassinated in 1914.

NOTES

[1] See G. Stolper, *The German Economy: 1870 to the Present* (New York, 1967).
[2] V. L. Lidtke, *The Outlawed Party: Social Democracy in Germany 1878–1890* (Princeton, 1966), p. 12.
[3] Mehring, op. cit., p. 252.
[4] ibid., pp. 251, 308.
[5] ibid., p. 256.
[6] M. M. Drachkovitch (ed.), *The Revolutionary Internationals, 1864–1943* (Stanford and London, 1966), p. 7.
[7] Mehring, op. cit., pp. 323–4.
[8] Drachkovitch, op. cit., p. 14.
[9] Mehring, op. cit., p. 334.
[10] Manfred Kliem, *Karl Marx Dokumente seines Lebens* (Leipzig, 1970), pp. 394–5.
[11] Mehring, op. cit., p. 340.
[12] ibid., p. 336.
[13] ibid., p. 497.
[14] ibid., pp. 499–500.
[15] Heinz Göhler (ed.), *Der demokratische Sozialismus zwischen Tradition und Fortschritt* (Munich, 1967), p. 22.
[16] Mehring, op. cit., p. 508.
[17] Engels to Bebel, 18–28 March 1875, as given in Karl Marx, *Critique of the Gotha Programme* (London, 1943), p. 35.
[18] ibid., p. 27.
[19] ibid., pp. 27–8.
[20] ibid., p. 45.
[21] Göhler, op. cit., p. 30.
[22] H. Bartel *et al.*, *Geschichte der deutschen Arbeiterbewegung* (East Berlin, 1966), I, 603–5.
[23] F. Mehring, *Geschichte der deutschen Sozialdemokratie* (East Berlin, 1960), Zweiter Teil, 674.
[24] ibid., 514.
[25] Lidtke, op. cit., p. 98.
[26] Mehring, *Karl Marx*: this and the following quotations are from pp. 528–32.
[27] Kliem, op. cit., p. 501.
[28] Berlin, op. cit., p. 158.
[29] Golo Mann, in *Karl Marx 1818/1968* (Inter Nationes, Bad Godesberg, 1968), p. 16.
[30] Mehring, *Karl Marx*, p. 503.
[31] George Lichtheim, *Marxism: an Historical and Critical Study* (London, 1961), p. 266.
[32] Karl Kautsky, *Programme der deutschen Sozialdemokratie* (Hanover, 1963), pp. 77–8. Introduction by Willi Eichler.
[33] Lidtke, op. cit., p. 234.
[34] ibid.
[35] G. D. H. Cole, *The Second International 1889–1914* (London, 1956), pp. 254–5.
[36] Lidtke, op. cit., p. 329.
[37] See the analysis by Hal Draper, 'Dictatorship of the Proletariat', in Curtis, op. cit., p. 290.
[38] Quoted W. O. Henderson (ed.), *Engels: Selected Writings* (London, 1967), pp. 111–12.

[39] Engels's Introduction (1895) to Karl Marx, *The Class Struggles in France 1848 to 1850* (Moscow, 1952), pp. 28–39.

[40] ibid., pp. 15–16.

[41] Peter Gay, *The Dilemma of Democratic Socialism: Eduard Bernstein's Challenge to Marx* (New York, 1962), p. 183. For this section the author has also used Helmut Hirsch (ed.), *Ein revisionistisches Sozialismus Bild* (Hanover, 1966).

[42] Göhler, op. cit., p. 35.

[43] H. Gemkow (ed.), *August Bebel, Diesem System keinen Mann und keinen Groschen* (East Berlin, 1961), p. 74.

[44] Gay, op. cit., p. 81.

[45] J. P. Nettl, *Rosa Luxemburg* (London, 1966), p. 960.

[46] Quoted Tony Cliff, *Rosa Luxemburg* (London, 1959), pp. 28–9.

[47] Nettl, op. cit., p. 459.

[48] ibid., p. 457. See C. Schorske, *German Social Democracy: 1905–1917* (Cambridge, Mass., 1955).

[49] This brief outline of American socialism is taken from Daniel Bell, *Marxian Socialism in the United States* (Princeton, 1967); James Weinstein, *The Decline of Socialism in America, 1912–1925* (New York, 1967).

[50] Bell, op. cit., p. 71; Weinstein, op. cit., p. 116.

[51] James Joll, *The Second International 1889–1914* (London, 1968), pp. 14–15.

[52] ibid., pp. 16–17.

[53] ibid., p. 35.

[54] ibid., p. 36.

[55] Gerhart Niemeyer, in Drachkovitch, op. cit., p. 123.

[56] Joll, op. cit., p. 112.

[57] Karl Drott (ed.), *Sozialdemokratie und Wehrfrage* (Berlin and Hanover).

[58] Joll, op. cit., p. 138.

[59] ibid., p. 198. The full text of the resolution is found here.

[60] ibid., p. 140.

# III

## Mensheviks and Bolsheviks in Russia

AS Edmund Wilson reminds us,[1] it was with considerable surprise that Marx learned in the fall of 1868 that a translation of *Das Kapital* into Russian was being printed in St Petersburg, then Russia's first city. Up to then he and Engels had held little of the Russians, an attitude they shared with most West European liberals and socialists. Marx had denounced Russia in a series of articles which later appeared under the title of *Secret Diplomatic History of the Eighteenth Century*. From 1868 onwards he took an interest in Russian affairs and even learned the language. It is not certain just how far he developed his thinking on the subject.

Engels, too, turned his attention to Russia. In 1875 in his *Social Conditions in Russia* he set out his thoughts on revolution in that country. He believed that no revolution in western Europe could finally conquer as long as the then Russian state existed beside it. Germany was particularly vulnerable to 'the shock of the Russian armies of reaction'. The overthrow of Tsarism and the dissolution of the Russian Empire were consequently the first conditions for the ultimate victory of the German workers. Defeat in war would hasten this dissolution, but inside Russia itself there were forces working strongly for the ruin of Tsarism. In Russia there were all the conditions for a revolution: 'in spite of the primitive simplicity of bourgeois society, capitalistic parasitism is so developed, so covers and enmeshes the whole country' that revolution seemed inevitable. Possibly this revolution would be started by the upper classes of the capital, 'even perhaps by the Government itself'. It must be rapidly carried further by the peasants. Clearly, Engels was not thinking in terms of a proletarian revolution, but one which would enable Russia to embark on bourgeois, democratic, capitalist development. What were the forces within the Russian Empire working so strongly for its ruin?

## I. PLEKHANOV AND THE ROLE OF THE INDIVIDUAL

The revolutionary movement in Russia stretched back to Napoleonic times when officers, infected with the ideas of the French Revolution, tried to overthrow the Tsar. They became known as the Decembrists and hoped to establish constitutional government in Russia. Most of them were either killed or exiled in December 1825. In the following years many other groups were crushed. They were given the composite name of *narodniki* and believed in the theory of peasant revolution and the practice of terrorism against the imperial family and its officials. Russian democratic thought was from the start associated with some vague sort of socialism. Political opposition to absolutism was part of a wider opposition not only to serfdom, but also to the nascent capitalism as well. Many of Russia's brightest intellects – Herzen, Turgenev, Chernyshevsky, Tkachev, and, of course, Bakunin – took part in this movement.

Russia was changing. Serfdom was abolished in 1861. In theory this gave the peasants more freedom, in practice they were weighted down with the burdens of heavy mortgages. Capitalism was spreading to agriculture. Urban capitalism was also developing. The number of factory-workers, miners, and railway employees increased from $1\frac{1}{2}$ million in 1887 to 2.8 million in 1900. In the ten years between 1887 and 1897 the numbers of those employed in these categories increased by 64 per cent, while the increase of population was not greater than 15 per cent. There was a rapid extension of railways towards the turn of the century. The Trans-Siberian railway 'will always rank as one of the most daring railway projects of modern times'.[2] More astonishing, the Tashkent railway had been an early innovator in diesel traction and had actually built a gas turbine locomotive. There were even diesel electric Russian-built ships! In fact, an American expert has summed up Russian development before 1914 as follows:

Although industrialization was restricted to a few population centers, it utilized modern, efficient plants operating on scales comparable to those elsewhere in the world. Further, there were obvious signs of indigenous Russian technology in chemicals, aircraft, automobiles, turbines, and railroad equipment.[3]

Some social progress could also be recorded. In 1882 a factory inspectorate was introduced, children under twelve were not allowed to work, and restrictions were placed on the employment of adolescents. Other laws followed, including one restricting the work of women and another abolishing payment in kind. By fits and starts progress was being made in education too. In the 1897 census, it was found that in European Russia 35.8 per cent of the men and 12.4 per cent of women were literate. By 1913, 73 per cent of army recruits were literate, compared with only 31 per cent in 1890.[4]

In this situation it was only to be expected that sooner or later some revolutionaries would begin to analyse Russia's problems in Marxist terms. This happened after 1880 when George V. Plekhanov (1856–1918) broke with the *narodniki*, because he believed acts of individual terrorism to be futile, and became a Marxist while living in western Europe. Plekhanov, son of a minor landowner, soon gained sympathy for the Russian peasant. After education at the St Petersburg Mining Institute and revolutionary activity in Russia, he went abroad not to return until the revolution of 1917. Whereas earlier revolutionaries had looked into Russia's own institutions for inspiration, Plekhanov looked to the Social Democratic movements of the West. He became known as the father of Russian Marxism. In 1883, in Switzerland, he, together with Vera Zasulich (1852–1919), a veteran of revolutionary conspiracy, and some others, set up a Marxist group called the 'Liberation of Labour'. Plekhanov, who despite his later break with Lenin is still venerated in the Soviet Union, is mainly known for his elaboration of the theory of historical materialism, and the Marxist view of the role of the individual in history. It is illuminating to quote at some length from his essay on the latter subject. He attacked the idea that Marx's conception of history meant a direct, causal line between the realm of ideas and the economic base. Following Engels, he tried to demonstrate that the Marxist view of history is not merely economic determinism, that, as Marx put it, men make their own history, and that the leader has an important role to play in making that history, but that, in the long run, the underlying economic development explains the 'superstructure', the institutions and ideas of a society. In rejecting the allegation that historical materialism leads to fatalism and paralysis of the will because it regards socialism as inevitable, he continues:

There cannot be the slightest doubt that the materialist conception of the human will is quite compatible with the most vigorous practical activity. . . .

. . . Let us, however, examine more closely the case when a man's own – past, present or future – actions seem to him to be entirely coloured by necessity. We know already that such a man, regarding himself as a messenger of God, like Mohammed, as one chosen by ineluctable destiny, like Napoleon, or as the expression of the irresistible force of historical progress, like some of the public men in the nineteenth century, displays almost elemental strength of will, and sweeps from his path like a house of cards all the obstacles set up by the small-town Hamlets or Hamletkins.[5]

Although he did not yet know it, Plekhanov had already met the man to prove his point, though that man – Vladimir Ilyich Ulyanov (Lenin) – was to accuse him, in so many words, of behaving like a small-town Hamlet when faced with the decisions of making history.

## II. 'WHAT IS TO BE DONE?'

Vladimir Ilyich Ulyanov was born in April 1870, the son of an inspector of schools who because of his office gained an hereditary title of nobility. His mother was the daughter of a Volga-German physician turned landowner. Vladimir was therefore brought up in comfortable, bourgeois surroundings. But his mother's Lutheran German origins probably raised certain questions in his mind. The social-class realities of his very provincial town – 935 miles from St Petersburg – must also have caused him to think. There were those from the old nobility who looked down on his kind and with the merchants of the town his family had little in common. His father's liberal tendencies were another important factor in his development. The event which turned him from a detached, intellectual opponent of the regime to a ruthless, practical one was the execution of his brother Alexander for taking part in a plot to assassinate Tsar Alexander III. The same event led him, like Plekhanov before him, to reject assassination as a means of overthrowing Tsarism in favour of the broader strategy of Marxist political activity. In the winter of 1888–89 he read the first volume of *Capital* and became a Marxist.[6] By this time he had been expelled from the University of Kazan for taking part in an illegal demonstration. With difficulty his mother was able to persuade the university to allow him to take his final examinations in law. He graduated first among 124 students. He then tried to practise law, but most of his funds, then and for years to come, he got from his mother. (His father had died when Vladimir was sixteen.)

In 1893 Vladimir Ulyanov arrived in St Petersburg and became a member of an underground Social Democratic group. This gave him useful organizational experience. He caught pneumonia and was forced to seek medical attention abroad in the spring of 1895. It was on this trip that he met Plekhanov in Switzerland. On his return to the Russian capital later that year he met and collaborated with Martov (Jules Tsederbaum; 1873–1923). They were arrested in December with the proofs for the first issue of the clandestine newspaper they were to publish.

The popular image of Tsarist Russia would lead us to expect the worst for Ulyanov. This was not so. Prison conditions in Russia do not seem to have been worse than in most countries. Russia differed from the advanced countries in that the lack of political freedom turned many politically-minded citizens into criminals. Secondly, the punishment of exile was widely used against offenders. In St Petersburg prison visitors were allowed twice a week; they could bring books and food several times a week; and there was a 'splendid' library. Controls were lax enough to allow Ulyanov to direct his group outside from his cell. After fourteen months he emerged from prison in excellent health and was banished for three years to a village in eastern Siberia.[7] He was given three days' leave to put his affairs in order.[8] During his exile he received from the authorities a regular monthly allowance, enough to pay for room, board, and laundry.[9]

Once again, reading the account left by his widow, it is difficult not to be impressed by the way Ulyanov was treated compared to the treatment meted out after 1917 to most of those who fell foul of Lenin and Stalin. It must be added, however, that not all political prisoners were as well treated as he. When his wife arrived to take up voluntary exile with him, he was out hunting. His room, 'though small, was spotlessly clean'. Krupskaya, his wife, and her mother were given the rest of the cottage. They had a vegetable garden and a girl to help them with the domestic chores. They received mail twice a week and carried on a social life with others like themselves or with the peasants. 'Practically, surveillance did not exist'.[10]

In 1900 Lenin – he had used the name for the first time in connection with his pamphlet *Aims of the Russian Social Democrats* – left Siberia. Later in the same year he turned up in Germany where it had been decided to publish the party paper *Iskra* (the Spark). Copies of it were then smuggled into Russia with the aid of the SPD. Lenin ran the paper, though he was assisted by Martov, Vera Zasulich, and A. N. Potresov. He wanted to turn it from an intellectual discussion journal into a fighting paper. Difficulties in Germany caused *Iskra* to be moved to London where Lenin, accompanied by Krupskaya, arrived in April 1902. They spent an eventful year in Britain. There Lenin met Leon Trotsky whose support and co-operation he welcomed. In that year too he published his decisive work *What Is To Be Done?* It appeared in Russian under the imprint of the SPD publishing company of Dietz. It was a scornful attack on all forms of revisionism, but especially against the Russian 'Economists', who believed that the backwardness of Russia left only one possibility for the intellectual – to fight for liberal bourgeois reforms, and support the trade union, economic, struggle of the workers. Thus the 'Economists' became 'indistinguishable' from the bourgeois liberals.[11] Had Lenin's work been merely an attack on revisionism, it would probably have been forgotten. In it Lenin demanded nothing less than the complete transformation of the party. He attacked the idea that the workers, left to themselves, could develop a socialist, as opposed to merely a trade union, consciousness.

> The history of every country teaches us that, by its own ability, the working class can attain only a trade union consciousness, that means, the conviction of the need to join together in organizations, to carry on a struggle against the employers, to wrest from the government this or that law for the benefit of the workers. Socialist doctrine, on the other hand, comes from the philosophical, historical, and economic theories, worked out by the cultured representatives of the propertied class, of the intelligentsia. By their social origin, Marx and Engels, the founders of modern, scientific Socialism, belonged to the bourgeois intelligentsia.[12]

Leadership, then, was very important, indeed decisive, for the working-class movement, 'without "a dozen" talented (and talented individuals are not born by the hundred), tried leaders, armed with the necessary knowledge, who have gone through a long schooling, and work excellently together, there can be no persistent class struggle in today's society'.[13] These leaders must be professional revolutionaries, no matter whether they are former students or workers.[14] But not only the leaders are the professionals, 'an organization of revolutionaries must contain primarily and chiefly people whose occupation is revolutionary activity'. And among the members all the differences between intellectuals and workers must disappear. Further, this organization must necessarily be not very broad, and as secret as possible.[15] In these circumstances party democracy was out. 'Whoever wants a wide workers' organization with elections, reports, voting, etc., under [Tsarist] Absolutism is an incorrigible utopian'.[16] It must be stressed that in this work Lenin is demanding such an organization to suit Russian conditions. He is not advocating it for other parties. In fact, time and again, he cites with admiration the SPD!

It was at the Second Congress of the Russian Social Democratic Party in 1902 that Lenin met with opposition to his ideas. He had clashed with Plekhanov over *Iskra* and over their work on a draft party programme. These differences were overcome and the programme, of which they were joint authors, was adopted by the congress. One unique feature of the programme was that it included the term Dictatorship of the Proletariat, defined as 'the conquest of political power by the proletariat'. As a first step towards its socialist ends it called for the overthrow of autocracy and the setting-up of a constituent assembly freely elected by the whole people. The programme remained party policy until 1919.[17]

The big clash of the congress, which commenced its work in Brussels and then moved to London because of police interference, came over the party statute. In line with his ideas in *What Is To Be Done?*, Lenin wanted membership restricted to activists, professional revolutionaries. Martov proposed a wider membership and his view carried the vote. Trotsky supported Martov, Plekhanov voted with Lenin.[18]

Lenin faced more opposition to his attempts to reduce still further the leadership group and increase their power over the rest of the party. He succeeded in reducing the *Iskra* – now official party organ – board from six to three, and in reducing the

Central Committee – responsible for organization – to three. This left a small Party Council of five, nominated by the other two bodies, and headed by a President elected by the congress, as the only other leading organ. With Plekhanov's help, as Party President, Lenin could virtually run the party. Martov, who was offered a seat on the *Iskra* board, refused to serve. Shortly after the congress the tables were turned on Lenin. Pressure mounted on Plekhanov to return to the pre-congress position. By this time he was having second thoughts about his protégé and he relented. It was Lenin's turn to withdraw into the wilderness.

It was at the Brussels-London Congress that Lenin's supporters became known, rather dubiously, as the Bolsheviks (after *bolshinstvo*, the Russian word for majority). Their opponents, around Martov, were dubbed Mensheviks (after *menshinstvo*, meaning minority).

Plekhanov, Martov, Zasulich, and Trotsky, freed from Lenin's presence in *Iskra* circles, tried to rid the party of his ideas. In a series of articles they sought to demolish him intellectually. In varying degrees they foresaw what would happen when he gained power. In his *Our Political Tasks* Trotsky described Lenin's tactics as 'a dull caricature of the tragic intransigence of Jacobinism' and predicted that Leninism would lead to a situation in which 'the party is replaced by the organization of the party, the organization by the central committee, and finally the central committee by the dictator'. It would be a dictatorship not *of* the proletariat but *over* the proletariat.[19] From Germany Rosa Luxemburg strongly condemned Lenin's position. His plan looked like 'a mechanical transfer of the organizational principles of the Blanquist movement of conspiratorial circles' to the Social Democratic movement.[20]

Lenin was under fire from all sides for allegedly turning from Marxism. He attempted to defend himself in *One Step Forward, Two Steps Backward*. Who was right? Was he, as his critics believed, returning to pre-Marxist forms of struggle? Or was he, as he was convinced, merely relating Marxism to Russia's special historical circumstances? No definitive answer can be given. So much depends on one's view of Marxism, and its two creators. Had Engels lived another eight to ten years he would probably have sided with the orthodox Social Democrats in Russia and elsewhere. On the other hand, it is perfectly legitimate to point out that Marx did say that the road to socialism would vary from country to country. It is legitimate to recall Engels's view of the Russian terrorists that their activities were inevitable in Russia's situation. Might he not have been similarly indulgent to Lenin? Further, Lenin could enlist a passage from the *Manifesto* in defence of his position on a small, élite, party:

> The Communists are, therefore, on the one hand, practically, the most advanced and resolute section of the working-class parties of every country, that section which pushes forward all others; on the other hand, theoretically, they have over the great mass of the proletariat the advantage of clearly understanding the line of march, the conditions, and the ultimate general results of the proletarian movement.[21]

Against this, Lenin's opponents could quote another well-known passage from the *Manifesto*, describing the proletarian movement as 'the independent self-conscious movement of the immense majority'.

Whether Lenin was or was not a Marxist, he was not a very attractive person. At best we can see him as a singleminded fanatic, a puritan by nature, as Gorky put it.[22] Or as a Jacobin giving up his music and his chess to concentrate his efforts even more on purely political tasks. Generally, historians have treated him kindly. One can readily think of reasons why they have done so. Most have seen Lenin as the man who did so much to bring down the detested Tsarist regime, as the sincere leader whose ideals were betrayed by others. Lenin's early death made it much easier to foster this image. Perhaps too, Stalin's subsequent actions made Lenin appear very mild by comparison. In addition, much of what has been written about him has been written by witnesses subject to editorial control in Moscow. This writer finds it difficult to believe that he was not an arrogant man ruthlessly pursuing his own personal power (which is not to say that he was not motivated by ideals and intellect as well). So many other revolutionaries, brilliant men, had failed in Russia. There were older men, experienced and erudite, like Plekhanov on the scene. He faced an array of highly intelligent and articulate contemporaries. Yet Lenin was certain he knew better than them all. He alone possessed the key to the future and he wanted to be in a position of supreme command to use it. When the time for action came, neither he nor the party, partly as a result of Lenin's actions, was ready.

### III. TROTSKY AND 1905

In 1904 the old imperialist power, Russia, collided with the new imperialist power, Japan. Russia was soundly defeated. The dislocation and suffering caused by the war brought on a revolutionary upsurge. Demands for greater freedom had been made in 1904. Tsar Nicholas II made promises after the assassination of his Minister of Interior, Vyacheslav von Plehve. In January 1905 there occurred an event which was to raise the temperature still higher. This was the shooting-down of scores of peaceful demonstrators in front of the Tsar's Winter Palace. They had been led by Father Gapon, a priest who headed a workers' union set up by the authorities themselves. A wave of strikes, disorders, and demands for reform followed, gaining momentum through the spring and summer. By autumn the Tsar realized that further delay would be fatal for his cause. He appointed a liberal, Count Sergius Witte, premier, and on 30 October 1905 issued a manifesto granting the election of a legislative Duma on an indirect but wide suffrage. It also provided for the reorganization of the government with a Western-style Prime Minister.[23]

In that same month a new institution was set up, the significance of which was not entirely clear at the time. This was the St Petersburg Soviet (or Council) of workers' deputies. Its job was to give political direction to a general strike which was paralysing the nation's services and industries. Delegates were elected from the factories but the leadership was intellectual. Trotsky became one of two vice-chairmen and, after the chairman's arrest, took over the leadership until the Soviet disappeared a short time later. This work gave Trotsky very useful practical experience of revolutionary organization on a large scale. It also enhanced his reputation considerably.

Trotsky (1879–1940) started life as Lev Davýdovich Bronstein in a village near the Black Sea. His father was a Jewish, self-made, farmer of considerable standing. Lev suffered in his education because of his ethnic background and was natural material for the revolutionary circles which he came into contact with as a secondary-school pupil. His associations, and his refusal to follow his father's advice on a choice of career, led to the end of his schooling. He tried to earn his keep as a tutor but seems to have spent more time as an organizer of strikes. It was in connection with one of these that he was arrested, jailed, and then exiled to

Siberia. From all accounts, his period in prison was more of an ordeal than was Lenin's. A *narodnik* at the start of his revolutionary activity, he gradually turned to Marxism through the influence of Alexándra Lvóvna, who was six years older than he and whom he married. His wife went with him into exile. There he fathered two girls, wrote literary criticism for a local paper, read Marx and Lenin, and finally escaped alone to western Europe. His marriage did not stand the strain of long separation. In Vienna he met Victor Adler, in Paris his second wife, Natálya Ivánovna Sedóva, in London Vladimir Ilyich Lenin. He had admired Lenin's writing; Lenin was impressed by his ability; both were subsequently disappointed by the other's political stance. The two men were very different. Trotsky was flamboyant, literary, and enjoyed the good things of life. Lenin was more reserved, without literary sense, and austere. Trotsky 'followed the tradition of Lassalle and Engels rather than that of Marx and Lenin: the tradition of the socialist as a man of the world and all-round personality'.[24]

Trotsky was one of the first exiles to return to participate in the revolutionary outbreaks of 1904–05. Lenin heard the news of the January massacre in Geneva. He became convinced that an armed uprising could be successfully launched, so he set about procuring arms. Before attempting to return home he did one other thing. He tried to convene a Third Congress of the Russian Social Democratic Party. This was held in London, but was ignored by the Mensheviks and served merely to strengthen Lenin's position in the eyes of his followers. He only returned to Russia in November. He pushed ahead with his plans for an insurrection and, taking advantage of the temporary press freedom, published his own paper. Remarkably he even found time for a little extra-marital romance.[25]

Spontaneous rather than planned, the revolution began to disintegrate. The authorities kept their heads and struck back. They decided on armed force against strikers, peasants in revolt, and navy and army mutineers. The St Petersburg Soviet was surrounded by armed police and Cossacks and its members arrested. In Moscow strikes turned into armed rebellion only to be put down by artillery. Lenin, whose faction alone had encouraged this, left St Petersburg.

The end of armed resistance in Moscow by no means marked the end of the first Russian Revolution, though it was a decisive turning-point. The revolutionary tide now started to ebb. By 1907 the Tsar was strong enough to dismiss the parliament (Duma) and arrest its Social Democratic members.

The defeat of the armed rising in Moscow did nothing to increase Lenin's stature. He was accused of adventurism and recklessness even by members of his own faction. He remained unshaken in his view of his destiny and regarded the revolution of 1905 as a 'general rehearsal' for the final revolution.

The years between 1905 and 1912 were bad ones for the Russian revolutionary movement. There were attempts to patch up the quarrel between Mensheviks and Bolsheviks, and for a time some sort of vague unity was established. Lenin carried on as though he regarded his left-wing critics as worse than his Tsarist enemies. There were quarrels about the money left to the party by wealthy benefactors. There were quarrels about the methods used to obtain money for the party. The majority disagreed with the Bolsheviks' use of armed robbery and extortion to get money for their movement. On occasion they even got their members to marry suitably wealthy potential donors. Even his friends, Maxim Gorky the writer among them, sickened by his methods and the shady characters who executed them,[26] abandoned him at this time. Lenin's attitude was clear: 'Revolution is a difficult matter. It cannot be made with gloves or manicured nails . . . party members should not be judged by the narrow standards of petty bourgeois morality. Sometimes a scoundrel is useful to our party precisely because he is a scoundrel'.[27]

After the fall of the St Petersburg Soviet, Trotsky was sentenced to an indefinite period of banishment. He escaped before he had even reached his place of exile and spent the next years in western Europe studying conditions for himself and developing his ideas. Politically, he claimed to stand aside from the factions of the Russian party.

During these years another actor in the drama of Russian Marxism was quietly establishing his position in the Bolshevik wing of the Russian Social Democratic movement – Joseph Vissarionovich Djugashvili, better known as Stalin (1879–1953).

## IV. STALIN ON THE NATIONALITY QUESTION

Like Trotsky, Stalin belonged to one of the oppressed peoples of Russia. His parents were Georgians and like so many other

Georgians he must have felt the pain of his nation's colonial status. Unlike Trotsky, Lenin, and so many other leading Marxists, he could really claim to be of proletarian background. His father was a cobbler and his parents had been born serfs. In view of his background he was lucky to go to the local religious school, and luckier still to be admitted, on scholarship, to the Theological Seminary in Tiflis, the Georgian capital. There he spent five years until expelled in 1899.

The seminary was a hotbed of revolutionary agitation. One Russian director had been assassinated by the pupils. It was spiritually 'half monastery and half barrack. . . . Any infringement of regulations was punished by confinement to the cells'.[28] The staff spied on the students and even denounced them to the police. Stalin picked up many radical ideas there and joined a secret socialist society in 1898. When he got the chance to read *Iskra*, he found he agreed with its ideas and analysis. When the party split came, he sided with Lenin.

After a period of unemployment Stalin secured a job as a clerk in the Tiflis observatory until a police raid forced him to go underground in 1901. In the same year he was elected to the nine-member Social Democratic committee in Tiflis. Only weeks later he was organizing the workers at the new oilfield in Batum. After a few months there, Koba, as he was then calling himself, was arrested. Eighteen months' imprisonment was followed by a sentence of three years' exile. He escaped before completing his sentence to find that he had been promoted in his absence.

The first time Stalin met Lenin, and the first time he saw the western part of the Tsarist Empire, was in 1905 when he attended a Bolshevik congress at Tammerfors in Finland. There he joined other delegates in opposing Lenin's resolution calling for participation in the Duma elections. Lenin withdrew his proposal. Stalin was the sole Bolshevik delegate from the Caucasus to the 'unity' congress of the Social Democrats at Stockholm in 1906, and he was at the London Congress in the following year. By the time the revolution came in 1917, he had risen from relative obscurity to become one of the national leaders of the Bolsheviks. Here we can do no better than quote Isaac Deutscher:

His rise appears the more puzzling as, of the ten years between 1907 and 1917, he spent nearly seven in prisons, on the way to Siberia, in Siberian banishment, and in escapes from the places of his deportation. . . . The clue to his promotion lay in his practical activities rather than in any talent for letters or journalism. . . . Except for two brief trips to Cracow and Vienna, he spent all those years in Russia, entrenched in the underground, immersed in the drudgery of the revolution's working day that was so different from its stormy, exciting festivals. This was to be the source of great strength as well as great weakness in him. He had no inkling of the broad international vistas that life in western Europe opened before the émigré leaders.[29]

Impressed by Stalin's practical work, and by his businesslike reports, Lenin took him under his wing. In January 1912 Lenin convened in Prague a congress of Bolsheviks and constituted the Bolsheviks as a separate party. He proposed Stalin for the Central Committee, but the proposal was turned down. Later he saw to it that his protégé was co-opted on to the committee. When a four-man committee was set up a short time later to run the party's activities in Russia itself, Stalin was elected to it. He edited the first issue of *Pravda* (in April 1912), the paper which is still the official organ of the Soviet Communist Party. One other item in Stalin's life during this period deserves mention: an essay he wrote at Lenin's urging.

The essay, published in 1913, dealt with the (for Russia) very important problem of the national question.[30] The Russian Empire was made up of many nationalities and races. In 1914 only 65.5 per cent of its inhabitants were classed as Russians and even this percentage included the Ukrainians.[31] There were quite distinctive national groups such as the Finns, Poles, Lithuanians, and Georgians. There were more scattered groups such as the Jews, who made up 3.9 per cent of the population and the Germans (1.6 per cent). As in other parts of the world, nationalism was rising in Russia. What should be the attitude of the Social Democrats to it?

Marx and Engels had not left a fully developed doctrine on this. They had written in the *Manifesto* that 'working men have no country' because they had no property or political power in their respective countries. They also believed that once the workers achieved power in the major countries, national differences would rapidly disappear. Nevertheless, until such times the working-class parties operated within the national framework and had to express themselves on the claims of various nationalities for independence. Marx and Engels had supported such claims where they considered them either historically progressive or likely to weaken a reactionary power, and where the units concerned would be able to produce viable nations. Thus they supported the Poles, Hungarians, Italians, and later the Irish. They rejected the claims of the Croats, Slovaks, Czechs, and Scots (among others).

Stalin's answer to the rising tide of nationalism was to urge Social Democracy 'to resist nationalism and to protect the masses from the general "epidemic". For Social-Democracy, and Social-Democracy alone, could do this, by bringing against nationalism the tried weapon of internationalism, the unity and indivisibility of the class struggle'. He strongly opposed the Austrian socialists and the Russian Jewish Social Democrats who favoured the organization of workers within multinational empires in federal parties based on national groups. He assailed the idea of a federal state. However, he recognized the right of self-determination, 'an essential element in the solution of the national problem'. And he preached that 'national equality in all forms (language, schools, etc.) is an essential element in the solution of the national problem'. Thus a nation could secede from the Empire, but those which did not would only have regional, rather than national, autonomy, and all minorities would have the right to their own language, schools, and religion. The party organization, though, would be a single body uniting all nationalities.

This essay has remained the basic Soviet theoretical text on the national question. Later we shall see in which ways it was, and in which ways it was not, observed after the Bolsheviks got power.

In the period from about the last decade of Marx's life to 1913 Marxism had become a mass movement. In Germany it completely monopolized the working-class movement and in many other countries, where there were rival socialist ideologies, it exercised a great deal of influence. Yet 'Marxism' already meant different things to different men. Some chose, like the Germans and the Mensheviks, to rely on the works written by Marx and Engels later in life, mature and mellowed with growing age. Others, notably Lenin, revived the Marxism of the *Manifesto*, believing they could adapt it to their 'historical circumstances'. It could be argued that neither was really Marxism, that the SPD used its Marxist jargon to mask its growing caution and conservatism, while Lenin invoked the founding fathers to hide his return to pre-Marxist revolutionary organization and methods. And there were other 'Marxists'. Rosa Luxemburg combined many of the attractive features of both Marx and Lenin. She took up the belief of Marx and Engels in democracy, their emphasis on building up a broad, democratic, mass movement, and grafted on to this her own theory of rising class-consciousness, which developed spontaneously from the workers' own experiences of struggle. On the other hand, like Lenin, she stressed Marx the revolutionist. Bernstein, too, was another variety of 'Marxist'. His strength was his intellectual honesty. He saw the SPD as it was rapidly becoming, a parliamentary reform party, and he tried to get everyone to admit the fact. He remembered that Marx and Engels had modified their theories in the light of new research and events. His weakness was that he took too short a span of time. There was some evidence that the workers were improving their lot, though this was not conclusive, and the peasants were taking a long time to die, though this has been the overall tendency. The crisis, concentration of property, and proletarianization of the *petit bourgeoisie* came in the 1920s rather than the 1890s, though their arrival did not result in the workers' revolution. Bernstein's greatest mistake was his optimism about Germany's ability to transform herself, gradually, without violent eruption, into a parliamentary, social, republic. Above all, he, together with all other types of Marxist, greatly underestimated the explosive character of nationalism and imperialism, the force which was finally to split the International, and later the world.

### NOTES

[1] Edmund Wilson, *To the Finland Station* (London, 1970), p. 351.
[2] The figures on the labour force are from James Mavor, *An Economic History of Russia* (London, 1925), p. 386. Quote: Margaret Miller, *Economic Development of Russia 1905–1914* (London, 1967), p. 185.
[3] Antony C. Sutton, *Western Technology and Soviet Economic Development 1917 to 1930* (Stanford, 1968), pp. 174, 344.
[4] Alec Nove, *An Economic History of the USSR* (London, 1969), p. 26.
[5] George V. Plekhanov, *The Role of the Individual in History* (London, 1950), pp. 11–16.
[6] Wilson, op. cit., p. 366.
[7] David Shub, *Lenin* (London, 1969), pp. 47–9.
[8] Wilson, op. cit., p. 381.
[9] Shub, op. cit., p. 49.

[10] N. K. Krupskaya, *Reminiscences of Lenin* (Moscow, 1959), pp. 32–40.

[11] E. H. Carr, *The Bolshevik Revolution 1917–1923*, I (London, 1966), 22.

[12] W. I. Lenin, *Was Tun?* (What Is To Be Done?) (East Berlin, 1970), p. 62.

[13] ibid., pp. 163–4.

[14] ibid., p. 166.

[15] ibid., p. 153.

[16] ibid., p. 161.

[17] Carr, op. cit., pp. 39–40.

[18] ibid., p. 41.

[19] ibid., p. 45.

[20] S. M. Schwarz, *The Russian Revolution of 1905* (Chicago, 1967), p. 208.

[21] Marx and Engels, *Manifesto of the Communist Party* (Moscow, 1955), p. 78.

[22] L. Schapiro and P. Reddaway (eds.), *Lenin, the Man, the Theorist, the Leader* (London, 1967), p. 62.

[23] Hugh Seton-Watson, *The Decline of Imperial Russia* (London, 1964), p. 223.

[24] Wilson, op. cit., p. 422. The above account is based on Wilson, op. cit., and on Leon Trotsky, *My Life* (New York, 1960).

[25] Shub, op. cit., pp. 104–5.

[26] ibid., p. 131.

[27] ibid., p. 130.

[28] Isaac Deutscher, *Stalin* (London, 1966), p. 33. This is based on an earlier version (London, 1949).

[29] ibid., pp. 107–8.

[30] The quotations below are taken from J. V. Stalin, *Marxism and the National Question* (Moscow, 1950).

[31] Miller, op. cit., p. 30.

# IV

## *The Great Divide*

IN the summer of 1914 the hopes of the International were dashed, its worst fears realized. On 28 June the Austrian Archduke Franz Ferdinand was assassinated by Serb nationalists at Sarajevo. This gave Austria-Hungary the opportunity to 'settle accounts' with Serbia. Encouraged by Germany, the Austrians sent an ultimatum to Serbia containing deliberately unacceptable conditions. The Russians went to the aid of the Serbs. On 1 August Germany declared war on Russia and on 3 August, on France. A day later Britain came into the war when Germany invaded neutral Belgium.

On 25 July the SPD executive committee had condemned, in no uncertain terms, the Austrian demands – 'the most brutal demands ever presented to an independent state'. The SPD called on the German government to stay out of the war. Fearing the possible arrest of their leaders, the Social Democrats sent two of them to Switzerland, and another on an unsuccessful mission to discuss joint action with the French socialists. Despite this apparent determination to oppose the threatening war, the entire SPD parliamentary group voted for the military appropriations, and thus for the war, in the Reichstag on 4 August. At their private party meeting before the Reichstag session seventy-eight members of parliament favoured approving the appropriations, only fourteen wanted to reject them. The majority used the argument that the SPD had always stood for national defence and that the war had been forced on Germany by Russia. They believed they could not stand aloof as Tsarist troops poured into the country. The minority did not want to sanction a war about whose immediate causes they had only one-sided reports; the party had always rejected military credits and besides, they were committed by the International to oppose war.[1] Though he had wanted the party to oppose the appropriations, Hugo Haase

(1863–1919), chairman of the SPD Reichstag group, read the formal statement in which he said that Social Democracy would not leave its own fatherland in the lurch in its hour of danger.[2]

The decision of the SPD fell, as Kautsky put it, like a hammer-blow.[3] The SPD had been the leading party of the International. The other parties regarded the Reichstag vote as a betrayal of all the International stood for. Most of the socialists in the other countries had little difficulty in persuading themselves that they should support the war efforts of their respective governments. They felt they were merely opposing German militarism. The small Serbian party opposed the war, and the Italians branded it 'imperialist'. But most of the French, Belgian, and British socialists supported their governments against Germany. Nor were the German Social Democrats the only Marxists to vote for war. Plekhanov encouraged Russian emigrants in France to volunteer to fight against Germany. In Britain the executive of the small Marxist British Socialist Party, led by Hyndman, whole-heartedly supported the Allied cause.[4] On the other hand, non-Marxists such as the British Labour members Keir Hardie, Ramsay MacDonald, and Philip Snowden refused to endorse it. MacDonald (1866–1937) resigned as chairman of the party, and became 'the best-hated man in Britain, decried and derided by the man in the street as a pacifist, a pro-German, and even as a traitor'.[5] He asked: 'We dislike the autocracy in Germany – but is that a reason why we should throw ourselves into the arms of the Tsar and give our aid in extending Cossack rule in Eastern Europe?'[6]

Had the SPD's parliamentarians rejected the military appropriations, they would not have stopped the war. They might even have come into conflict with the mass of their members and voters. But this would, as likely as not, have paid off later, once the casualties began to mount, once the shortages occurred, once the full horror of the war was revealed.

## II. LENIN ON WAR AND IMPERIALISM

When the war broke out, Lenin was in Cracow, then part of the Austro-Hungarian Empire. He was arrested but subsequently released on the intervention of Victor Adler, the Austrian socialist parliamentarian.[7] He left for neutral Switzerland in September.

There does not appear to have been any doubt in Lenin's mind about the nature of the war or what socialists should do about it. He soon got down to writing articles denouncing it. It was a year after its outbreak before he managed to set out his ideas in systematic fashion. In his pamphlet *Socialism and War* he repeated the traditional Marxist argument that there were offensive and defensive wars:

> If Morocco were to declare war against France tomorrow, or India against England, or Persia or China against Russia, etc., those wars would be 'just', 'defensive' wars, no matter which one was first to attack. Every Socialist would then wish the victory of the oppressed, dependent, non-sovereign states against the oppressing, slave-holding, pillaging 'great' nations.
>
> But imagine that a slave-holder possessing 100 slaves wages war against a slave-holder possessing 200 slaves for a more 'equitable' redistribution of slaves. It is evident that to apply to such a case the term 'defensive' war or 'defence of the Fatherland', would be an historical lie; in practice it would mean that the crafty slave-holders were plainly deceiving the unenlightened masses, the lower strata of the city population. It is in this very fashion that the present-day imperialist bourgeoisie . . . deceive the peoples . . .[8]

He urged socialists to 'turn the imperialist war into civil war'. The socialists must explain to the masses that there was no salvation outside of a revolutionary overthrow of 'their' governments. The difficulties caused by the war should be taken advantage of.[9]

Without doubting his sincerity, it is worth underlining that Lenin was preaching from his Swiss sanctuary and that he personally was not responsible for the fate of any large socialist organization.

Lenin's views on war led him to a particular interpretation of the imperialism of his time. His *Imperialism, the Highest Stage of Capitalism*, written in 1916, became known as one of his major works. It owed a good deal to the earlier researches of J. A. Hobson, a British liberal critic of imperialism, and the Austrian Marxist Rudolf Hilferding. Like other socialists, and many liberals, Lenin had been appalled by the 'scramble for Africa' in the last quarter of the nineteenth century, and the increasing pressure of the industrial nations, including here his own, on China and Persia. He had been impressed by the Spanish-American War of 1898, the Boer War (1899–1902), and the brutalities of the colonial regimes. He had been brought up in 'the age of imperialism' and felt there was a connection between this imperialism and war. He sought to expose it.

He linked imperialism closely with the growth of monopolies and cartels which changed the nature of capitalist exports: 'Under the old capitalism, when free competition prevailed, the export of *goods* was the most typical feature. Under modern capitalism, when monopolies prevail, the export of *capital* has become the typical feature'.[10] This export of capital resulted from the abundance of capital, despite the misery of the masses, which had accumulated in the advanced countries. In the

> backward countries profits are usually high, for capital is scarce, the price of land is relatively low, wages are low, raw materials are cheap. . . . The necessity for exporting capital arises from the fact that in a few countries capitalism has become 'over-ripe' and (owing to the backward state of agri-culture and the impoverished state of the masses) capital can-not find 'profitable' investment.[11]

The hunt for raw materials is another factor in imperialism:

> The more capitalism is developed, the more the need for raw materials is felt, the more bitter competition becomes, and the more feverishly the hunt for raw materials proceeds throughout the whole world, the more desperate becomes the struggle for the acquisition of colonies.[12]

In this situation, in the epoch of modern capitalism:

> certain relations are established between capitalist alliances, *based* on the economic division of the world; while parallel with this fact and in connection with it, certain relations are estab-lished between political alliances, between states, on the basis of the territorial division of the world, of the struggle for colonies, of the 'struggle for economic territory.'[13]

Having divided the world among themselves, can the imperialist powers redivide it without force? For given the uneven develop-ment of the productive forces in one country compared with another, given that some powers have arrived late on the scene, there will be demands for a redivision:

> Is there *under capitalism* any means of removing the disparity between the development of productive forces and the

accumulation of capital on the one side, and the division of colonies and 'spheres of influence' for finance capital on the other side – other than by resorting to war?[14]

Lenin's theory of imperialism has been criticized on many grounds. It has been pointed out that the formation of monopolies and cartels in Germany and the United States, on which Lenin concentrated, came after the high point of imperial expansion had been passed, in many cases after 1900. It is difficult therefore to account it a cause of imperial expansion. Trusts and cartels were by no means as important in Britain and France as they were in Germany or the United States; yet it was Britain and France which were the leading colonial powers. Secondly, although it appeared plausible to argue that Britain had completed her development and had surplus capital for export, this was not so in the cases of France, Germany, Italy, and Portugal. Nor is it certain that interest rates in the colonial and semi-colonial areas were sufficiently higher than in the European countries to attract capital.[15] Another weakness of Lenin's analysis is that much of the capital exported in this period did not find its way into the new colonial areas. This is clear from figures given by Lenin himself. According to him, in 1910 Britain had about 29 billion marks invested in Asia, Africa, and Australia; 37 billion in America; and 4 billion in Europe. The bulk of French investments abroad were in Europe, as were the major part of German investments.[16] To some extent he would be able to answer this apparent contradiction by claiming that countries such as Portugal and Russia were being reduced to a semi-colonial status or at least to dependencies of colonial powers. But the fact remains that neither Britain nor Germany could induce investors to sink large amounts in their new colonies. In the case of Germany investment in the whole of Africa amounted to only two-thirds of German investment in Austria.[17]

More modern, and less partisan, researchers believe they have discovered reasons other than economic for the imperialistic surge-forward before 1914. Some see the colonial policies of the European states formed in the light of the balance of power and designed to serve European ends.[18] Others see them as the inevitable result of the development of the steamship and the railway making possible the imposition of 'civilization' on 'backward' peoples.[19] Others stress the nationalistic aspect. Newly united nations felt they had not really 'arrived' unless they possessed colonies. For most students of imperialism the question is not whether economic motives were an important factor – that is usually admitted – but whether other factors were important as well. As one writer summed up the reasons for American imperialism at this time:

> The Roosevelt-Lodge expansionists who took the American people into an imperialist struggle for world power were not primarily concerned with American economic interests around the world. Nor did they attempt to justify expansion chiefly on economic grounds. Where they were interested in economic matters it was because economic advantages won converts to imperialist policies or enhanced the prestige of the country. Economic factors *were* important in imperialism and were to become important in American expansionist foreign policy in the twentieth century. But the primary concern of Roosevelt and his fellow-expansionists was power and prestige and the naval strength that would bring power and prestige. They gloried in the thought of American greatness and power that their expansionist policies would create.[20]

The other question connected with Lenin's theory is whether imperialism, as defined by him, inevitably led to the outbreak of the 1914–18 War. Though few Western historians support the Leninist thesis (not surprisingly), they are not agreed on the reasons for the outbreak of hostilities. Views changed, especially as more documents became available and greater objectivity was gained with the passage of time. Many would go along with the views of G. P. Gooch:

> The war was the child of the European anarchy, of the outworn system of sovereign states. The Old World had degenerated into a powder-magazine, in which the dropping of a lighted match was almost certain to produce a gigantic conflagration. No conflict, strictly speaking, is inevitable, but in a storehouse of high explosives it required statesmen of exceptional wisdom and foresight in every country to avoid a catastrophe.[21]

Certainly the war was an indictment of 'the system' and the ruling circles of Europe, as socialists claimed. But whether there was a causal connection between the export of capital, and colonialism, and that war, as Lenin claimed, is another matter.

### III. THE REVOLUTIONS IN RUSSIA

Despite the importance of the armed forces in Russia, despite the weaknesses revealed by the Russo-Japanese War, the Tsarist forces entered the War of 1914 in a poor state. The troops were badly led and poorly equipped compared to their adversaries. For instance, the Russian infantry division had seven field-gun batteries compared with fourteen in the German division. The whole Russian army had sixty batteries of heavy artillery compared with 381 in the German army.[22] For every one man employed on the lines of supply in France four were needed in Russia.[23] Behind this poorly equipped army stood an inadequate and badly organized economy. By the spring of 1915 it was clear that Russian industry was incapable of dealing with the problems imposed by the war.[24] Equally clear by this time was the plight of the Russian army: its losses were reaching the staggering figure of nearly 4 million.[25] On the home front life was tough, with the rapid rise in the price of food and other essential goods, with queues, regulations, and restrictions. In Petrograd (as St Petersburg was now called), prices in late 1916 had increased in comparison with 1914 as follows: milk, 150 per cent; white bread, 500; butter, 830; shoes and clothing, 400 to 600 per cent.[26] Wages had been left well behind. Starting in April 1915 there were demonstrations and riots over the food shortage. Over half a million workers went on strike in 1915; in 1916 nearly a million did so. The situation in Petrograd became so critical that the authorities threatened absentee workers with the firing squad. In these circumstances it is not surprising that the activities of those opposed to the regime should increase, nor that there should be many within the Tsarist 'establishment' plotting to overthrow the ruling house. However, 'in the end, the Revolution was not planned, or led. It simply happened'.[27]

The beginning of the end for Russian Tsarism was 8 March, celebrated by the working-class movement as Women's Day. According to Trotsky,[28] even the most militant Bolshevik organization in Petrograd opposed strikes for that day, fearing they would lead to an open fight for which the time was 'unripe'. But the women textile-workers, angered by the frustrations of queueing for meagre rations, were in no mood for passivity. In the end about 90,000 men and women downed tools that day. A mass of women, not all of them workers, flocked to the town hall demanding bread: 'It was like demanding milk from a he-goat'. The demonstrations passed off with enthusiasm yet without bloodshed.

During the following days the strike movement spread, political slogans competing with economic ones. The authorities were unable to control the situation because this time, unlike 1905, the troops started to fraternize with the revolutionary crowds. They had made the strategic mistake of dispatching the crack Guard regiments to the front, leaving only recruits, untrained, poorly fed and housed, and convalescent soldiers in the capital. Remarkably, even the Cossacks, 'those age-old subduers and punishers' of the Russian people, sick of war, showed their sympathies for the masses.[29]

Nevertheless, the authorities did not capitulate yet. Armed with an order from the Tsar, who was not in the capital, General Khabalov, the military governor, on 10 March forbade assemblies and public meetings, arrested leading leftists, and ordered the workers back to the factories within three days. The following day troops were used against the demonstrators. Though some soldiers fired into the sky, others obeyed orders to fire into the crowds. About sixty people were killed and as many wounded. The demonstrators went wild with anger. Before they had looted bakeries, they turned their attention now to the symbols of the regime – the police stations and the court buildings. A day later a decisive turning-point came. Disgusted with themselves and their comrades for shooting on their own unarmed people, troops in one unit after another mutinied. The crowds of soldiers and civilians successfully stormed the secret police headquarters, the Fortress of St Peter and St Paul, and the arsenal. Weapons were distributed. They then headed for the Duma. Under pressure from outside, the parliament, conservative-dominated though it was, recognized what was happening and set up an emergency committee which took over the government.[30]

The Duma committee immediately had a rival in the Petrograd Soviet of Workers' Deputies formed at the same time. Based on elected delegates from the factories and the garrison, one deputy per thousand workers or soldiers, the Soviet could claim to be more representative than the Duma committee. Housed in the Duma building, the Soviet immediately got to work. It organized a military section which set about the job of defending the city. Although the Soviet was socialist in complexion, the Bolsheviks were very poorly represented on it in those early days, with only about forty deputies out of between 2,000 to 3,000.[31] The leaders of the Soviet were not aiming at power for their organization. They were quite prepared to let power reside in the Duma and the government, but they wanted the introduction of a wide range of reforms.

Agreement on reforms was reached on 16 March when a joint Soviet–government statement was issued. The provisional government was to rule until a constituent assembly could be elected by the people. It was to grant an amnesty for political prisoners, freedom of speech, equal rights for all citizens whether of foreign nationality or not, and to defend the country against the German and Habsburg forces. The statement concealed the political differences between Soviet and government. The latter was concerned with law and order, preservation of middle-class society, and the struggle against Germany. The former wanted to improve the lot of the worker, to move in a vaguely egalitarian direction, and to end the fighting (though it was prepared to defend Russia against the enemy).[32] Yet in those spring days there was hope that a working compromise, a readiness to co-exist, had been achieved. The regime had some sort of support throughout the country. The remainder of the armed forces – thousands of troops had simply deserted – were more or less loyal either to the Soviet or to the government. The Tsar abdicated without fuss, and the imperial family were held under house arrest. Russia's allies were prepared to accept the new regime: the United States, not yet at war, greatly welcomed the change.

Lenin had not expected the revolution. In January 1917 he had addressed a youth meeting in Zürich and had rather sadly prophesied: 'We of the older generation may not live to see the decisive battles of this coming revolution'.[33] At first he received the news with great scepticism.[34] Once the situation became clear he naturally wanted to get to Russia as quickly as possible. With most European countries involved in the war, this was not easy. The German government offered its help, hoping that the anti-war revolutionaries would do its work for it and destroy Russia's will to resist. As Krupskaya herself admitted:

The German Government gave permission for us to travel through Germany in the belief that revolution was a disaster to a country, and that by allowing emigrant internationalists to return to their country they were helping to spread the revolution in Russia. The Bolsheviks ... did not care what the German bourgeois government thought about it.

Nor did they care what other socialists thought about it. They expected a 'mud-slinging campaign' against themselves, but were confident that in the long run the masses would follow them.[35]

Once an agreement was reached, thirty-two revolutionaries – nineteen Bolsheviks, six members of the Jewish (socialist) *Bund*, three left-Mensheviks, and four others[36] – left Switzerland under German auspices. The Germans, as Churchill put it, 'transported Lenin in a sealed truck like a plague bacillus from Switzerland into Russia'.[37] They did the revolutionaries well, serving them 'good square meals' on the way.[38] Travelling via Germany and Sweden Lenin's group arrived at the Finland Station in Petrograd on 16 April. They might have expected to have been arrested as German agents. Instead a crowd of supporters, a military band, and a guard of honour awaited them. The Bolshevik leader was 'taken by surprise' at this reception.[39] It was a harbinger of things to come.

Other key figures in the coming Bolshevik revolution – Kamenev, Stalin, and Muranov – were able to greet Lenin on his arrival. They had benefited from the amnesty and had made their way to the capital from Siberia. In May another key figure appeared. Trotsky returned from America. Had he not been removed from the (neutral) Norwegian ship in which he was travelling, and interned by the British, he would probably have got back about the same time as Lenin. His internment helped further to enhance his already considerable reputation. He too was met on arrival by a crowd with red banners. In July Lenin and Trotsky joined forces: 'It was the most ruthless and formidable combination that one could well imagine and there is a certain fascination in watching it grow in power from day to day'.[40] Trotsky, claiming that past differences were insignificant compared with future revolutionary possibilities, joined the Bolshevik party. The old weaknesses of the Bolsheviks on the organizational side were being eliminated as the party became a mass party.

In May a new government was formed which was to the left of the old one. It consisted of ten bourgeois and six socialists approved by the Soviet.[41] This was an advantage from the

Bolshevik point of view. As the sole opposition Lenin's party could take advantage of the difficult times while their rivals were held responsible for the worsening situation. Urged on by the Allies, and backed by the Soviet, the government played into the hands of the Bolsheviks by ordering an offensive which failed almost as soon as it had started. The Bolsheviks seemed rapidly to be gaining the upper hand when they too suffered a severe reversal.

Early in July, when the army was going over to the offensive, a rising of Bolshevik supporters, including soldiers, sailors from Kronstadt, and workers from the Vyborg district of Petrograd, shook the capital. After some confusion the rebellion was put down. Although they had not at this time planned a take-over bid, the Bolshevik leaders became wanted men. Most of them were soon in jail. Lenin was accused of being a German agent. Trotsky called this a 'great slander'. But though conclusive evidence was never produced, many serious writers believe that Lenin, at the very least, received funds from the Germans.[42] Would this have been so serious from the Bolshevik standpoint? Surely not. The argument in favour of taking money was no different from that in favour of accepting German travel facilities and hospitality. And Krupskaya admitted that they had accepted this aid.

Either because he feared assassination, or because, as his enemies claimed, he was guilty of the charges, Lenin fled from Petrograd to Finland. Trotsky, who was not accused and who was not yet actually a member of Lenin's party, defended the Bolsheviks and insisted on being treated as one of them. His wish was granted. He found himself in the same prison as in 1905. The conditions were much worse and he reflected that Lenin was not so mistaken when he decided to take refuge.[43]

With the Bolsheviks apparently finished, a struggle for power started between Kerensky, who as a result of another government reshuffle had emerged as Prime Minister, and General Kornilov. The general, a man of humble origin and an able soldier, wanted to establish himself as dictator. He found sympathy among those who wanted an energetic prosecution of the war and those who feared the growing influence of the workers' organizations. He was appointed commander-in-chief of the armed forces by Kerensky and wanted to reorganize the army on traditional lines. He intended to rescind the famous Order No. 1, issued on its own authority by the Petrograd Soviet on 14 March. The Order had put the troops, in political matters, under the control of the Soviet. It weakened the position of the officers and even gave control of the armouries to the soldiers' committees.[44] After restoring discipline in the army, Kornilov planned to deal with the Petrograd Soviet.

The general launched his abortive *coup* on 6 September. It was badly conceived and poorly executed. As Trotsky put it: 'The government troops were nowhere obliged to resort to force in stopping the onslaught of the Kornilov army. The conspiracy disintegrated, crumbled, evaporated in the air'.[45]

The outcome of the attempted *putsch* was the final breach between Kerensky and the army leaders as well as the conservative elements. Kerensky took over command of the forces himself. This changed little in practice. Kornilov and some other officers were arrested. A five-man directory headed by Kerensky and including two officers became the official government. In the hope of appeasing left-wing opinion Russia was declared a republic. Increasingly Kerensky was dependent on the Petrograd Soviet: increasingly that body was subject to Bolshevik influence. The shock of the *putsch* made it easier for the Bolsheviks to gain converts and win the co-operation of other left-wing groups. The new climate led to the release of the Bolshevik leaders. By mid-September Lenin's friends constituted the majority in the Moscow Soviet. A few days later Trotsky was elected chairman of the Petrograd Soviet. Bolshevik majorities were gained in major provincial centres.

All this time life was getting more and more difficult. Russia's armies were disintegrating. Industry was coming to a halt as strikes, lockouts, and famine spread across the land. In the countryside the peasants, with 'revolutionary barbarism', were destroying the manors and driving out the landlords. Many famous manorial homes were to disappear. As Trotsky commented, 'Gone are the nests of the gentility celebrated by Pushkin, Turgeniev, and Tolstoi. The old Russia has gone up in smoke'.[46] No wonder the Bolshevik press poured out a message which grew in popularity from day to day:

All power to the Soviets – both in the capital and in the provinces.
Immediate truce on all fronts. An honest peace between peoples.

Landlord estates – without compensation – to the peasants.
Workers' control over industrial production.
A faithfully and honestly elected Constituent Assembly.[47]

The government and its backers became associated with the policy of forced requisitions of grain and with continuing (what was assumed to be) a lost war. Had the government put itself at the head of the agrarian revolution, which it was powerless to control, it might have won more support for its defence policy and gained more authority in general.

Convinced that his hour had come, Lenin urged insurrection. He overcame considerable opposition among his party colleagues and, backed by Trotsky and Stalin, committed the Bolsheviks to an armed rising.

The decision of the Bolsheviks was widely known. And many voices were raised against them. *Delo Naroda*, organ of the Socialist Revolutionaries (the agrarian socialists), commented: 'The Bolsheviks are getting ready for action . . . this action is intended to be an armed one'. This was at a time of 'our heaviest defeats on the front, which is almost at Petrograd'. Unity of the revolutionary front was needed, not civil war. The demand for a takeover by the Soviets was being made 'on the eve of the convening of the Constituent Assembly'. Even though the government had made an official denial, the Bolshevik press went on speculating about the evacuation of Petrograd. Maxim Gorky denounced the impending Bolshevik *coup*, asking: 'Is it possible that the adventurers, seeing the decline of the revolutionary zeal on the part of the thinking proletariat, hope to stimulate this zeal by abundant bloodletting?' *Izvestia*, the paper of the All-Russian Central Executive Committee of the Soviets, forecast dislocation of food supplies to the capital and the front, and a strengthening of the reactionary war party in Germany, as consequences of the Bolshevik *coup*.[48]

The Central Executive Committee, still dominated by the Mensheviks and the Socialist Revolutionaries, rejected a Bolshevik demand that the Soviets should take over power from the government. On 5 November the government moved. It declared the Bolshevik leaders under arrest, and the Petrograd Soviet Military Revolutionary Committee, which had become Leon Trotsky's instrument for planning the *coup*, illegal. Before these orders could be acted upon the Bolsheviks struck. They claimed they were acting as the Military Committee of the Soviets and not merely as a political faction, to defend the revolution against another attempted rising of the Right similar to Kornilov's July *putsch*. Thus some of the participants of the 'October Revolution' must have been confused about the issues.

On 7 November (25 October according to the old-style calendar) in the early hours, Bolshevik-led forces occupied the key points in the city. The members of the government were either arrested or became fugitives. There was little actual fighting, for the government of Kerensky had controlled few military units.

The Bolsheviks had used a temporary majority in the Soviet of the capital to seize power. The victory had been due to the cunning, opportunism, and ruthless determination of Lenin, and the oratorical and organizational talents of Trotsky. Lenin intended to present the Second Congress of the All-Russian Soviets and, later, the newly elected Constituent Assembly with a *fait accompli*. Later on the day of the *coup* Trotsky told the delegates of the Second Congress: 'The will of the All-Russian Congress has been anticipated by the rising of the Petrograd workers and soldiers!'[49] Perhaps, years later, some of the delegates reflected that the leaders of the 'workers' and peasants' power' had started as they intended to go on: by 'anticipating' and interpreting the 'will' of the proletariat without ever giving it a chance to manifest itself from below. With the noise of gunfire in the background, the delegates got down to business. John Reed described the scene:

> So we came into the great meeting-hall, pushing through the clamorous mob at the door. In the rows of seats, under the white chandeliers, packed immovably in the aisles and on the sides, perched on every window-sill, and even the edge of the platform, the representatives of the workers and soldiers of all Russia waited in anxious silence or wild exultation. . . . There was no heat in the hall but the stifling heat of unwashed human bodies. A foul blue cloud of cigarette smoke rose from the mass and hung in the thick air.[50]

In the election to the praesidium the Bolsheviks won a majority. Many of the minority decided to withdraw from the congress. The majority did not care. Trotsky,

> standing up with a pale, cruel face, letting out his rich voice in cool contempt, 'All these so-called Socialist compromisers,

these frightened Mensheviki, Socialist Revolutionaries, *Bund* –
let them go! They are just so much refuse which will be swept
away into the garbage-heap of history'.[51]

The congress resolved that all power in the land should pass to
the local Soviets. It called for an immediate truce on all fronts;
promised free transfer of land to the peasants; democratization of
the forces; workers' control; and 'the convocation of the Constituent Assembly at the proper date'; as well as bread for the
towns; 'articles of first necessity to the villages'; and the right to
an independent existence for all nationalities in the former
Russian Empire.[52]

The congress adjourned at 6 a.m. Later the same day it re-
assembled and set up, 'until the Constituent Assembly provides
otherwise', a government, 'The Soviet of the People's Com-
missars'. Among the key appointments were: President, Lenin;
Interior, A. I. Rykov; Foreign Affairs, Trotsky; Military and
Naval Affairs, V. A. Avseenko (Antonov), N. V. Krylenko, and
F. M. Dybenko; Nationalities, Stalin.[53]

Having seized the capital, the question now was whether the
Bolsheviks could extend their writ throughout the country. A
few days later, after some confused fighting, Moscow fell to
them. Yet Kerensky had escaped and twelve of the fifteen Russian
armies did not recognize the new regime.[54] Had they relied solely
on force, especially military force, the Bolsheviks would have
failed. They rightly interpreted the desperation, anger, and
weariness of the troops and fired a political bombshell. This was
the 'Proclamation to the Peoples and Governments of all the
Belligerent Nations'. It called for immediate negotiations for a
'just and democratic peace'. It was to be a peace without annexa-
tions or indemnities. It abrogated all agreements concluded by
the earlier Russian governments and promised the publication of
secret treaties and open diplomacy in the future.[55] A land decree
followed. The peace offer seems to have been decisive for the
troops. General Dukhonin, the chief of staff, refused the orders of
Lenin and was slain by a mob of soldiers. A few Bolshevik sailors
and soldiers led by Krylenko had little difficulty in taking
Moghiliev, the army headquarters. Negotiations with the
Germans began at Brest-Litovsk.

## IV. 'THE STATE AND REVOLUTION'

What kind of man had Lenin become at the time of his assumption of power? And how had his ideas developed on the vital question of the exercise of power? Maxim Gorky, the writer, who knew him well, believed:

> a man of talent, he possesses all the qualities of a 'leader' and also the lack of morality necessary for this role, as well as an utterly pitiless attitude, worthy of a nobleman, towards the lives of the popular masses.[56]

We get some interesting impressions of Lenin from Bertrand Russell who met the Bolshevik leader on a visit to Russia in 1920:

> He has no love of luxury or even comfort. He is very friendly, and apparently simple, entirely without a trace of hauteur. If one met him without knowing who he was, one would not guess that he is possessed of great power or even that he is in any way eminent. I have never met a personage so destitute of self-importance. . . . He laughs a great deal; at first his laugh seems merely friendly and jolly, but gradually I came to feel it rather grim. He is dictatorial, calm, incapable of fear, extraordinarily devoid of self-seeking, an embodied theory. . . . He resembles a professor in his desire to have the theory understood and in his fury with those who misunderstand or disagree, as also in his love of expounding. I got the impression that he despises a great many people and is an intellectual aristocrat.[57]

Lenin had hurriedly set down his interpretation of the Marxist view of the state in August 1917 when he was avoiding arrest in Finland. This appeared under the title *State and Revolution* and has been compulsory reading for Communists ever since. Lenin wanted, in the first place, to resurrect Marx the apostle of violent revolution who had been buried by the 'opportunism' of the Second International. The fate of Marx and Engels had been the same, he argued, as that of earlier revolutionaries. Subjected to 'lies and slanders' in their lifetime, after their deaths there were attempts to canonize them. The object of this was to emasculate 'the revolutionary doctrine of its content, vulgarising it and blunting its revolutionary edge'.[58] To those who argued that

Marx had later modified his view and stated that in certain countries peaceful change was possible, he replied emphatically:

> In the epoch of the first great imperialist war, Marx's exception is no longer valid. Both England and America, the greatest and last representatives of Anglo-Saxon 'liberty', in the sense that militarism and bureaucracy are absent, have today plunged headlong into the all-European, filthy, bloody morass of bureaucratic-military institutions to which everything is subordinated and which trample everything under foot.[59]

In those countries too the bourgeois state machine would have to be 'smashed'. He condemned parliamentary democracy as a sham: 'the actual work of the "state" is done behind the scenes and is carried on by the departments, the government offices and the General Staffs. Parliament itself is given up to talk for the special purpose of fooling the "common people" '.[60] If 'parliamentarianism' was to go, this did not mean that the proletarian revolution would be without representative institutions. These would be, like those of the Commune of 1871, executive and legislative at the same time. Their members 'would have had to execute their own laws, they themselves would have to test their results in real life; they would have been directly responsible to their constituents'. There would be no 'privileged position for deputies'. There would be no career politicians, no gulf between rulers and ruled. Indeed, such officials who were needed would receive 'ordinary workmen's wages'.[61]

Though he was mainly concerned with discrediting the orthodox Social Democratic conception of the road to socialism, Lenin devoted some space to an attack on anarchism. He denounced 'anarchist dreams' of 'dispensing *at once* with all administration, with all subordination'. The state could not be abolished. In time it would, as Engels had put it, 'wither away'. Before this withering-away mankind would live under the dictatorship of the proletariat which would last until the enemies of the proletariat had been destroyed, until the economy had been transformed and the workers educated to rule and human nature changed. How long this dictatorship would last 'we do not and *cannot* know'.[62] But in 1919 he promised that those 'who have not passed the age of 30 or 35 will see the dawn of communism'.[63] Until that glorious dawn 'we shall establish strict, iron discipline supported by the state power of the armed workers'. And there would be subordination, for 'we want the socialist revolution with human nature as it is now, with human nature that cannot dispense with subordination, control and "managers" '.[64]

Lenin's sketch of the future was to remain a dream. Only the hints of authoritarianism found in *State and Revolution* were to become grim reality.

In the first few days after the *coup* the Bolsheviks did not deal too harshly with their opponents. Some members of the Kerensky government, for instance, were quickly released and subjected only to a nominal form of supervision.[65] In December a new (Bolshevik) secret police was set up, the *Cheka*, to combat 'counter-revolutionary sabotage'.[66] Press freedom had been curtailed in the previous month. Lenin later justified this by saying: 'The dictatorship of the proletariat will wipe out the shameful purveying of the bourgeois opium'.[67] The bourgeois Cadet Party was outlawed at the beginning of December. Much of what was done in this direction could be regarded as the 'normal' acts of a new regime with large parts of its territory in the hands of opponents or foreign powers. However, the Bolsheviks, with at the very most only a fig leaf to cover their illegality, had got themselves in a position where terror became the only means of retaining power. That this was so was indicated by the results of the elections to the Constituent Assembly and Lenin's and Trotsky's reaction to them. Out of a total of 41.7 million votes, only 9.8 million were given to the Bolsheviks – about 24 per cent. Their allies, the Left Socialist Revolutionaries, won roughly 5 per cent. The majority of the votes went to the Socialist Revolutionaries. The bourgeois parties got under 2 million votes. Thus the majority of the voters had opted for socialism but not for Bolshevism. Of 707 deputies the Bolsheviks elected 175, their allies 40. The centre and right-wing Socialist Revolutionaries gained 370 seats, a clear majority.[68] Some of the deputies were simply arrested, others were prevented from attending by other means. An unarmed, peaceful demonstration in Petrograd in favour of the Assembly was fired upon with many casualties. Finally, the Assembly was forced by Bolshevik sailors to adjourn, not to be given the chance to meet again.

Had Lenin attempted to rule though the Assembly, as well as the Soviet, he would have found it anything but reactionary. Its composition and its brief deliberations had revealed that it wanted land for the peasants and peace negotiations. In any case, the Bolsheviks were a large group in it, and were far more disciplined than the other parties. It is likely that they would have been able to win majorities on key issues. The Assembly would probably have opted for an economic policy of the kind Lenin was forced to introduce in the twenties. It would have given the regime far greater prestige abroad, probably avoiding both the isolation Russia was to suffer and the nightmare of political and economic Stalinism.

Lenin's dictatorship led to a good deal of condemnation from left-wing critics inside and outside Russia. The dying Plekhanov said that the Assembly represented the labouring masses of Russia. By dissolving it Lenin was fighting not the enemies of the workers, but the enemies of the Bolsheviks.[69] Maxim Gorky, later literary parade-horse of the regime, called his friend 'a deliberate juggler, who has no feeling either for the lives or the honour of the proletariat'.[70] The two greatest names in the international working-class movement to denounce Lenin's policy were Rosa Luxemburg and Karl Kautsky. Lenin later canonized Luxemburg with the words 'in spite of these mistakes, she was and is an eagle, and not only will she be dear to the memory of Communists in the whole world, but her biography and the *complete* edition of her works . . . will be a very useful lesson in the education of many generations of Communists'.[71] One of 'these mistakes' was her clear condemnation of Lenin's abolition of democracy. She admired Lenin's earlier anti-war stand and his courage, and her attack was more in sorrow than in anger. The critique, *Die Russische Revolution*, was written in autumn 1918:

> To be sure, every democratic institution has its limits and shortcomings, things which it doubtless shares with all human institutions. But the remedy which Lenin and Trotsky have found, the abolition of democracy as such, is worse than the disease it is supposed to cure; for it stops up the very living source from which alone can come the correction of all the innate limitations of social institutions – the active, uninhibited, energetic political life of the broadest masses of the people.[72]

And again:

> Freedom only for the supporters of the government, only for the members of one party . . . is no freedom. Freedom is always only freedom for one who thinks differently.

Because the Bolsheviks were experimenting, and this was what all revolutionaries would have to do, their measures were not perfect and needed criticism. But they were interpreting the dictatorship of the proletariat as if socialist transformation could be a completed prescription in the pocket of the revolutionary party.[73] She correctly predicted what was going to happen:

> Without general elections, without unrestricted freedom of the press and assembly, without a free struggle of opinion, life dies away in every public institution, becomes a mere sham, in which only the bureaucracy remains the active element. Public life gradually goes to sleep, a few dozen party leaders of inexhaustible energy and limitless idealism direct and rule. Among them, in reality only a dozen outstanding heads lead, and an élite of the working class is invited from time to time to meetings, to clap the speeches of the leaders, and approve proposed resolutions unanimously. This is therefore at bottom a clique – a dictatorship to be sure, but not the dictatorship of the proletariat. It is the dictatorship of a handful of politicians, that is, dictatorship in the bourgeois sense, in the sense of Jacobin rule. . . .[74]

Such a situation, she continued, would lead to assassination attempts, the shooting of hostages, and so on. She claimed that both Trotsky and Kautsky were wrong in posing the alternative, 'Either Democracy or Dictatorship?' Proletarian dictatorship was only dictatorship in so far as the immense majority were prepared to use force to prevent the handful of officials, officers, land-owners, and capitalists of the old order from regaining power. In this she was more of a Marxist than the Bolsheviks. Had Lenin tried to rule through the Assembly, he might have erected the first real dictatorship of the proletariat in the Marxist sense (though for Marx this was the Paris Commune). As we saw in the last chapter, Rosa Luxemburg had criticized Lenin's conception of the party. She was now attacking his second major deviation from Marx on the dictatorship. In the same pamphlet she put her finger on what was to be his third great mistake – from the Marxist point of view:

> The danger begins there where they [the Bolsheviks] make a virtue of necessity, theorise about the tactics forced on them by these fatal circumstances, and recommend them to the inter-national proletariat as a model.[75]

Kautsky wrote his first criticism of the Bolsheviks about the same time, published under the title *The Dictatorship of the Proletariat*. Kautsky likened the Paris Commune to the events in Russia and commented: 'In one important aspect, the Paris Commune was superior to the Soviet Republic. The former was the work of the entire proletariat. All shades of the Socialist movement took part in it, none drew back from it, none was excluded'. In Russia, the Bolsheviks had gained power by fighting the other socialist parties.[76] There could be no socialism without democracy. The Bolsheviks might claim that the ruling classes used force against socialists, but this did not prove that democracy should be dispensed with: 'Should a ruling class . . . resort to force, it would do so precisely because it feared the consequences of democracy. And its violence would be nothing but the subversion of democracy'.[77]

Trotsky made a brave, but not very successful, attempt to defend the Bolshevik position. He used the argument of history that terror had been widely used in the past by progressive forces – in the Reformation, the Civil War in England, the Revolution in France, the Paris Commune, the American Civil War. In any case, terror had been used first against the Bolsheviks. This was not entirely true. Even if it were, the Bolsheviks were the ones who were usurping the authority of the democratic institutions. He further claimed: 'Our Extraordinary Commissions shoot landlords, capitalists, and generals who are striving to restore the capitalist order'. This was not true then and, as Trotsky was to find out to his own cost, it became less and less true. He defended the lack of press freedom on the grounds of wartime conditions.[78] The Constituent Assembly had been dismissed because

> As we saw the organization of revolutionary power only in the Soviets, and as at the moment of the summoning of the Constituent Assembly the Soviets were already the de facto power, the question was inevitably decided for us in the sense of the violent dissolution of the Constituent Assembly, since it would not dissolve itself in favor of the Government of the Soviets.

If they did not repudiate the Assembly beforehand, 'it was only because it stood in contrast, not to the power of the Soviets, but to the power of Kerensky himself, who in his turn, was only a screen for the bourgeoisie'.[79] Such tortuous arguments had become necessary in order to cover up the plain facts.

We left the Bolshevik emissaries at Brest-Litovsk negotiating peace with the Germans and their allies. We need not go into the details of the long, involved talks with Trotsky trying to buy time, time to proclaim the Bolsheviks' peace aims, to 'gauge the intensity of the revolutionary ferment in Europe; and to test the attitude of allied and enemy governments'.[80] The German generals were not prepared to give the Russians respite. They were afraid of the Bolsheviks turning 'the whole of Europe into a pig-sty' and, in the words of General Max Hoffmann, regarded Russia as 'a vast heap of maggots – a squalid, swarming mass'[81] to be exploited by Germany. They therefore presented the Bolsheviks with an ultimatum at the same time as they renewed their advance. Trotsky at first opposed acceptance of this. Lenin argued in favour. The Bolshevik Central Committee prevaricated and then by one vote accepted. The agreement was signed on 3 March 1918. The terms were crushing. 'Never yet had any peace brought so much suffering and humiliation as the "peace" of Brest had brought to Russia.[82] Russia lost one-third, or 62 million, of her population, one-quarter of her territory, one-third of her croplands, 27 per cent of her income, and more than half her industries. She was left defenceless.[83] In addition, the Russians had to pay reparations disguised as reimbursement 'for expenses incurred by the other party for its nationals who have been made prisoners of war'.[84] The Germans had in fact profited from the use of Russian prisoners whose labour had helped boost their economy. Both sides agreed to cease hostile propaganda, something which was of far greater importance to the Germans than to the Bolsheviks.

The terms of Brest-Litovsk were cruel, but had the Bolsheviks any alternative? The German advance was meeting virtually no resistance. In the short run the Allies could do little to help even if the political obstacles to such help were quickly overcome. The British military attaché in Petrograd had independently come to the same view as Lenin about the impossibility of continued Russian resistance.[85] Yet the workers were ready to enlist 'in their tens of thousands for the defence of the Revolution'.[86] No organization existed to harness this feeling. In the Ukraine many peasants were putting up a desperate struggle against the occupiers.[87] Under the treaty the Russians were to come to terms with the German puppet regime there and to abandon the partisans.

It is not surprising that the treaty provoked widespread revulsion both in Russia and outside.

If the capacity to withstand criticism be the criterion of greatness, then upon this score alone Lenin's place among the great ones of the earth would have been assured. From the moment that the terms of the treaty became public, there was no more vilified man in Russia or in Europe.[88]

Revulsion and vilification turned to anger and opposition. On 6 July the German ambassador was assassinated by two Left Socialist Revolutionaries, high officials of the *Cheka*, hoping to provoke a new Russo-German war. This was followed by a Left Socialist Revolutionary insurrection which was suppressed. Within the Bolshevik Party there was much opposition, with Nikolai Bukharin leading the Left Communists (or left wing of the Bolshevik Party) against Lenin. But the party soon found it had to unite in order to survive.

For Britain and France Russia's defection from the Allied cause was a disastrous blow. Under the old regime the Russians had fought hard and had tied up more than half the total number of enemy divisions.[89] After Brest-Litovsk the Germans were able to transfer many divisions from the east and hurl them against the hard-pressed Anglo-French forces. This was reason enough for Allied intervention in Russia to attempt to mobilize anti-German forces. The Brest Treaty gave them another reason: the grain, livestock, timber, and oil Germany and her allies were to get from the occupied territories. These would defeat the Allied naval blockade of Germany and prolong the war. After Brest-Litovsk, it was commonly feared in the Allied states that 'Germany was about to reduce Russia to the status of a satellite'.[90] Other reasons for intervention were fear that large stocks of war material sent to Russia would fall into German hands, and the Bolshevik repudiation of all the debts of earlier regimes – including a great deal owed to France, Britain, and the United States – and nationalization of foreign undertakings. In the case of the United States, the trickle of goods and investments of pre-war years became a flood in the years 1914–17. The result was that, 'as the war advanced, the United States found itself . . . more deeply engaged than ever, economically and financially, in the Russian scene'.[91] By intervening the Allies hoped 'to unseat the Bolsheviks and install a regime more favourable to Russian and foreign property-owners', and set 'the Germans and Russians at each other's throats'.[92]

In May 1918 Lloyd George, the British Prime Minister, sent to Russia 'as his secret service agent the international adventurer, Sydney Reilly, a Jew from Odessa, whose object was nothing short of the organization of a coup against' the Bolsheviks.[93] By the time the Western powers were negotiating with the Germans in Paris at the end of 1918 Bolshevik Russia was surrounded by a ring of enemies, foreign and domestic:

> In the east was the Japanese-protected regime at Chita. . . . There was the central hub of anti-Bolshevik power at Omsk, where . . . Kolchak . . . had arrested his colleagues with the connivance of the Allies and given himself the title of Supreme Ruler of Russia. His chief source of supply for munitions was Britain. . . . In the Ukraine, Denikin was the spearhead of the French penetration. The forces against Moscow in the north-west were the new Baltic states and Finland . . . threatening Petrograd. . . . In the far north the Murmansk-Archangel regime relied upon British and United States support.[94]

Yet against all odds the Bolsheviks held on to power. Their doing so 'can only be regarded as a great, almost miraculous achievement'.[95]

Even to have a chance of survival the Bolsheviks had to create armed forces. Their earlier propaganda was their first problem. They had helped, only helped, to produce a pacifist abhorrence of war. They had helped to create the illusion that the Red Guards could protect the revolution and that soldiers had a right to elect their commanders. Under the Brest-Litovsk Treaty they were obliged to demobilize those troops who had not already demobilized themselves. In March 1918 Trotsky was appointed Commissar of War. He soon had to utter words which 'sounded like a profanation of revolutionary taboo'.[96] He had to re-establish a standing professional army. The Red Guards and partisans were disbanded. Worse still, from the point of view of many idealists, he had to engage the services of any former professional soldiers who could be bought, bullied, or persuaded. He told his comrades: 'As industry needs engineers, as farming needs qualified agronomists, so military specialists are indispensable to defence.'[97] In order to ensure loyalty the death penalty was brought back and officers knew that treachery or

desertion could lead to reprisals against their families.[98] In the
summer of 1918 conscription was reintroduced. Both Reds and
Whites were forced to rely on peasant masses who were little
interested in getting killed and who deserted *en masse*. Suffering
all these disadvantages the Bolsheviks persevered and won.

The reasons for the Bolshevik victory are not completely clear.
The lack of a co-ordinated effort on the part of the intervention-
ists and the geography of the country helped. Mutinies among
French and British troops, war-weary, cold, and tired, not
understanding why they were in Russia, panicked politicians into
withdrawing them. Opposition from sections of opinion in the
Allied countries did the same. Yet it would be wrong to attribute
the Bolshevik victory to outside factors only. Their leadership
was important:

> Lenin (and also Trotsky in his sphere) had a grip on men and
> events that none of the White leaders could ever acquire. And
> they were realists. Trotsky's flaming rhetoric never obscured
> the practical difficulties to be overcome. . . . As against this,
> Kolchak, Denikin, Miller . . . were romantics.[99]

The Bolshevik Party itself was another key factor. It brought 'a
cohesion to the Red war effort that was lacking on the other
side'.[100] Perhaps the patriotism of the ordinary Russian peasant
and worker was another cause. Even if they were not Bolsheviks,
they were suspicious of regimes kept going by foreign powers.
Intervention failed. It has embittered Soviet-Western relations
ever since. But its supporters would claim that by 'containing'
Bolshevism in Russia they saved the rest of Europe from a similar
fate. Certainly, by the end of intervention the Bolsheviks could
take little hope from the disorder and turmoil which had swept
across many of the lands beyond their frontiers.


### V. ROSA LUXEMBURG AND THE GERMAN REVOLUTION

Hardly any country had been spared social upheaval as a result
of the war – even Switzerland had had a general strike – but only
in the Habsburg Empire, Germany, and Bulgaria were there
attempts at Marxist revolutions on the Soviet model.

In Hungary a bourgeois-Social Democratic coalition had taken
over from the Habsburg regime in the 'Autumn Rose Revolution'.[101] It set about creating a democratic republic in the

impoverished rump of old Hungary divested of about half her former territory. But it was soon overthrown by an ill-assorted company of Communists and Left Social Democrats. The guiding spirit of this 'proletarian' revolution was Béla Kun (1886–1939). Kun, son of a village clerk who had joined the Social Democratic movement at sixteen, worked as a clerk for the Workers' Insurance Bureau and then as a journalist. As a prisoner-of-war officer he had witnessed the Russian Revolution and had been inspired by Bolshevism. His Soviet regime lasted 133 days. Its fall was the result of external opposition – from the Western powers and its neighbours – and its own incompetence, lack of unity, and ill-advised policies. It failed to win the peasants, tried to cut off the faithful from their Church and the workers from their liquor. It was also the victim of popular anti-semitism, as most of the Communist leaders were Jews. It was replaced by a White dictatorship under Admiral Horthy which ruthlessly extirpated all manifestations of the Hungarian Soviet Republic. Thousands were killed, thousands more, including many non-Marxists, fled. Kun and many of his colleagues perished later in Stalin's purges.

In Austria, the old regime had fallen victim of the war as well. There, the socialists, who also regarded themselves as Marxists, chose the parliamentary road, and found themselves in a minority. They then withdrew from the government. In practice the country then had two governments – one in Vienna and another in the rest of the country. This was possible because of the federal system. The national government was clerical and re-actionary. In the province of Vienna, where the socialists had a majority, the government embarked on an impressive pro-gramme of housing, education, and welfare, based on a system of local taxation 'bearing with unexampled severity on the wealthier classes'.[102] The working-class housing projects became celebrated throughout the world because of the high standard of design. All this ended in 1934 when the socialist experiment was smashed after a brief civil war. The party's Linz Programme of 1926, although Marxist, had by implication rejected the dictatorship of the proletariat. The programme of 1934, based on the experience of right-wing terror, spoke of 'a revolutionary dictatorship' as a transitionary form.[103]

The Russian Bolsheviks set great store by the German prole-tariat. In Germany mass opposition to the war was widespread from 1916 onwards. This led to a split in the SPD and the setting-up of the Independent Social Democratic Party (USPD) in April 1917. The new party united all those opposed to the war from Bernstein and Haase to Luxemburg and Karl Liebknecht (1871–1919). Later in that year a mutiny broke out in the German navy, but was suppressed. After the failure of the German offensive on the Western front in 1918 the country's military leaders were ready for negotiations with the Allies. In the hope of presenting a better 'image' they advised the formation of the broadest-based coalition government. This included two majority Social Democrats, Philipp Scheidemann (1865–1939) and Gustav Bauer. Legislation was approved making the Reichstag a responsible parliament. Early in November renewed naval mutinies spread throughout the coastal towns and then inland to the main urban centres. In some cases workers' and soldiers' councils took over the local administration. On 7 November the first of the German royal houses, the Wittelsbachs of Bavaria, fell and was replaced by a democratic republic ruled by a coalition of USPD and majority SPD members. The pressure for change mounted.

Fearing they would be outmanoeuvred by the Left, the majority SPD resigned from the government. On 9 November Karl Liebknecht, just freed from prison where he had served a sentence for anti-war activities, proclaimed a German socialist republic at a demonstration in front of the royal palace in Berlin. For his action he had no authority but himself. The revolutionary situation appeared to be developing so rapidly that Scheidemann felt obliged to proclaim a free German republic on the same day. He too had no authority other than his own good political sense. He was criticized by the head of the majority SPD, Friedrich Ebert (1871–1925), but there was no going back. The next day, as the Kaiser fled to Holland, a mass meeting of Berlin workers' and soldiers' councils formally elected six People's Commissioners to rule Germany. There were three from each wing of Social Democracy and Ebert, Haase, and Scheidemann were among them. Ebert was elected chairman.

On 11 November a German delegation, led by a Centre Party politician, Matthias Erzberger, signed an armistice agreement with the Allies.

The Ebert government, now the only German government, faced grave decisions. Its chairman wanted to avoid anarchy, which would cause suffering to the people and Allied intervention. He rejected the revolutionary road, believing that it would lead to tyranny. (The Russian Bolsheviks had been in power for about a year by this time.) He desired to create conditions in which a democratic, fully representative parliament could be elected to run the country. To achieve his objects he made a fatal pact with the army High Command, to fight Bolshevism in Germany.[104] The army estimated that 'a tiny minority could simply overthrow the whole German Empire'.[105]

On 20 December the first all-German Congress of Workers' and Soldiers' Councils voted in favour of holding elections for a national assembly on 19 January. They rejected extreme left-wing demands for a republic based on workers' and soldiers' councils. In fact, Luxemburg and Liebknecht could not even get themselves elected to the congress. Nevertheless, the congress did not go entirely as Ebert would have liked. It passed resolutions calling for the establishment of a people's militia to replace the regular army, a militia with elected officers and responsible to the People's Commissioners. It further demanded the nationalization of ripe industries, especially coalmining. The resolution regarding the army was a great embarrassment to Ebert. Its realization would have meant the destruction of German militarism. It need not have led to Bolshevism, for Switzerland had such a system (though there the officers are not elected). The army High Command, increasingly impatient, put pressure on the government. Realizing that the old army units were rapidly disintegrating, it also commenced recruitment of reliable officers and other ranks for its new 'Volunteer Corps'. Towards the end of December, a left-wing naval unit, angry because it had received no pay and dissatisfied with the general situation, had occupied the Berlin Palace and taken Otto Wels, Social Democratic Berlin City Commandant, hostage. Troops of the army High Command tried unsuccessfully to bring the rebels to heel. In the end negotiations led to the marines getting their pay, the evacuation of the palace, and the release of Wels. One important result of the fighting was the withdrawal of the USPD from the government. The Independent leaders wanted the resolutions of the congress on nationalization and the armed forces implemented. They too agreed on the parliamentary road to socialism, but they wanted the government to carry through fundamental reforms at once.

With the resignation of the USPD leaders vanished the last

possibility of mediation between the government and the increasingly restless left-wing elements in Berlin. 'It was clear that a violent eruption was inevitable'.[106]

This became more inevitable still when the Spartacists broke away from the USPD at the end of December. The Spartacist League had been set up at the beginning of the war as an extreme internationalist, revolutionary socialist group backed by Rosa Luxemburg and Karl Liebknecht. It now formed itself into the Communist Party of Germany (KPD). Official KPD policy was to engage in relentless agitation among the workers until, without need for a *putsch*, the party was summoned to power by the masses.[107] The leaders of the fragmented Left met at the Berlin police headquarters. The meeting was called to decide what to do about the dismissal of Emil Eichhorn, a USPD member, from his post as head of the Berlin police. He refused to be sacked and called upon the Left to support him. A huge demonstration in his favour took place in front of the police building. Inside, the leaders of the left wing of the Berlin USPD, the revolutionary shop stewards from the Berlin factories (not associated with any party), and Karl Liebknecht and Wilhelm Pieck of the KPD, all carried away by the crowd's enthusiasm, agreed to call a general strike and launch an armed assault upon the government. Liebknecht and Pieck were later reproved by Luxemburg for committing the KPD to this action, but she felt they could not back out.

The day following the meeting, 6 January 1919, leftists started to take over key buildings. Similar outbreaks took place in other major cities. For some hours the issue appeared undecided, but the determination of Gustav Noske, government minister in charge of the *Freikorps*, and the bad organization of the revolutionaries, led to the defeat of the Left. One by one the buildings were recaptured, often with the massacre of those found in them. Within a week all was lost. The left-wing leaders were hunted down. Liebknecht and Luxemburg were captured and shot. Whether their murder, for the authorities later recognized their deaths as such, was connived at by Noske, is not known for certain. Leaving aside the human aspects, the deaths of the two revolutionaries was a tragedy from the political point of view. As one writer who had little time for them put it:

A curse clung to this wretched deed: by helping destroy distaste for violence and respect for human lives in Germany it helped teach the nation to accept brutal and bloody force as a legitimate tool of domestic politics.[108]

It is also possible that had Luxemburg and Liebknecht lived, they might have led the KPD out of the cul-de-sac of Leninism-Stalinism, which it was soon to enter, and contributed to uniting the working class in face of the rising tide of Nazism which swept over Germany just over a decade after their deaths.

Early in March renewed fighting exploded in Berlin. It was put down with great ruthlessness by the *Freikorps*. In Bavaria an attempt to set up a republic based on workers' councils was drowned in blood. The promised elections were held with the majority SPD emerging as the largest party (with 38 per cent of the vote), the USPD gained 7.6 per cent; the Catholic Centre Party was the second largest group with 20 per cent of the poll. The KPD did not contest the elections. A Left-Centre government was formed with seven majority socialists, three Catholics, three democrats, and one non-party. Ebert was elected President of the Republic and a democratic constitution was agreed, but fundamental reforms of German society were not carried through. The republic faced the continued antagonism of the old right-wing classes, including the armed forces, the heavy burden of Versailles, and widespread dissatisfaction among the workers who felt cheated of their revolution.

## VI. LENIN'S INTERNATIONAL

The divisions in the socialist movement over the war and the revolutions and disorders which followed it, shattered the old International. Yet it is possible, indeed likely, that had Lenin not embarked upon a policy of splitting the international socialist movement, most socialist groups would have eventually reunited in their own countries, and come together again in one international organization. As it was, Lenin set up the Third, or Communist, International in Moscow in March 1919: an attempt to dish the non-Leninist socialists who were planning to revive the earlier International.[109]

Many socialists in Europe, including many in Britain, admired the courage of the Bolsheviks, respected their power, and paid homage to them as the architects of the only successful 'proletarian' revolution. Few of them understood either Leninist theory or Soviet reality. The forty-four, mainly unrepresentative, delegates to the First Congress of the Communist International did not do justice to the prestige of Lenin and his revolution abroad. Once it became clear that Leninism would represent a break with the traditional forms of organization and practice of the main socialist parties, and that they would have to accept outside control, enthusiasm for affiliation to the Communist International waned. Lenin, however, believed the trend was towards him and he was in no mood to compromise. Parties which did not accept the 'twenty-one points', the statutes of the Communist International, were not admitted. The British Independent Labour Party, then an important part of the Labour Party, and the American Socialist Party, despite the fact that its Left had already split off, were among those organizations which initially favoured affiliation and then had second thoughts. Eugene V. Debbs, one of the greatest figures in the history of American socialism, called the 'twenty-one points', 'ridiculous, arbitrary and autocratic'.[110]

The statutes of Lenin's International were adopted by its Second Congress, held in Moscow in July-August 1920. One of the key paragraphs reads:

> It is the aim of the Communist International to fight by all available means, including armed struggle, for the overthrow of the international bourgeoisie and for the creation of an international Soviet republic as a transitional stage to the complete abolition of the state. The Communist International considers the dictatorship of the proletariat the only possible way to liberate mankind from the horrors of capitalism. And the Communist International considers the Soviet power the historically given form of this dictatorship of the proletariat.[111]

On organization it was decided that there must be a strongly centralized body, that the International must 'in fact and in deed' be a single party 'of the entire world. The parties working in the various countries are but separate sections'. Among the twenty-one points were the obligations to set up 'parallel illegal organization[s]', to establish party cells in the trade unions and co-operatives to accept Democratic Centralism,[112] to be bound by the decisions of the International, to change their names to 'Communist' parties, and to expel 'centrists' and 'opportunists'.

The splits provoked by Leninism made it more difficult for the workers to take advantage of the situation created by the aftermath of the war. They weakened the workers' movement in face of the menace of Fascism and Nazism. Had Lenin not advocated imitation of his policies by other parties, had he not set up his own International, it is likely that his party would have been eventually accepted in the Labour and Socialist International reconstituted in 1923. This would at least have lessened the isolation of Russia.

Lenin's greatest mistake, then, was his refusal to accept that his theories were, at very best, the product of Russian conditions, and relevant only to those conditions. The Communist International, or Comintern as it became known, was from the start the instrument of the Soviet Communist Party, or rather its leader, and remained so until it was disbanded in 1943. After Lenin's death in January 1924, the defects of his intellectual, spiritual, and material heritage which he left his followers were magnified by Stalin. Here too the consequences were serious for the international socialist movement as well as for the world in general, and the peoples of the Soviet Union in particular.

## NOTES

[1] Julius Braunthal, *History of the International, 1914–1943* (London, 1967), II, 12.
[2] *GDAB*, II, 217.
[3] Braunthal, op. cit., p. 7.
[4] Walter Kendall, *The Revolutionary Movement in Britain 1900–21* (London, 1969), p. 85.
[5] Peter Stansky (ed.), *The Left and War: The British Labour Party and World War I* (Stanford, 1969), p. 62.
[6] Braunthal, op. cit., p. 27.
[7] Krupskaya, op. cit., p. 281.
[8] V. I. Lenin, *Socialism and War* (London, 1940), pp. 10–11.
[9] ibid., p. 24.
[10] V. I. Lenin, *Imperialism the Highest Stage of Capitalism* (London, 1948), p. 76. The emphasis is Lenin's throughout.
[11] ibid., p. 77.
[12] ibid., p. 101.
[13] ibid., p. 92.
[14] ibid., p. 119.
[15] These arguments are well set out in M. E. Chamberlain, *The New Imperialism* (Historical Association, London, 1970), pp. 21–2.
[16] Lenin, *Imperialism*, p. 79.
[17] Chamberlain, op. cit., p. 22.
[18] H. M. Wright (ed.), *The New Imperialism* (Boston, 1961), p. 95. This contribution is by Nicholas Mansergh.

[19] Chamberlain, op. cit., p. 39.

[20] Howard K. Beale, *Theodore Roosevelt and the Rise of America to World Power* (Baltimore, 1956), p. 38. See also G. E. Mowry, *The Era of Theodore Roosevelt* (New York, 1958), p. 144.

[21] G. P. Gooch, *Recent Revelations of European Diplomacy* (New York, 1967), p. 470. The various standpoints of the causes of the war are given in Dwight E. Lee (ed.), *The Outbreak of the First World War* (Boston, 1958).

[22] Barbara W. Tuchman, *August 1914* (London, 1962), p. 72.

[23] Alan Moorehead, *The Russian Revolution* (London, 1958), p. 111.

[24] Peter I. Lyashchenko, 'Economic and Social Consequences of the War', in Arthur E. Adams (ed.), *The Russian Revolution* (Boston, 1968), p. 15.

[25] Moorehead, op. cit., p. 113.

[26] Lyashchenko, op. cit., p. 19.

[27] G. D. H. Cole, *Communism and Social Democracy, 1914–1931* (London, 1958), I, 69.

[28] Leon Trotsky, *The History of the Russian Revolution* (London, 1932), I, 119–23.

[29] ibid., p. 123.

[30] Moorehead, op. cit., pp. 160–8.

[31] Oskar Anweiler, *Die Rätebewegung in Russland 1905–1921* (Leiden, 1958), p. 136.

[32] Moorehead, op. cit., p. 176.

[33] Krupskaya, op. cit., p. 335.

[34] Moorehead, op. cit., p. 192.

[35] Krupskaya, op. cit., pp. 344–5.

[36] Moorehead, op. cit., p. 200.

[37] ibid., p. 191.

[38] Krupskaya, op. cit., p. 345.

[39] ibid., p. 347.

[40] Moorehead, op. cit., p. 213.

[41] ibid., p. 211.

[42] Shub, op. cit., pp. 243–8; Moorehead, op. cit., p. 229.

[43] I. Deutscher, *The Prophet Armed: Trotsky 1879–1921* (London, 1954), p. 279.

[44] Moorehead, op. cit., pp. 171–2.

[45] Trotsky, *History of the Russian Revolution*, I, 229.

[46] ibid., III, 37.

[47] John Reed, *Ten Days that Shook the World* (London, 1928), p. 25.

[48] For *Delo Naroda* and Maxim Gorky, see R. P. Browder and A. F. Kerensky, *The Russian Provisional Government 1917*, III (Stanford, 1961), 1764–6. For *Izvestia*, see Shub, op. cit., p. 277.

[49] Reed, op. cit., p. 73.

[50] ibid.

[51] ibid., p. 79.

[52] ibid., p. 91.

[53] ibid., p. 114.

[54] Shub, op. cit., p. 295.

[55] Reed, op. cit., pp. 105–6.

[56] This is from Gorky's magazine *Novaya Zhizn*, No. 177 (10[23] Nov. 1917), as quoted in S. W. Page (ed.), *Lenin: Dedicated Marxist or Revolutionary Pragmatist?* (Lexington, Mass., 1970), p. 181.

[57] Bertrand Russell, *The Practice and Theory of Bolshevism* (London, 1951), pp. 33–4.

[58] V. I. Lenin, *State and Revolution* (London, n.d.), p. 7.

[59] ibid., p. 31.

[60] ibid., p. 37.
[61] ibid., p. 40.
[62] ibid., p. 73.
[63] Carr, op. cit., p. 247.
[64] Lenin, *State and Revolution*, p. 39.
[65] Carr, op. cit., p. 161.
[66] ibid., p. 167.
[67] Shub, op. cit., p. 312.
[68] For votes, see Shub, op. cit., p. 315.
[69] ibid., p. 328.
[70] ibid., p. 301.
[71] Nettl, op. cit., p. 792.
[72] Rosa Luxemburg, *Die Russische Revolution*, edited by Peter Blachstein (Hamburg, 1948), p. 48.
[73] ibid., p. 54.
[74] ibid., p. 56.
[75] ibid., p. 62.
[76] Karl Kautsky, *The Dictatorship of the Proletariat* (Ann Arbor, 1964), pp. 1–2.
[77] ibid., p. 8.
[78] Leon Trotsky, *Terrorism and Communism* (Ann Arbor, 1963), p. 59.
[79] ibid., p. 44.
[80] Deutscher, *The Prophet Armed*, p. 355.
[81] John W. Wheeler-Bennett, *Brest-Litovsk: The Forgotten Peace* (London, 1956), p. 244.
[82] Deutscher, *The Prophet Armed*, p. 399.
[83] Moorehead, op. cit., p. 303.
[84] Wheeler-Bennett, op. cit., p. 273.
[85] R. H. Ullman, *Intervention and the War* (Princeton, 1961), p. 48.
[86] Wheeler-Bennett, op. cit., p. 247.
[87] Deutscher, *The Prophet Armed*, p. 394.
[88] Wheeler-Bennett, op. cit., p. 275.
[89] John Swettenham, *Allied Intervention in Russia 1918–1919* (London, 1967 p. 17.
[90] George Kennan, *Russia Leaves the War* (London, n.d.), p. 458.
[91] ibid., pp. 33–4.
[92] F. S. Northedge, *The Troubled Giant* (London, 1966), pp. 66–7.
[93] ibid., p. 69.
[94] ibid., pp. 75–6.
[95] Swettenham, op. cit., p. 275.
[96] Deutscher, *The Prophet Armed*, p. 406.
[97] ibid., p. 408.
[98] ibid., p. 414.
[99] David Footman, *Civil War in Russia* (London, 1961), p. 304.
[100] ibid., p. 305.
[101] Rudolf L. Tökés, *Béla Kun and the Hungarian Soviet Republic* (Stanford, 1967), p. 83. The facts on Hungary are drawn from this source.
[102] Cole, *Communism and Social Democracy*, p. 228.
[103] Klaus Berchtold, *Österreichische Parteiprogramme 1868–1966* (Munich, 1967), pp. 260, 266.
[104] Waldemar Erfurth, *Die Geschichte des deutschen Generalstabes* (Göttingen, 1957), p. 16.
[105] F. L. Carsten, *The Reichswehr and Politics* (London, 1966), p. 12.
[106] Rudolf Coper, *Failure of a Revolution* (Cambridge, 1955), p. 186.
[107] R. W. Watt, *The Kings Depart* (London, 1969), p. 257.

[108] Erich Eyck, *A History of the Weimar Republic* (Cambridge, Mass., 1962), I, 53.

[109] Shub, op. cit., p. 390.

[110] Bell, *Marxian Socialism*, pp. 114–15.

[111] Braunthal, op. cit., p. 534.

[112] This classic Leninist formulation in theory meant that all higher organs were elected from below, but once elected they had very wide powers to make decisions binding on all members. In practice even the elections were beyond the control of the ordinary members.

# V

## 'Socialism in One Country'

ON the evening of 7 March 1921 cannon boomed at each other across the Gulf of Finland. This time Lenin's troops were in action not against foreigners or White guards but against their own comrades. The sailors of the Kronstadt garrison, once the pride of the Bolshevik Revolution, had raised the standard of revolt and told Lenin to go.

The sailors' revolt was merely the climax of a series of insurrections and disturbances which had affected large areas of the country. The rebels were peasants made desperate by the requisitioning of grain, seed, and stock, and workers, weary, hungry, and angry. They wanted to end the 'nightmare rule', as the sailors put it, of Leninism, and restore the effective power of the Soviets.[1] The sailors stood for 'power to the soviets but not the parties, for the freely elected representation of the toilers. The soviets that have been captured and manipulated by the Communist party have always been deaf to all our demands and needs; the only reply we have ever received has been shooting'.[2]

With some difficulty government troops under Tukhachevsky crossed the ice and stormed the forts of Kronstadt. Hundreds, perhaps thousands, were killed on both sides. Some of the rebels managed to escape to nearby Finland. Those who fell into Bolshevik hands were either butchered on the spot, shot later, or sent to forced labour.

Kronstadt was a body-blow to the prestige of the Soviet regime and caused the first major crop of resignations from Communist groups around the world. The rising brought home to Lenin the urgency of the need to introduce measures to alleviate the daily suffering of his people. Such measures were approved at the Tenth Congress of the Communist Party in the month of the Kronstadt rising. The measures had been planned before. It is interesting that Trotsky had proposed one of the key changes in agriculture as early as February 1920, but his proposal had been defeated.[3] By February 1921 Lenin was advocating what

amounted to the same policy: abolition of the requisitioning of
grain surpluses in favour of a tax in kind calculated on a percentage of production; the lowering of the percentage of tax in
proportion to the increase of effort by the cultivator; freedom for
the cultivator to sell his surplus over and above the tax. Hitherto
this had been denounced as a return to 'free trade' and petty
bourgeois capitalism. Starting in May 1921 a series of decrees
were approved according to which the small artisan and the petty
industry of the countryside were granted the same legal security
and the same opportunity to trade as had been offered to the
peasantry.[4] Another important reversal of policy was the leasing
of nationalized industrial enterprises to private individuals or
co-operatives. Leases were generally granted for periods of from
two to five years, rent was paid in kind. Foreign companies were
also encouraged to take up concessions in Russia and, as we shall
see, a considerable number of important ones did so. According
to Lenin, the state would hold on to the 'commanding heights'
of the economy.

Increasingly under the New Economic Policy (NEP), enterprises had to rely on their own resources. State subsidies were cut
off for the majority which had to look to their own profits for their
future. Only essential sectors of heavy industry continued to
receive state support.

The NEP did stimulate both agriculture and industry, but it
favoured the consumer goods industries at the expense of the
long-term, slow-maturing projects of heavy industry. The
desperate situation of Russia before NEP and in its early years
was revealed by official figures. They indicated that large-scale
industrial production as a whole had by 1920 fallen to 15 per cent
of the 1912 level. By 1922 it had recovered to 20 per cent of that
level. The leather, textile, woollen, and linen industries had
recovered much more. But the metallurgical industry, the
greatest of Russia's pre-war large-scale industries, had slumped
to 6 per cent of the 1912 figure in 1920, only managing 7 per cent
in 1922.[5] The industrial collapse was, for the most part, *not* the
result of the war or intervention. The main manufacturing areas
were not affected by these events. The collapse followed the
breakdown of discipline and the dispersal of skilled workers,
engineers, and managerial personnel which occurred after the
revolution.[6]

More than the above figures the desperation of Russia was

exposed by the famine of 1921–22. The British Communist Party journal, *Communist Review* (April 1922), called it 'one of the world's greatest tragedies', claimed that cannibalism was breaking out, and blamed the disaster on Russia's past and Churchill's intervention policy. Obviously, it was also due to the policy of 'War Communism' before March 1921 (quite apart from any responsibility the Bolsheviks had for provoking intervention). NEP had come too late to effect the immediate food situation.

The Tenth Congress exposed Lenin's political differences with the so-called 'Workers' Opposition'. These were Communist Party members, comparatively young men, who were largely either former workers or, in some cases, still workers.[7] They had been prepared to accept iron discipline during the struggle to get and retain power but felt the time had come for some relaxation. They demanded that control over industry should be exercised by a central organ elected by the unions – 'by which they meant elected by those who almost alone now enjoyed any voice inside the unions, the communists in the trade union committees'.[8] Lenin had little difficulty in defeating this and other demands of the 'Workers' Opposition'. The entire leadership of the party feared that any loosening of its grip would undermine its own authority. Trotsky made 'the Ten' – headed by Lenin, Zinoviev, Kamenev, Stalin, and trade union leader Tomsky – look almost like moderates by advocating the fusion of trade union and state bodies, and military discipline as the normal method of achieving results in industry. And to be sure, resolutions were passed which seemed to herald some limited turning-away from dictatorial methods. However, these resolutions were to remain a dead letter. Two others were to be of key importance for the future. One of these condemned the views of the 'Workers' Opposition' on the control of industry. More significant still, the other called for the immediate dissolution of all groups with a separate platform. Immediate expulsion was to be the penalty for non-compliance.[9] In the same year Lenin called party purges 'enormously important work', saying that if the party were purged from top to bottom, it would be one of the great achievements of the revolution.[10]

By the time Lenin died in January 1924 the struggle for power which ended with Stalin's supremacy had already begun. And Lenin's theories and practice, as well as Russia's history and the strengths and weaknesses of the contenders, had very largely determined the form of that struggle, its limitations, and outcome. For Lenin bequeathed to his lieutenants the dictatorship of a few men – in the Politburo, the Secretariat, the Orgburo (Organization buro), and to some extent the Central Committee, to which the others were formally subservient, of the Party. As Leonard Schapiro so aptly reminds us: 'However much more democratic the regime in the party in Lenin's day might appear in retrospect, there was no period in its history when the masses participated in the leadership'.[11] Lenin left his followers the example of Kronstadt on how to deal with popular dissent. He left them the political police and the entrenched bureaucracy. He left them the resolutions and texts to justify the purges, terror, and centralization. And although he always eschewed the trappings and pomp of power, his style, personality, and great belief in his own theories, paved the way for his own canonization – manifested by his embalmed corpse in the mausoleum in Red Square, Moscow – and for the pattern of Stalin's personal rule. The doubts which he felt towards the end, expressed in his testament in which he criticized both Stalin and Trotsky, were withheld from his adherents.

## I. STALIN DEFEATS TROTSKY

Lenin did not leave his party any blueprint for Russia's way forward. (Apart, that is, from such generalizations as 'Communism is Soviet power plus the electrification of the whole country'.[12]) Its members therefore had plenty to argue about regarding what was 'socialist' and what was 'Leninist' as well as continuing to argue about democracy in the party and NEP.

From the time of Lenin's illness in 1922 the conduct of affairs lay virtually in the hands of Stalin, Zinoviev, and Kamenev. This was the situation when Lenin died. Stalin was General Secretary of the Party from early 1922. It seemed that a dull person had got another dull job; and with powerful armed forces and police organizations, and powerful personalities in the party leadership, Stalin's appointment did not seem very significant. Stalin was also a member of the Politburo, the highest party organ with five, and then (1922) seven, members, Commissar of Nationalities, and Commissar of the Workers' and Peasants' Inspectorate. The Inspectorate was set up to control every branch of the administration and to eliminate inefficiency and corruption. At the head of these three bodies Stalin had great opportunities for patronage. His party appointment was the most significant, for the party was gradually extending its control over everything. Zinoviev (1883–1936) was head of the powerful Petrograd party organization and Chairman of the Communist International. Kamenev (1883–1936) was in charge of Moscow. The three had prestige as old Bolsheviks. They disliked Trotsky as a 'newcomer' in the party and were jealous of his fame as co-author of the revolution. Perhaps too they feared that as head of the Red Army he was the natural candidate for a 'Bonapartist' plot.[13] They could bring up his anti-Leninist past and use the contempt with which the trade unions held him in any argument. In the Politburo the three had almost a majority, and when in 1923 Lenin proposed the expansion of the Central Committee, Stalin saw to it that his men were elected. It was difficult for Trotsky to quarrel with this move. The motions of the three, on which they usually agreed before every session of the Politburo, were invariably carried. Their colleagues were the prisoners of party discipline. Public discussion of Politburo or Central Committee matters was regarded as betraying party secrets. The 'triumvirate' or 'troika' lasted until early 1925, until Stalin succeeded in getting the already isolated Trotsky to resign from the Commissariat of War. He remained in the Politburo.

In the debates during 1923–25 Trotsky took, broadly speaking, a 'left' line – for more democracy in the party, for greater industrial development and planning, for a less conciliatory attitude to the peasants. Stalin – and this was another reason for his success – appeared to take a middle-of-the-road position between Trotsky and Bukharin on the Right. Trotsky was hamstrung by his own past and the Leninist norms of the party. As Deutscher put it, Trotsky was

> at cross-purposes with himself: he wanted Lenin's rules, that he himself had endorsed, to stand; but he claimed that they had been abused. It was on this point that Stalin concentrated his fire, compelling Trotsky to retreat, to vacillate, to give up one position after another, and then to attempt to regain the lost ground when it was too late, when Trotsky's followers had already been confused and disheartened.[14]

Trotsky threw away two of his last opportunities which might have made some difference to the result of his struggle with

Stalin. One of these was Lenin's testament, which had been written at two periods, separated by an interval of ten days: 25 December 1922 and 4 January 1923. In the first part, written in December, Lenin expressed the view that Stalin 'has concentrated an enormous power in his hands; and I am not sure that he always knows how to use that power with sufficient caution'. He described Trotsky as 'the most able man in the present Central Committee', but thought him too self-confident. He feared that the struggle between the two would cause a split and proposed an increase in the membership of the Central Committee so that such an outcome would be avoided. (Apparently he did not realize this would merely increase Stalin's hold.) He also had some critical remarks to make about other Bolshevik leaders. In the January postscript Lenin expressed a more definite dislike and fear of Stalin:

> Stalin is too rude, and this fault, entirely supportable in relations among us Communists, becomes insupportable in the office of General Secretary. Therefore, I propose to the comrades to find a way to remove Stalin from that position and appoint to it another man who in all respects differs from Stalin. . . . This circumstance may seem an insignificant trifle but . . . it is such a trifle as may acquire a decisive significance.[15]

The testament was brought to the attention of the top echelons of the party, but withheld from the mass of the members. Trotsky, no doubt under pressure from his political enemies, repudiated a book containing large extracts from the testament published by an admirer in the United States.[16] This later made it more difficult to establish the existence of such a document.

Trotsky's second missed opportunity was his failure to attend Lenin's funeral. His enemies attended as pall-bearers.

Others in the Politburo saw too late the truth of Lenin's assessment of the danger from Stalin. In the spring of 1926 Zinoviev and Kamenev joined Trotsky and some others in the party against Stalin. They had already clashed with the General Secretary on the interpretation of NEP, had been defeated, and had lost some of their posts. At a meeting of the Central Committee in April 1926 the new allies demanded a programme of more intensive industrialization. This cost Zinoviev his Politburo membership. In October he was ousted from the Communist International, and Trotsky and Kamenev were expelled from the

Politburo. In a 'gesture of despair'[17] they had staged a series of demonstrations in party factory-cell meetings, demanding full discussions of vital issues. They then repudiated their action and disowned their left-wing supporters. Trotsky was apparently still at 'cross purposes' with himself. He, and his new associates, were apparently still not clear, as Lenin had not been clear, of the consequences of the lack of free discussion in Russia after 1917. Now no member of the opposition was in the Politburo. A year later Trotsky and Zinoviev were even expelled from the party. During the official celebrations of the tenth (1927) anniversary of the October Revolution they had led their followers through the streets of Moscow and Leningrad in an act of defiance. As the secret police quickly dispersed them, 'the proletariat watched with disinterested apathy'.[18]

The Fifteenth Congress of the party in December passed the resolutions required by Stalin and expelled another large number of oppositionists. The atmosphere at the congress and its decisions were significant because they helped to bring about a split in the opposition. The Trotskyite group refused to bow to the ultimatum of the majority to renounce and denounce their own views or lose their party membership. Trotsky was deported to Alma Ata, at that time a town without waterworks, electricity, or paved roads, a town of earthquakes, floods, and malaria.[19] Zinoviev and Kamenev recanted their ideas only to have their surrender rejected by the congress. The General Secretary was given discretion about their future. They lived to regret their disavowal. In January 1929 Stalin felt strong enough to get the Politburo to agree to Trotsky's expulsion from Russia. He did not yet feel strong enough to have him jailed or liquidated.

Almost simultaneously Stalin dealt with the right wing in the leadership. Chief among them were Bukharin, who was dismissed from chairmanship of the Comintern and from the Politburo; Tomsky, who lost his position as head of the trade unions; and Rykov, the Soviet premier. They survived for a little while longer by renouncing their views.

Thus by the end of 1929 Stalin had won the power struggle and emerged as dictator of the Soviet Union. This was shown by the celebrations which followed his fiftieth birthday:

The whole Soviet press displayed vast headlines, large portraits and articles of enormous length. The eulogies of the Dictator

were not less portentous. According to the incense-burners of
his entourage, all human and some superhuman virtues were
incarnate in Stalin. His modesty, courage and devotion were
paralleled by his knowledge and wisdom. . . . He was, moreover, the leader of the world proletariat. The man of action
proved himself as great as the theorist, and both are infallible;
there is no instance of a mistake made by Stalin.[20]

## II. THE FIVE-YEAR PLANS

One of the key ideological weapons in Stalin's struggle for
ascendancy was his theory of 'Socialism in one country'. It was
first formulated in 1924. It replaced the Leninist dogma, also
accepted by Stalin, that for the building of socialism in backward
Russia it was necessary for the proletariat to be victorious in one
or more of the advanced industrial states. Stalin changed the
doctrine to mean that there was

> the possibility of solving the contradictions between the
> proletariat and the peasantry with the aid of the internal forces
> of our country, the possibility of the proletariat assuming
> power and using that power to build a complete socialist
> society in our country, with the sympathy and the support of
> the proletarians of other countries, but without the preliminary
> victory of the proletarian revolution in other countries. . . . It
> is no use building Socialism without being sure that the tech-
> nical backwardness of our country is not an *insuperable*
> obstacle to the building of a complete socialist society. To deny
> such a possibility is to display lack of faith in the cause of
> building Socialism, to abandon Leninism.

But

> What do we mean by the *impossibility* of the complete, final
> victory of Socialism in one country without the victory of the
> revolution in other countries? We mean the impossibility of
> having full guarantees against intervention, and consequently
> against the restoration of the bourgeois order, without the
> victory of the revolution in at least a number of countries. To
> deny this indisputable thesis is to abandon internationalism, to
> abandon Leninism.[21]

This theory, based on two truncated quotes from Lenin written
in 1915 and 1923, was used against Trotsky and Zinoviev. They

were more international in outlook and expected revolutions abroad, above all in Germany. Against Stalin's theory they had no coherent alternative. It is easy to see why Stalin was able to attract the majority of the party with such a formulation. The revolutions had failed in other countries and the Soviet Communists had to decide what to do next. Even under Lenin they had started to 'normalize' their relations with the outside world and had concluded a particularly significant agreement with Germany at Rapallo in 1922. The new doctrine appealed to the party members' patriotism, their 'longing for stability',[22] and their belief in themselves. Unexpectedly they had got power: more unexpectedly they had held power. Could they not yet again achieve the unexpected?

The logic of the new doctrine would seem inevitably to lead to the conclusion that socialist industrialization and socialist transformation of agriculture should follow in Russia. Yet these practical implications were not clear at the time, for only in 1929 was an all-out drive in this direction made.[23] And this 'second revolution' was neither foreseen nor prepared by Stalin.[24] However, Western experts have noted a 'warming-up period' marked by the Party Congress of December 1927. Apart from expelling the opposition, the congress laid down general directives for the future (first) Five-Year Plan, emphasizing the need for speed as well as for balance, and urging greater support for collective farming.[25] This 'warming-up period' gave way, in the autumn of 1929, to the period of all-out industrialization and collectivization. The publication of Stalin's 'The Year of the Great Turn' in *Pravda*, the party paper, on 7 November 1929 is the specific date when the period started.[26] The original targets of the plan were swept aside. 'Not a single Bolshevik group, faction, or coterie thought of an industrialization so intensive and rapid or of a collectivization of farming so comprehensive and drastic as that which Stalin now initiated'.[27]

The exact reasons for this 'third revolution' are not known. Some believe Stalin wished to end the relative independence from party control which the peasants enjoyed under NEP. The view is also expressed that Stalin needed a crisis in order to maintain the tension necessary to justify his dictatorial methods. Others see Stalin as forced by economic necessity: he had either to industrialize and collectivize at breakneck speed or succumb to the peasant. The need to build up a defence capacity has been another factor stressed. One sophisticated pro-Soviet line of argument, not accepted by most students of Soviet affairs, runs as follows:

> The situation that Soviet economy had reached was regarded as being one of those crucial stages in the process of history where, if progress along a certain line of development is to be made with any rapidity at all, it has to be made under the impetus of an initial rush; where the inertia-forces that have accumulated and crystallised over a whole preceding epoch of history have to be overborne by the momentum of this sudden move, if they are not to retard and deflect the course of movement over several decades; where the process of sapping and infiltration must needs give way before the simultaneous and abrupt assault.

The writer went on to describe it 'as one of those acts of faith and courage without which history is not made'.[28] Others would admit the courage while condemning the inhumanity.[29]

The Five-Year Plan of 1928–32 brought fear, famine, chaos, and death to the countryside. Even pro-Soviet writers admit this now:

> The gravest loss suffered by Soviet economy in the battle for the village was the widespread slaughter of livestock. . . . The *kulaks* had struck a damaging counter-blow against those who had decreed their 'elimination as a class'. . . . By 1931 the number of cattle had fallen by nearly a third (and by 1932 more than a third) of the 1929 level; sheep and goats had fallen by a half; and horses by a quarter. Moreover, the fall in the animal population continued of its own momentum until 1933.[30]

The kulaks, the 'rich' peasants, were not the only ones to suffer the revenge of the police and the Politburo. All who were reluctant to accept the new ways, 'rich' or poor, were struck down. No one knows how many perished. But as one disillusioned American journalist recorded, their liquidation was

> one of the most brutal episodes of such dimensions in all modern history. Millions of peasant homes were destroyed, their occupants packed into cattle cars and dumped in the frozen North or parched Central Asia. . . . I saw batches of these wretched men, women, and children at railroad sidings,

peering out of air-holes in the cattle cars like caged animals. By pre-revolutionary standards, let alone Western standards, they were themselves poverty-stricken.[31]

In the industrial sector, by concentration on certain key objectives, positive results were achieved in the course of the first and second (1932–37) plans. But the planners' forecasts were by no means all fulfilled. For half the products whose targets were listed in physical terms, output reached less than 76 per cent of the target by the terminal year of each plan.[32] An exact appraisal of the results has not been possible because of faulty and misleading statistics. Nor is it possible to say just how much the 'planning' helped or hindered industrial development. After all, considerable industrial development had taken place under NEP. It was claimed, for instance, that by 1928 the Soviet Union was producing two and a half times as much electricity as had Tsarist Russia.[33] It is also important to remember that, as under the Tsars, many of the new industrial undertakings were foreign built and equipped. In the 1920s Krupp and other German firms erected armaments plants in the Soviet Union. The Swedish firm SKF built a ball-bearings factory there in the same period. As under the Tsars, the textile equipment still came from Manchester and the saw-mill equipment from Sweden. The sheds of the Stalingrad tractor factory were constructed by a Detroit firm and the locomotive section of the Kirov Dynamo Works by Metro-Vickers of Sheffield. Much of the new steel capacity was the responsibility of American firms and 'The Bolshevik motorcar industry was born in the United States'. The Ford Company signed an agreement with the Soviets in May 1930. Even the famous Dnieper Dam with its great power-station was the work of an American, Colonel Hugh Cooper.[34] The Red armed forces were also heavily dependent on foreign prototypes for their arms. As mentioned above, Weimar Germany was an important supplier.[35] Fascist Italy provided torpedo and other boats in 1931.[36] Many of the planes developed in the 1930s were modified versions of American types such as the Gee Bee racer and the Boeing YB19A bomber.[37] The Russians traditionally admired German ideas and efficiency; the Soviet leaders seemed to admire the Americans more. Back in the twenties Stalin said:

American efficiency is that indomitable force which neither knows nor recognizes obstacles; which with its businesslike

perseverance brushes aside all obstacles; which continues at a
task once started until it is finished, even if it is a minor task;
and without which serious constructive work is inconceivable.

He was not just talking about economic affairs: 'The combination
of the Russian revolutionary sweep with American efficiency is
the essence of Leninism in Party and state work'.[38]

Remembering all this foreign participation in Soviet economic
development one must conclude that the Soviet claim to have
done it all alone, to have pushed through an industrial revolution
in spite of foreign hostility, is largely propaganda. It is true,
though, that the Soviet Union found it difficult to get foreign
loans, partly because she refused to pay the debts of the earlier
regime. Finally, let a British expert sum up the argument about
the Five-Year Plans:

> There is general agreement among students of Soviet economics
> that the hectic pace of development imposed heavy sacrifices
> on the Russian people. There is much disagreement, inevitable
> in view of the difficulty of assessing the evidence on Soviet
> economic activities, about the degree of efficiency with which
> planning has done the job, and whether other methods would
> have been more efficacious. Some hold that a slower rate of
> development, with more attention paid to consumer needs,
> would have yielded better results from the strictly economic
> point of view. . . . On the broad effectiveness of the indus-
> trialization drive in achieving the politically-inspired aims of
> the government there can be no doubt.[39]

### III. THE GREAT TERROR

In 1933 the situation in the Soviet Union looked as though it was
becoming a little more relaxed. The harvest of that year had been
a good one and the worst of the crisis in agriculture was over.
Some consumer goods appeared in the shops. The Seventeenth
Congress of the party at the beginning of 1934 seemed to confirm
that better times were on the way. Some of the oppositionists
were allowed to resume ordinary, if no longer prominent, lives.
Though the cost of living went up, rationing was abolished. The
reintroduction of pre-revolutionary emblems, ranks, conven-
tions, and ideas led some to believe that indeed the worst had

passed and that Russia was at last settling down to a 'normal' existence once again. Yet all this proved to be the calm before the storm.

It is usually accepted that it was the murder of S. M. Kirov, Secretary of the Leningrad party and member of the Politburo, in December 1934 which proved to be a turning-point. The full story of the murder is still unknown. Some believe Stalin himself was implicated in it. Whatever the truth of this, he certainly knew how to exploit it for his own ends. He claimed that it was all part of a larger plot hatched by the opposition in the party. As the (now discredited) party history put it:

> The assassin was caught red-handed and turned out to be a member of a secret counter-revolutionary group made up of members of an anti-Soviet group of Zinovievites in Leningrad. . . . As it later transpired, the murder of Comrade Kirov was the work of this united Trotsky-Bukharin gang . . . later it became known that the actual, real and direct organizers of the murder of Kirov were Trotsky, Zinoviev, Kamenev and their accomplices. . . .[40]

The secret police were given even more power than before. A law was passed in the same month as the assassination which provided for the summary infliction of death sentences by virtue of Article 58 (viii) (terror) of the criminal code. The same law proclaimed the duty of denouncing one's close relatives and provided for the taking of drastic measures against an accused's relatives, even if they were entirely unconnected with the case.[41] Those actually charged with Kirov's murder were tried *in camera*, condemned, and shot. Zinoviev and Kamenev were also tried for allegedly having inspired the assassins. They were sentenced to imprisonment. In the spring of 1935 tens of thousands of party members and Young Communists, and their families, were deported from Leningrad to northern Siberia. Many others were deported from other towns.[42] Yet it was still not clear what was to come. Two months after Kirov's death the Congress of Soviets passed a resolution calling for a new constitution and elected a commission to draft it. Among its members were former oppositionists Bukharin and Radek, as well as Stalin. This misled many at home and abroad into thinking things really were changing for the better.

Yet in the party the purge went on. After an apparent lull came

the whirlwind once again. Many in the lower echelons were dispatched to slavery or death without even the fiction of a trial.
The big-shots, or former big-shots, ended their careers in the
dock at the notorious 'show trials'. The major ones were those of
Zinoviev, Kamenev, and others in August 1936; the trial of
Radek and others in January 1937; and the trial of Rykov,
Bukharin, and others in March 1938. Marshal Tukhachevsky,
the man who had smashed Kronstadt, was the main accused in a
purge of top Soviet officers. Together, the defendants at these
trials constituted all the members of Lenin's Politburo, except
Stalin and Trotsky. They included men who had held most of
the top civil and military positions in the USSR including two
chiefs of the secret police. The charges were fantastic:

> The trials showed that these dregs of humanity . . . had been in
> conspiracy against Lenin, the Party and the Soviet State ever
> since the early days of the October Socialist Revolution.

It was claimed that they had participated in the plot against Lenin
in 1918, the attempt to assassinate him, the assassination of
Kirov, the death of Maxim Gorky in 1936, and:

> The trials brought to light the fact that the Trotsky-Bukharin
> fiends, in obedience to the wishes of their masters – the
> espionage services of foreign states – had set out to destroy the
> Party and the Soviet state, to undermine the defensive power
> of the country, to assist foreign military intervention, to pre-
> pare the way for the defeat of the Red Army, to bring about the
> dismemberment of the USSR, to hand over the Soviet Mari-
> time Region to the Japanese . . . [etc., etc.][43]

These old Bolsheviks, 'Whiteguard pigmies', 'Whiteguard insects',
'contemptible lackeys of the fascists', were virtually all shot.

The confessions of the defendants were as fantastic as the
charges. Almost all of the accused confessed to the above charges
in full view of foreign diplomats, journalists, legal observers, as
well as well-drilled groups of Soviet loyalists.

Perhaps more fantastic still was the fact that many people
believed in the guilt of the old Bolsheviks in the dock. If they
were not guilty, it was asked, why on earth did they confess? How
could such hardened revolutionaries be persuaded to humiliate
and accuse themselves? Many explanations were advanced at the
time. Since then the world has become more familiar with Soviet

police methods. We have the testimonies of those who survived the purges in eastern Europe after 1945, and we have the revelations of Party Secretary Khrushchev in 1956. Old-fashioned tortures were used as well as newer psychological tortures. The victims were deprived of sleep, forced to stand, etc. There were threats against their families. Those with children were told their children would be put into homes for waifs and strays under false names so that they could never be found again. Some were promised their lives or eventual rehabilitation if they would perform this last service for the party.

The purges of the 1930s eventually engulfed millions. Particularly vulnerable were old Bolsheviks, accused of having been recruited by the Tsarist police; technicians, accused of sabotage; foreign refugees and experts, 'enemy agents'; those with foreign contacts or experience, likewise 'enemy agents'; minorities, 'bourgeois nationalists'; army officers, 'German agents'; secret police officials, who became scapegoats and witnesses Stalin could not afford. Many foreign Communists, refugees from Fascism, were arrested for allegedly supporting the Soviet opposition. Among those who perished were Béla Kun, the Hungarian revolutionary leader, most of the leaders of the Polish party, and many Germans, Finns, Yugoslavs, and others. Later, over five hundred German Communists who had survived their ordeal in the camps were handed over to the Nazis at the time of the Hitler-Stalin Non-Aggression Pact.[44]

The conditions in the camps were such that there was little to choose between Stalin's and Hitler's. One can ignore the many accounts by escapees who reached the West and rely on those published in the Soviet Union to confirm this. During the Khrushchev era a few such reports were allowed to appear. Best known of these was Alexander Solzhenitsyn's *One Day in the Life of Ivan Denisovich*, published in Moscow in 1962. Solzhenitsyn, a former officer, had been a prisoner in the camps after 1945 when conditions were somewhat improved: Reveille at 5 a.m.:

'clad in all their rags'; 'the skilly was the same every day . . . nothing but salted carrots last year'; 'tommy-guns . . . pointing right at your face . . . grey dogs'; 'a step to the right or left is considered an attempt to escape and the escort has orders to shoot without warning'; 'warm up with the work, that was your only salvation'; 'if the authorities had any gumption, d'you think they'd put men on to pecking away at the ground with pickaxes in a frost like this?'; 'how often had Shukhov in his youth fed oats to horses! Never had it occurred to him that there'd come a time when his whole soul would crave for a handful of them'; 'Shukhov had the right to two letters that year'; 'Sleep apart, the only time a prisoner lives for himself is ten minutes in the morning at breakfast, five minutes over dinner and five at supper'.[45]

Western experts have tried to estimate the numbers in the camps and the mortality rate from eyewitness accounts and from Soviet census returns. But it is impossible to be sure. One authoritative estimate is that there were 8 million in the camps and prisons in 1938.[46] Certainly millions were incarcerated and millions died.

Equally perplexing is the reason why Stalin engaged in the mass purges with the large-scale forced labour programme. It is easy enough to understand why he attempted to rid himself of his rivals for power, but not why he tortured, starved, and worked millions of loyal Soviet citizens to death. Some believed the mass purges were merely an extension of Stalin's drive for power; he felt he dared not leave anyone capable of organizing an alternative to himself. Another theory was that the Soviets were going through a period of 'primitive accumulation' similar to that undergone by the capitalist West. Edward Crankshaw is among those who have argued this explanation:

> The camps served two purposes: they isolated and worked to death genuine oppositionists and assisted the security police in the maintenance of Terror as an instrument of compulsion; they also provided a vast pool of unskilled labour to dig canals, fell timber, and develop the mineral resources of the frozen areas of the North and the desert areas of the South, where no free citizen would dream of living of his own accord. This process was wasteful beyond imagination; but it seems to have been a calculated waste. The work had to be done somehow, and life was cheap, machines were dear. The period of forced labour . . . corresponds in many striking ways with the early days of the English industrial revolution. . . .[47]

At the beginning of 1939 Yezhov, head of the secret police, then called the NKVD, was removed. He was replaced by Stalin's fellow-countryman Lavrenti Beria. Some were released from the camps. There were even trials of NKVD officials.[48] In March Stalin announced to the Party Congress that the purges were at an end.


## IV. STALIN DECEIVES THE WORLD

The 1930s are often referred to as the 'Red decade'. In terms of votes and representatives elected the Communists did not add up to much. But the economic troubles of the 1920s and the world economic crisis from 1929 onwards, led many thinking people to look for novel solutions to their countries' problems. Some chose Fascism, others communism. A greater number, though not becoming Communists, thought the Soviet system, somewhat modified, had much to offer a world with so much poverty in the midst of plenty. People wanted hope and Moscow provided it. People who by virtue of their training and experience should have known better became apologists for some of the worst features of the Soviet way of life. They thought that by so doing they were aiding the cause of progress in their own countries. They felt they needed an example to prove the practicability of their proposed reforms. Often the people who seemed so indifferent to poverty at home were those who attacked the Soviet Union most. This seemed to 'prove' the Soviets had something. Later they saw the Soviet Union as the bastion of democracy against Nazism. They accepted the spurious argument that to attack the Soviet Union was to play into the hands of the Nazis and reactionaries. Others saw Hitler's Germany as a bulwark against Bolshevism which should therefore be courted.

The purges, trials, and concentration camps were the features of the Soviet system most likely to put off those who were free to choose. Yet there seemed to be battalions of experts and prominent visitors to the USSR quite ready to defend them. One of the most ardent professional advocates of Soviet ideas in Britain from the 1930s to the 1970s, Pat Sloan, wrote of Soviet prisons: 'Compared with the significance of that term in Britain, Soviet imprisonment stands out as an almost enjoyable experience'.[49] Sloan's views were shared by many others who went to the Soviet Union during this period. Those who popularized Soviet explanations of the trials found they had some distinguished allies. Professor Sir Bernard Pares, who had spent a lifetime studying Russia, wrote in the *Spectator* (18 September 1936): 'the guilt of the accused is completely brought home'. He was joined by the Moscow correspondent of the London *Observer* (23 August 1936): 'It is futile to think that the trial was staged and the charges trumped up. The Government's case against the defendants is genuine'. D. N. Pritt, then a Labour Member of Parliament who as a lawyer had distinguished himself in exposing the Nazi Reichstag Fire trial, believed it was 'obvious to anyone who watched the proceedings in court that the confessions as made orally in court could not possibly have been concocted or rehearsed'.[50] Another lawyer, Joseph E. Davies, United States Ambassador to Moscow, reached the 'reluctant conclusion that the state had established its case'.[51] In the United States, as in Britain and other countries, the Communists were busy organizing support for the trials and against the Trotskyists. They did this usually through 'front' organizations which were not at first glance recognizable as Communist-dominated bodies. Typical of their activities was a letter published in *Soviet Russia Today* (March 1937) which claimed that 'the trials were properly conducted and the accused were fairly and judicially treated'. It was signed by prominent members of the liberal intelligentsia, including such writers as Theodore Dreiser, Ring Lardner, Jr, Dorothy Parker, Lillian Hellman, Carey McWilliams, Anna Louise Strong, the former head of the American Red Cross in Russia, Colonel Raymond Robins, and left-wing economist Paul M. Sweezy. Even the London *Times* seemed to draw consolation from the trials, and concluded that they reflected the triumph of Stalin's 'nationalist' policy over that of the revolutionary diehards.[52] It was only with the 1938 trial that this paper expressed doubts about the way things were going in the USSR. Undoubtedly one of the most sophisticated pro-Soviet arguments was put by Maurice Edelman in his *G.P.U. Justice* (1938) and *How Russia Prepared* (1942). Edelman, who speaks Russian and worked for a London firm engaged in trade with the Soviet Union between 1932 and 1939, claimed in his second book:

At crucial periods, the *de facto* martial law has become martial law *de jure*, as when Kirov, Stalin's closest friend, was assassinated by Trotskyists in Leningrad. Repressive measures under administrative law, including the execution of suspects and the exile to Siberia of Trotskyist sympathizers shocked democratic friends of the Soviet Union but consolidated the State. To view these measures in true relation to their circumstances, let us imagine that a group of Fifth Columnists in Manchester assassinated a Cabinet Minister. Quite certainly, there would be a round-up of suspects; many, including for caution's sake a number of innocents, would be interned by the Minister for Home Security; the trial of accused would be held *in camera*, and a brief announcement in the newspapers that the guilty were hanged in Pentonville Prison would follow. These strong and appropriate steps would be endorsed by public opinion. So, too, in Russia.

Edelman went on to claim that the Russian people 'heard the death sentence on the traitors as a death sentence on Hitler's hopes. The Moscow Trials were a Munich reverse; instead of a military victory for Hitler in a conference room, they were a military defeat for Hitler in a court room'.[53] Maurice Edelman, now a Member of Parliament, abandoned his pro-Soviet position long ago. But he retained that concern for the underprivileged which had originally led him to seek hope in Moscow.

Among the most incredible apologists for the Soviet regime were Dr Hewlett Johnson, 'Red' Dean of Canterbury, and Sidney (Lord Passfield) and Beatrice Webb. Sidney Webb had behind him a distinguished career as a civil servant, reformer, writer, and Cabinet Minister. His wife's career was only slightly less distinguished. Many had benefited from their good works and they had helped to arouse the middle-class conscience to the suffering of the poor. They surprised many of their admirers, and no doubt their left-wing opponents, with their *Soviet Communism: A New Civilization?*, first published in 1936. Two quotes from this will suffice to indicate just how off course it was. They asked the rhetorical question, 'is the USSR a political democracy? – it is clear that, tested by the Constitution of the Soviet Union as revised and enacted in 1936, the USSR is the most inclusive and equalised democracy in the world'.[54] As for Stalin's position:

unlike Mussolini, Hitler and other modern dictators, Stalin is not invested by law with any authority over his fellow-citizens, and not even over the members of the Party to which he belongs. He has not even the extensive power which the Congress of the United States has temporarily conferred upon

President Roosevelt, or that which the American Constitution entrusts for four years to every successive president.[55]

Writers like the Webbs had greater influence, and therefore were more dangerous, because they were not Communists. Well-intentioned, they unwittingly misled many other well-intentioned people who sought only to end unemployment, inequality, racial discrimination, and war. The lesson of their folly is relevant today.

In conclusion it is worth noting that Stalin failed to convince the Socialist International or the International Federation of Trade Unions. These bodies, which represented most of the non-Communist Left in Britain and the rest of Europe, sent telegrams of protest on the occasion of each of the trials. They shared the view of H. N. Brailsford about the trials: 'In one Judas among twelve apostles it is easy to believe. But when there are eleven Judases and only one loyal apostle, the Church is unlikely to thrive'.[56]


## V. 'THE REVOLUTION BETRAYED'

Purges, trials, and firing squads apart, what kind of 'socialist' society had Stalin established in the USSR between 1929 and the outbreak of war? For the great mass of the people the life of unremitting toil they had always known went on. The villages remained as they had always been – a single street of thatched cottages without water, gas, or electricity, separated by a dirt road. Before the revolution the majority of peasants had worked for others; now they did so again, though in theory, as collective farmers, they worked for themselves. Although films and show farms exhibited gleaming new equipment and tractors, on the majority of farms the old ways prevailed. In 1932, at the end of the First Plan, the total tractive-power in agriculture, both animal and mechanical, was actually less than in 1929. The leeway was only fully made up after 1935.[57] The *kolkhoz* (collective farm) members were allowed private plots with a few animals, the produce of which they were permitted to sell. They spent a relatively large amount of time working on these to the neglect of their other duties.

For the younger generation life was changing. Though no doubt some avoided it or were unable to attend, compulsory schooling was introduced for children between the ages of eight and fifteen. Because of the lack of buildings, schools operated on a shift system. And, as one pro-Soviet writer admitted: 'In many of the smaller places the school-buildings are still poor and poorly equipped by our standards'.[58] Nevertheless, the Soviet regime had much to its credit in this direction in both town and village. Under the plans there was a great expansion of both secondary and higher technical education, creating a new class of Soviet technical intelligentsia.

Though perhaps life was harder for them than for their menfolk, women had gained formal equality with men. In practical terms this meant greater educational opportunities, greater employment opportunities, equal pay, modest family allowances, and other social benefits. Because the state favoured it, and wages were low, many women were forced to go out to work. Despite the much-publicized nurseries, the fact that consumer amenities were poorer than in other countries meant that Soviet women had, and have, a harder lot than working women in West European countries.

Urbanization was another feature of life under Stalin's plans. Between the censuses of 1926 and 1939 the rural population had declined by 5 per cent. The decline of the farm population was greater still. Some 20 million migrated from the villages to the towns.[59] The housing situation was actually getting worse. Pat Sloan, who lived in the Soviet Union from 1931 to 1936, recorded some years later: 'Housing was appallingly overcrowded, one family to one or two rooms being common in the main towns'.[60] This was probably an optimistic estimate.

The workers in the new industrial enterprises were offered training, paid holidays, canteens, and fairly secure jobs in exchange for severe discipline, long hours, hard work, and low pay. Strikes were illegal, as this would be 'striking against themselves'. Whenever possible the system of payment by results was introduced. By the later 1930s something like three-quarters of all workers were paid according to this system.[61] 'Socialist competition' was introduced by the Stakhanov movement. This was named after a coalminer who had produced coal far in excess of his work norm, by rationalizing his work motions. Stakhanov became a 'hero of labour' and the other workers were judged by his example.

Better off were the members of the technical intelligentsia.

Starting in the early thirties, in particular after Stalin's speech of 23 June 1931, enterprises were encouraged to assign special dining-rooms and living quarters to the technicians and managers. A government order of 25 March 1932 instructed Gosplan, the official planning body, to arrange for the allocation of special housing facilities for engineers and technicians, in addition to those that were already being provided on new industrial sites. In Moscow, Leningrad, Kharkov, Stalingrad, and other centres, apartment blocks were put aside for them. These flats contained three or four rooms, in addition to kitchen and bathroom. Wage and salary differentials were increased. Other preferential treatment followed.[62] They were more likely to get places in holiday sanatoria owned by the enterprise or trade union, more likely even to get theatre tickets. They got first choice of consumer goods in short supply. Special shops were set up for them and the other favoured groups – the party and state officials, officers of the armed and security services, and top members of the professions. These were the groups on which Stalin relied. His 'Socialism in one country' thesis appealed to their patriotism; his industrial and educational programmes, and his purges, provided them with opportunities for quick promotion. Their privileged position has remained despite other changes in the Soviet Union since then. The price they had to pay for their privileges was complete conformity.

The worst aspect of this conformity was in the arts. The experimentation and variety which characterized the arts and architecture in the 1920s gave way to the unreal 'socialist realist' stereotypes of the 1930s. More and more, writers, publishers, film directors, and theatre managers looked to the safer themes of the past. Even then they had to tread very cautiously, for the party line on history was changing. In the cinema, to take just one example, the revolutionary themes of the earlier Eisenstein, with ordinary people as the actors, were replaced by his patriotic, staged, historical works *Alexander Nevsky* and *Peter the Great*.[63] As in Soviet reality, the individual 'hero' had replaced the heroic masses of the earlier period. The Soviet Union could boast about the numbers of theatres which had been built, the gigantic production of books, special celebrations to mark the 375th anniversary of Shakespeare's birth (in 1939), and the countless editions of Dickens's works. But little of interest was published by Soviet writers. Replacements were not found for Gorky and

Mayakovsky, the popular revolutionary writers whose deaths were reported in the 1930s.

The new constitution of 1936 remained mere fiction. If it was meant to divert the opposition, give hope to the masses, and deceive foreign liberals, it probably achieved its objective. Though mainly drafted by oppositionists headed by Bukharin, who were dealt with shortly afterwards, it became known as the 'Stalin Constitution'.[64] It claimed that the Soviet Union was 'a socialist state of workers and peasants' based on the 'socialist ownership of the instruments of production'.[65] It replaced the two earlier Soviet constitutions of 1918 and 1922. Under this constitution, which is still in force, the highest organ of state is the Supreme Soviet which comprises the Soviet of the Union and the Soviet of Nationalities. The former is elected on a constituency basis with one deputy for every 300,000 of the population; the latter is elected on the basis of 25 deputies per Union Republic. Both chambers have equal rights. Both jointly elect a Presidium with presidential-style powers. The Supreme Soviet at a joint sitting appoints the government, the Council of Ministers. The short, infrequent, and purely formal nature of its deliberations over the years exposes the unimportance of the Supreme Soviet. The elections to it further reveal that it cannot be considered seriously as the expression of the views of the Soviet electors. There is no known instance, in the years since elections under the new constitution were introduced, of there being more than one candidate in any constituency. All the electors have to do is collect their ballot papers and drop them into the ballot-box. If they wish to vote against the official candidate by crossing out his name, they draw attention to themselves. Only official organizations are permitted to nominate candidates and all such organizations are controlled by the Communist Party. It is impossible, therefore, even in theory, for *ad hoc* groups of citizens to contest elections. High turn-out of electors has been ensured not only by months of propaganda, a high level of organization, and the opportunity to vote on ships, trains, planes, in army units, etc., but by fear of being regarded as an anti-party element if one does not vote. Any open protest against these arrangements is taken care of under Article 125, which guarantees Soviet citizens freedom of speech, of the press, of assembly, and of street processions, but only 'in order to strengthen the socialist system'. And it is the party which decides what does, and what does not, serve this end. In any case, the party controls all publications and dominates all organizations for, under Article 126, it 'is the leading core of all organizations . . . both public and state'. In theory, Soviet citizens have the right to work, to rest and leisure, to maintenance in old age, sickness, or disability, and to education. In practice they have no way of ensuring they get their rights. It was only in the 1960s, for instance, that pensions were introduced for collective farmers. As there are no independent labour unions, it is very difficult for any Soviet worker, or group of workers, to rectify grievances. Strikes could be punished under Article 130, which obliges citizens to 'maintain labour discipline'. The other duties of the citizen include military service (no question of conscientious objection), to safeguard and fortify public, socialist property (pilfering becomes a serious offence), and to work.

It is worth pointing out that there is no judicial review in Soviet Law. In other words, a constitutional enactment is not much use to the individual who cannot challenge either a law or an administrative act in the courts on the grounds that this conflicts with the constitution, let alone enforce any right conferred by the constitution in the courts.

The constitution proclaims the USSR a federal state, a voluntary union of equal republics. One unique features is Article 17 which gives the 'Union Republics' the right to secede. (There are lesser republics which do not have this right.) This right, and indeed the federalism of the Soviet Union, is purely theoretical, a sop to the national feeling of the former subject nations of the Tsarist empire still under Moscow control, and useful propaganda among colonial peoples. Moscow domination is secured not just through the armed forces but through party control. The party is not even in theory a body organized on federal lines.

The new constitution removed all the restrictions hitherto placed on former members of the old propertied classes, Tsarist supporters, etc. It was claimed that the Soviet Union had achieved socialism and that therefore such restrictions were no longer necessary. This also provided the justification for the maintenance of the one-party state. Parties, it was said, were manifestations of antagonistic classes: as these no longer existed in the USSR, only one party was necessary. As Trotsky commented in his *Revolution Betrayed*, it was nonsense to argue from the Marxist standpoint that socialism had been built in Russia. Material surplus and a high cultural level were necessary prerequisites of socialism. Both were absent in the Soviet Union.

In the same work Trotsky had delivered a comprehensive analysis and critique of Stalinist Russia. On being expelled from his homeland, he had been dumped in Turkey, staying at first as a guest at the Soviet consulate. But Turkey was too near Russia and too far away from the advanced labour movements of Europe. Fearing his reputation, most European governments refused him entry. They could claim that they had enough agitators of their own without adding to their troubles. He was eventually admitted to France, where he held court to socialists from many lands, among them Jennie Lee, future British Minister for the Arts, Paul-Henri Spaak, later NATO Secretary-General, and André Malraux, in the 1960s Minister of Culture under President de Gaulle. The large Moscow-orientated Communist Party in France worried Trotsky and he sought a safer place. In 1935 the Norwegian Labour government offered him sanctuary, only to abandon him for fear of offending Stalin. (Trade with the Soviets was a major consideration at a time of slump.) At the end of 1936 he was invited to Mexico by President Cárdenas. Mexico had been in a state of revolutionary ferment since before the First World War. The President was an agrarian radical and anti-imperialist, but no Marxist. Trotsky lived, and worked, in Mexico until assassinated by one of Stalin's agents in 1940. Stalin liquidated most of Trotsky's relatives either inside or outside Russia.

*The Revolution Betrayed*, finished in 1937, was Trotsky's last complete work and, 'in a sense, his political testament'.[66] Trotsky paid tribute to the 'unexampled' upsurge of Soviet industry and pointed out that Stalin had taken over, in an exaggerated form, the opposition's programme on industrialization. He believed:

> Socialism has demonstrated its right to victory, not on the pages of *Das Kapital*, but in an industrial arena comprising a sixth part of the earth's surface – not in the language of dialectics, but in the language of steel, cement and electricity. Even if the Soviet Union, as a result of internal difficulties, external blows and the mistakes of its leadership, were to collapse – which we firmly hope will not happen – there would

remain as an earnest of the future this indestructible fact, that thanks solely to a proletarian revolution a backward country has achieved in less than ten years successes unexampled in history.[67]

He compared this to the 'mouselike fussing' of the reformist socialists. He admitted Soviet industry was based on 'high production costs and poor quality of product', and quarrelled with the 'tendentious manipulation of statistics'. He labelled the collectivization drive 'this adventurism' which had carried the 'nation to the edge of disaster'. But 'the blame for these sacrifices lies not upon collectivization, but upon the blind, violent, gambling methods with which it was carried through'.[68]

Trotsky characterized the Soviet regime as a 'Bonapartist bureaucracy'.[69] Under it, the 'scope of inequality in the payment of labor . . . has not only caught up to, but far surpassed the capitalist countries'.[70] And he estimated 'that 15 per cent, or, say, 20 per cent, of the population enjoys not much less of the wealth than is enjoyed by the remaining 80 to 85 per cent'.[71] This inequality was manifested by:

> Limousines for the 'activists', fine perfumes for 'our women', margarine for the workers, stores 'de Luxe' for the gentry, a look at delicacies through the store windows for the plebs – such socialism cannot but seem to the masses a new re-facing of capitalism, and they are not far wrong.[72]

How had this situation arisen, and how could it be remedied? He seemed to lay the blame on the historical circumstances of the Russian Revolution, with its 'material want, cultural backwardness':

> The tendencies of bureaucratism, which strangles the workers' movement in capitalist countries, would everywhere shoe themselves even after a proletarian revolution. But it is perfectly obvious that the poorer the society which issues from a revolution, the sterner and more naked would be the expression of this 'law', the more crude would be the forms assumed by bureaucratism, and the more dangerous would it become for socialist development.[73]

The solution to this state of affairs was not just changing the leadership:

but of changing the very methods of administering the economy and guiding the culture of the country. Bureaucratic autocracy must give place to Soviet democracy. A restoration of the right of criticism, and a genuine freedom of elections, are necessary conditions for the further development of the country. This assumes a revival of freedom of Soviet parties, beginning with the party of Bolsheviks, and a resurrection of the trade unions.[74]

Trotsky believed this would lead in the direction of socialism. Many of the liberties he was now advocating were liberties which the Bolsheviks, himself included, had suppressed. He claimed that such suppressions were meant to be temporary. It is worth recalling here that Trotsky did criticize Leninism long before the revolution (see above, p. 70). In many ways he seemed to be returning to that position without actually denying his Leninism.

It is easy to understand why Trotskyism has remained so worrying to the Soviet leadership; why, when they later denounced Stalin, they could not rehabilitate Trotsky or even admit his contribution to 1917. Trotsky was second only to Lenin in bringing about the revolution which released the nation from the 'bad old days'. Yet still speaking as a Leninist, he offers the dissatisfied, patriotic, Soviet student a way forward, from the wilderness of Stalin's heritage to the true Jerusalem of Marx, Engels, and Lenin. It does not matter if this does not square up completely with the facts of history.

What kind of man was at the head of the 'Bonapartist bureaucracy'? What kind of man was Trotsky's adversary and murderer? It is very difficult to know. Those who knew Stalin best, his close colleagues in the Politburo, have not been able to speak freely about him. They would not have been very reliable witnesses anyway. The only reminiscences we have from someone who knew him intimately are those of his daughter Svetlana, published after she fled to the West in 1967. From her we get the picture of a tragic figure troubled by the suicide of his wife in 1932, and by his son's capture by the Germans in 1941. For her he is the victim of friends and circumstances, a man who did not like pomp, fuss, and adulation:

Nowadays when I read or hear somewhere that my father used to consider himself practically a god it amazes me that people who knew him well can even say such a thing. It's true my father wasn't especially democratic but he never thought of himself as a god.[75]

Svetlana completely rehabilitates her father as a human being, a good family man, and a Russian patriot who, remarkably, liked Churchill.[76]

It is hard to believe we get the *whole* picture of the Soviet dictator from Svetlana. The likelihood is she knew only one side of him. She admits that from the time of the German invasion she did not see him frequently. Our other witnesses only saw certain sides of him. The author will let them speak without comment. They help to bring Stalin alive, but he remains an enigma.

Lord Avon (Anthony Eden), as British Foreign Secretary, negotiated with Stalin on a number of occasions. Writing in 1962 he related:

> Stalin impressed me from the first and my opinion of his abilities has not wavered. His personality made itself felt without effort or exaggeration. He had natural good manners, perhaps a Georgian inheritance. Though I knew the man to be without mercy, I respected the quality of his mind and even felt a sympathy which I have never been able to analyse. Perhaps this was because of Stalin's pragmatic approach. It was easy to forget that I was talking to a Party man, certainly no one could have been less doctrinaire. I cannot believe that Stalin ever had any affinity with Marx, he never spoke of him as if he did. . . . I have never known a man handle himself better in conference. Well informed at all points that were of concern to him, Stalin was prudent but not slow, seldom raising his voice, a good listener, prone to doodling, he was the quietest dictator I have ever known, with the exception of Dr Salazar. Yet the strength was there, unmistakably.[77]

Lord Strang, onetime Head of the British Foreign Office, had very similar impressions of Stalin.

Clement Attlee, the British Labour premier, got his first impressions of the Soviet leader at Potsdam in 1945:

> He was clearly a pretty ruthless tyrant but a man you could do business with because he said yes and no and didn't have to refer back. He was obviously the man who could make decisions, and he was obviously going to be difficult. It was plain

to me from the beginning at Potsdam that the Russians were going to ask for everything on the grounds of their immense sufferings and so forth. Stalin was genial enough. He could make jokes and take jokes.[78]

Milovan Djilas, former Yugoslav Communist leader and later opponent of communism, gives us a vivid description:

. . . he was of very small stature and ungainly build. His torso was short and narrow, while his legs and arms were too long. His left arm and shoulder seemed rather stiff. He had quite a large paunch, and his hair was sparse. . . . His face was white, with ruddy cheeks. . . . His teeth were black and irregular, turned inward. Not even his moustache was thick or firm. Still the head was not a bad one; it had something of the common people, the peasants, the father of a great family about it – with those yellow eyes and a mixture of sternness and mischief. I was also surprised at his accent. One could tell he was not a Russian. But his Russian vocabulary was rich, and his manner of expression very vivid and flexible . . . Stalin had a sense of humour – a rough humour, self-assured, but not entirely without subtlety and depth. His reactions were quick and acute – and conclusive, which did not mean that he did not hear the speaker out, but it was evident that he was no friend of long explanations.[79]

This was Stalin in his sixties.

## NOTES

[1] Paul Avrich, *Kronstadt 1921* (Princeton, 1970), p. 160.
[2] ibid., p. 162.
[3] Carr, op. cit., II, 280. Earlier still the Mensheviks had urged what became the new economic policy.
[4] ibid., p. 300.
[5] ibid., p. 310.
[6] Sutton, op. cit., p. 344.
[7] Leonard Schapiro, *The Communist Party of the Soviet Union* (London, 1970), p. 203.
[8] ibid., p. 202.
[9] ibid., p. 214.
[10] W. I. Lenin, *Über die Normen des Parteilebens* (Berlin, 1964), p. 537.
[11] Schapiro, op. cit., p. 311.
[12] V. I. Lenin, *Collected Works*, vol. 31 (Moscow and London, 1966), 516.
[13] Schapiro, op. cit., p. 271. Both Zinoviev and Kamenev had joined the Social

Democratic movement in 1901 and its Bolshevik faction in 1903. Kamenev had been banished in 1914 as head of the Bolshevik deputies in the Duma. Both, however, had opposed Lenin's seizure of power of 1917.

[14] Deutscher, *Stalin*, p. 267.

[15] Leon Trotsky, *On the Suppressed Testament of Lenin* (New York, 1970), p. 7.

[16] Schapiro, op. cit., p. 300.

[17] ibid., p. 305.

[18] ibid., p. 310.

[19] Trotsky, *My Life*, pp. 548–9.

[20] Boris Souvarine, *Stalin* (London, n.d.), pp. xii–xiii.

[21] J. Stalin, *The Foundations of Leninism on the Problems of Leninism* (Moscow, 1950), pp. 234–5.

[22] Deutscher, *Stalin*, p. 292.

[23] ibid., p. 294.

[24] ibid., p. 297.

[25] Alexander Erlich, *The Soviet Industrialization Debate, 1914–1928* (Cambridge, Mass., 1960), p. 191.

[26] Naum Jasny, *Soviet Industrialization 1928–1952* (Chicago, 1961), p. 14.

[27] Deutscher, *Stalin*, pp. 319–20.

[28] Maurice Dobb, *Soviet Economic Development since 1917* (London, 1966), p. 244.

[29] Schapiro, op. cit., p. 465.

[30] Dobb, op. cit., p. 246.

[31] Peter G. Filene (ed.), *American Views of Soviet Russia* (Homewood, Ill., 1968), p. 102.

[32] G. W. Nutter, *Growth of Industrial Production in the Soviet Union* (Princeton, 1962), p. 205.

[33] M. Dobb, *USSR — Her Life and Her People* (London, 1945), p. 37.

[34] Werner Keller, *Are the Russians Ten Feet Tall?* (London, 1961).

[35] E. H. Carr, *German-Soviet Relations between the Two World Wars 1919–1939* (Oxford, 1952), pp. 60–1.

[36] Keller, op. cit., p. 240.

[37] Maurice Edelman, *How Russia Prepared* (London, 1942), p. 49.

[38] Stalin, op. cit., pp. 161–2.

[39] Margaret Miller, *The Rise of the Russian Consumer* (London, 1965), p. 18.

[40] *History of the Communist Party of the Soviet Union (Bolsheviks)* (Moscow, 1948), pp. 401–2.

[41] F. Beck and W. Godin, *Russian Purge* (London, 1951), pp. 28–9.

[42] Deutscher, *Stalin*, p. 355.

[43] *History of the Communist Party*, pp. 427–8.

[44] Robert Conquest, *The Great Terror* (London, 1968), p. 430. This is the most comprehensive account of the purges and camps in English.

[45] Alexander Solzhenitsyn, *One Day in the Life of Ivan Denisovich* (London, 1963).

[46] Conquest, op. cit., p. 532.

[47] Edward Crankshaw, *Khrushchev's Russia* (London, 1959), pp. 12–13.

[48] Deutscher, *Stalin*, p. 381.

[49] Pat Sloan, *Soviet Democracy* (London, 1937), p. 111.

[50] D. N. Pritt, *The Zinoviev Trial* (London, 1936), pp. 12–14.

[51] Quoted Walter Laqueur, in *Survey* (April 1962), p. 9. This issue is devoted to 'The Western Image of the Soviet Union 1917–1962'.

[52] Hugo Dewar, in *Survey* (April 1962), p. 94. For a comprehensive study of the trials see his *The Modern Inquisition* (London, 1953).

[53] Edelman, op. cit., pp. 10–11.

[54] Sidney and Beatrice Webb, *Soviet Communism: a New Civilization?* (London, 1944), p. xxi.

[55] ibid., p. 333.

[56] Dewar, op. cit., p. 94.

[57] Dobb, *Soviet Economic Development*, p. 246.

[58] Dobb, *USSR*, p. 95.

[59] Dobb, *Soviet Economic Development*, p. 286.

[60] Pat Sloan, *Commonsense about Russia* (London, 1960), p. 3.

[61] Dobb, *Soviet Economic Development*, p. 464.

[62] ibid., pp. 258–9.

[63] The most comprehensive book on the Soviet cinema is Jay Leyda's *Kino: A History of the Russian and Soviet Film* (New York, 1960).

[64] V. Karpinsky, *The Social and State Structure of the USSR* (Moscow, 1950), p. 9.

[65] The text used is that in *Constitution (Fundamental Law) of the Union of Soviet Socialist Republics* (Moscow, 1955).

[66] Deutscher, *The Prophet Armed*, p. 298.

[67] Leon Trotsky, *The Revolution Betrayed* (London, 1967), p. 8.

[68] ibid., p. 40.

[69] ibid., p. 290.

[70] ibid., p. 125.

[71] ibid., p. 142.

[72] ibid., p. 120.

[73] ibid., p. 55.

[74] ibid., p. 289.

[75] Svetlana Alliluyeva, *Twenty Letters to a Friend* (London, 1967), p. 215.

[76] ibid., p. 184.

[77] Lord Avon, *The Eden Memoirs: Facing the Dictators* (London, 1962), p. 153.

[78] Francis Williams, *A Prime Minister Remembers* (London, 1961), p. 71.

[79] Milovan Djilas, *Conversations with Stalin* (London, 1962), pp. 59–60.

# VI

## *Communism, Fascism and the Popular Front*

THE history of Lenin's International is a sad one. It started out as a genuinely internationalist-minded body working for world revolution. It soon degenerated into the tool of one man's view of Soviet interests. It failed to bring off a single successful revolution and impotently sat by while its revered leader massacred more Communist leaders than Hitler, Mussolini, and the other dictators together managed.[1] It suffered from the embarrassing zigzags of Soviet policy culminating in the Hitler-Stalin Pact of August 1939. Finally, it was sacrificed on the altar of the 'anti-Hitler coalition' in 1943.

Roughly speaking, after Lenin's death in 1924, there were five periods in the development of the Comintern. The first ran from 1924 to 1928. It ended with the Bolshevization of the parties of the Third International in the same way as in the Soviet party. In the second period, the International went over to the offensive. It saw little distinction between Fascism and bourgeois democracy, or, for that matter, between Fascists and non-Communist socialists. By contrast, between 1934 and 1939 it called for United Fronts (of workers), together with Popular Fronts of Communists, socialists, and bourgeois democrats, and an alliance between the Soviet Union and the Western democracies. The fourth period was again in sharp contrast, dominated as it was by the fight against 'the imperialist war', but with more emphasis on that fight in Britain, France, and the United States than in Nazi Germany. Finally, between 1941 and its disbandment in 1943, it was once again dominated by the struggle against the Fascist powers, and its alliance with the democracies. Whereas in Lenin's time there was still hope that revolutions would develop in the West – in which case, Moscow would cease to be the centre of the international revolutionary movement – after 1924 Comintern policy was increasingly subservient to the 'Socialism in one country' theme. The defence of the 'Socialist Fatherland', the 'Socialist Sixth', became of overriding importance.

This writer still finds it difficult to understand how it was that the Communist parties followed the Soviet line so blindly for so long. Part of the explanation is that they were mesmerized by the apparent success of the Bolsheviks. They had dared, had succeeded against great odds and against all expectations. Their success was due to their formula, Leninism, which gave hope even to seemingly insignificant groups of revolutionaries. If everything was not perfect in Russia, this was the legacy of Russia's historical backwardness, and criticism of Russian weaknesses would only play into the hands of the reactionaries. This argument was used with even greater conviction after the recognition of the Fascist danger. Many parties were, in any case, little more than scattered clandestine groups with their leaders living as guests of the Soviet party and therefore forced to do its bidding. Most of the parties which remained legal after 1933, with the exception of the French and the Czechoslovaks, remained small and probably depended on financial assistance from Moscow.[2] Another important factor was the purges of Trotskyists and others from the Communist parties in the 1920s. These removed many of their best brains and most independent-minded cadres. For those who remained, going to Moscow was a holiday with a spiritual uplift. They were fêted and flattered so long as they did not deviate. At home they were a harassed minority and it would have been extremely difficult for the full-time officials to find alternative sources of income. Finally, it was difficult for men and women fighting against unemployment and poverty, and seeing at close hand the failure of Social Democracy, to admit that the Bolshevik Revolution too had failed. It was like despairing of the possibility of all progress. All this was before the welfare state, the 'affluent society', and the Western 'economic miracles' of the 1940s and 1950s.

By 1924 Western capitalist society had returned to 'normalcy'. Moscow's allies in the West were floundering. Apart from the 'objective situation', they were having difficulties transplanting Bolshevik organization and techniques in their own countries, and they were soon to be consumed in arguments about Trotsky. As we have seen, attempts at revolution in Hungary, Bulgaria, and Germany had failed. The French party was in a state of chronic crisis. The Communists in the United States were already revealed as

> essentially irrelevant and as a divisive political force among radicals. . . . Their relationship with the Third International attracted radicals and others who sought identification with the world revolutionary movement, but their attempts to duplicate the Russian experience and form of party organization alienated the Communists from American radicals, from labor, and from the farmers. [3]

The Bolshevization of the party in 1925 led to a decline in membership of almost 50 per cent. It took seven years to climb back to the pre-1925 figure of about 16,000, and that achievement in 1932 owed more to the slump than to anything else. [4] In Britain, a country of particular concern for the Comintern, the party's membership stood at a mere 3,900 in May 1924, [5] and the Labour Party had decided to prohibit Communists from individual membership. The first Labour government had held office for only a few months, yet the Communists were unable to exploit its failings or, later, the situation created by the General Strike of 1926. As we shall see, in another key country, China, the party leadership was soon threatened with extermination. For the Italian Left the post-war situation had looked promising, but there, by 1924, the Communists had fallen victim of a new force – Fascism. As for the KPD, bitter personal rivalry and deep political differences existed among the leadership. Nevertheless, that party was to enjoy great expansion in the late twenties and early thirties, only to be exposed as essentially weak in 1933, when it collapsed before the Nazi onslaught.

'Nazi-Fascism' became a decisive concern of Comintern policy, and a justification for much of that policy. Without Fascism, communism would certainly have been weaker in many countries in the second half of the 1930s, for fear of Fascism bred Communists (just as fear of communism produced Fascists). We must, therefore, say something about Fascism and communism in Italy and Germany.

### I. THE RISE OF FASCISM IN ITALY AND GERMANY

The original Fascist movement was, of course, that born in Italy at the end of the 1914–18 War. If its father was disappointed nationalism, its mother was fear of Bolshevism. Officers, intellectuals, students, and journalists joined together to take for Italy, by direct action, what the armed forces had failed to gain on the battlefield, or the politicians in the peace negotiations: namely, a greater slice of the dismembered Austro-Hungarian Empire. Led by the poet D'Annunzio, they occupied the town of Fiume, which had been declared a free state by the powers. The Italian government was forced to use the army to expel them.

Just as the government seemed incapable of asserting Italy's claims abroad, so did it appear incapable of keeping order at home. In 1919–20 Italy was hit by a wave of strikes, factory occupations, riots, and rural disorders. Many former officers, having little political sophistication, felt quite simply that the socialists, having failed to destroy society with their pacifist propaganda during the war, were now having a second go with class-war slogans. The old-line politicians could not be trusted to stop them, perhaps Fascism would. Such ex-servicemen knew little of the problems of the working classes and were attracted by the fasces emblem, with signified the power of the state in ancient Rome, the nationalist rhetoric, and the emphasis on action, of the Fascist movement. Benito Mussolini, in his contempt for his erstwhile socialist comrades, and his lust for power, presented his Fascist movement as an antidote to socialism. In this way he attracted the money of industrialists and landowners, as well as the energies and abilities of the ex-officers.[6] But Mussolini, himself a former soldier, failed to convince the mass of the conscripted soldiers and their families. At elections which were relatively fair and free he did not gain a mandate from the nation. After the elections of May 1921 the Fascist deputies numbered only 35 out of a total of 535. This did not dismay Mussolini. He continued his struggle for power by terror, infiltration, and persuasion of the powerful and the wealthy. He gained considerable numbers of supporters in the armed forces, police, civil service, and even the royal family. For everyone who joined him, ten thought there was something in what he said. Thus when he launched his 'March on Rome' in October 1922 there was no opposition from the forces of 'Law and Order', forces which could easily have dispersed the lightly-armed Fascists.[7] He was given the chance by King Victor Emmanuel III to form a government to replace the discredited Facta cabinet.

Mussolini's first government was a coalition of four Fascists and ten non-Fascists. The latter were Liberals, Catholics (of the *Partito Popolare*), and some others. Within a short time, many deputies elected as Liberals or Popolare moved over to the Fascists.[8] In 1923 Mussolini got the same parliament to amend the electoral law so that the list heading the poll obtained two-thirds of the seats. In the elections which followed, some popularity and more terror, combined with prudent window-dressing of his 'national' list, produced the desired result. By 1928 the Duce was strong enough to introduce single-list elections. During these years various laws were introduced establishing the paraphernalia of the totalitarian – Mussolini coined the term – state.

The Left could do little to halt Mussolini's rise to power. The working-class movement was divided in Italy as elsewhere. From 1917 onwards there had been a group within the Italian Socialist Party (PSI) which gave unreserved support to the Bolsheviks. Prominent in this group were Antonio Gramsci (1891–1937) and Palmiro Togliatti (1893–1964). They found strong support in the northern industrial town of Turin and there promoted a general strike and occupation of factories in 1920. In January 1921 the Communist group in the PSI seceded and formed the Communist Party of Italy (PCI). In the elections of November 1919 the socialists, united, had returned 156 deputies to parliament, the largest number of any party. In May 1921 the PSI gained only 124 seats, the PCI only 13. Instead of uniting in face of the growing threat of Fascism, even the remaining members of the PSI could not agree on policy and a further split occurred. By 1926 both the socialists and the Communists had ceased to exist as organized political parties.

The Left had clearly underestimated Fascism and went on doing so for some time. This was not so surprising as Fascism was a novel development on the political scene and not even Mussolini was absolutely clear what he was about. But the failure of the Left to analyse accurately the nature of Fascism exposed the weakness of their Marxist theory which they claimed to be scientific.

In Germany the rise to power of Adolf Hitler was in some respects more remarkable than Mussolini's in Italy; the failure of the Left was even greater.

Germany, like Italy, suffered from frustrated nationalism. The peace settlement imposed heavy burdens on Germany in territory lost and reparations to pay. Defeat had humiliated the armed forces, the Versailles Treaty reduced them to a mere 100,000 or so men. Many officers who felt they had given of their best for the country were either unemployed or doing jobs they considered inferior. Germany like Italy suffered from political instability. The democratic mass parties of socialist and Catholic were antagonistic to each other. As in Italy many officers, civil servants, and other members of the middle classes distrusted democracy. They regarded the Weimar Republic, born as it was of revolution, as somehow illegitimate. Finally, as in Italy the working-class movement was divided. But in Germany the feud was more bitter than that which fragmented the Italian Left.

Despite all these difficulties the young Weimar Republic managed to withstand the initial shocks from Left and Right. In 1923 Adolf Hitler's National Socialist German Workers' Party (NSDAP) staged a *coup* in Munich reminiscent of Mussolini's March on Rome. This was put down by a few resolute policemen. For a short time at least Hitler was forced to ponder his fate in Landsberg jail.

Adolf Hitler had much in common with Benito Mussolini, whom he greatly admired. They came from similar, lower-middle-class, backgrounds. Neither had succeeded in gaining admission to a satisfactory profession. Both had served in the ranks in the World War. Both were impressive nationalist orators. Eventually both seized power while still young. Hitler, however, seemed to have stronger political beliefs. Unlike Mussolini, he was a virulent racist. Racial purity, discrimination against races judged by him to be inferior, was one of his most fundamental principles, probably *the* most fundamental. He was also more austere than the Duce and lacked his sense of humour.

In the years of 'capitalist stability', 1924–29, the Nazis did not make any visible headway, though they were strengthening their organization, against the 'Jew Republic' of Weimar. In the election of 1928 they actually lost seats, dropping from 14 to 12 in a 491-seat Reichstag. Even their respectable nationalist friends had lost support. The Communists had been doing somewhat better. They had won 62 seats. In May 1924, falling to 45 in December of that year, but climbing back to 54 in 1928. Their Social Democratic rivals, the largest party, won 153 seats in 1928. After their election success the Social Democrats formed a 'grand coalition' of democratic parties.

The stability of Weimar was undermined by the world economic crisis which followed the Wall Street crash in autumn 1929. As Germany was heavily dependent on exports, and her industrial expansion rested to a considerable extent on short-term, mainly American loans, she was worse hit than most other industrial nations (the United States being the exception). The political crisis which grew from this increased the flow of funds out of the country. In this situation, the coalition broke up after disagreement over the financing of unemployment relief.

Though the Social Democrats held on to most of their support in the elections of September 1930, the Nazis shot up into second place with 107 seats. The Communists, too, improved their position and became the third largest party with 77 seats. It appears that many of the votes for the two extremes were from the young, from those who had previously not bothered, and, in the case of the Nazis, from radicalized nationalists.

Between 1930 and 1933 Germany moved steadily deeper into crisis. The number of registered unemployed rose from 1.3 million in September 1929 to 5.1 million in 1932. Many more were on short-time or were non-registered unemployed. Yet the unemployment alone cannot explain the fall of democracy in Germany in 1933. Other nations suffered large-scale unemployment, and Germany had faced crisis in the early years of the republic. This earlier crisis had been resolved by the statesmanship of the Social Democratic President, Friedrich Ebert.[9] After Ebert's death in 1925 the Presidency was in the hands of Field Marshal Hindenburg, an aged, politically naïve, authoritarian monarchist. As the crisis deepened his increasingly unrepresentative governments relied more and more on emergency decrees. In January 1933 when the Nazis, by then the largest party, were actually losing support,[10] Hindenburg was persuaded to appoint Hitler Chancellor. Hindenburg, then, was one of the guilty men who played a decisive part in bringing about the fall of Weimar. Ironically, he had been the candidate of the Social Democrats and Catholics in the Presidential election of April 1932 when Hitler was the only other likely contender. Behind Hindenburg stood the great majority of the *Reichswehr* officers and civil servants, landowners and businessmen, academics and professional men, who rejected Weimar and yearned for the 'good old days'. Their votes, and in some cases money, helped Hitler into power. The conservative nationalist leader, Alfred Hugenberg, eased Hitler's path to respectability and to the funds of a section of industry. When the crisis came, the right-wing trend won out in the Catholic Centre Party. This party voted for the Enabling Act which made Hitler's dictatorship legal in 1933. Had they joined the Social Democrats in opposing it, it is conceivable that history would have been different. They too, therefore, must share responsibility for what happened. And what of the Communists?

The policy of the German Communist Party[11] was increasingly drafted in Moscow. That policy was to entice Germany into an alliance with the Soviet Union. Russia needed German know-how, Germany needed the Russian market. Both were victims of the Western powers, both were aggrieved with Poland. If Russia could not have an alliance with a Bolshevik Germany, then she would be prepared to have one with a capitalist Germany. For the Soviets one capitalist state was much the same as another. Strangely enough, in view of the activities of Communists in Germany, the German military leadership, and a section of the bourgeois political élite, agreed with this assessment. The result was the Treaty of Rapallo of 1922 which, among other things, brought about secret military co-operation between the two countries. When Foreign Minister Stresemann signed the Locarno treaties of 1924, which guaranteed Franco-German and Belgian-German frontiers, and took Germany into the League of Nations, the Russians feared that Berlin was turning against Moscow. But in 1926 Stresemann signed another agreement with Soviet Russia based on Rapallo.

The policy of the German Communists had followed that of Moscow in all this. The Social Democrats, too, wanted friendship with Russia as much as with the West, but they were against Russo-German military co-operation (which was contrary to the Versailles Treaty). This co-operation the Social Democrats had brought to light in 1926 without, however, stopping it. The Russians saw the SPD as the main obstacle to either revolution in Germany or a Soviet-German alliance. The Social Democrats had to be smashed one way or another. At the Fifth Congress of the Comintern in 1924 they were denounced as Fascists, and a little later as Social Fascists. But the Communists still aimed at United Fronts (not only in Germany) from below, which meant attempts to draw ordinary Social Democrats into alliance with the Communists, leading to the isolation and 'exposure' of the

SPD leadership. The Communists remained indifferent to 'bourgeois democracy'. In line with this, in 1925, they refused to withdraw their candidate, Ernst Thälmann, in the Presidential election, in favour of the Social Democratic-Catholic nominee, Marx. As a result Hindenburg was elected.

In the summer of 1928 the Sixth Congress of the Comintern adopted a new 'Left' line. The two main points of this were: that the capitalist world was entering upon a new period of crisis which would lead inevitably to wars and revolution; that the Social Democrats (and Labourites) were the main obstacle to revolution and were 'playing a Fascist role',[12] and should be fought accordingly. This new militancy even led the Communists into occasional actions with the Nazis against the Social Democrats. For instance, in 1931 they formed a common front against the Social Democratic government of Prussia which led to the defeat of that government. Another joint Communist-Nazi action took place during the strike of Berlin transport-workers in November 1932. Typical of the Communist attitude was a statement made about this time by Ernst Thälmann (1886–1944), the former docker who led the KPD:

> . . . the main blow must be directed against the Social Democratic party, and it must be made clear to the masses that the Hitler party and the possibility of a Hitler government cannot be fought if the mass influence of the 'moderate wing' of Fascism, namely the S.P.D., is not first overthrown. . . .[13]

The official history of the German working-class movement put out by the East German Socialist Unity Party in 1966 recognized that the Communists had been mistaken in regarding the Social Democrats as Fascists. Unfortunately this recognition came too late for many thousands of Communists as well as Social Democrats. The KPD was the first victim of the Nazi-dominated coalition government which took over in January 1933. Alleging that the Communists had set fire to the Reichstag as a signal for revolution, Hitler banned the KPD and rounded up its leaders. Thälmann died in a Nazi concentration camp in 1944. Whether he ever recognized the folly of his earlier line we do not know.

Historians and political scientists are still arguing about the nature of Fascism. One thing is certain: it was, and is, a more complicated phenomenon than the classic Communist definition allowed: 'fascism is one of the methods which may be adopted by the capitalist class when the threat of the working class to the stability of monopoly capitalism becomes acute'.[14] Though they kept to this basic interpretation, they were soon forced to revise many of their judgements connected with Fascism. However, before examining those revisions, we must look to another key area of Comintern interest – China.

## II. NATIONALISTS AND COMMUNISTS IN CHINA

Throughout the nineteenth century a decaying China had been increasingly prey to interference, incursions, and invasions from more technically advanced nations which sought commercial rights and territory. Early in the century Britain took control of Burma, until then a vassal state of Peking. In the First Opium War (1839–41) Chinese defeat meant the loss of Hong Kong and five 'treaty ports' to Britain. A second war (1856–58) opened the way for the penetration of the Yangzte basin. A war with France in 1884 lost China her suzerainty over Indo-China. Defeat at the hands of the Japanese in 1895 resulted in Peking handing over Korea and Formosa to Tokyo. Russia had earlier extended her empire enormously in Siberia and Central Asia at China's expense. Germany, too, had not been left out of the scramble for concessions.

In 1900 the Boxer Rebellion against foreign influence was put down by the Imperialist powers, including the United States. Reforms followed, but they did not go far enough to satisfy the growing number of Chinese who, though they looked to Japan and Europe for ideas, resented foreign interference in their country's affairs. A revolution overthrew the monarchy in 1911 and set up a republic. A British-educated doctor, Sun Yat-sen, had inspired this revolution through his Alliance Society, a largely urban middle-class affair. The society influenced many thousands of Chinese students and officers who studied abroad to adopt Sun's ideology. This was summed up in his three principles of nationalism, democracy, and people's livelihood, or socialism. It was these foreign-educated Chinese, especially the officers in the modern units of the army, who were the backbone of the revolution. Money from the overseas Chinese, collected by Sun on world fund-raising tours, helped the revolutionaries, as did the sympathy and support of the foreign powers.[15] Sun Yat-sen returned from exile abroad to become China's provisional President.

For their victory Sun's friends had to pay a heavy price. They had come to terms with Yuan Shih-k'ai, the man who had modernized the Imperial Chinese Army, and who had been recalled from retirement by the Empress-Dowager to take command. Instead of saving the monarchy, he agreed to support the rebels in return for the Presidency. By 1913 he had made himself dictator. He gained recognition by agreeing to British influence in Tibet and Russian influence in Mongolia.

Seeking to take advantage of the World War, Japan presented in 1915 her Twenty-One Demands to turn China into a *de facto* dependency. With only words for help from the European powers, Yuan made major concessions to the Japanese. The result was an upsurge of anti-Japanese feeling which probably weakened Yuan's position. In 1916 Yuan attempted to make himself emperor, but resistance and then his sudden death ended this dream. China then plunged into the warlord era which lasted until 1928, and during which the foreign powers backed rival generals.

It was in 1921 that the Chinese Communist Party was set up from a number of Marxist study groups. Inevitably Chinese intellectuals had started to examine Marxism together with other Western ideas in their search for a modern approach to China's problems. But Lenin's policies stirred them more than Marx's theories. Lenin, under the Karakhan Declaration of July 1919, renounced all the privileges of Tsarist Russia in China. This contrasted with the attempts of the European powers to maintain their privileges, and of the Japanese to extend theirs. The Comintern also sent emissaries into China to exploit the growing anti-imperialist fervour. This had manifested itself on 4 May 1919 when angry students had demonstrated in Peking against the upholding of Japanese privileges at the Versailles Peace Conference. Comintern representative G. N. Voitinsky persuaded his Chinese friends that Leninism would be the salvation of China and that the time had come to set up a Leninist party. Among the twelve delegates to the First Congress of the Chinese Communist Party who gathered in a girls' school in Shanghai on 1 July 1921 was a twenty-eight-year-old librarian, Mao Tse-tung.

Mao was born in 1893 in Hunan province, the son of a prosperous peasant. From eight until he was thirteen he attended the local primary school. He was then forced to work on his father's land. A year later he was formally married, though the marriage was never consummated. In the teeth of strong opposition from his father he returned to full-time education at the age of sixteen. In his new school he had a difficult time because he was older than his classmates and poorer. At this time he developed patriotic indignation against the humiliations of China and a liking for stories about George Washington, Napoleon, and other great men. In general he was enthusiastic about 'warriors and nationbuilders'.[16] His search for education next took him to the provincial capital, Changsha. There he witnessed the 1911 Revolution; served for six months as a private in a revolutionary army; read, in translation, Adam Smith, Darwin, J. S. Mill, Rousseau, and other Western writers, before getting five more years of formal education. In the spring of 1918 Mao graduated from an establishment classed as a secondary school, but 'the standards at the school were high, and in fact he learned as much as he might have done at a provincial university'.[17] He had distinguished himself both as a student and as a radical student leader.

Mao left Changsha for six months in Peking, working as an assistant librarian at Peking University. Teaching and writing in Changsha followed and then another stay in Peking, where Mao became a Marxist by the summer of 1920. After 1921 he devoted his time increasingly to revolutionary activity, becoming a full-time revolutionary from 1923. Yet he had found time to marry the daughter of one of his teachers. In June 1923 he was elected to the Central Committee of the Chinese Communist Party; simultaneously he was making his way in Sun's National Party, the Kuomintang. This dual membership was in line with Comintern policy at that time.

The Comintern had concluded that countries like China were not yet ripe for proletarian revolutions, but should complete their bourgeois national revolutions, including their reassertion of their national independence. Communists should therefore work with genuine 'bourgeois nationalists' to this end. On 26 January 1923 Adolf Joffe, Comintern representative, and Sun Yat-sen issued a joint statement agreeing on co-operation between Moscow and the Kuomintang. The Soviets helped in the reorganization of the Kuomintang on Leninist lines (the party did not embrace Leninism), the Kuomintang admitted Communists on an individual basis.

Sun Yat-sen died in 1925 and his place was taken by an ambitious general trained in the new Russia, Chiang Kai-shek. Chiang received military aid from Soviet Russia, and in 1926 felt he was strong enough to set out from nationalist-held Canton to destroy the warlords in the north and unify the country. Before embarking on this venture, however, he executed a *coup* in Canton which neutralized the Communists and the Russian advisers in that city. Why precisely Chiang did this we do not know. Perhaps he feared the Russians were getting too much influence. More likely, he feared the Communists would take over the Kuomintang and oust him. No doubt he realized that interested foreign powers had been worried by Communist-led strikes.

The strikes had broken out in Japanese textile-mills in Shanghai in May 1925 and they had quickly turned into anti-British demonstrations, Britain being one of the major concessionaires. At one stage British police had fired on demonstrators and had killed thirteen people. The Chinese nation, in the words of the American magazine *Christian Century*, rose up 'into a single body of protest'.[18] Strikes spread to all the main industrial centres, and a year-long boycott of Hong Kong started. The Communists greatly benefited from these developments. Party membership leapt from about a thousand in May to 10,000 six months later.[19]

Following Chiang's *coup*, Ch'en Tu-hsiu, Communist Secretary-General, believed the time had come for his party to assume greater independence from the Kuomintang. Moscow saw things differently and continued to put its weight behind the alliance with Chiang.

Increasingly Mao had turned his attention to the peasants. In 1925 he had been put in charge of the Kuomintang's college for peasant agitators. He was made head of a largely non-existent Communist Party Peasant Department in 1926. In the winter of 1926–27 he was among the peasants of Hunan, gathering material for his *Report on an Investigation of the Peasant Movement in Hunan*. The *Report* was intended for Kuomintang rather than Communist consumption, but it has been called 'a classic of Chinese Leninism'.[20] But although Lenin had been for an alliance with the poor peasants, he placed them essentially in a secondary, auxiliary role. Mao was beginning to work out a completely new strategy. It was 'the marriage of Marxism-

Leninism to the traditional pattern of the Chinese peasant revolt by which Mao has changed the entire concept of revolution in China – perhaps also in other backward countries'.[21] Whether, as has been suggested, Mao was 'caught by the revolutionary tempest he had witnessed in Hunan',[22] or whether he attempted to force the pace of revolutionary change, is not clear. His *Report* and his activities were too radical for the Kuomintang Right. He took care not to attack all landlords, only 'local tyrants and evil gentry' and 'lawless landlords'.

Many landowners in the Kuomintang and its armies were disturbed. As for Chiang, he saw the Left of the Kuomintang and the Communists drawing closer together and decided he must act against them. Instead of making for Peking, he headed for Shanghai. An insurrection by the Communist-led masses in the city opened the way for him. In return he struck down the Communists in April 1927, executing hundreds of them. Thus the first alliance between the Communists and the Kuomintang came to an end in practice.

Chiang had set up his capital in Nanking, but armed with funds from Shanghai's business community his troops pressed on to Peking in 1928.

The Communists' response to Chiang's onslaught was armed risings in both urban and rural centres. A rising failed in Nanchang in August 1927. A conference of the CCP leadership later in the month decided, however, on a 'putschist line'.[23] Mao was ordered to carry through an 'Autumn Harvest Rising' in Hunan and Kiangsi. This failed.

While the Communist leaders continued with the Moscow-endorsed[24] policy of urban insurrection, Mao led the remnants of his forces to the Ching-kang-san area on the Kiangsi-Hunan border. There, later joined by Chu Teh, he set up an outpost of revolution, based on the peasants and defended by a Red Army. He was able to extend this area until in 1931 a Chinese Soviet Republic was set up. Mao was elected Chairman of the Central Executive Committee which ran the republic. Also on the committee were: Chu Teh, Liu Shao-ch'i, Chou En-lai, and Ch'en Shao-yu, who had replaced Ch'en Tu-hsiu as Party Secretary. To what extent the republic was based on the revolutionary enthusiasm of the peasants or merely their half-hearted collaboration[25] is debatable.

From November 1930 Chiang made several unsuccessful

attempts to crush Mao's republic. But by 1934 his large, foreign-equipped and German-advised, armies, and his blockade, forced the Communists to attempt a breakout. The 'Long March' of Mao's supporters began. Of the 90,000 men who set out, only a few thousands reached northern Shensi, over one year and some 6,000 hard miles later. Mao, who had been in disgrace for his unorthodoxy six years before, was made party leader in January 1935.

As Mao's personal situation was improving, China's was deteriorating. In 1931 the Japanese had taken Manchuria and set up a puppet regime there. In the 1930s they put mounting military and political pressure on Chiang's regime. Mao's response was to offer a United Front against Japanese aggression in July 1934. Whether this was his own idea or in line with Moscow's changing policy is not clear. In December 1936 Chiang formally accepted this offer. He did so only after being held prisoner by a pro-United Front general whom he had gone to berate for not prosecuting the war against the Communists.

### III. THE SPANISH CIVIL WAR AND THE POPULAR FRONT

Early in 1934 the Comintern line began to change again. Instead of indiscriminate condemnation of all 'bourgeois' states, a distinction was made between the role of the aggressive Fascist states (Germany, Italy, and Japan) and the non-aggressive capitalist states (Britain, France, the United States, and others). By 1935 'there had unfolded in Comintern statements the drama of a great struggle between the "war-mongering" forces of world fascism (the fascist dictatorships and movements) and the anti-fascist forces'.[26] Stalin felt that the Soviet Union was threatened by the rise of Nazism in Germany, a Nazism which claimed to be militantly anti-Communist, which was rearming Germany, and which was looking menacingly eastwards. In this situation the Soviets needed allies to help them contain Nazi Germany. The most likely ally in any such venture was France. France had fought two wars against Germany and was also apprehensive about German rearmament. France and Russia had been allies in 1914, their different political systems notwithstanding. Why should they not be so again? On 2 May 1935 the Franco-Soviet Mutual Assistance Treaty was signed in Moscow. At the request of the French government Stalin publicly endorsed French rearmament. Thus 'At one blow, the Communist dogma of opposition to national defense had been demolished'.[27] The French Communist Party obeyed the call from Moscow to abandon its opposition to rearmament plans. In effect they now moved to the Right of the French Socialists, who opposed rearmament, on the defence issue.

It followed that if it was correct for the Soviet Union to collaborate with bourgeois states against Fascism, it must be correct for Communist parties in those states to collaborate with bourgeois and reformist politicians, who were themselves collaborating with the Soviet Union. The French Communists worked with the Radicals, whose government had signed the pact with the USSR. Together they ensured ratification of the treaty by the French Chamber of Deputies.

Since July 1934 the French Communists, again in line with the latest edict of Moscow, had a pact with the Socialists under which they co-operated against Fascism and in support of democratic liberties. In Communist parlance this was a 'United Front from above' because it had been reached by the leaderships of the two parties. The pact between France and the Soviet Union caused some friction in the United Front as the Socialists of Léon Blum were less enthusiastic about national defence than the Communists of Maurice Thorez now were. Nevertheless, this difficulty was overcome because of the enthusiasm of the rank-and-file Socialists and the determination of the Communist leadership. The continued activities of the Fascist leagues were also a powerful stimulus to united action. The Radicals too were worried by the activities of the French Fascists and needed the electoral support of the Socialists to maintain their position.

In their efforts to woo the Socialists and the Radicals the Communists dropped all their earlier emphasis on 'class against class', the 'dictatorship of the proletariat', and 'revolutionary defeatism'. Later they sided with the Radicals against Socialist demands for nationalization. Instead they took to waving the (previously despised) tricolour, and singing the *Marseillaise*. The Communists even changed the name of their party from 'French Section of the Communist International' to the 'French Communist Party', stopped their campaign for national independence for the colonial peoples, and supported the League of Nations. When the 14 July celebrations of 1935 came round the Communists had become respectable enough to celebrate the storming of the Bastille with the Socialists and the Radicals. This was the first major public manifestation of what became known as the Popular Front.

In Communist theory the Front meant:

> Aggressive action by the mass of the people against their enemies, on an unprecedented scale: substantial progress towards real unity of the working class, in both trade union and party spheres: extension of the struggle against Fascism from the streets, the factories, the ballot box, to the battlefield itself, with the anti-Fascist forces organized as a Government: fiercer fighting but on a higher plane than ever before, and therefore nearer victory.[28]

Some Socialists – members of the French Socialist Party, the British Independent Labour Party, the Trotskyists, and others – saw the new Communist line as a 'sell out', as 'class collaboration'. The Communists were willing to postpone indefinitely all socialist measures, such as widespread nationalization and land collectivization, even though they presented the Popular or People's Front as a step towards the victory of socialism. Others, like the leaders of the British Labour Party, remained unconvinced of the Communists' sincerity or that there was anything to gain by association with them.

The Seventh Congress of the Communist International in Moscow in July 1935 confirmed the new line and praised the French party's successes in carrying it through. Whatever the private doubts of delegates about this *volte-face* by the Comintern the façade of unity was maintained. The United Front and the Popular Front tactics had become the law for Communists from Paris to Prague and Chicago to Chunking.

The French Popular Front parties entered the national elections of April 1936 with a programme which 'contained little to frighten the middle classes'. But 'there was promise enough in this cake for anyone who felt at all hungry. Vague though it was, no program like it had ever been seen before in France'.[29] On the first ballot the Communist vote doubled over the previous election, giving them 15 per cent of the total vote. In all the Popular Front parties received 54.5 per cent of the votes. Communist representation in the Chamber of Deputies increased from 10 to 72 seats. Of these 41 were due to their alliance with the Radicals and Socialists.[30] The Socialists emerged as the strongest of the Front parties and it was they, somewhat to the Communists' disappointment (for they preferred the Radicals), who formed the major part of the new government.

The victory of the *Front Populaire* in France was seen at the time as 'the means . . . of keeping Fascism well in check'. But in Spain a similar development

> the victory of the *Frente Popular* at the General Election of 1936 was the prelude to civil war. It gave the signal for armed military revolt, subsidised and aided not only by the rich in Spain, but by the Fascist Governments of Italy and Germany, and conducted with a ruthless savagery.

This is how G. D. H. Cole, a British non-Communist supporter of the Popular Front, analysed the impact of the Popular Front on the two countries.[31] The developments in both countries were to disappoint Professor Cole and the Left in general, the more so in Spain, for Spain became the centre of a modern crusade.

The Spanish Communist Party had been very weak up to 1936, greatly outnumbered by the other parties of the Left. The extreme policies of the Comintern up to 1934 had been a factor, but by no means the only one, promoting this weakness. The new policy, in itself a recognition of Communist weakness, was welcomed by the Spanish Communists. But in Spain the initiative for a Popular Front came not from them and would have occurred without them. The main parties of the Left, the Socialists, the Left Republicans and the Republican Union, the Syndicalist Party, the 'Trotskyist' POUM, had come themselves to realize that some kind of alliance was needed to defeat the Right in the elections. Even the powerful Anarchists had come to this view. Although they did not sign the Front pact, they supported it.[32]

The Spanish Popular Front had a small but clear majority of votes over an alliance of right-wing parties calling itself the National Front. If anything, the results underestimated the Left feeling in the country. Many peasants living in a position of extreme dependence were not free to vote as they liked. And not all the Anarchists cast their votes. Many of those elected as Centre candidates, that is independent of the two Fronts, later sided with the Republic, as did the Basque nationalists. A liberal government of Left Republicans emerged, supported by the working-class parties, and based on a programme of 'extremely

mild'[33] reform covering land and education, an amnesty for
political prisoners, autonomy for Catalonia, and a review of the
situation in the Basque country. But 'from the moment of the
election onwards a trail of violence, murder, and arson spread
across the face of the country'.[34] This was partly caused by
spontaneous outbursts by the Left masses stimulated by the sweet
smell of victory, and partly the 'conscious work'[35] of the Fascist
Falange attempting to spread disorder to give the Right the
pretext for revolt. Such a revolt, long contemplated by many of
Spain's generals, was in the final stages of preparation.

Military rebellion actually broke out in July 1936. What
followed was a three-year conflict regarded by both sides as a
holy war. It impressed the world by its brutality. Arthur Koestler
commented: 'I am convinced that enough acts of brutality have
been committed on both sides to satisfy Europe's demand for
horrors for the next hundred years'.[36] In his 'Christian crusade',
the leader of the Right, General Franco, unleashed his Muslim
Moroccan troops, his Foreign Legionaries, and his Nazi experts
in aerial bombardment against Spain. About 16,000 Germans
aided the Francoists. Italian forces were about 50,000 at their
peak. There were also about 20,000 Portuguese fighting for
Franco, and small groups of right-wingers from several other
countries.[37] Without them the 'Christian crusade' would not
have succeeded. The Republicans would certainly have failed
earlier had not the Soviet Union sent them war material, food,
and specialists. The democracies, fearing an extension of the
conflict, imposed an arms embargo which, in practice, helped the
Francoists. Roosevelt, for one, later regretted his decision.[38]

The dependence of the Republic on Soviet aid furnished the
Communists with the opportunity to gain more and more
influence in Spain. From being a tiny group of about a thousand
in 1931, they had developed into a party of nearly half a million
by 1939, had secured dominance in the Defence Ministry,[39] and
had much influence in other areas of political life. This growth
of Communist influence is one of the lessons of the Spanish war:
that aid and influence go together, and that Communists will
never be slow to exploit such opportunities. The second is how
the Communists gained influence outside Spain because of
Soviet help and their untiring efforts in various front organizations.

In a way the International Brigades were one of these. Their members were by no means all Communists, but the Brigades were a creation of the Comintern. They attracted 40,000 men from many nations. Among the 2,000 Britons, of whom over 500 were killed, were Esmond Romilly, nephew of Winston Churchill; Fred Copeman,[40] a Roman Catholic, who had led the Invergordon naval mutiny in 1931 and later became an Officer of the Order of the British Empire, and Moral Rearmer; Alexander Foote, future Soviet spy; Will Paynter, for many years secretary of the National Union of Mineworkers; and George Nathan, ex-'Black and Tan' and in 1918 the 'only Jewish officer in the Brigade of Guards'.[41] The United States were represented by 2,800, of whom 900 did not return. About a thousand Canadians also participated.[42] Of the American veterans, 600 fought in the Second World War; many were later victims of McCarthyism.

Many intellectuals who did not fight, wrote. Ernest Hemingway's *For Whom the Bell Tolls* was of course the most successful literary work inspired by the war. But there were many others. Roy Campbell was the best-known writer (and one of the very few) on the other side of the barricades. A dazzling array of Hollywood celebrities also gave varying degrees of support for the Republic – Fredric March, Errol Flynn, Robert Montgomery, Paul Muni, Edward G. Robinson, Orson Welles, and even Shirley Temple.[43]

Two other lessons which emerged from the Spanish Civil War were the Soviet Communists' attitude to other Left groups, and the Soviet Union's readiness to drop a holy cause once that cause has become an embarrassment.

What the fate of other left-wing parties would be once the Communists got in a dominant position was indicated by the savage attempt to exterminate the POUM in 1937. Together with the Anarchists, the POUM were the main working-class movement in Catalonia which since 1936 had become an autonomous region of the Republic. There the main working-class movements had been enaged in a social revolution. There land was being collectivized, factories brought under workers' control, small businesses run by the communes, ranks abolished, wage and salary differences greatly reduced, and 'almost every church had been gutted and its images burnt'.[44] All this was completely against Comintern policy. As Orwell tells us, the POUM line was that bourgeois democracy was capitalism: Fascism was another form of capitalism; so that, for the workers, these were not real alternatives: 'The only real alternative to Fascism is workers' control'.[45] To counter this, the Comintern ran an international campaign of vilification against the POUM and the Anarchist CNT, even claiming that they were agents of Franco![46] The bitterness and rivalry between the POUM-CNT and the Communists led to open clashes in Barcelona in April 1937. Hundreds were killed. The Communists demanded the dissolution of these groups. As the Socialist Prime Minister Largo Caballero would not agree, the Communists forced him to resign. He was replaced by the more right-wing Juan Negrín, who did agree. A wave of terror descended over the POUM, the Anarchists, and all who opposed the Stalinist domination of the Republic. The murder squads and the torture experts of the Soviet secret police and their Comintern helpers went to work. Though there was much to criticize in the activities of the extreme Left, this Soviet purge must have greatly weakened Republican resistance.

After the Munich Agreement of 1938 under which Britain and France, Germany and Italy, sealed the fate of Czechoslovakia without even consulting the Soviet Union, Stalin started to reappraise his country's foreign policy. He wanted to withdraw from Spain which appeared a potentially dangerous entanglement, hindering his manoeuvrability. The International Brigades were withdrawn, the pro-Republican propaganda tuned down, the aid phased out. Slowly the scene was set for another political *volte-face.*

One final point about Stalin and Spain. The tactic of United Front followed by Popular Front, followed by People's Government and then a parliamentary democracy of a 'new type' became the Communists' theoretical model as an alternative to the Soviet model. It was applied in eastern Europe after 1945, but there were many differences between Spain and the People's Democracies. For one thing, Spain was never a Moscow satellite, because this would not have fitted in with Stalin's attempt to win Britain for an Anglo-Soviet alliance.

## IV. THE HITLER-STALIN PACT

In the period August 1939 to June 1941 Stalin's communism lost much of the credibility and goodwill it had built up in left-wing liberal, and anti-Fascist circles since 1935. This was the result of the Hitler-Stalin Non-Aggression Pact announced on 25 August 1939. In the treaty, valid for ten years, Germany and the USSR resolved that neither party would attack the other. Should one of them become the object of belligerent action by a third power, the other would not lend its support to this third power. Nor would either of the parties to the treaty join any coalition directed at the other. The additional secret protocols placed Finland, the Baltic states, and eastern Poland, 'in the event of a territorial and political transformation', in the Soviet 'sphere of interest'. Bessarabia was also so placed. This gave Hitler the green light for his planned action against Poland. He did not believe that without the USSR, Britain and France would go to war on behalf of Poland.

On the face of it the treaty was pretty damning. The two powers which for years had preached holy war against each other were suddenly concluding a treaty of peace and friendship. But it would be unfair to leave it simply at that. As we have seen, Stalin had tried to get Britain and France to agree to take action to prevent Nazi aggression. In particular, in April 1939 the Soviet Union presented proposals to London and Paris for a mutual assistance agreement. Under these proposals the parties would assist each other in case of attack; all three would render all manner of assistance, including military, to East European states situated between the Baltic and the Black Sea in case of aggression against these states.[47] In Britain public opinion had been moving in the direction of a pact with the Soviet Union. The Labour Party favoured such a pact, as did many Liberals and some Conservatives. Anthony Eden was one of the latter. Such outspoken anti-Bolsheviks of the past as Churchill and Lloyd George agreed with him. Prime Minister Chamberlain remained sceptical on both military and political grounds. But he had given a guarantee to Poland after the fall of the rump of the Czecho-Slovak state in March 1939. How could he stand by that guarantee without the support of the USSR, his critics asked. Chamberlain relented a little and sent a Foreign Office mission to Moscow in June. Although progress was being made, the going was slow, and an Anglo-French military mission only reached Moscow on 12 August. The British team was not very high-powered. In any case, the Poles refused to agree to having Soviet troops, to assist them or anyone else, on their soil. The negotiations ended when the Hitler-Stalin Pact was signed.

The Russians had put out feelers to Berlin earlier in August and Hitler had jumped at the chance of doing a deal. Unlike Chamberlain, he was willing to send his Foreign Minister to Moscow. On 15 August Soviet Foreign Minister Molotov, who had replaced the 'anti-Fascist' Jew Maxim Litvinov on 3 May, asked if Berlin would agree to a non-aggression pact. In addition, he sought a guarantee for the Baltic states, and German help in improving Soviet-Japanese relations. Hitler reacted positively and without delay. Critics of Chamberlain pointed out that he had gone twice to see Hitler but had not been prepared to send anyone of authority to negotiate with Stalin. Had he been prepared to do so events might have taken a different course.

Churchill saw the Hitler-Stalin Pact as an act of political realism on Stalin's part.[48] Many Communists felt embarrassed by it; some felt betrayed and broke with the movement. The ranks of the Popular-fronters and fellow-travellers were thinned as people like John Strachey and Louis Fischer left the Moscow-organized parade. In the words of Fischer: 'The Pact produced my "Kronstadt" '. It was 'the gravestone of Bolshevik internationalism and the cornerstone of Bolshevik imperialism'.[49]

Most Communists were slow to see the implications of the Pact. When the war broke out, they simply supported Britain and France as anti-Fascist states. Harry Pollitt, leader of the British Communist Party, wrote: 'To stand aside from this conflict, to contribute only revolutionary-sounding phrases while the Fascist beasts ride roughshod over Europe, would be a betrayal of everything our forefathers have fought to achieve in the course of long years of struggle against capitalism'.[50] The French, Scandinavian, and other parties took a similar line. Even the German Communist Party still called for the overthrow of Hitler on 3 September.[51]

The line was, however, soon to change. Four weeks after the signing of the Hitler-Stalin Pact came an authoritative statement by Georgi Dimitrov of the new line. This was contained in an article entitled 'The War and the Working Class of the Capitalist Countries'. Dimitrov claimed: 'In its character and essence the present war is, on the part of both warring sides, an *imperialist, unjust* war'.[52]

Any doubts that Communist parties had about what their line should be were dispelled on 17 September when the Red Army crossed the Polish frontier from the east. The Russians claimed they were protecting the rights of the Ukrainian and Belorussian minorities in the area, and to be sure, the area they occupied, in agreement with Berlin, was roughly along the Curzon Line which the British Foreign Minister had suggested should be the Western frontier of Russia after the First World War. Originally the Russians were to get more of Poland, but they secretly traded their extra share for a free hand in Lithuania.[53] Within the next few months Stalin swallowed up the three Baltic states and, after the 'Winter War' with Finland, forced that country to cede territory and grant Moscow a naval base. A little later Romania was forced to hand over Bessarabia and northern Bukovina. One wonders why Stalin engaged in this aggression. The most charitable interpretation one can put on these events is that the Soviet leader was improving the defensive position of the USSR. A look at the map, especially as regards the Baltic states, Finland, and eastern Poland, would show that this is plausible. However, the value of such territory in defence terms is greatly reduced if the population is hostile. The Russians learned this in 1941. Another explanation, also plausible, is that Stalin simply wanted to re-create the old Tsarist Empire. The Hitler-Stalin Pact was almost a Brest-Litovsk in reverse. A third explanation, less plausible in this writer's view, is that Stalin was remembering his Communist mission and exporting revolution. Hitler needed Stalin during this period. He needed Soviet strategic materials,[54] and he needed Soviet diplomatic and propaganda aid. Above all, he needed the Red Army neutralized while he dealt with the Western powers. Stalin exploited this situation and increased his demands on Hitler. Did he thus make the Nazi attack on Russia more likely? We can ask this question, but we cannot answer it with any degree of certainty.

The London *Daily Worker* (20 September 1939) had coyly told its readers: 'The Red Army is bringing bread to the starving peasants', as the Soviet tanks rolled into Poland. And in the months which followed the world's Communist parties spent their time explaining away the new Soviet moves and bashing the British and French governments. The comments on Germany grew milder and milder. In Britain the Communist line was 'so anti-Chamberlain as to be virtually pro-Hitler'.[55] In France the Communist Party had been banned after its switch of line. But its underground organization pushed a defeatist line which perhaps was a contributory cause of the downfall of France in

1940. After the French capitulation the Communists were once again allowed to publish their papers openly. The same thing happened in Norway. In the United States the Communists fought for isolation against American involvement in the war. The American party criticized American help for Britain.

In Britain itself the Communists called for a People's Government without spelling out what that was. Even when the anti-appeaser Churchill replaced Chamberlain and the Labour Party joined in what really was a national government, the Communist Party still opposed the government and the war. It is remarkable that they were allowed to carry on their activities openly and legally. In September 1940, they launched a campaign for a People's Convention as a kind of counter-Parliament. The appeal to support the Convention was signed by such well-known fellow-travellers as D. N. Pritt, K.C., M.P., and the 'Red' Dean of Canterbury, but also by the Reverend Mervyn Stockwood (later bishop of Southwark) and actor Michael Redgrave.[56] On 12 January 1941, 2,234 'delegates' met, including 'plenty of people present who were not habitual fellow-travellers'.[57] Among the speakers was the future Indian Foreign Minister Krishna Menon. (The Indian Congress was at that time opposed to the British war effort.) The Convention's programme, and how it intended to achieve it, was never really very clear. As D. N. Pritt outlined it, it did not add up to much. He asked the rhetorical question: 'What are these necessary measures?' (to get out of 'this present very serious situation . . . for the working class'). Firstly, 'there is the whole situation in production, the inability of the present Government to increase the home production of food because it dare not touch the privileges of the Landlords, together with the chaotic situation . . . existing in factories'. Secondly, 'there is the necessity for a radical change in foreign policy which would include an entirely different orientation towards the Union of Socialist, Soviet Republics, the Republic of China and the Peoples of India'. Thirdly, 'amid the worsening situation of the Spring and Summer, new hope can only be built upon a Government which shows it is able to lead the way and bring the British people out of this present crisis'.[58] The British government under Churchill was of course trying to engage in closer relations with Stalin. It was cold-shouldered to the cost of the USSR.

## V. BARBAROSSA AND THE ANTI-HITLER COALITION

In the early hours of 22 June 1941 Wilhelm Schultz, a Communist mechanic from Eisenach then serving as a N.C.O. in the *Wehrmacht*, reached the Soviet side of the Hitler-Stalin frontier running through Poland. He was mortally wounded, but before he died he revealed that in one hour's time Barbarossa, Hitler's plan for the invasion of Russia, would be set in motion. A few other ordinary German soldiers had done the same even days earlier. These Germans need not have bothered; the Soviets had the information from their own agents, including Dr Richard Sorge who operated from the German embassy in Tokyo, and from the British and American governments. In fact, Hitler's planned attack was one of the worst-kept secrets of the war. Rumours even circulated in the world's press.

Stalin rejected such warnings and thought the rumours were a plot of the British to get Russia involved in the war. At the same time he made frantic efforts to placate his erstwhile, and still official, German partner. The world's Communists naturally echoed Stalin's line. Typical was an article which appeared in the British Communist journal *Labour Monthly*, in the very month of the attack. It attempted to show in great detail why Hitler would not invade the USSR. The article commented:

> If there is one statement that appears almost daily in the press of this country it is the constant refrain that Nazi Germany is about to march into the Ukraine. This was Hitler's aim until it was postponed in August, 1939, when he sent von Ribbentrop to Moscow to sign a Non-Aggression Pact.

If Hitler dared so much as attempt any hostile action, the article went on:

> . . . the whole Red Army would be set in motion, the march on Danzig, the envelopment of the Nazi Armies in Poland and the vital sweep down to Budapest, and this would mean the end of the Hitler hold in the East and South. The possibilities of Red uprisings in Holland, Belgium, France, Spain, and even Germany herself should not be overlooked. Perhaps this fact growing in the consciousness of the Nazi leaders makes them look with apprehension at this sword of Damocles, this iron hand at present in a velvet glove.

Despite such appalling lack of judgement resulting in the need for another political somersault later in the month, the leaderships of the various Communist parties had little difficulty in winning their members for the new line of resistance to Nazism. In Britain the transformation from an anti- to a pro-war line was made much easier by Winston Churchill. In an act of great political wisdom the Prime Minister offered the Russians, in a radio broadcast made only hours after the start of the invasion, an alliance against Hitlerism. By 12 July the Anglo-Soviet mutual assistance agreement was signed. In the following month Britain and the Soviet Union acted in concert in their joint occupation of neutral Iran. Towards the end of September an Anglo-American mission, even though the United States was not yet in the war, arrived in Moscow to discuss aid to the Soviets. In the remainder of the year over 360,000 tons of such aid was dispatched by the Western powers. The Japanese attack on Pearl Harbor in December 1941 led to Hitler's reckless declaration of war on the United States. Thus the anti-Hitler coalition was forged.

Many in Britain thought the coalition with the Soviet Union would not yield much in military terms. Stalin had boasted about Soviet military might, but the spectacular German advance appeared to expose this claim. Chaos reigned on the Soviet side. The inadequate communications system broke down. Troops had arms but no ammunition, or ammunition but no spades to dig defensive positions, or all three but no food. Within a very short time the *Wehrmacht* had crossed the old, pre-September 1939 Soviet frontiers, having destroyed most of the Soviet Air Force and vast quantities of armour, and inflicted very heavy punishment on the Red Army. By the end of 1941 there were nearly 4 million Soviet troops in German hands[59] which represented many more men than in the entire United Kingdom armed forces at that time. Soviet losses in killed and wounded were also very heavy. By October Leningrad was cut off to face its long, tortured martyrdom. In Moscow 'a large mass of Muscovites' panicked and fled 'just as in Paris people had fled'.[60] In the south the Potemkin city of Odessa had fallen to the 'crawling locusts' of 'Hun soldiery'[61] and their Romanian satellites. What had gone wrong?

It remains one of the mysteries of the war why Stalin ignored the numerous warnings of imminent attack. His forces suffered quite unnecessarily from the element of surprise. Much of their equipment was obsolete; they had not learned the lessons of tank warfare; and their officer corps was still suffering from the results of the purge. In Stalin's defence it can be argued that boasts are a normal part of psychological warfare; that anyway Pearl Harbor need not have happened; that the French, British, and Americans started the war with out-of-date ideas; and that at least some of their high officers were incompetent. There is much truth in the anti-Stalin view that Russia would have fallen by December had not space and climate helped out, but is it not at least as true that Britain would have fallen had the Channel not stopped Hitler? There is, though, one difference between Britain and America and the USSR: Stalin had lavished funds on the Red Army; the Anglo-American forces had been starved of funds. The Soviet forces faced one other disadvantage in that most of them were without combat experience. The Germans had a string of the most impressive victories behind them. The Russians, too, traditionally respected the Germans as soldiers and technicians; the Germans had long regarded the Russians as inferior. Even so, the Red Army often put up stiff resistance; units went on fighting in hopeless situations; and German casualties mounted. By the end of November over 743,000 German casualties were recorded by the *Wehrmacht*. Of these nearly 200,000 were dead. These losses were more than four times the number of German casualties in the West in 1940,[62] and more than German's entire losses before June 1941.

If the Red Army had not lived up to the claims made for it by Communist propagandists before June 1941, it had performed at least as well as any forces which had stood against the Nazis and better than most. What of Stalin's subjects? It is impossible to get an objective picture of what ordinary Russians felt during the early stages of the war, but from all accounts their traditional patriotism soon stirred them and they soon came to fear the Germans for their inhumanity. As for the non-Russian peoples of the USSR in the path of the Nazi panzer divisions, many of them either welcomed the *Wehrmacht* at first, or at least were not disposed to resist. This was especially so in the areas annexed by Stalin from 1939 onwards.

This is not the place to go into the details of the Russo-German campaign. It must do to mention a few significant highlights. The Soviet success in holding Leningrad was one of these. This act of desperate defiance and sacrifice has few equals in the history of war. The Soviet counter-offensive which threw the Germans back from Moscow was another. It did not achieve all its objectives, but for the first time since 1939 the *Wehrmacht* was clearly taking a beating. Here winter clothing was an important factor, something the German generals neglected. At this time, 'The comic "Winter Fritz", wrapped up in women's shawls and feather boas stolen from the local population, and with icicles hanging from his red nose, made his first appearance in Russian folklore'.[63] The resistance of the Red Army stiffened still further after this success and after they had seen what German occupation had meant in the recaptured areas.[64] The Russians had lost more men in their winter offensive than had the Germans, and exhausted many of their stocks. In the summer of 1942 they suffered new disasters at the hands of the *Wehrmacht*. In the south the Germans swept forwards once again, taking the great naval base of Sebastopol. This was after a nine-month siege and for the Russians was one 'of the most glorious defeats of the Soviet-German war'. Once again the Germans were paying a heavy price for their victories. Up to September 1941 the German General Halder recorded over 1,637,000 casualties (excluding the many sick).[65] In addition there were the casualties of the satellite armies – the Finns, Italians, Hungarians, Romanians, Bulgarians, Spanish 'Blue Division', French Fascists, Scandinavian SS, etc.

The winter of 1942–43 brought another turning-point in the Soviet-German campaign. This was the disastrous German defeat at Stalingrad. By the middle of October it had looked as though this important river port, industrial and communications centre, on the Volga would fall to the Germans. But somehow the Red Army held on. The Soviet defenders caught the imagination of their grateful allies. At last in January 1943 the world saw the pictures of the 'long black serpents of German war prisoners',[66] and even more impressive, those of the twenty-four or so German generals, headed by Field Marshal Paulus, going into captivity. It was the greatest single psychological blow of the war against Nazi Germany. It was also pretty impressive in material terms. The Germans had lost at least 200,000 men either dead or prisoners.[67] As for materials, to name just one item, they lost 490 transport planes.[68] Stalingrad showed the world that the *Wehrmacht* was not invincible, and that high-ranking German officers preferred captivity in 'Bolshevist, Jewish, subhuman' hands than death.

Important though Stalingrad was, the battle of Kursk in July 1943 was more important still and really did mark the beginning of the end on the Eastern front. At Kursk in the Ukraine Hitler hoped to engage and destroy the major part of the Red Army. The Soviet units were in heavily entrenched positions reminiscent of the First World War, but Kursk was possibly the greatest tank battle of the war. This defeat was the military turning-point in the East; after it, the Germans lost the initiative on the Eastern front, never to regain it.

After Stalingrad and Kursk and the other Soviet victories which ultimately led them to Berlin, the Communists claimed that the Red Army had won the war. They could even cite Winston Churchill as a witness. In 1944 in a message to Stalin he had admitted that 'Russia is holding and beating far larger hostile forces than those which face the Allies in the West, and through long years, at enormous loss, has borne the brunt of the struggle on land'. Certainly a look at the numbers of Nazi men and material engaged on the battlefronts indicates that this was so. On 1 July 1943, for instance, Hitler had 175 *Wehrmacht* and SS divisions in the East plus seven in Finland, as against only 38 in the West, 6 in Italy, 14 in the Balkans, and 15 in Norway and Denmark. Of the 22 *Luftwaffe* divisions 12 were in the East.[69] Of course this is not the whole story. What about Anglo-American aid for one thing?

The Russians claim that this aid was only a fraction of the material they used. We can readily agree to this regarding tanks, planes, artillery, and infantry weapons. The items which were extremely important were motor vehicles. At the end of the war over 50 per cent of all vehicles in the Red Army were of American origin.[70] Wireless and railway equipment, food, fuel, and even clothing were also important. Without American trucks and jeeps the Russians could not have exploited their breakthroughs. Lack of motorized transport severely handicapped them in their Moscow offensive of winter 1941.[71]

Another thing conveniently forgotten by Soviet historians is the importance of Britain 'standing alone' in 1940. The fact that Britain did not seek terms from Hitler served to strengthen the resolve of all those who were against the Nazis, especially in the United States. Britain later provided the Americans with a strategic base for the liberation of western Europe (quite apart from the British contribution to that venture). Thirdly, the Allied bombing of Germany, while it proved much less effective than was supposed at the time, did tie up large formations of the *Luftwaffe*. This was a great help to the Russians who were weaker in the air than on the ground. Finally, by engaging the Japanese fully, the Americans and British prevented them from stabbing the Russians in the back.

In the summer of 1944 the last Axis forces were being driven out of the Soviet Union and Stalin could therefore take stock of the Soviet Union, assess how the non-Russian people had reacted to the invasion, and take appropriate action. The 'appropriate action' was drastic when Stalin suspected disloyalty. Over 1.6 million Muslims from the North Caucasus and the Crimea, alleged to have collaborated with the Germans, were rounded up and deported. Unlike purges and deportations of the past 'this time it was whole peoples that were being sent into oblivion'.[72] It was 'an act of brutality barely paralleled in the whole history of imperialism'.[73] Whole areas became depopulated, 'Autonomous Soviet Socialist Republics' disappeared overnight from the map. Their land was then colonized by Russians and Ukrainians. Most of the deported seem to have ended up in Siberia, Kazakhstan, or Uzbekistan. Behind them were appalling journeys under primitive conditions. The citizens of the Volga-German Autonomous Soviet Socialist Republic, about half a million of them,[74] had already had their republic dissolved and been removed in August 1941 – as a precautionary measure.[75] Under Khrushchev these nations were rehabilitated. It was said that Stalin's policy was anti-Leninist, but many of the peoples concerned were deemed to have settled permanently outside their original homelands.[76]

The fate of these 'republics' exposed the fictitious nature of the Soviet constitution when it came to the rights of the Union's peoples. Yet at the very time of the deportations, Stalin was proclaiming the extension of the rights of the Union Republics.[77] They were to have their own military formations and the right to diplomatic representation abroad. This was largely to impress foreign opinion with a view to increased Soviet representation in the United Nations.

As the limitations of space will not permit a return to this subject, let us briefly examine the question of what Soviet rule has meant for the non-Russian peoples. Somewhat oversimplifying, one can say that, in the period up to the war, providing there was no opposition to Moscow, the non-Russian peoples were helped to develop their national cultures. Though they too suffered in the collectivization drive, the attacks on religion, and the purges (here as 'bourgeois nationalists'), there was much educational, social, and industrial progress. Since 1945 the tendency, on the whole, has been to put rather more emphasis on Russification, though there have been variations from place to place and under different Secretaries. The pace of industrialization in these areas, especially in Asia, has quickened, and again there has been great progress in education. On the whole, the more 'backward' the society, the more the progress achieved. For instance, the Baltic states enjoyed a high degree of literacy, and relatively high living standards, before Soviet rule. In the Central Asian republics, on the other hand, the progress in education

> must be seen as one of the most remarkable achievements of the Soviet, or indeed of any other imperial regime . . . there can be no doubt that the standard of literacy and of higher and technical education in Central Asia is far higher than that of any Muslim country in the world and indeed higher than of any Asian or African country with the exception of Japan and Israel.[78]

This generalization – the more backward, the more progress – seems broadly true of economic development as well. In purely economic and educational terms, Western scholars have concluded that the Asian Soviet republics have progressed more than their non-Soviet neighbours.[79] What is not clear is the extent to which these peoples accept rule from Moscow. Few informed Westerners with a knowledge of the appropriate languages penetrate very deeply or for very long into the more distant republics. The actual state of affairs must vary from republic to republic, according to the length of time under Soviet rule, according to how much contact the people have with fellow-countrymen or co-religionists abroad, etc. For instance, the Muslim Asian republics of the USSR have been subject to a great deal of immigration by Russians and Ukrainians. This is true also of the Baltic republics. It would be surprising if this had not created some friction. And the Baltic states have only been under Soviet rule continuously since 1944; many of their citizens, therefore, are likely to consider what it would be like to enjoy an independent existence again. Many have relatives abroad who are a constant reminder of old times and alternatives. Armenians too are scattered beyond the frontiers of the USSR; but they have no recent experience of lengthy independence, so 'Soviet Armenia is the only available focus of Armenian nationalist pride and cultural creativity . . . few Armenians condemn all aspects of life there'.[80] In the largest non-Russian republic, the Ukraine, nationalist feelings were revealed under the Nazi occupation. According to Khrushchev, in his secret speech in 1956, Stalin would have deported the entire population had it not been too large to handle. In conclusion, it seems likely that, despite material progress, the Soviet Union will have to face, in a more or less violent form, the problems connected with nationality which have afflicted so many other states in recent times.

In Britain, the Commonwealth, and the United States, from June 1941 the Communists threw their efforts into raising production to aid the Soviets. Strikes were now regarded by them as serious breaches of discipline which aided the enemy.[81] The Communists also clamoured for a Second Front. This was in line with Soviet demands that the Western Allies should attack Nazi-held Europe as soon as possible – even in 1941! This was impossible because of British losses and American unpreparedness. Yet it was a good line for the Communists who could basically support their governments – a patriotic stance – and at the same time criticize them for dragging their feet in preparing the invasion of Europe (thus giving an issue to those still distrustful of the Establishment).

When the Russians did not capitulate within 'six weeks' as many right-wingers and military experts had suggested they would,[82] their prestige grew. Interest in the Soviet Union grew. With the great Soviet victories of 1943 and 1944 this interest reached a climax. If the Soviet system was so bad, it was asked, why had Russia not collapsed as in the First World War? And why were there no traitors?[83] Why had the Soviet Union stood up to Hitler in a way which the Poles and French – assessed as great military powers before 1939 – had not? The answer must be that the Soviet system was intrinsically better than the systems of pre-war Europe. And so, ran the argument, 'we could learn a thing or two from the Soviets'. We could learn how they beat unemployment, carried on without capitalists, developed mass education, promoted a welfare state, gave equality to women, eradicated racial prejudice – in short, how they had organized society on a rational and just basis. The demand for information on the Soviet Union was so great that it could only be satisfied by relying to a great extent on domestic Communist or Soviet sources. Between 1941 and 1945 the Communists had a field day getting their propaganda into the mass circulation press, into the cinemas, libraries, and the many discussion groups.[84]

The task of the Communists outside the USSR was made easier still in May 1943 by the announcement that the Communist International had been dissolved. It was claimed that the organizational form of uniting workers chosen by the First Congress of the International was now outmoded through the growth of the working-class movement and the growing complexity of the problems facing the parties in the different countries. Thus the International had actually become a drag on the further strengthening of the national working-class parties.[85]

In this situation it is not surprising that membership of the Communist parties should rise. In the case of the British party, membership rose from 12,000 in June 1941 to 56,000 in September 1942. The party's influence was much greater because of its interest in the trade unions and its use of 'front' organizations. To say the least, by 1945 the Communists could reasonably expect that their influence in the post-war world would be far greater than it was before the war.

## NOTES

[1] M. M. Drachkovitch and B. M. Lazitch (ed.), *The Comintern: Historical Highlights* (New York, 1966), p. 170.

[2] L. J. MacFarlane, *The British Communist Party* (London, 1966), p. 139, quotes the *Workers' Weekly* (2 July 1926) as admitting financial dependence on Moscow. In more recent times such financial assistance takes many forms. For instance, large quantities of Western Communist newspapers are bought for distribution in the USSR and East Europe.

[3] Weinstein, op. cit., p. 332.

[4] Theodore Draper, *American Communism and Soviet Russia* (London, 1960), p. 187.

[5] James Klugmann, *History of the Communist Party of Great Britain* (London, 1968), I, 331.

[6] F. Chabod, *A History of Italian Fascism* (London, 1963), p. 50.

[7] Denis Mack Smith, *Italy: A Modern History* (Ann Arbor and London, 1959), p. 372.

[8] ibid., p. 373.

[9] See comments of Karl Dietrich Bracher, *The German Dictatorship* (London, 1970), p. 170.

[10] In the last free elections in November 1932 they had lost 2 million votes.

[11] The best history of the KPD is Hermann Weber, *Die Wandlung des deutschen Kommunismus* (Frankfurt/M, 1969).

[12] The Communist view of Fascism is contained in Theo Pirker, *Komintern und Faschismus 1920–1940* (Stuttgart, 1965).

[13] Braunthal, op. cit., p. 369.

[14] John Strachey, *The Coming Struggle for Power* (London, 1932), p. 261. This was one of the classic Marxist texts in English published during this period.

[15] C. P. Fitzgerald, *The Birth of Communist China* (London, 1964), p. 45.

[16] Stuart Schram, *Mao Tse-tung* (London, 1966), p. 25.

[17] ibid., p. 37.

[18] Jerome Ch'ên, *Mao and the Chinese Revolution* (London, 1965), p. 99.

[19] ibid., p. 100.

[20] Conrad Brandt *et al.*, *A Documentary History of Chinese Communism* (Cambridge, Mass., 1959), p. 79.

[21] Ch'ên, op. cit., pp. 114–15.

[22] Schram, op. cit., p. 99.

[23] Ch'ên, op. cit., p. 130.

[24] Was it Moscow endorsed? Richard C. Thornton, 'The Emergence of a New Comintern Strategy for China: 1928', in Drachkovitch and Lazitch, op. cit., questions the usual thesis, arguing that Comintern policy in China at that time was not for urban uprisings.

[25] Chalmers A. Johnson, *Peasant Nationalism and Communist Power* (Stanford, 1962), p. 2, believes that co-operation before 1937, when full-scale war broke out, was half-hearted; patriotism, not communism, was the stimulus.

[26] K. E. McKenzie, *Comintern and World Revolution, 1918–43* (New York and London, 1964), pp. 144–5.

[27] D. R. Brower, *The New Jacobins* (Ithaca, 1968), p. 50.

[28] See 'Spain and the People's Front', by 'U.H.P.', in *Labour Monthly* (March 1937).

[29] Brower, op. cit., p. 119.

[30] ibid., p. 138.

[31] G. D. H. Cole, *The People's Front* (London, 1937), p. 121.

[32] David T. Cattell, *Communism and the Spanish Civil War* (New York, 1965), p. 15.

[33] ibid., p. 16.

[34] Hugh Thomas, *The Spanish Civil War* (London, 1965), p. 138.

[35] ibid.

[36] Frederick R. Benson, *Writers in Arms* (London, 1968), p. 224.

[37] Thomas, op. cit., p. 793.

[38] ibid., p. 720.

[39] Cattell, op. cit., p. 211.

[40] See his autobiography, *Reason in Revolt* (London, 1948).

[41] Vincent Brome, *The International Brigades* (London, 1965), p. 120.

[42] These figures are from Thomas, op. cit., pp. 796–7.

[43] Stanley Weintraub, *The Last Great Cause* (London, 1968), p. 289.

[44] George Orwell, *Homage to Catalonia* (London, 1938; 2nd edn., 1968), p. 8.

[45] ibid., p. 60. See also Burnett Bolloten, *The Grand Camouflage* (London, 1961), chapter 16.

[46] See, for instance, George Soria, *Trotskyism in the Service of Franco* (London, n.d.).

[47] Martin Gilbert, *Britain and Germany between the Wars* (London, 1964), p. 135.

[48] Winston Churchill, *The Second World War*. I: *The Gathering Storm* (London, 1948), p. 394.

[49] Louis Fischer, in *The God that Failed*, edited by R. H. S. Crossman (London, 1950), p. 223.
[50] Quoted Victor Gollancz, John Strachey, and George Orwell, *The Betrayal of the Left* (London, 1941), pp. 175–6.
[51] *GDAB*, V, 524.
[52] McKenzie, op. cit., p. 170.
[53] William L. Shirer, *The Rise and Fall of the Third Reich* (London, 1960) gives a comprehensive account of the Hitler–Stalin negotiations.
[54] Experts differ on how important Soviet materials were. The Russians were getting certain military-technical advice in return. Before rushing to condemn Stalin too hard we must remember Sweden's and Switzerland's trade with Hitler.
[55] Angus Calder, *The People's War* (London, 1969), p. 243.
[56] ibid., p. 244.
[57] ibid., p. 246.
[58] *Labour Monthly* (June 1941).
[59] Alexander Dallin, *German Rule in Russia* (London, 1957), p. 409.
[60] Alexander Werth, *Russia at War 1941–1945* (London, 1964), pp. 236–7.
[61] Churchill's terms in his speech of 22 June 1941.
[62] Werth, op. cit., p. 260.
[63] ibid., p. 264.
[64] ibid., p. 271.
[65] ibid., p. 403.
[66] ibid.
[67] Albert Seaton, *The Russo-German War 1941–45* (London, 1971), p. 336.
[68] ibid., p. 333.
[69] ibid., p. 353.
[70] ibid., p. 589.
[71] Werth, op. cit., p. 265.
[72] Robert Conquest, *The Nation Killers* (London, 1970), p. 65.
[73] Geoffrey Wheeler, *The Peoples of Soviet Central Asia* (London, 1966), p. 83.
[74] Based on the figures given by Dallin, op. cit., p. 288n.
[75] It is legitimate to argue that the fate of the Japanese Americans in 1942 was little better considering American traditions and living standards.
[76] There is no doubt that some of the populations of those areas went over to the Germans. But before jumping to condemn them one should remember that the Soviet system had been forced on them, they had experienced its brutalities, and they knew little of Germany, less of Nazism.
[77] In the Soviet constitution the Union Republics have in theory more rights than the Autonomous Republics.
[78] Wheeler, op. cit., p. 101.
[79] See Alec Nove and J. A. Newth, *The Soviet Middle East* (London, 1967). It would be interesting to compare development in Finland since 1945 with that of the Baltic states.
[80] Mary Matossian, 'The Armenians', *Problems of Communism* (USIA), Sept.–Oct. 1967.
[81] The British Trotskyists of the Revolutionary Communist Party led by Jock Haston were the only Marxists to continue to oppose the war. They had little success.
[82] Seaton, op. cit., p. 215. The British Chiefs of Staff thought the Germans capable of reaching Moscow within six weeks.
[83] The case of General Vlasov and his anti-Stalin army was not known.
[84] See comments of Douglas Hyde, *I Believed* (London, 1950), pp. 114–15.
[85] *World News and Views* (London), 29 May 1943.

# VII

## Stalin's New Empire

NO completely satisfactory analysis has been advanced to explain the origins of the 'Cold War' – the break-up of the wartime alliance of the West with the Soviet Union, the war of words, and the arms race which followed. The difficulty is that whereas much has been published on the attitudes of American and British leaders, little has been made public in the Soviet Union about Stalin's motives in the early post-war period. Obviously the wartime allies did not entirely lose their deep-rooted suspicion of each other, and when the *raison d'être* for their alliance was eliminated – the menace of Nazi Germany – the earlier attitudes reasserted themselves. In 1944 Kim Philby was appointed by the British Secret Intelligence Service head of a newly created section designed to operate against the USSR.[1] But for years he had been operating as a Soviet agent. Such was the trust of the 'anti-Hitler coalition' partners for each other.

Perhaps the change in leadership in the West was a factor in the breakdown. Despite their differences Stalin, Roosevelt, and Churchill had got some regard for each other. Harry Truman, who took over the Presidency of the United States on Roosevelt's death in 1945, was more hostile to Soviet Russia than his predecessor[2] (though the latter was disappointed with Stalin). He was also ill-equipped for the job. Churchill was a veteran anti-Bolshevik who even before the end of hostilities had ordered that German arms be carefully stacked so that they could easily be reissued to German troops if the Soviets did not halt their advance as agreed.[3] And his 'iron curtain' speech at Fulton in March 1946 was regarded as stoking the fires of the Cold War. Yet Stalin probably valued the old warrior more highly than he did the Labour premier, Clement Attlee.

In Germany Soviet policy appeared to be initially concerned with seizing as much booty as possible to make up for enormous losses. Britain and the United States were not fully aware, partly owing to Soviet secrecy, of what the Nazis had done in Russia; they had suffered much less and their priorities were different. They had learned the dangers of a severely punitive policy after the First World War. They expected that a united Germany, democratic and re-educated, would eventually re-enter the community of nations.[4]

Some Western 'doves' have claimed that Stalin could have been pacified by a massive reconstruction loan.[5] There may well be some truth in this. Others claim that the refusal of the United States to share her nuclear secrets made the Cold War inevitable.[6] The use of the A-bomb against Japan has also been seen, wrongly in this writer's view, as an attempt to blackmail the Soviets.[7] It has also been argued[8] that though Stalin was not necessarily looking for trouble, he naturally took advantage of the situation which presented itself in eastern Europe to strengthen Soviet defences by the creation of buffer states. In addition, economic advantage and belief in the historical inevitability of communism provided every inducement to Stalin to remain in eastern Europe.[9] Finally, the point was sometimes made that although the Soviets kept the West out of the countries they had overrun, so the West denied the USSR any influence in Italy, France, and Japan.

Whatever the influences on him, whatever his motives, Stalin seemed to be pursuing a policy in many respects akin to traditional Russian, Tsarist, foreign policy. The Baltic states, first seized in 1940, were again absorbed into the USSR; Bessarabia was taken from Romania; pressure was exerted on Turkey, in northern Iran, and in Manchuria. The Japanese victory over Tsarist Russia was revenged in a lightning move instigated by the West on the assumption that Soviet forces would be needed to finish off the Japanese. Japan subsequently lost territory to the USSR. In Poland a Moscow-subservient regime was installed, which angered the British. As Averell Harriman has pointed out:[10] Britain had gone to war over Poland, but to Stalin the Polish plains were 'the classic invasion route from the West'.

Nevertheless, in eastern Europe, where the old order had crumbled under the impact of Soviet tanks, an order incidentally which in most cases deserved to crumble, Stalin's policy was initially varied enough to cause doubts to linger on: that all that subsequently did happen need not have done so. In Hungary reasonably free elections were held in 1945 with a genuine coalition, largely non-Communist in character, emerging. Free elections in Czechoslovakia in 1946 indicated that the Communists had more support than any other party, though not a majority. In Bulgaria the path of communism was eased by the traditional pro-Russian feelings of the people and their hatred of the old system. In Romania the Communists, backed by the Red Army rather than the people, held sway from the start behind the façade of the monarchy. The Albanian and Yugoslav Communists, on the other hand, could claim to have brought off their revolutions themselves with just a little help from British arms parachuted to them because they were the most effective anti-Axis forces in their countries. The Finns were forced to pay heavy reparations to the Soviet Union for their part in the war against the USSR, but they were allowed to retain their Western-style democracy. Austria, too, had in effect to pay, but was treated officially as a victim of Nazi aggression. Elections there produced an overwhelmingly non-communist parliament; yet it was 1955 before Austria was freed from Four-Power occupation. In Greece the Communist-dominated partisans had been crushed by the British in 1944. The partisans got more sympathy from *The Times* and British public opinion than they did from Stalin.

Soviet policy, then, varied. Perhaps Stalin and Churchill really did genuinely misunderstand each other on the future of eastern Europe. It will be remembered that in October 1944 Churchill proposed to Stalin that the Soviet Union should have a 90 per cent say in Romania, Britain a 90 per cent influence in Greece; their shares should be 50:50 in Yugoslavia and Hungary, with Russia being pre-eminent in Bulgaria.[11] Later on Stalin decided it was not enough to have governments in his 'sphere of influence' which were merely broadly friendly to the USSR, as Churchill claimed he understood the agreement. The Soviet leader insisted on turning these states into satellites dominated by Moscow in every detail of their internal, as well as their external, policies.

### 1. PEOPLE'S DEMOCRACY

The Communist regimes which arose or were installed in eastern Europe called themselves People's Democracies. In the case of Albania and Yugoslavia, the defeat of the Axis states resulted in the swift destruction of the old regimes and the establishment of Communist rule. The Yugoslav and Albanian Communists came down from the hills with great prestige as patriots. Many people who were not Marxists were sympathetic to them. In both countries the Communists felt strong enough to dispatch the opposition; proclaim – somewhat to Stalin's chagrin – republics with Soviet-type constitutions; and start transforming their economies and societies along Soviet lines.

In the other East European countries there was a three-stage development towards Communist rule.[12] Firstly, there was a period of genuine coalition of Communists and non-Communists, followed by bogus coalitions. The third period was one of artificially monolithic unity.

In the first stage the parties, usually four or five of them – Communist, Socialist, Peasant, Christian, Liberal – were joined together in a People's, National, or Anti-Fascist Front. The parties agreed on practical reform programmes: measures to provide a more even distribution of land; nationalization of key industrial enterprises, especially those belonging to Fascists or pro-Germans; welfare measures; and foreign policies based on friendship with the Soviet Union. In the interest of the reconstruction of their countries they agreed on coalition governments. The Soviet Union could not be criticized, but otherwise discussion of political issues was fairly free. Yet already the Communists had secured for themselves key ministries – police, defence, information, and nationalized industries. They started to infiltrate the other parties and attempted by promises or blackmail to turn non-Communist politicians into their tools. They used the opportunities for patronage in the nationalized industries and in re-allocation of land.

In the second stage non-Communist parties still functioned, but with increasing difficulties. They found it difficult, for instance, to get police permission to hold meetings or protect meetings which were allowed. Their allocation of paper for publicity material was modest compared to that of the Communists. Most of the transport available went to the Communists. By this time independent-minded non-Communist leaders had been forced out of office or arrested on trumped-up charges. The Communists attempted to set up bogus bourgeois parties to weaken their opponents. The socialist parties were forced to merge with the Communists who then had the right to

speak for the whole of the working class. All the 'mass organizations' – trade unions, youth organizations, and women's organizations – were Communist-dominated and were used to bolster the
Communists' positions.

In the period of monolithic unity 'socialist construction' began
in earnest with widespread nationalization, collectivization of the
land, measures to bring the Churches to heel, and an 'intensification of the class struggle' in general. No opposition of any kind
was tolerated. All bodies were subject to 'democratic centralism',
the members formally and infrequently ratified the policies of
their leaders. The real centres of power in the state were the
Politburo of the Communist Party, the Soviet embassy, and
secret police headquarters.

Of course, nowhere did the development run entirely as set out
above. For one thing the three stages were by no means so clear
cut. In Poland, for example, there was no first stage. In the
Soviet Zone of Germany, on the other hand, there was in some
respects a slower development. The basic policy was, however,
the same.[13] By the time the zone was transformed into the
German Democratic Republic in 1949 monolithic unity had been
virtually established behind the façade of a multi-party state with
a liberal constitution. Czechoslovakia seemed, for a time, to be an
exception to the rule. Despite some friction, it appeared that there
at least non-Communists and Communists could work together
on the basis of compromise. This compromise ended in February
1948 when the Communists staged a *coup* based on their control
of the police, the army, and, above all, the workers' militia. A
crisis had broken out in the previous year over Czech participation in the Marshall Plan for European recovery. This American
plan was largely conceived to meet the challenge of communism
by creating a prosperous Europe. The terms were such that it was
not expected that the USSR would participate.[14] The agreement
of the West European states to participate in Marshall Aid, and
the Communist refusal to do so, marked a fresh deterioration in
East–West relations.

In that same year the Soviet blockade of the Western sectors of
Berlin was embarked upon. This was in response to the decision
of the Western powers to introduce their 'reformed' mark,
already in circulation in West Germany, into Berlin. Had the
Soviets not countered this, it would have led to the whole of the
city becoming financially incorporated into West Germany. The

Soviet blockade, designed to force the West out of their part of
Berlin, failed because of the ability of the Anglo-Americans to
supply the Western sectors by air. The Prague *coup* and the
Berlin blockade convinced many people in the Western nations
of the aggressive, expansionist nature of communism, and were
important in preparing opinion for the setting-up of NATO
(1949) and the eventual rearmament of West Germany (1955).

Three other events hastened this reversal of Western policy.
One was Stalin's war of words against Tito of Yugoslavia, which
started in 1948. The other was the Soviet Union's first nuclear
explosion, much earlier than anticipated in the West, in 1949.
The invasion of South Korea by the Communist North in 1950,
an event never fully explained, was the final proof for most in the
West of Stalin's global designs. From the Communist point of
view the Stalin-Tito split was the most significant of these three
events.

## II. THE BREAK WITH TITO

In 1947 the Communist Information Bureau or Cominform was
set up. It comprised only the Communist parties of eastern
Europe, excluding the East German Socialist Unity Party
(SED) and the Albanians, and including the two largest West
European parties, the French and the Italians. Thus, with only
nine member parties the Cominform differed from the earlier
Comintern. In practice its function was to co-ordinate the work
of the East European parties with Moscow, and ensure that the
two major parties in the West were advancing Stalin's cause. The
Cominform was a flop. The only thing for which it is remembered
is its expulsion of the Yugoslav party in June 1948.

The expulsion of Tito's party was a political bombshell at the
time. Of all the Communist leaders Tito stood second only to
Stalin in popularity. His partisans had gained fame for their wartime struggle against the Nazis and could claim to have made
their own revolution. And although the Yugoslavs' image had
been dented by their eagerness to imitate the Russians, Tito's
love of showy uniforms, the imprisonment of Archbishop
Stepinac, and their toughness with Italy over Trieste, they were
still popular even among non-Communists in the West.[15] In the
ranks of international communism they had appeared closest to
Moscow.

The resolution of the Cominform expelling the Yugoslavs claimed that they had 'pursued an incorrect line on the main questions of home and foreign policy, a line which represents a departure from Marxism-Leninism'.[16] It charged the Yugoslavs with spreading slanders about Soviet military experts in Yugoslavia, putting Soviet citizens there under secret police surveillands, and attacking the Soviet Union in Trotskyite terms in the Central Committee of the Yugoslav party. The chief culprits were Tito and his closest associates, Kardelj, Djilas, and Rankovich. The resolution further charged that the Yugoslav leaders did not recognize the sharpening of the class struggle necessary in the transition to socialism, were pursuing an incorrect policy in the countryside, and underestimated the role of the industrial working class and the Communist Party. Finally, the Cominform alleged that Tito and his colleagues had introduced a 'Turkish regime', a system of military despotism exercised by a small power-group from above, into the party.[17] By not heeding the criticisms of the Cominform the Yugoslavs were taking the road of bourgeois nationalism.

To Stalin's surprise the Yugoslavs did not genuflect to Moscow. They did protest their friendship for the USSR and their loyalty to Marxism-Leninism and even their love of Stalin.[18] But they defended themselves. Luckily there were no Soviet troops in the country. Stalin perhaps hoped that there would be a pro-Cominform rising. If so he was to be disappointed. As was only to be expected, there were some Yugoslav Communists who supported Moscow. Andriya Hebrang, Minister of Industry, and Streten Zhuyovich, a Central Committee member, were exposed and jailed after it became known that they were sending secret reports to Moscow. The deputy chief of the air force fled to Romania and made propaganda broadcasts against Tito.[19] But the party as a whole stood behind its leaders and as the split got daily more bitter, the regime increased in stature in the eyes of its people.

Yet the price the Yugoslavs had to pay for their heresy was great. Maybe they were unmoved by the increasingly hysterical flow of abuse which poured forth from the press and radio of the neighbouring capitals. Perhaps they cared little when they were told by Communists in the West, as well as in the East, that the 'Tito clique' were leading them back to capitalism 'in a more and more openly fascist form'.[20] But they had to face economic realities. Their trade which was orientated Eastwards lost its markets overnight. Supplies were cut off without ceremony. Half-completed projects had to be abandoned. Petroleum from Albania and Romania – 80 per cent of the total – dried up. As petroleum supplied 90 per cent of the lighting in the country, many Yugoslavs went without light. Worse still, the air force was virtually grounded. This Soviet-equipped force was in any case increasingly non-operational as it could not get any more spare parts. Even the housing programme was hit. As Yugoslavia was dependent on Cominform countries, mainly Czechoslovakia, for such things as taps, pipes, lavatories, and other sanitary ware, many apartment blocks and other buildings could not be completed. Technical co-operation of all kinds was suspended. Yugoslav students in Cominform countries were forced to give up their studies and return home. The frontiers with the 'fraternal' states were closed, their ambassadors withdrawn. There were constant manoeuvres of Cominform troops near the Yugoslav frontiers[21] and the number of frontier incidents multiplied. All in all, it was a grim and painful lesson in what it means to cross a state like the USSR when you are totally dependent on it. Yet, remarkably, Stalin did not go to the ultimate length to remove the 'Tito clique'. And soon, if he ever had any such ideas, he must have realized he had missed his chance, for help started to arrive from the West.

The Cominform campaign against Titoism was not confined merely to the Yugoslavs. Soon a wave of heresy-hunting spread throughout eastern Europe. The main aim of this seems to have been to remove any Communist who showed the slightest signs of independence of Moscow. This meant in the first instance all those who had formulated the doctrine of separate national roads to socialism. This line had been put out after the war with the express approval of Moscow. Before the war Communists had talked about working for a Soviet Britain, a Soviet Germany, etc. After 1945 they indignantly denied they aimed at any such thing. As the British Communist programme of January 1951, significantly called 'The British Road to Socialism', put it:

The enemies of Communism accuse the Communist Party of aiming to introduce Soviet Power in Britain and abolish Parliament. This is a slanderous misrepresentation of our policy. Experience has shown that in present conditions the advance to Socialism can be made just as well by a different road. For example, through People's Democracy, without establishing Soviet Power, as in the People's Democracies of Eastern Europe.[22]

Obviously Moscow had favoured this formulation in 1945 either because it was uncertain about eastern Europe's future, or as a tactical move to allay the fears of non-Communists. It certainly helped to make the Communists a little more respectable and, though this was not very important, it was good Marxism. After the break with Tito it became opportunist deviation or bourgeois nationalism. In a few Western countries where it was too embarrassing to throw out the national road, it had to be reinterpreted.

In removing 'independent' Communists in eastern Europe Stalin thought it best to blacken them as much as possible so that it would be that much easier to have them liquidated and to justify other extreme measures. For instance, Traicho Kostov, former President of the Bulgarian Council of Ministers and Secretary of the Central Committee of the Bulgarian Communist Party, was charged with having been a Trotskyist in the 1930s, with having betrayed his comrades when interrogated by the police in 1942, and with having 'criminal contact with the British Intelligence Service'. It was further alleged that he and 'his group' were plotting to overthrow the Bulgarian state.[23] The remarkable feature of the Kostov trial of December 1949 was that the chief accused denied in open court the charges of betrayal and treason which he had allegedly confessed to.[24] Otherwise, the Kostov trial, and the others which took place up to 1953, followed the pattern set in the Soviet show trials of the 1930s.

No country was spared its share of 'traitors'. In Hungary László Rajk and other prominent Communists had been charged with treason in September 1949. The Albanians had got in first with their trial in the previous May. The Czechs were more sluggish. It was 1952 before Rudolf Slánský, formerly Secretary of the Czech party and deputy Prime Minister, and others were charged with various capital crimes. Most of the defendants in these trials were later executed. In Poland Party Secretary Władysław Gomułka was only charged as a 'nationalist deviationist', eventually placed under house arrest, but not put on trial.[25] The East German Socialist Unity Party, too, avoided a show trial. Lex Ende, editor-in-chief of *Neues Deutschland*, the East German party paper; Paul Merker, a Politburo member; and some others were arrested, but managed to avoid the fate of Kostov, Rajk, and Slánský. This was also true of Ana Pauker, one of the most widely known women Communists. Some of the other Romanian Communists who fell with her were, however, executed as late as 1954.[26]

The trials were supposed to reveal that Tito's deviations were due not merely to a mistaken policy but were 'the result of a deliberate, counter-revolutionary, anti-Communist plot carried out by a gang of police-informers, *agents provocateurs* and intelligence agents, centred around the leading Titoites'.[27] In fact they revealed that there was no place in Stalin's empire for anyone who did not blindly follow Moscow. One particularly nasty aspect of the purges in Czechoslovakia, Hungary, East Germany, and Romania was the anti-semitic flavour, as many of the victims were of Jewish origin. As for the trials themselves, they had their nightmare world of *1984* flavour. The Czech trial had one touch of Kafka about it when the proceedings had to be interrupted because, due to his loss of weight, one of the defendants' trousers fell down![28] Another tragi-comic aspect of that trial was the accusation against Konni Zilliacus. Zilliacus, a multilingual Labour Member of the British Parliament, was expelled from the Labour Party for his anti-NATO, pro-Moscow views. At the trial he was accused of being a British intelligence officer who sought to corrupt Czech Communists. *His* story had a happy ending: he was later reconciled with the Labour Party and with Moscow.

The trials led the world once again to ask, as in the 1930s, 'Why do they confess?' Arthur Koestler had given a brilliant answer of sorts after the Moscow trials in his *Darkness at Noon*. But more recently we have had the most authentic answers possible from two of the very few survivors. Artur London, a Czech Communist, tells us that in his case old-fashioned methods were used along with persuasion. As with Koestler's hero, he was told that by confessing in court he would be doing a service to party and state. If he did disown his confession in court, his family would suffer.[29] Another Czech victim, Eugene Loebl, narrates how he was defeated by standing hours on end, lack of sleep, hunger, humiliation, drugs, fake executions, and despair: 'What was the point of clinging to ideals when everything had been sullied, become pointless, when such atrocities, such Gestapo methods were possible in a Socialist State?'[30]

Again, as just over a decade before, Western Communists took on the unrewarding task of trying to justify the split and the purges. They rightly argued that ruling-class spies were not unknown in the working-class movement. Spies had been used against the Chartists, against the Bolsheviks, and in America. The British Special Branch and the American FBI were busy against Communists now. They rightly pointed out that Western intelligence agencies were waging a secret war against the Soviet bloc states.[31] They argued that there had been traitors before, like Mussolini, Ramsay MacDonald, and Leon Trotsky. They quoted the admiration expressed for Tito by Western statesmen, forgetting what the same people had said about Stalin during the war. They made much of the precarious state of the Yugoslav economy, neglecting the Cominform's part in this. They gave much currency to stories told by refugees from Yugoslavia, ignoring similar accounts by refugees from the Cominform states. Worst of all, they failed to ask themselves how the People's Democracies could have been established in the first place if they were so riddled with spies.

As the years went by Tito must have got some satisfaction from the fact that roughly half of the twenty Communists who originally attacked him at the Cominform meeting in Romania were either purged as Titoists or removed in post-Stalin purges. By 1971 all of them, except Suslov of the Soviet party, had disappeared from the political scene; Tito remained. As we shall see, two of the three Yugoslavs accused with Tito later broke with their leader.

### III. ECONOMIC DEVELOPMENT AND THE CULT OF PERSONALITY

Any government in eastern Europe after the war would have had problems. Most of the area suffered before the war from traditional poverty, and the war had inflicted severe punishment on all the countries concerned (with the possible exceptions of Bulgaria and Romania). Poland suffered the most, though her acquisition of partly industrial territory from Germany helped her back on to her feet. Bulgaria, Hungary, and Romania (and of course East

Germany) were treated as enemy states and had to pay reparations to the Soviet Union. They also had to help maintain Soviet troops on their soil. Bohemia and East Germany apart, these countries were mainly agrarian and their agriculture suffered as badly as, or more than, the other sectors of their economies. United Nations estimates put losses in Polish agriculture as heaviest (43 per cent of horses, 60 per cent of cattle, 70 per cent of pigs);[32] Yugoslavia and eastern Slovakia were hit almost as hard. Bulgaria, Romania, and East Germany got off fairly lightly. In addition, communications had been badly affected, homes destroyed, markets dislocated. All nations had suffered manpower losses; but in the case of Poland and Yugoslavia these were of staggering proportions.

As explained above, the coalition governments which emerged took over the commanding heights of the economies from the start. Former German property was seized by the Soviet Union, and either shipped off to the USSR or run as Soviet companies on the spot. All the People's Democracies adopted short-term development plans to rehabilitate their economies. These plans were ambitious, demanding high investment in basic industries to the neglect of the consumer and agriculture. As in the Soviet Union, the emphasis was on the quantity of production rather than its quality. Nevertheless, as Seton-Watson tells us, 'immense material progress was made'.[33]

By the early 1950s all the Soviet satellite states had embarked on longer-term plans similar to those of the USSR and with the same priorities – defence and basic industries. Well-developed traditional industries which were no longer rated very highly were neglected. This was especially true of East Germany and Czechoslovakia, but also of Hungary and Romania. In the German Democratic Republic, for example, the textile and leather industries were starved of investments. On the other hand, costly steel-mills were erected, a shipbuilding capacity was created, the port of Rostock was greatly expanded, and the chemical, machinery, and electro-technical industries were developed.[34] In Czechoslovakia, the consumer goods sector, so important before the war, was restricted to the advantage of mining and heavy engineering. Slovakia was industrialized at great cost.

The proclaimed aims of economic policy in the People's Democracies were sensible enough – to overcome inherited economic backwardness by industrialization, thus raising living

standards; ending dependence on foreign suppliers; and improving the defence capacities of the nations concerned. But there was
little co-ordination between states as one would have expected
under socialist planning even though the Council for Mutual
Economic Assistance was set up in 1949. There was little attempt
made to analyse which countries were best suited for particular
industries. And though it must be admitted that planning was a
new and difficult technique, little chance of experimentation was
given to the able economists who were enthusiastic members of
the Czech, East German, Hungarian, and Polish parties. They
were shackled by party dogmas, by agreements which put supposed Soviet interests above those of their own countries, and
were even hindered by the dwindling amount of genuine statistics.
As in the Soviet Union, the dogma of collectivization of agriculture was pushed through and with the same difficulties and
consequences. The new collectives lacked trained managers and
technicians. They could not placate the peasants by dazzling
before them consumer goods and a high degree of mechanization;
and many peasants, even after they had decided to make their
peace with the new regime, found it difficult to adjust to the new
ways.

In the absence of hard and reliable statistics it is impossible to
say just how much progress was made in these years, but one can
say that there was a rapid development of industry.

This rapid development was paid for by holding back living
standards and the regimentation of labour. The trade unions
became part and parcel of the state system, and strikes, or even
free discussion, became impossible. Wherever possible, payment
by results was introduced together with direction of labour and
severe penalties for breaches of labour discipline. Forced labour
was one such penalty which was widely applied. In Romania, for
instance, on the Danube–Black Sea Canal project, the camps of
Galati, Craiova, Vlahita, and Ialimota, and the sites of the hydro-
electric installations at Stejar-Bicaz, became notorious for the
way in which forced labour was extracted.[35]

The 'monolithic unity' covered not only political and economic
life, but intellectual life as well. Admittedly, in all the People's
Democracies there was a great expansion of all forms of education
(in most cases hitherto neglected) with special emphasis given to
technical education. And attempts were made to give greater
opportunities to the children of workers and peasants. But even

here a price had to be paid. Stalinist indoctrination was introduced into the system from the kindergarten to the university. Marxism-Leninism and Russian were made compulsory subjects and military sports were encouraged. Membership of the official youth organization was essential for those hoping to go on beyond the basic education.

The position of the intellectuals was a sorry one. True, those intellectuals who were prepared to justify the regimes' policies were granted privileges of all kinds from priority in housing and holiday accommodation, to monetary rewards and honours, scarce consumer goods and trips abroad. Those who would not conform or who wished to remain 'non-political' were simply denied all means of communication with their public, if they were lucky, and were jailed if they were not so lucky. In the main, during these years the regimes had to rely on a few Communist parade horses of pre-war vintage such as Bertolt Brecht and Arnold Zweig in East Germany, and György Lukács and Gyula Hay in Hungary. Even these intellectuals had their difficulties (Brecht took out Austrian citizenship as a precaution) and produced little of interest. All art and letters had to advertise, popularize, and promote 'Socialist construction'. Books, plays, painting, films, even music had to conform to the norms of Socialist Realism as taught in Moscow. It could rightly be said that it was neither socialist nor realist. Luckily, Marx, Engels, and Lenin had extolled the virtues of many eighteenth- and nineteenth-century writers whose work was therefore above suspicion and could be enjoyed by an even wider public than before.[36]

Despite their seemingly omnipotent position the Communist parties of East Europe could not control every organization in their respective countries. They failed to bring the Churches completely to heel. The situation differed somewhat from country to country. On the one hand, in Romania the Communist Party got its man elected as Patriarch of the important Orthodox Church in 1948.[37] In Bulgaria,[38] too, some sort of arrangement was arrived at between Orthodox Church and the state. On the other hand, throughout the bloc the Communists found they could not break the independence of the Roman Catholic Church. In Poland, Hungary, and to a lesser extent in Czechoslovakia, that Church was very influential indeed because of the loyalty to it of millions of ordinary people. Before the war it had been very wealthy too. It had not always used its influence

and wealth for good purposes. To say the least, the princes of the
Catholic Church had not done all they could to encourage the
spirit of tolerance, progress, and democracy in their lands. Yet
they fulfilled the spiritual needs of very many of their countrymen. In Poland it was even said, 'Pole equals Catholic'. The
Communists seemed at first to recognize this. Yet later, as the
People's Democracies were sovietized, the Churches were
assaulted. In Poland Cardinal Wyszyński was interned in a
monastery, in Hungary Cardinal Mindszenty was subjected to a
show trial and jailed, and in Czechoslovakia Archbishop Beran
was forced out of office. If anything, such tactics strengthened
Catholicism.

In the Soviet bloc states between 1948 and 1953 the old
religions were under attack as reactionary, feudalist, Fascist, and
obscurantist. Doubtless there would have been friction between
any left-wing government and such privileged and conservative
institutions, especially in Slovakia, Hungary, and Yugoslavia.
But the main reason for the severity of the anti-Church measures
was not the past mistakes or privileges of the Churches; rather it
was that they represented an obstacle to the new secular religion
of Stalinism, what the Communists later described as the 'cult of
personality'. Stalin was everywhere. His portrait, suitably
touched up, was found in every public building. Statues of him
were being erected in all the capital cities from the relatively
modest one in East Berlin to the giant-sized one in Budapest.
Streets, factories, settlements, and towns were named after him.
The main reading in Marxist-Leninist classes were Stalin's
*Problems of Leninism* and the notorious *Short History of the
CPSU (B)* inspired by him.

IV. 'ECONOMIC PROBLEMS OF SOCIALISM IN THE USSR'

As they watched the firework displays in Moscow to mark the
victory over Germany the Soviet people must have wondered
what the peace would bring. Surely, they concluded, things could
only get better? Having survived the war, they could survive anything. Having beaten the German *Herrenvolk*, they could *do*
anything. They needed such feelings in view of the task which
faced them. As Edward Crankshaw, who served in Russia during
the war, has reminded us, the retreating Germans had so

scorched the Russian earth that hardly a house, a barn, a plough, a telegraph pole remained. Nobody who did not live through that first terrible starvation winter [of peace] with the Russians can have the least conception of the suffering of the people and the total ruin of the Soviet economy. . . . These things are too easily forgotten over here, if only because they were never properly understood.[39]

Manpower losses were between 20 and 30 million[40] – that is, more than the United States, Britain, France, and Germany together had lost in *both* World Wars! Production was well below the pre-war level. In 1940 the USSR produced 18.3 million tons of steel, in 1945 11.2 million. Coal extraction, which had reached 166 million tons in 1940, was down to 149.3 million tons. Oil output had dropped from 31 million tons to 19.4 million.[41] And there was little else. For many years to come such basic things as razor blades, safety pins, buttons, and pots and pans were luxuries. And there was bitter truth in the joke that even if there was no news in the party organ *Pravda*, it was still good value for money as it could be used for wrapping or in the toilet.

To such a situation Stalin's answer was a policy of 'blood, sweat, and tears' to make good the war losses and secure the country's defences. There was the struggle to develop nuclear weapons, rockets, radar, and modern jet warplanes. By concentrating the bulk of resources on such projects and with the help of spies – Klaus Fuchs, Bruno Pontecorvo, Harry Gold, and others – and German experts, success was achieved.[42] In 1952, 34 million tons of steel were produced, 300 million tons of coal, and 119 million tons of oil. The Soviet Union possessed nuclear and other modern weapons. The cost of all this was greater privation for the people and their isolation from the outside world, and mental slavery for the intelligentsia. In 1952 the standard of living remained very low, perhaps lower than in 1928. Agriculture, so important for the Soviet standard of living, lagged badly. In 1953 cattle stocks were below the 1913 level.[43]

The pressure on the intellectuals was associated with the name of Politburo member Andrei A. Zhdanov (1896–1948) who was given the task of rooting out foreign influences in the arts and re-establishing complete party authority in this sphere. (This had lessened slightly during the war.) His commission embraced everything from architecture and literature to philosophy and music.

In the case of architecture, Western styles were subjected to constant attacks for their alleged rejection of the 'heritage of the past'. Buildings were supposed to demonstrate the grandeur, permanence, and might of the Soviet system. Structures resembling medieval fortresses, Florentine palaces, or Byzantine churches were erected throughout Stalin's empire. Among these were the apartment blocks and shops in East Berlin's Stalinallee (now Karl-Marx-Allee), the Palace of Culture in Warsaw, the arches spanning the Volga-Don Canal, and Moscow University.[44]

Zhdanov became most notorious for his criticisms of Soviet composers who, he felt, were not 'Russian' enough. Typical of his ideas were his remarks that

> Internationalism arises from the very flowering of national art. To forget this truth is to lose sight of the guiding line, to lose one's own face, to become a homeless cosmopolitan. Only the nation which has its own highly developed musical culture can appreciate the music of other peoples.[45]

Part of the campaign against 'homeless cosmopolitans' was directed against those Jews who did not cast off their 'Jewishness'.

Traditionally the socialist and Communist movements had attracted many Jews: Lassalle, Bernstein, Luxemburg, and of course Marx, among them in Germany; Trotsky, Kamenev, Radek, and Zinoviev, among the Bolshevik leaders. The Marxists had always rejected Jewish nationalism, Zionism, as a solution to the problem of anti-semitism. Lenin had fallen out with the leaders of the Jewish labour *Bund* on this issue. After the revolution, policy had fluctuated. Jewish religious bodies had suffered along with others, but Jews were no longer subject to official discrimination. For some years there had been an 'Autonomous Jewish Region' near the Manchurian frontier. Jewish theatres, periodicals, and publishing houses were permitted. During the war the 'socialist solution' to the Jewish question was given much greater emphasis in Soviet propaganda abroad in order to win more sympathy for the USSR. In 1948 Stalin supported the establishment of the state of Israel and weapons from Communist states were supplied to Jewish military formations in Palestine. But Moscow's line soon changed as Israel and the United States developed close ties. In the Soviet Union itself many Jews were attracted to Israel and this frightened Stalin who started to doubt their loyalty and regarded them as a potential fifth column. From his daughter we know that he harboured a dislike for Jews. In the last years of his reign Stalin unleashed a purge of the Jewish intelligentsia, many of whom perished. Nevertheless, prominent 'non-Jewish' Jews such as the writer Ilya Ehrenburg and Politburo member Kaganovich remained. The culmination of Stalin's campaign against 'rootless cosmopolitans' was the announcement of the so-called 'doctors' plot' a few months before his death. Seven of the nine accused were Jews. It was claimed that these prominent doctors were trying to eliminate Soviet leaders on the instructions of the Americans. After Stalin's death the accusations were dropped.[46]

Space does not permit a full discussion of the CPSU after 1945. Suffice it to say it was in a state of atrophy. Its constitution was even less regarded than before the war. The Eighteenth Congress had been held in 1939. The Nineteenth followed only in 1952! Like the earlier congress, the Nineteenth was largely a ceremonial affair. It is mainly remembered for Stalin's prognostications about the future, the emergence of G. M. Malenkov as the dictator's heir apparent, and the minor changes introduced in the party constitution. The Politburo was abolished and replaced by a larger Praesidium, which included understudies for the 'old guard' who, as witnesses to Stalin's crimes, were likely to have been purged had the Generalissimo lived much longer.[47] The congress also agreed to drop the term 'Bolshevik' from the party title.

Stalin's thoughts on the future, contained in his *Economic Problems of Socialism in the USSR* published on the eve of the congress, offered hope to the Soviet workers of better times to come. In it Stalin, who was ostensibly replying to an earlier discussion of Soviet economists, dealt with the transition from socialism to communism. In order for the USSR to 'pave the way' for a real transition to communism 'at least three main preliminary conditions have to be satisfied'. Firstly, 'a continuous expansion of all social production with a relatively higher rate of expansion of the means of production'. Secondly, 'to raise collective-farm property to the level of public property'. Thirdly, 'to ensure such a cultural advancement of society as will secure for all members of society the all-round development of their physical and mental abilities'.[48] To bring about this cultural advance it was necessary to 'shorten the working day at least to six, and subsequently to five hours', to give everyone 'the necessary free time to receive an all-round education'. Polytechnical education was also needed 'in order that the members of society might be able freely to choose their occupations and not be tied to some one occupation all their lives'. Likewise, 'housing conditions should be radically improved and . . . real wages of workers and employees should be at least doubled, if not more'.[49] Many of the peasants on the collective farms must have been worried by Stalin's references to them. If collective-farm property was to be raised to the level of public property, their private plots would go. And from their experience to date, they could be forgiven for concluding that the introduction of a 'products-exchange' system, under which the farms would barter their produce at government agencies, would only make their conditions of life harder still.

Stalin indicated in his pamphlet that his aim was still that of the founding fathers, Marx and Engels:

> Only after *all* these preliminary conditions have been satisfied in their entirety will it be possible to pass from the socialist formula, 'from each according to his ability, to each according to his work', to the communist formula, 'from each according to his ability, to each according to his needs'.[50]

In his analysis of the international situation, too, Stalin gave the Soviet people some comfort. He saw Germany and Japan 'languishing in misery under the jackboot of American imperialism'. It was like believing in miracles not to believe that these nations would try to alter this situation. He therefore concluded that 'the inevitability of wars between capitalist countries remains in force'.[51] Once again, as after the First World War, the struggle for markets meant that in practice the contradictions between capitalist states were stronger than the theoretically greater contradictions between the capitalist and socialist camps. But, it still remained true that to 'eliminate the inevitability of war, it is necessary to abolish imperialism'.[52]

The more thoughtful Soviet citizens no doubt had their reservations about this analysis, for the West stood united in NATO and the Korean War, which was still dragging on, carried with it the danger of a Soviet-American nuclear confrontation. On the other hand, the USSR now had a formal alliance with her new, mighty, and respected (outside the USSR) eastern neighbour, the People's Republic of China.

## V. MAO'S VICTORIES

China emerged from the war strengthened rather than weakened. The important industrial area of Manchuria and the industrialized island of Formosa were returned to China, most of the extra-territorial rights of the powers were ended, the Chinese Nationalist armies were American-trained and equipped. Diplomatically, China had Great Power status, having been awarded a permanent seat on the Security Council of the United Nations; she had treaties of friendship with the United States and the Soviet Union. Under China's treaty with Moscow the USSR recognized the Chiang Kai-shek regime as the legitimate government of China. In exchange the Chinese recognized the independence of the Mongolian People's Republic, agreed to joint Sino-Soviet operation of the Chinese Eastern and South Manchurian railways, and guaranteed the USSR's use of Port Arthur and Dairen.

The Americans were even more friendly to the Nationalists than were the Soviets. They supported them in all their negotiations with the Communist Chinese. They ensured that all aid to China went to the Nationalists, even though the latter did little fighting against the Japanese.[53] When Japan surrendered on 15 August 1945 the Americans air-lifted Nationalist troops to the cities of north China to forestall Communist takeovers. In some cases American troops were sent in. The Americans could, of course, claim that they were only aiding the internationally-recognized government of China. But American actions made the Communists more suspicious of the United States and perhaps made civil war more likely by increasing Chiang's appetite.[54]

With all their advantages the Nationalists failed. They alienated many of the liberal middle classes by their corruption, incompetence, and intolerance.[55] And the Nationalist armies often behaved as conquerors rather than liberators – looting and raping as they went. If not put off the Nationalists by any of these things, the middle classes suffered from the chronic inflation which hit post-war China.

At the time of their Seventh Congress in Yenan in April 1945 the Communists felt more confident than before. From control of about 35,000 square miles with a population of about 1,500,000 at the beginning of 1937, the Communists had expanded their control to about 225,000 square miles with a population of some 85 million.[56]

The re-entry of Nationalist troops into north China led to renewed fighting between them and the Communists. It looked as though China was in for another long period of civil war. However, despite their superiority in numbers and weapons, the Nationalists soon revealed that they were no match for the Communists, who had control of the countryside and were able to isolate their enemy in a few urban centres. In pitched battles in 1948–49 the Nationalists were badly led and their morale was low. Thousands of them defected.[57] By the time the Communists crossed the Yangtze in April 1949, the Nationalists were effectively defeated. When the People's Republic was established in the following October, only Hainan, Tibet, and Taiwan (Formosa) remained to be taken.

What were relations between Moscow and the new regime going to be like? the world asked. Communists took it for granted that Mao's China was simply one more mighty addition to the 'socialist camp'. Yet there were already reasons for suspicion and discord between the two states. The Chinese could feel resentful about failures through following Moscow's advice in the 1920s. Perhaps they resented aid to the Nationalists from Moscow in the 1930s. And Stalin admitted to Yugoslav leaders that he had wrongly advised Mao to come to terms with Chiang in 1945.[58] Soviet dismantling of Manchurian industry and penetration of that area did not endear the Soviets to the Chinese Communists or Nationalists. At that time too, the Russians had, like the Americans, helped the Nationalists to take over the urban centres of the north. Finally, Stalin must have feared that, on a purely personal level, he had in Mao a rival for canonization in the Communist church. After all, in 1946 Mao's deputy, Liu Shao-ch'i, in a much-quoted interview with Anna Louise Strong, the American writer, claimed that Mao had developed Marxist thought to fit Asian conditions. 'He uses Marxist-Leninist principles to explain Chinese history and the practical problems of China. He is the first that has succeeded in doing so. . . . There are similar conditions in other lands of southeast Asia. The courses chosen by China will influence them all'.[59] In other words, Mao's works belonged to the classics of Marxism. The Soviets never accepted this.

Despite the past, relations between Moscow and Peking were amicable from 1949 until after Stalin's death. Possibly both sides felt they needed each other as security to enable them to concentrate on their internal problems. Possibly knowing little of the Soviet Union, but warming to the Russians as fellow-Marxists and representatives of a nation which had also suffered at the hands of foreigners, Mao resolved to turn a marriage of convenience into a marrage of love. In July 1949 warmly and at length he praised the Soviet Union:

> The Chinese were introduced to Marxism by the Russians. Before the October Revolution, the Chinese were not only unaware of Lenin and Stalin but did not even know of Marx and Engels. The salvoes of the October Revolution helped the advanced people of China and of the whole world to adopt a proletarian world outlook as an instrument for looking into a nation's future or for reconsidering one's own problems. Follow the path of the Russians – this was the conclusion.[60]

And again:

> Internationally we belong to the side of the anti-imperialist front, headed by the Soviet Union. We can only turn to this side for genuine and friendly assistance, not to the side of the imperialist front. . . .
>
> The Communist Party of the USSR is our very best teacher, and we must learn from it.[61]

On 16 December 1949 Mao Tse-tung arrived in Moscow. Remarkably, he stayed until 17 February 1950. Perhaps he discussed with Stalin the coming North Korean invasion of the South. This we do not know. We do know that the results of the visit were three separate agreements. The first was a Treaty of Friendship, Alliance, and Mutual Assistance between the two states. Aimed ostensibly against Japan, it really sought to protect the two against the United States. The second virtually confirmed the Soviet position in Manchuria as set out in 1945. Soviet credits were the subject of the third agreement. The People's Republic was to receive, over a five-year period, credits worth US $300 million. The treaty of 1945 was declared void, but the independence of Mongolia was reaffirmed. Later in the year a Soviet military mission was established in Peking and Sino-Soviet joint-stock companies were set up.[62]

After Stalin's death the Soviet leaders made greater efforts to woo the Chinese. In January 1953 the People's Republic's first Five-Year Plan was announced; in September, that is after

Stalin's death, it was made known that there would be Soviet aid for it. Up until the spring of 1956 the Soviet Union pledged support for a total of 211 industrial projects.[63] Though it had to be paid for, Soviet aid was important as China was under economic blockade imposed by America through the United Nations. This was the result of Chinese participation in the Korean conflict on the side of the North Koreans. In 1954 Khrushchev and Bulganin visited Peking and offered lavish praise and practical aid to China. They relinquished Soviet privileges in Manchuria and sold the Chinese their share in joint companies.

Up until the Twentieth Congress of the CPSU the relations between Moscow and Peking were good. Only when the Soviet leaders started to reassess the role of their state, its priorities and objects, did the Sino-Soviet alliance crack.

## VI. COMMUNISM IN WESTERN EUROPE

With the exception of Germany the Communists of western Europe had greatly benefited from the war. They were associated in the public mind with the victorious Red Army, and had played leading roles in the resistance movements. Moreover, their opponents were often associated with pre-war appeasement, or wartime collaboration. Those who were not, like the new Christian Democrats, were badly organized. Everywhere, therefore, the Communists went forth into the post-war era as patriots, as well as apostles of a better life.

In France the Communist vote increased from 12.6 per cent of the registered voters in 1936 to 20.3 per cent in 1945, and 22.2 per cent in November 1946. They thus replaced the Socialists as the main party of the Left. In Italy the same thing happened. In June 1946 the Socialists and Communists in alliance polled nearly 40 per cent of the vote, the Socialists getting rather more than the Communists. But in 1947 a minority of the Socialist Party broke away in protest against the alliance with the PCI. Italian Communist strength went on growing. Despite Pope Pius XII's threat to excommunicate Catholics who voted Communist, the party managed to win 22.6 per cent of the votes in 1953. Only the Christian Democrats were stronger. In Belgium the Communists won 14 per cent of the poll in 1946, and they got decent polls in Denmark, Sweden, and, more remarkably in view of the war, in Finland. In France and Italy and most other countries of western Europe the Communists entered coalition governments, usually with the Socialists and Christians.

In Britain too there was more sympathy for communism than before. But the two-party system and the great flexibility of the Labour Party in catering for socialists of many different shades, the popularity of the Labour leaders, and their radical yet civilized appeal, made the Communists seem irrelevant. In the election of 1945 which produced a Labour landslide they doubled their parliamentary representation, from one to two members in a Parliament of over 600!

At this time the Communists were not presenting the electorates with very radical programmes. In some cases they were less radical than their socialist rivals. Some comrades in Italy were surprised to see, for instance, that the Communist Party favoured the adoption, in the new Italian constitution, of the privileges accorded to the Catholic Church by the Lateran Pacts, concluded between Mussolini and the Vatican in 1929.

All this changed in 1947. In line with a hardening of Soviet attitudes, the Communists took a tougher line. They went, or were thrust, into opposition. In France and Italy, where the Communists controlled the main trade unions, violent strikes were launched. The countries of western Europe were faced with the problems of reconstruction, as well as the backlog of social problems from the 1930s, and, in most cases, with decolonization. There was much explosive stuff here to exploit. In some cases the fear of communism was used once again, as before the war, by the propertied classes to block reform. Italy in particular lagged behind in social and educational progress.

As well as the basic bread-and-butter issues, the main campaigns of the Communists were against Marshall Aid, against 'U.S. nuclear blackmail', and later, against alleged American germ warfare in Korea and German rearmament. Peace campaigns, suitably window-dressed, were a prominent feature of Communist activities. Young people were a special target with massive subsidized Youth Festivals in various Communist capitals. Western reactions, often over-reactions, such as indulgence shown to Fascists in the Italian paramilitary police forces, attempts to prevent young people going to Youth Festivals, etc., seemed to confirm Communist beliefs.

The biggest crisis the Communists had to face up to the death of Stalin was the expulsion of Tito. Leading 'traitors' were exposed and expelled – André Marty and Charles Tillon in France, Axel Larsen, the Danish party leader, being among the most prominent. On the whole, however, the Communists clung to the belief, here expressed by the British Communist, the late William Gallacher:

> Whoever is a Socialist is for the Soviet Union – not because the people of the Soviet Union are Russian, but because they are the first workers to break and throw off the shackles of capitalism. Whoever is against the Soviet Union, whether it be Churchill, Bevin, Tito or Zilliacus, is not a Socialist. Tito has repudiated Lenin and is now, like the traitors here, selling his country for dollars.[64]

Isolated by their subservience to Moscow's whims, the parties began to decay. Only the Italian party, which always tempered the Soviet line to suit local conditions, went on improving its position.

### VII. COMMUNISM IN THE UNITED STATES

Like the other fraternal parties, the United States Communist Party improved its standing during the war. At its peak, membership reached between 70,000 and 80,000 in 1944–45. A significant proportion of the membership was Jewish.[65] Negroes and immigrants were other significant groups. Geographically much of the membership was concentrated in New York and Los Angeles. Relatively few members belonged to the industrial proletariat. Nevertheless, good candidates, hard work, the favourable political climate, and the apathy of the non-Communists, helped the Communists to penetrate the leadership of a considerable number of CIO unions.[66]

The leader of the party at this time was a Kansas teacher's son, Earl Russell Browder (b. 1891). The end of the war meant the end of the road for him as party leader. Under his leadership, in 1944, the Communists dissolved their party which became the 'educational' American Communist Political Association. In April 1945 he was denounced by Jacques Duclos, the French Communist leader, for his 'notorious revision of Marxism'. It is assumed that this was done with Moscow's approval. Shortly afterwards Browder was ousted from the leadership and then expelled from the party.

Browder's successor was William Z. Foster. Born in 1881 in Taunton, Massachusetts, of Anglo-Irish immigrant parents, Foster had little schooling, a variety of jobs, and a variety of left-wing affiliations before joining the Communists in 1921. In 1928 and 1932 he was Communist candidate for the Presidency. He was a tough, ruthless, operator in the 1920s and 1930s and was angered when his former ally in party faction disputes, Browder, was promoted by Stalin to be General Secretary. He was never very happy with the wartime, 'soft' line of playing down the class war for the war against Hitler. Both for political and personal reasons, therefore, he was ready to strike at Browder.

With Foster at its head the American party adopted an increasingly hard line, a line which mirrored Moscow's hardening attitude. At the same time, influenced by Communist tactics in eastern Europe, it attempted to gain more influence by seeking to set up a third party to challenge the traditional Democratic and Republican parties. Its unlucky and unwitting ally in this was former Vice-President, for nearly a decade a cabinet member, Henry Wallace. Wallace had been forced out of office for opposing Truman's foreign policy. He fought the 1948 Presidential election on the peace issue as candidate of the Communist-backed Progressive Party. He was heavily defeated. By that time the Communist Party was on the road to virtual oblivion. Membership was down to 60,000, falling to 54,000 in 1950 and a mere 25,000 in 1953. Its influence in the unions was being eliminated. The Communists were suffering from defections brought on by Stalin's policies, their own purges, and, not least, the harassment, between February 1950 and December 1954, associated with the McCarthy era.

Senator Joseph McCarthy sought to advance his own political career by spectacular exposures of real, and alleged, Communists and former Communists, in high places. His charges were taken seriously because of the international climate, and because of one or two serious espionage cases involving nuclear secrets or State Department documents. It was in February 1950, for instance, that German Communist atom spy Klaus Fuchs confessed in London to having given A-Bomb information to the Soviets. Fuchs had worked on the original nuclear bomb project in the United States. His evidence later led to the American Jewish couple Ethel and Julius Rosenberg, who were convicted and executed for spying in 1953.

During this period the American Communists were fighting for mere survival. Their Politburo members were convicted of sedition and by the end of 1954, ninety-two Communist leaders had been indicted and tried under the Smith Act of 1940.[67] Most suffered imprisonment. Communists were barred from many areas of national life. The fear of communism reached such a pitch that, for example, in Indiana professional boxers had to take a non-Communist loyalty oath before they could work.[68]

The Twentieth Congress of the CPSU and the Hungarian Revolution of 1956 revealed to many comrades that their near martyrdom had been for nothing. Despite some relaxation in the American attitude to communism, a further period of decline set in. Today an insignificant sect, the American party still clings to its Soviet patriotism. The party faithful visit the USSR and are most impressed by 'such zest, such enthusiasm, such a sense of purpose' of the Soviet people. They sound glad to admit how Soviet students 'put us to shame in discussing world events and a wide range of other subjects'.[69] As for Maoism: 'Never before has adventurism camouflaged with revolutionary talk presented such a danger as today'.[70] No wonder that most young American radicals look elsewhere for leadership.

## NOTES

[1] Bruce Page, David Leitch, and Phillip Knightley, *Philby: the Spy who Betrayed a Generation* (London, 1969), p. 171.

[2] See K. Ingram, *History of the Cold War* (London, 1955), p.15.

[3] *Manchester Guardian* (24 Nov. 1954).

[4] Wilfrid Knapp, 'The Partition of Europe', *The Cold War: a Reappraisal*, edited by Evan Luard (London, 1964), p. 47.

[5] This was the *New Statesman and Nation*'s editor Kingsley Martin's opinion. See *International Journal* (Toronto), autumn 1951, p. 284. Also M. F. Hertz, *Beginnings of the Cold War* (Bloomington, 1966), p. 253; and W. Knapp, *A History of War and Peace 1939–1965* (RIIA/Oxford, 1967), p. 112.

[6] Professor H. J. Laski held this view. See D. N. Pritt, *The Labour Government, 1945–51* (London, 1963), p. 71.

[7] See M. Armine, *The Great Decision* (London, 1960), p. 232 – for Professor Blackett, British scientist and government adviser.

[8] D. F. Flemming, *Cold War and its Origins* (London, 1960).

[9] Knapp, *A History*, p. 97.

[10] *The Times* (15 March 1971).

[11] Winston Churchill, *The Second World War*. VI: *Triumph and Tragedy* (London, 1954), p. 227.

[12] This section is based on Hugh Seton-Watson, *The East European Revolution* (London, 1956). For the fate of Socialists in East Europe, see Denis Healey

(ed.), *The Curtain Falls: the Story of the Socialists in Eastern Europe* (London, 1951).

[13] For the Soviet Zone's development, see Wolfgang Leonhard, *Die Revolution Entlässt Ihre Kinder* (Cologne, 1955).

[14] Knapp, *A History*, pp. 112–13.

[15] For a summary of Yugoslav policy at this time see G. W. Hoffman and Fred Warner Neal, *Yugoslavia and the New Communism* (New York, 1962), chapter 6.

[16] James Klugmann, *From Trotsky to Tito* (London, 1951), p. 8.

[17] ibid., p. 10. This notorious book was typical of Communist attacks on their erstwhile comrades.

[18] Jan Yindrich, *Tito v. Stalin* (London, 1950), p. 121.

[19] ibid., p. 75.

[20] Klugmann, *From Trotsky . . .*, p. 189.

[21] Phyllis Auty, 'Yugoslavia's International Relations', in *Contemporary Yugoslavia*, edited by W. Sayne Vucinich (Berkeley, 1969), p. 169, doubts Stalin ever intended attacking Yugoslavia.

[22] *The British Road to Socialism* (Communist Party, London, 1951), p. 14.

[23] *The Trial of Traicho Kostov and his Group* (English version, Sofia, 1949).

[24] ibid., p. 68.

[25] M. K. Dziewanowski, *The Communist Party of Poland* (Cambridge, Mass., 1959), pp. 208–12.

[26] Seton-Watson, *East European Revolution*, p. 375.

[27] Klugmann, *From Trotsky . . .*, p. 32.

[28] Eugene Loebl, *Sentenced and Tried* (London, 1969).

[29] Artur London, *On Trial* (London, 1970). For a British view of a Communist prison at this time, see Edith Bone, *Seven Years Solitary* (London, 1957).

[30] Loebl, op. cit., p. 17.

[31] They did not know that the East German deputy premier, Professor Hermann Kastner, actually was an American agent (*Der Spiegel*, 19 April 1971).

[32] Seton-Watson, *East European Revolution*, p. 232.

[33] ibid., p. 246.

[34] Heinz Kohler, *Economic Integration in the Soviet Bloc with an East German Case Study* (New York, 1965), p. 42.

[35] Ghita Ionescu, *Communism in Rumania* (London, 1964), p. 199. For forced labour in general in the Soviet bloc see *Report of the Ad Hoc Committee on Forced Labour* (UN/ILO, Geneva, 1953).

[36] For a study of the Polish intellectuals at this time, see Czesław Miłosz, *The Captive Mind* (New York, 1953).

[37] Ionescu, op. cit., p. 180.

[38] For the situation in Bulgaria see J. F. Brown, *Bulgaria under Communist Rule* (New York and London, 1970).

[39] Crankshaw, op. cit., p. 14.

[40] Crankshaw, ibid., p. 15, says 30 million.

[41] ibid., p. 26.

[42] By mentioning spies and foreign experts the writer is not trying to diminish the very real achievements of Soviet scientists. On the value of Soviet espionage in the atom bomb, see David J. Dallin, *Soviet Espionage* (London, 1955), p. 473.

[43] Deutscher, *Stalin*, p. 586.

[44] See Paul Willen, 'New Era in Soviet Architecture?' in *Problems of Communism* (USIA), July–August 1956, for some interesting comments.

[45] A. A. Zhdanov, *Essays on Literature, Philosophy and Music* (New York, 1950), p. 92. S. Finkelstein, *How Music Expresses Ideas* (London, 1952) gives a pro-

Zhdanov view. See also A. Werth, *Musical Uproar in Moscow* (London, 1949).

[46] Schapiro, op. cit., p. 548.

[47] Deutscher, op. cit., pp. 602–3.

[48] J. Stalin, *Economic Problems of Socialism in the USSR* (English version, Moscow, 1952), pp. 74–6.

[49] ibid., p. 77.

[50] ibid.

[51] ibid., pp. 38–40.

[52] ibid., p. 41.

[53] Robert C. North, *Moscow and Chinese Communists* (Stanford, 1963), p. 205.

[54] Fitzgerald, op. cit., pp. 91–2.

[55] George Moseley, *China since 1911* (New York, 1968), English edition: *China – from Empire to People's Republic* (London, 1968), pp. 91–3.

[56] North, op. cit., p. 206.

[57] John Gittings, *The Role of the Chinese Army* (London, 1967).

[58] V. Dedijer, *Tito Speaks* (New York, 1953), p. 322. When the author met Dedijer in 1962 he certainly believed Stalin was telling the truth.

[59] Donald S. Zagoria, *The Sino-Soviet Conflict 1956–61* (Princeton, 1962), pp. 14–15.

[60] Mao Tse-tung, *On People's Democratic Dictatorship* (English version, Peking, 1950), pp. 7–8.

[61] ibid., pp. 15, 25.

[62] Franz Schurmann and Orville Schell, *China Readings*, 3: *Communist China* (London, 1968), pp. 255–8.

[63] Moseley, op. cit., p. 107.

[64] William Gallacher, *Rise Like Lions* (London, 1951), p. 161. Zilliacus supported Tito.

[65] David A. Shannon, *The Decline of American Communism* (London, 1959), p. 96.

[66] The CIO was one of the two main trade union organizations. It later merged with the AF of L.

[67] Shannon, op. cit., p. 189.

[68] ibid., p. 190. For another account of American communism at this period, see Irving Howe and Lewis Coser, *The American Communist Party* (New York, 1958).

[69] Gertrude and Robert Decker, 'We visited the Soviet Union', *Daily World* (New York), 4 Sept. 1971.

[70] *Daily World*, 4 Sept. 1971, p. 7, under *quote unquote*.

# VIII

## The Twentieth Congress and the New Revisionism

ON the morning of 6 March 1953 the death of Stalin was announced in Moscow. As he died of a brain haemorrhage his closest colleagues watched him with a mixture of 'sorrow and relief'.[1] Many of them shed genuine tears. In Moscow many ordinary people, too, had tears in their eyes. The world wondered what would happen next. Would there be a renewed struggle for power similar to Stalin's own? The Soviet leaders stressed their unity. Yet of the eight men who stood by the coffin at Stalin's funeral only two, Voroshilov and Mikoyan, retired voluntarily. Remarkably, however, only one died a violent death.

The top leaders immediately carried through a reorganization of party and government. The party Praesidium was reduced in size to include: Malenkov, Beria, Molotov, Voroshilov, Khrushchev, Bulganin, Kaganovich, Mikoyan, Pervukhin, and Saburov. For a few days only Malenkov was head of both party and government. But on 14 March he lost his party position to Khrushchev. In July followed the downfall of Beria, the security chief and 'a magnificent modern specimen of the artful courtier, the embodiment of Oriental perfidy, flattery and hypocrisy'.[2] He was accused of having worked for the British for over thirty years and was shot! Svetlana Stalin attributed many of the crimes of the 1939–53 period to him.[3]

With Beria out of the way the power struggle in the Kremlin continued, but started to take on a somewhat more civilized form. Malenkov's next step downwards was in February 1955 when he was replaced as Chairman of the Council of Ministers by Marshal Bulganin. When Stalin died, Malenkov as heir apparent with a grip on the party organization expected to fill the dead man's shoes. This was his undoing. Older party leaders such as Molotov, Kaganovich, and Voroshilov had resented him while Stalin was alive and were suspicious of him after the dictator's death. This paved the way for the relative outsider, Khrushchev. Malenkov also made the mistake of trying to go too far too quickly to gain popularity by a policy of butter before guns. This alienated the conservatives among the Soviet leaders including those mentioned above. This switch of emphasis was partly in response to unrest in the satellites. Its need was underlined by a revolt of workers in East Germany in June 1953 and disorders in Poland. Though he had originally lined up with the conservatives, Khrushchev was aware that changes must come. In any case, Malenkov's policies could not so easily be dispensed with. Khrushchev strengthened his position in the Politburo with the promotion to full membership in July 1955 of Kirichenko, from the Ukraine, and Suslov, the party theoretician. He also believed that by cutting a figure abroad he would strengthen his hand in the Politburo still further.

Although at the Foreign Ministers' conference in Geneva in 1955 there were no signs of major Soviet concessions to the Western view, Malenkov's new-style friendlier, diplomacy remained in vogue. Towards the end of the year Khrushchev and Bulganin embarked on an American-type Asian tour. More astonishing still were Soviet moves regarding Austria, where the Four-Power occupation was ended; West Germany, with whom the Soviet Union established diplomatic relations; and Yugoslavia. The two Soviet travellers went to Yugoslavia to ask Tito's forgiveness. Their visit ended with an agreement to reopen state relations and recognize that there were different roads to socialism. These foreign policy moves were too much for Molotov, who was replaced as Foreign Minister in 1956.

If 1955 had been a dramatic year for the USSR, 1956 was to be about as dramatic as any since 1917. The man who will always be most closely associated with this drama was Nikita Khrushchev (1894–1971).

Khrushchev's life had been a remarkable journey, the ticket for which he owed to the Russian Revolution and the Bolshevik regime. As far as is known,[4] his father was a poor peasant who worked, like many others in his region, as a coal-miner in winter. Nikita was born in a village on the Russian-Ukrainian frontier. After some basic education, he was a shepherd boy and then was lucky enough to get an apprenticeship with a German engineering firm. At this time he does not seem to have had more than average interest in politics. He was not called to do service in the Tsarist army, but later joined the Red Army to fight in the civil war. His membership of the Bolshevik Party dates from 1918, which means that many of his colleagues in the leadership, even some younger than he, could point to a longer party membership. At the end of the civil war he was picked to study at the Workers' Faculty of the Don Technical College. It was there that he got his first formal introduction to Marxism, met his second wife (his first died in the famine), and got his first party commission – to act as Party Secretary at the college. In 1930, after a number of posts in the Ukrainian party organization, he was delegated to study at the Industrial Academy in Moscow. There followed appointment as Second, and then First, Secretary of the Moscow city party committee and membership of the Central Committee of the CPSU in 1934. After a relatively late start he had arrived, at the age of forty. What was the basis of his success? Certainly native intelligence, hard work, and ambition. Probably help from his wife Nina, a school-teacher. Above all, the times – the purges and expansion providing opportunities for rapid promotion even for the half-trained and inexperienced – and the kind of mentality which does not question the acts of whoever happens to be leader at the moment.

Khrushchev's standing with his leader can be gauged when one remembers that about a hundred of the 139 members of the Central Committee to which he was elected in 1934 were arrested. Most of them were shot. This helps to explain how he became First Secretary of the Ukrainian party organization at the beginning of 1938. The Russian Khrushchev now had responsibility for a population about the same as England's which produced half the USSR's coal, about a third of her steel, and a large amount of her agricultural produce. In 1939 he was promoted to full membership of the Politburo. As CPSU Secretary in the Ukraine, he had the task of integrating eastern Poland into the Soviet Union in 1939 and must have carried a major responsibility for the mass deportations which took place. Hitler's attack on the Soviet Union two years later must have been a profound shock to him as his 'empire' was quickly swallowed up by the *Wehrmacht*. Surely this shook his confidence in Stalin?

In the war Khrushchev lost a son, but his career was enhanced. Already in 1944 he was back in Kiev directing the work of reconstruction and the operations against the Ukrainian national-ist guerrillas who were challenging Soviet authority. For this

work he came under fire from Zhdanov and Malenkov, at that
time two of Stalin's inner circle. The former accused him of being
soft on Ukrainian nationalism in the arts, the latter of concentrating on economic tasks to the neglect of political. Nevertheless,
Stalin still thought enough of him to recall him to Moscow in
1949 to work in the party's secretariat – the headquarters. Once
again he crossed swords with Malenkov. This time over agricultural policy.

It is difficult to understand how Khrushchev survived under
Stalin, for the world soon got to know him as 'an excitable,
petulant, occasionally impossible, but not unlovable extrovert'.[5]
When he was in a clowning mood it 'was one gag after another,
like sitting next to Abbott and Costello'.[6]

## 1. KHRUSHCHEV'S 'SECRET SPEECH'

It is doubtful whether the delegates who assembled for the
Twentieth Congress of the CPSU in February 1956 had any
inkling of the explosive effect the congress would have. On the
first day the comrades were treated to a long report by First
Secretary Khrushchev in which there was a clear indication that
the Soviet leaders realized that many reforms were needed at
home, together with a more flexible foreign policy, and a re-
assessment of the role of Stalin. There was, of course, the usual
confident assertion about the economic development of the USSR
which was contrasted with the allegedly unfavourable development in the Western nations. Yet the relatively good economic
conditions prevailing in the West had to be explained. These
were due, claimed Khrushchev, to technological advance, the
militarization of the economy, renewal of fixed capital, and the
intensification of the exploitation of the working class and the
reduction of the living standard of the working people.[7]

It was in the section of his speech on the Cold War that
Khrushchev heralded a new departure. He urged the leaders of
Western socialist parties to sweep aside 'mutual recriminations'
and, in the interests of peace, to co-operate with the Communists. Later on, he admitted the possibility that in certain
countries there could be a parliamentary road to socialism,
though

> in the countries where capitalism is still strong and has a huge
> military and police apparatus at its disposal, the reactionary

forces will, of course, inevitably offer serious resistance. There the transition to socialism will be attended by a sharp class, revolutionary struggle.[8]

He once again admitted that 'fraternal Yugoslavia' was a socialist state with 'specific concrete forms of economic management and organization of the state apparatus' arising in the process of socialist construction.[9]

Discussing living standards in the Soviet Union, the First Secretary admitted: 'we do not yet have an adequate quantity of consumer goods', and 'there is a shortage of housing'. Some communities were insufficiently supplied with basic foodstuffs. Yet Khrushchev seemed to be offering the Soviet people not just more, not just a larger cake, but one a little more evenly shared. For one thing he attacked the 'impermissible disparities in the size of pensions'.[10] He also called for changes in the education system, aimed at giving greater equality of opportunity. Fees in secondary schools should be abolished; free hot lunches should be provided for children whose parents earned little; there should be a better geographical distribution of higher educational establishments. Khrushchev also attacked Soviet education for being divorced from life and implied that it was producing 'an aristocratic caste deeply inimical to the people'.[11] He therefore advocated polytechnical education under which pupils would spend some time in the workshop as well as in the classroom. One other proposal he mentioned in education would, if anything, exacerbate the problem – the creation of boarding schools 'in picturesque suburban localities'.

In several other places in his speech Khrushchev expressed concern about the growing social stratification of Soviet society (though he did not put it in those terms). He pointed out that despite reforms, 'the administrative and managerial apparatus is still excessively large'.[12] And that

there are some 90,000 Communists in coal industry establishments, for example, but only 38,000 work in the mines, underground. More than 3 million party members and candidate members live in rural localities, but less than half work in the collective farms, machine and tractor stations and state farms.

(He might have added that very many of those who did were in managerial positions.) This, he concluded, was an 'abnormal situation'.[13]

Any comrades whose attention was beginning to flag must have pricked up their ears when Khrushchev talked about the necessity of re-establishing the party standards worked out by Lenin, including the principle of collective leadership. The Central Committee had 'vigorously condemned the cult of the individual as being alien to the spirit of Marxism-Leninism and making a particular leader a hero and miracle worker. At the same time this belittles the role of the party and the masses, and tends to reduce their creative effort'.[14]

Khrushchev's speech was one which the more serious Marxist and reforming elements in the CPSU and in the foreign parties could, with some reservations, welcome. It promised a consumer revolution, a bigger role for the elected organs in the Soviet state, collective leadership, unity with all Communist, socialist, and anti-colonial movements, and respect for others' views on the roads to socialism. Its cry was back to Marx and Lenin, even if it rather idealized what Lenin had stood for. Nevertheless, it did not involve any undermining of the CPSU's monopoly of power, or any change of the fundamentals of the Soviet system. And the delegates must have been amazed as much by what Khrushchev did not, as by what he did, say. Of Stalin he said simply: 'Shortly after the 19th Congress, death took Joseph Vissarionovich Stalin from our ranks'.[15] On the face of it, Stalin was already virtually an 'unperson'.

That might have been that, had not Anastas Mikoyan mentioned the unmentionable on the third day of the congress with an open attack on Stalin and his works. Only after the Mikoyan onslaught did Khrushchev make his famous 'secret speech'. The speech was secret in the sense that it was made in closed session and was not published by any Communist organ. A copy of it, however, reached the United States and was published by the State Department. Its authenticity was never in doubt and it was accepted by Communists in the West as genuine. It was also in line with all the statements made afterwards by East European Communist leaders. Briefly, Khrushchev reminded the delegates of the criticisms of Stalin contained in Lenin's testament, denounced the mass purges of the 1930s, rehabilitated the Marshals, accused Stalin of ignoring warnings of invasion in 1941, of playing a 'shameful role' in the conflict with Tito, and, among other things, of plotting the downfall of Voroshilov, Molotov, and Mikoyan.[16]

Let us be clear about what Khrushchev did *not* say. He did not rehabilitate the old Bolshevik leaders Bukharin, Kamenev, Zinoviev, Trotsky, and the others. In fact, he praised Stalin's efforts in this direction. Nor did he question the forced collectivization or the forced-labour system as such. And his speech contained no Marxist analysis explaining how a man like Stalin could gain dictatorial power in an allegedly socialist state. Finally, he avoided the potentially dangerous question of the part played by the present leaders in Stalin's policies and plots. At the Nuremberg Trials of the major associates of Hitler, the chief Soviet Prosecutor had said that these Nazis were 'necessary to Hitler just as much as he was necessary to them'. Khrushchev now ignored this truth as applied to Stalin and his accomplices. Of the existing leaders only Malenkov was slightly criticized.

We still do not know why Khrushchev embarked upon this potentially hazardous course at the Twentieth Congress. Of course, there were dangers in not doing so. We do not know whether Mikoyan made his critical remarks about Stalin with the prior knowledge and approval of his colleagues, or whether it was his own private contribution to putting the record straight. If Mikoyan was acting on his own, perhaps Khrushchev felt his position would be threatened if he did not take up the anti-Stalin campaign.[17]

It was a sad, as well as an amusing and nauseating, sight to see the Communist leaders falling over each other in their scramble to leave Stalin's sinking ship. The East European leaders could expect the least sympathy, for they had known the most and enjoyed the privileges of power. At the other end, there were those like the British working-class Communist leaders – Harry Pollitt, John Campbell, Willie Gallacher, and Arthur Horner – who had gained little in a material sense from being Communists. They were not evil men.[18] They had been moulded in their attitudes by the great poverty in the midst of plenty which they had witnessed. The Soviet revolution they had never really understood, nor the system which had been built from it. They knew about slums in London, Manchester, and Glasgow, about dole queues, means tests, and murderous industrial conditions, but were out of their depth when faced with the duplicities of a man like Stalin whose country they knew only from conducted tours. Often their intellectuals and their enthusiasm had triumphed over their commonsense. They had been impressed

by the failures, conservatism, and sometimes complacency, of the
Labour leaders of the MacDonald vintage, who, they felt, had
betrayed the working class. Often, like the Labour leaders, they
became so involved in day-to-day, bread-and-butter, campaigns,
that they had little time to think about other great issues. Doubts
they did have were rationalized by use of the fragments of theory
they had and, above all, by their overriding faith. Despite all this,
one shudders to think what would have happened to Britain, and
to them, had their party got power.

Typical of the kind of statement which had been made about
Stalin by such leaders was that of Harry Pollitt, Secretary of the
British Communist Party, at the time of Stalin's death. Stalin,
'whose lustre time can never efface', was 'always eager and
willing to understand another's point of view'. He was 'never the
dictator'.[19] Now he had to eat his words, but he tried to fight a
dignified rearguard action. Stalin had made serious mistakes (!)
'because the only people who do not make mistakes are people
who never do anything at all'. He still thought Stalin's contribution to the development of industry, the building of socialism,
and the defeat of Hitler would always remain.[20] The British,
American, French, and above all the Italian (among others)
parties were not satisfied with Khrushchev's explanation of
Stalinism. The most comprehensive, and searching, contribution
to the discussion of 'the cult of personality' was made by Palmiro
Togliatti (1893–1964).

Togliatti paid tribute to the achievements of both the CPSU
and Stalin, but concluded from the Soviet discussion so far of
the Stalin issue:

> At one time, all that was good was due to the superhuman
> positive qualities of one man; now all that is bad is attributed
> to the equally exceptional and even staggering defects of the
> same man. Both in the one case and in the other, we are outside
> the criterion of judgment which is proper to Marxism. The real
> problems escape notice, such as the method by which, and the
> reason why, Soviet society could and did stray so far from the
> democratic path and from the legality which it had traced out
> for itself, arriving as far as degeneration.[21]

Two other fundamental conclusions which the Italian leader
drew from the Twentieth Congress discussions were that the
Italian party was treading the parliamentary road to socialism, a

road which would not lead to a one-party state. Secondly: 'Today, the front of socialist construction in the countries where the Communists are the party in the government has widened to such an extent (it comprises one-third of the human race!) that even for this part the Soviet model cannot and should no longer be compulsory'.[22] These countries should be influenced by their individual objective and subjective conditions, traditions, and forms of organization. In the rest of the world:

> . . . there are countries in which they wish to find the way to socialism without the Communist Party being in the lead. In still other countries, the advance towards socialism is an objective for which there is a concentration of forces from different movements. . . . The whole system is becoming polycentric, and even in the Communist movement we cannot speak of a single guide; but rather of progress which is made by following ways which are often different.

This was certainly a very big change of front. It was a revision not only of Stalin's doctrine but also of Lenin's. One only has to think of Lenin's *What Is To Be Done?* and the Twenty-One Points of the Communist International to be clear that this is so.

The denunciation of Stalin was a great shock to Communists all over the world. Though some felt there was now more hope for communism than before, many felt betrayed and, in countries where they were free to do so, left the movement. As the situation seemed to be under control in the Soviet Union, the Communist leaders probably underestimated the reaction to the 'secret speech' in eastern Europe. The most explosive reactions were in Poland and Hungary.

## II. POLAND'S 'SPRING IN OCTOBER'

In the period between 1953 and 1956 Poland underwent a similar development to that in the Soviet Union. Without much publicity 'transgressions against socialist legality' were admitted and the victims quietly rehabilitated. Yet unlike the Soviet Union the old leadership remained and with it the old economic policies. As a result of these policies and the low living standards which resulted from them, an 'abyss' separated the party from the people, and the party bosses from the rank-and-file.[23]

Khrushchev's Twentieth Congress devaluation of Stalin naturally provoked more questioning of the way things had been going in Poland as well as in the Soviet Union. Poland's 'little Stalin', Bolesław Bierut, died less than a month later in Moscow. Edward Ochab took his place, officially rehabilitated Gomułka (without finding him an appropriate post) and others, and promised more investments for agriculture and better wages for the lowest-paid workers. Meanwhile trade unions, the youth organization, parliament, and the universities awoke from their stunned silence of the preceding years and began to discuss, debate, and to criticize.

A critical stage was reached in June when the strike of workers at the Stalin locomotive-works in Poznań led to demonstrations and then to armed fighting between crowds and security police. A combination of concessions and repression, promises and personal appearances, by party leaders prevented revolt becoming revolution. In July, under the watchful eyes of Marshals Bulganin and Zhukov of the CPSU, the Polish Central Committee came out in favour of a policy of reconciliation with the masses and reform. But throughout the summer of 1956 the ferment among the youth and intellectuals, and the unrest in the factories remained. Independent workers' councils were set up.

The next meeting of the party's Central Committee convened in mid-October, amid rumours of Stalinist *coups* and menacing Soviet troop movements. Unexpectedly, a Soviet delegation led by Khrushchev, but including hardliners Molotov and Kaganovich, flew to Warsaw and threatened armed intervention.[24] The majority of the Polish Central Committee stood firm, backed by pro-Gomułka crowds and by the security forces which by this time were in the hands of a Gomułka supporter. Sensibly the Poles emphasized that they were the best guarantee of a Communist Poland, and of a Poland in the Warsaw Pact. Sensibly the Russians backed down.

After a speech in which he offered 'a mild, gradual transformation of the country's social and economic structure, whenever possible achieved with support of the governed, an autonomous Poland as a member of the "socialist camp" ', Gomułka was unanimously elected First Secretary of the Party on 21 October. In the new nine-member Politburo his supporters included former socialists such as Józef Cyrankiewicz and former Stalinists such as Edward Ochab whose commonsense had done much to ensure a peaceful transition. Gone was the Soviet general who had been forced on the Poles as Defence Minister, the Polish-born Marshal Rokossovsky.

A week after Gomułka's election Cardinal Wyszyński was released from house arrest and by early December, after a series of moves to placate the Church had been introduced, the new First Secretary got the vital backing of the Cardinal.[25]

By behaving in a way most outsiders believed to be a non-Polish way, the Poles had achieved much in their 'spring' in October. Their success must have been due in great measure to the readiness of leaders of party and Catholic Church to compromise. Perhaps their success was also attributable to Soviet difficulties in Hungary and to Chinese backing for the Poles.[26]

## III. REVOLUTION IN HUNGARY

In Hungary events moved swiftly to a bloody climax. At the end of March 1956 Rajk was posthumously rehabilitated. The 'Stalin of Hungary', Mátyás Rákosi, fell on 18 July. The new party manager, Ernő Gerő, called for reconciliation with Tito, which, after all, was only following the Soviet line. In the same month Mikoyan visited Hungary to conduct an investigation and to inform the new leadership that the Soviet Politburo still regarded the Soviet Union, not Yugoslavia, as the model for the East European socialist states. The Yugoslavs apparently took objection to this and talks were held between Khrushchev and Tito in September.

Meanwhile, in Hungary the remains of Rajk were exhumed and on 6 October a public funeral was held with thousands joining the procession. Imre Nagy, a veteran Communist intellectual, who had spent the war years in Moscow and Siberia, and had held office as a Malenkov-style premier from July 1953 to April 1955, symbolically kissed Rajk's widow. A few days later Nagy was reinstated in the party and Rákosi's secret police chief was arrested. The press and radio started to call for a Hungarian way to socialism, praising developments in Poland and Yugoslavia. Students took up this demand. In Gyor, popular demonstrations called for the release of Cardinal Mindszenty and, more significantly, for the withdrawal from Hungary of all Soviet troops.

Apparently it was shots fired by frightened secret policemen of the Hungarian Political Police (AVH) on unarmed crowds in

Budapest which turned peaceful demonstrations into uncontrollable riots.[27] Gerő's response on 23–24 October was to ask for Soviet military assistance. This led to some Hungarian army units going over to the (by now) insurgents. On 25 October Mikoyan and Suslov from the Soviet Politburo flew in to order Gerő's removal and to give authority to Nagy, already official premier, to deal with the situation. János Kádár, ex-working-class Communist who had been jailed under the Stalinist regime as well as before 1945, was given Soviet backing as Party Secretary. Nagy was authorized to announce a programme of concessions, including the eventual Soviet withdrawal from Hungary. A genuine coalition government was formed, the secret police was abolished, and Soviet troops withdrawn from Budapest. On 30 October Nagy even announced that free elections would be held with the parties of 1945 taking part. These parties had been re-forming and in the factories workers' councils had been established.

An analysis of the Soviet press during this period[28] suggests that the Soviet leaders were prepared to accept the situation. However, on 31 October Zoltán Tildy, of the old Peasants' (Smallholders') Party, and Premier Nagy met Mikoyan and Suslov who had once again appeared in Budapest. According to one account[29] Mikoyan offered immediate withdrawal of all Soviet troops over and above those stationed in Hungary before the revolution. Withdrawal of those stationed there under the Warsaw Pact agreement would be negotiated later with all the Pact states. Tildy rejected this offer and demanded *immediate* evacuation of *all* Soviet troops. He declared that Hungary would, in any case, leave the Warsaw Pact. This seems to have been a vital turning-point, leading the Soviets to intervene reluctantly for the second time. They were reluctant because the massive invasion which followed on 4 November obviously put in jeopardy their policy of 'peaceful co-existence' with the West and dented their image as an anti-colonialist power. In this instance Chinese opinion might have tipped the scales in favour of intervention.[30]

Officially the Soviet forces were intervening at the request of the Hungarian authorities. But what authorities? It was claimed that a new 'Hungarian Revolutionary Workers' and Peasants' Government' had been set up on 1 November. This was headed by Kádár. Against the might of Soviet armour the legitimate

Hungarian government could do little. Thousands of Hungarians poured over the frontier into Austria. Nagy and some of his close associates were not so fortunate. The premier took refuge in the Yugoslav embassy and was tricked into leaving by the Soviets who then abducted him. He was taken to Romania and later killed after a secret trial in Hungary.[31] Moscow claimed that he had capitulated to reactionary forces. This was true to the extent that it was by no means certain that without Soviet intervention a Nagy-led reform communism would have managed to survive. The revolution released many forces from reform communism through Social Democracy to conservatism and beyond. At their worst some revolutionaries wreaked vengeance on Communists, descending to lynch law against the secret police.[32]

The world quite naturally regarded Kádár as a stooge of Moscow and a traitor to his country. But, as we shall see, he turned out rather differently than expected.

## IV. WOLFGANG HARICH

In the German Democratic Republic (GDR) the party leaders had found themselves in deep trouble long before the Khrushchev speech. After 1949 they were in daily competition with a larger, more powerful, and increasingly more prosperous West German state which claimed to speak for all Germans. Like the other satellite regimes, they had made the mistake of heaping adulation on Stalin and everything Soviet, which sickened and alienated the East German populace. They had their local Stalin, ex-cabinetmaker from Saxony Walter Ulbricht, who had spent the Nazi years in Moscow. Unlike the other East European states, they were ostracized by all states outside the Communist bloc. They had the problem of an open frontier in that before 1961 movement from the Western to the Eastern sectors of Berlin, and vice versa, was unrestricted. Their people were further open to Western influences from radio and from relations in the West. They had the very unpopular job of justifying the annexation by Poland and the USSR of roughly a quarter of German territory beyond the Oder-Neisse Line – the GDR officially accepted the frontier in a treaty with Poland in 1950 – when the West German government was attacking it. Their main parties suffered competition from parties with similar names in West Berlin and West Germany. Above all, the Socialist Unity Party (SED) was opposed from West Germany and West Berlin by the powerful Social Democratic Party (SPD) led, until his death in 1952, by Kurt Schumacher. Schumacher,[33] a tragic yet charismatic figure, had lost an arm in the First World War, and a leg as a result of his internment in a Nazi concentration camp. He advocated a strongly national policy, including a return of the lost territories, but rejected West German rearmament (on the terms available), and spoke as a Marxist and a democrat. No wonder the SED leaders feared his influence amongst their own workers! However, the East German leaders had a problem perhaps greater still.

Given that Germany was to remain divided into two mutually hostile states, the SED leaders had to make arrangements to secure the basic industrial raw materials, coal and steel, which before 1945 had come from West Germany. As we saw in the last chapter, they embarked on a costly expansion of basic industry. In 1952 they decided on 'building the foundations of socialism' and on the creation of armed forces. They were still paying reparations to the USSR. The result was that the workers were forced to work harder for the same pay. East Germans who did not like it could, unlike their Eastern neighbours, 'vote with their feet'. They could go to West Germany via Berlin and resettle without great difficulty.

It was on 28 May 1953 that the East German government ordered the raising of output norms without any corresponding increase in pay. Less than a month later, probably under orders from Moscow, they started to revise their plans, especially those which discriminated, in line with Stalin's intensification of the class-struggle theory, against the middle classes and the Churches. They failed clearly and explicitly to reduce the workloads of the industrial workers. The result was a strike by workers on the prestigious Stalinallee building site on 16 June. The next day the strike movement spread to other parts of East Berlin and the surrounding republic. Roughly 300,000 to 372,000 workers downed tools in 272 localities.[34] Demonstrations took place and in some cases violence, plundering, and arson.[35] In East Berlin demonstrators were joined by some from West Berlin.[36] On 16 June the SED leadership had not attempted to stop the demonstrations. They made known that the raising of the work norms had been rescinded and appealed to the workers to take part in official factory meetings the following day. It was only on the afternoon of the following day that Soviet troops together with the militarized People's Police (KVP) were sent into action to disperse the demonstrators. Apparently they were very cautious in their use of force.[37]

Although only between 4.5 and 5.5 per cent of East German workers went on strike, the regime was profoundly shaken. The SED admitted many of its 'mistakes', but claimed the revolt was part of a Western plot. Remarkably, Ulbricht survived, but some 'defeatists' were removed, including Wilhelm Zaisser, Politburo member and Minister for State Security, Rudolf Herrnstadt, editor of the party organ, and Max Fechner, Minister of Justice and a former Social Democrat. The 'New Course', as the more conciliatory policies were called, was continued.

By the time the Twentieth Congress of the CPSU approached, then, the SED had removed, unlike their colleagues in Poland and Hungary, some of the material causes of revolt. Nevertheless, they were completely taken by surprise by Khrushchev's denunciation of Stalin. On 4 March, about a week after the end of the Moscow Congress, the party paper, *Neues Deutschland*, published a statement from Ulbricht which largely repeated what by this time most party members had heard from other sources. On 18 March he returned to the attack, admitting that the party had a problem with its younger members who had joined since 1945. These young people now found that the few dogmatic phrases learnt by heart no longer fitted life. He further claimed that in the GDR there had been fewer distortions than in some other socialist countries and that the SED had earlier embarked on corrective measures. In July the Central Committee of the SED met to agree on action following the Twentieth Congress. It was decided to rehabilitate many of the comrades disgraced before 1953 and to allow 'honest discussion', but the party must not assume that 'under the flag of freedom, criticism, and scientific conflict of opinion the fundamental principles of Marxism and Leninism are being abandoned'.[38]

Some of the students were not satisfied with the party's explanation of Stalin's fall. They found a spokesman in Dr Wolfgang Harich, brilliant thirty-six-year-old SED academic. Basically, Harich wanted workers' councils as in Yugoslavia, an end of collective farms, the abolition of the secret police, greater social equality, freedom of discussion both inside and outside the SED, and a parliament worthy of the name. In its ideology the party should take into consideration the contributions of socialists as far apart as Kautsky and Trotsky, as well as the contemporary SPD, the Chinese, Poles, and Yugoslavs. He was in contact with the SPD, with groups in Poland and in Hungary including the literary historian György Lukács. The SED dealt with the situation by having Harich and some others arrested. They were tried in March 1957. Harich was sentenced to ten years' imprisonment. He was released in 1964.

Apart from the Harich group which was suppressed before it got very influential, Walter Ulbricht had to deal with his Politburo colleagues Karl Schirdewan and Fred Oelssner who were using the Twentieth Congress decisions to challenge his leadership. They were removed in 1958, but condemned only to a life of obscurity. All in all, the SED leadership got off with relatively little trouble from the aftermath of the Twentieth Congress. As mentioned above, material conditions were not the pressing problem they were in Hungary and Poland. And East Germany had no Rajks to grieve over. In addition, some who would have been the stuff of insurrections had gone West. Finally, it may well be that the workers had not yet got over the events of June 1953.

## V. EXPERIMENTS IN YUGOSLAVIA

As we have seen, especially after the Twentieth Congress, East Europeans seeking to improve the socialist system in their own countries were interested in Yugoslavia as a possible alternative model. As for the Yugoslav Communists themselves, at first, after their expulsion from the Cominform, they had been stunned. Then they tried to prove they were more orthodox Communists than the Cominformists. In 1949, for instance, they pressed forward with forced collectivization. But the continuing menacing attitude of their erstwhile allies forced them to take a fresh look at Stalin's Russia. When their shock had been replaced by anger, they decided that they, and not the Muscovites, were the true Marxist-Leninists. In practical terms they held that different countries had different roads to socialism and that one could not generalize from the experiences of any one attempt. This was good Marxism though not such good Leninism. This interpretation – aided no doubt by necessity – led them to take a more friendly look at the efforts of Social Democratic movements in western and north-western Europe. Their contacts with these movements multiplied. They came to believe that the Western democracies with their welfare programmes, state intervention in the economy, and powerful working-class movements were no longer quite what they had been in the time of Marx.

In her foreign relations Yugoslavia was *de facto* outside the blocs; she had had no choice, and this position was gradually built up to a fundamental principle. Yet by 1950 Yugoslavia had received loans and credits from the World Bank, the Export-Import Bank, and the British Treasury. In December the United States Congress voted aid to Yugoslavia on the assumption that it was in the Western interest to prevent this country from falling under Stalin's influence once more. During the next ten years Yugoslavia received from America $2,396,900,000 in aid, much of it military. Britain contributed another $120,400,000 and France gave small amounts as well.[39] Sneered Mikoyan: 'Tito can be bought with a hundred million dollars', forgetting that by the same token Lenin had been bought in 1917, and the USSR had been 'bought' in the Second World War by Anglo-American aid. In any case, it was the men in the Kremlin who had forced Tito into this position. In January 1954 Yugoslavia's relations with her non-Communist neighbours had improved so much that she concluded the Balkan Pact with the two NATO states Greece and Turkey. In the case of Greece the improvement in relations was made possible by Yugoslavia closing her frontier to Greek Communist rebels operating in the mountains. The military aspects of the Balkan Pact remained largely a dead letter.

In its internal policy the Yugoslav party saw centralization and bureaucracy as major causes of the existing state of affairs in the USSR. This led to some curtailing of the secret police, of party and state bureaucracy, a law introducing worker-management in 1950, the abandonment of Soviet-type planning, the end of compulsory collective farming in 1952–53, and party and constitutional changes at the same time.

Before saying a little more about these reforms let us look briefly at the men behind them.

Josip Broz Tito was born in 1892 not far from Zagreb. His parents were poor Croat peasants. He learned the trade of locksmith, and later became a metal-worker. Like some others, he was converted to communism while a prisoner-of-war in Russia at the time of the October Revolution. He had served in the

Austro-Hungarian Army. Soon after his return to the new Yugoslavia in 1920 he became a full-time revolutionary. He was jailed for his activities and on his release he was sent abroad by the party. It was Stalin's purges rather than his own ability which were the decisive factor leading to his appointment as General Secretary of the Yugoslav Communist Party in 1937. During the Spanish Civil War, on orders from the Comintern, he managed the flow of East European volunteers from a small hotel in Paris. He returned to Yugoslavia in 1938 with the mandate to select and appoint members of the party's Central Committee. From 1941 to the end of the armed struggle he was in command of the partisan forces. The commander of the British Military Mission and later Conservative Member of Parliament, Sir Fitzroy Maclean, summed up his qualities:

> courage, realism, ruthless determination and singleness of purpose, resourcefulness, adaptability, and plain common sense. . . . He possessed, and could inspire in his companions, an absolute devotion to their common cause which led them to count as nothing their own lives or the lives of others.[40]

After the war Tito became the 'Stalin of Yugoslavia' and his 'cult of personality', at least in its external manifestations, survived the breach with Moscow and subsequent changes in Yugoslavia. Thrice married, President Tito developed a lavish style of living and love of uniforms which contrasted with the general poverty of the country.

Among the men selected by Tito in 1938 for the Central Committee were Edvard Kardelj and Milovan Djilas. Both contributed much to the theory of Yugoslav communism after 1949. A Slovene, forty-one years old in 1951, Edvard Kardelj started his adult life as a school-teacher and some say his classroom manner has remained with him. 'Ask him a question', it is said, 'and you get a lecture'. Kardelj joined the Communists in 1927 and later spent some time at the Lenin University in the USSR. He was a wartime partisan and after 1945 became the party's top theorist. At the same time he held many leading positions. Kardelj has remained closest to Tito over the years and is most likely to succeed him.

Milovan Djilas was only thirty-eight in 1950, but behind him were years of illegal activity, armed struggle, high-level missions to Moscow, and experience in the highest party bodies. A native of Montenegro, he was elected a Vice-President of Yugoslavia. At the time of the split with Stalin he had the reputation of a fanatical and very pro-Soviet Communist. Later, however, he willingly, though not eagerly, exchanged the pomp and privileges of power for a prison cell. He felt compelled to speak out in criticism of the system he had helped to create, and would not, or could not, stop when ordered to do so by his comrades.

Undoubtedly, the reform which has caused the most interest is the law introducing worker management. The theory behind it is that mere nationalization of the means of production does not produce socialist relations in industry, does not alter the relations between the workers and the bosses, even if, in theory, the latter represent 'the People'. The law of 1950 abolished central control of industry by laying down the following basic principles:

> Manufacturing, mining, communications, transport, trading, agricultural, forestry, municipal and other public undertakings shall, as the property of the whole nation, be administered in the name of the community by the staffs employed therein, as part of the State economic plan, and on the basis of the rights and duties established by law.
>
> The staff of employees shall carry out their administration through the workers' councils and administrative committees [*upravni odbori*] of the undertakings . . .[41]

The workers' councils comprise, depending on the size of the enterprise, between fifteen to 120 members elected annually by universal, equal, and secret ballot. They must meet at least once every six weeks and are responsible for: approving the basic plans and the balance sheet of the undertaking; decisions regarding administration and carrying-through of the economic plan; electing, dissolving, and replacing the administrative committee; issuing enterprise regulations with the approval of the adminstrative committee or the public authority concerned; examining reports and activities of the administrative committee; carrying out the division of net profits. The administrative committees consist of from three to eleven members, including the enterprise manager who is an *ex officio* member. At least three-quarters of their members must be involved in production or in the basic economic activity of the enterprise. The administrative committees are in general responsible for the execution of the plan and the proper functioning of the enterprise, and thus such things as draft plans, internal organization, measures for improving labour discipline, appointment of leading officials, rationalization of production, staff training, etc. Under the original law of 1950 the manager was appointed by the administrative committee, not of the enterprise, but of the association of enterprises of the particular branch of industry. It is a sign of the difficulties connected with workers' management that this system of appointment has been changed several times since then.

Ideologically, the new arrangements of 1950 had more in common with the late G. D. H. Cole's Guild Socialism than with the theories of Lenin (though this would be contested by Yugoslav Communists). As to how they operated in practice, the writer makes no apologies for not being able to give any definitive answer. One obvious question is whether the Communists found ways to perpetuate their control of the enterprises. The Communist League, as the official Communist organization was known from 1952, is often organized on a factory basis. The Communists have kept a grip on the trade unions and an ILO investigation published in 1962 claimed that 98 per cent of the members of the workers' councils had been elected on the basis of the trade union lists.[42] And a survey of a sample of eighteen factories in Zagreb in 1958, with labour forces ranging from 200 to 1,500, indicated that between 5.3 and 15.3 per cent of the workers belonged to the League, whereas on the councils the proportions were between 8.3 and 65 per cent.[43] Another obvious problem is how you get meaningful participation when so many of the workers were, only yesterday, peasants with no experience of industry, unions, or democratic practices – workers, moreover, with the very minimum of education.[44] And if the workers' councils really have power, how do you get them to consider the wider public interest? On this, the ILO survey quoted above maintained that the Yugoslav system 'seems compatible with the pursuit of a policy of rapid economic expansion under a central development plan'.[45] One other point worth remembering is that workers' management has not prevented strikes, even without strike pay, which have become more frequent over the years. In conclusion, the writer feels he can only quote the rather innocuous conclusions of the ILO study that only the future will show the durability of the system but that its 'originality and interest can hardly be denied even today'.[46]

As mentioned above, in 1952 the Communist Party changed

its name to League. The change, reverting to a term used at the time of Marx, was supposed to be indicative of a change in approach by the Communists. The emphasis would now be on persuasion rather than force or administrative decree. The formal agencies of the state and the mass organizations would come more alive and not merely follow the dictates of the monolithic party. Indeed party organizations in such bodies were abolished. Henceforth Communists worked merely as individuals in them. (This did not apply to industry.) The People's Front was disbanded and replaced by the Socialist Alliance, but this remained completely dominated by the League.[47] The party, too, was promised more internal democracy with more power at local level, fewer full-time officials, open meetings, and so on. All these reforms were seen as fulfilling the Marxist prophecy that the state would wither away. And if the state withered away, so would the party eventually as well.

Many Yugoslavs remained sceptical about these changes; some thought they did not go far enough. One of these was Milovan Djilas. With Tito's blessing, in the party organ he called for more democracy and less dogmatism and opportunism. Only when he attacked the ultimate goal of communism in December 1953 did he meet with opposition from his comrades in the Central Committee. But he really went too far for them when he published an article attacking the 'inner circle of party bureaucrats'. He attacked their pseudo-aristocratic style, primitive greed, new-found pomposity, and material luxury. And he attacked the wives of these party officials more than he attacked the officials themselves. It was a bitter outburst which remarkably, in view of past Communist practice, only earned his removal from the Central Committee. In April 1954 he resigned from the League. It was for giving an interview to an American newspaper at the end of the year, in which he advocated the setting-up of a democratic socialist opposition party, that he was sentenced to jail for 'hostile propaganda'. He was, however, put on probation. More interviews with the foreign press followed until in December 1956 he was sent to prison. After his book *The New Class* appeared in the West, his sentence was increased to ten years. He was released in January 1961 only to be rearrested later in the year for a new book, *Conversations with Stalin*. On this occasion he was accused of divulging unauthorized information.

The basic point of *The New Class* is that communism had produced by terror and centralization a new class whose power over the people was more complete than any earlier ruling class. The workers had no genuine organizations; they faced one employer, the state; no opposition was allowed, however peaceful; and the education system and the news media were also subservient to the party. It was a system of control more complete than ever before. And Djilas condemned the Soviet as well as the Yugoslav variety.

In the case of Yugoslavia Djilas was less than fair in that, as we have seen, reforms, however imperfect, were being introduced. In the fifties and sixties there was far more genuine discussion there than in the period 1945–50, and in general, life was somewhat more relaxed. In the arts, to take just one example, Yugoslavia produced a brilliance in painting and sculpture which surprised the public abroad.[48] On a different plane, ordinary Yugoslavs, students, tourists, those seeking work, found it much easier to travel to the West. On the other hand, Djilas's charge that there were, and are, privileged groups, was obvious to anyone who visited the country. When the writer spent ten weeks in Yugoslavia in 1955 he found the ostentatious display of the new rich with their Cadillacs and Mercedes saddening as well as sickening. But he did meet other Communists still dedicated to the League's high ideals. The Djilas thesis was more applicable to the USSR.[49]

Some observers in the non-Communist world have seen the treatment of Djilas as in part conditioned by Yugoslav relations with the other Communist states. His imprisonment in 1956 could be seen as an attempt to placate the Soviets after disagreements over Hungary. Yet, by Communist standards, Djilas's treatment was lenient.

After Khrushchev and Bulganin visited Belgrade in 1955, relations between the two countries improved rapidly. Khrushchev was prepared to go to considerable lengths to win the approval of Tito, the anti-Stalinist. As a gesture to him the Cominform was dissolved in June 1956. Tito then visited Moscow in June. His stay ended with talk of party, as well as state, co-operation. A month after Tito's trip American aid to Yugoslavia was suspended. In that summer one delegation after another visited Belgrade to study Tito's system. There were more talks between Tito and Khrushchev about de-Stalinization in eastern Europe – in itself an indication of the Yugoslav's influence at that time. Yet by winter Tito's influence had slumped badly. To the orthodox Communists the revolution in Hungary seemed an indication of what could happen if Yugoslav theories were exported. On the other hand, the revisionists were dismayed because Tito upheld the second Soviet intervention as a necessary evil to avoid chaos, civil war, counter-revolution, and even a new world war. He did, however, indict Stalinism for the Hungarian situation.

After Hungary, Yugoslav relations with the Soviet Union quickly cooled without going back to where they had been between 1948 and 1954. American aid was restored. At the end of 1957 Yugoslavia recognized East Germany in an effort to appease the Russians and East Germans. This cost Belgrade its relations with Bonn. The Yugoslavs sent a delegation to the meetings of Communist parties in November 1957, and observers to similar meetings in January 1959 and November 1960, but they refused to sign the declarations which, in effect, were aimed at restoring Soviet hegemony, albeit in a modified form.

The Seventh Congress of the Yugoslav Communist League in 1958 exposed the hostility of the 'world socialist camp'. All Communist and socialist parties had been invited to send delegated to Ljubljana, but only the Norwegian and Danish Communists accepted, together with socialist delegates from Switzerland, Japan, Israel, and Chile.[50] Diplomatic representatives of the Communist countries attended, but they left demonstratively during the speech of Alexander Rankovich, the fifty-nine-year-old Serb who for many years ran the secret police, and who seemed then a likely successor to Tito.

The programme which was adopted by the congress repeated the theories outlined above. It also defined Yugoslavia's position on blocs, and on roads to socialism. The whole programme was based on the proposition that:

> Marxism is not a dogmatic system or established doctrine, but a theory of social processes which develops through successive historical phases. There it implies the creative application of scientific theory, which will continue to develop, primarily through generalization of practical experience in socialist development and achievement in the scientific thought of mankind.[51]

The idea that 'Marxism is not a dogmatic system' is, of course, good Marxism. It has always been the starting-point for any revision of doctrine.

Defending their non-alignment, the Yugoslavs claimed:

> The world to-day is in dire need of efforts by all peace-loving forces, by all states and responsible statesmen, to promote co-operation between East and West. A significant role in this respect is played by the non-committed countries which, by virtue of the fact that they are not aligned with any bloc, can contribute a great deal towards breaking down the exclusiveness of the blocs.[52]

The Yugoslavs' comments on the dictatorship of the proletariat were an interesting departure. They believed that the general growth of the 'forces of socialism' would cause an 'even greater abundance of diverse political forms of dictatorship of the proletariat ranging from revolutionary dictatorship to parliamentary government in which the working class and its social and economic interests wield decisive influence'. The Yugoslavs saw another possibility: 'various transitional political forms of specific dual rule and compromise in which the growing influence of working-class interests will be in evidence – until that influence becomes predominant in the political system'.[53] In other words, they were admitting the possibility of a gradual, parliamentary road to socialism.

The Seventh Congress led to vehement attacks from the Peking newspaper *People's Daily* and, a few days later, from the Soviet, Czech, and other East European presses.

By the beginning of the sixties the Russians were once again wooing the Yugoslavs. The men in the Kremlin felt they faced a much greater threat than Tito's to their position in the world Communist movement: that from Mao Tse-tung.

NOTES

[1] Svetlana Stalin in the *Observer* (London), 22 Sept. 1967.
[2] ibid.
[3] ibid.
[4] This account is based on Mark Frankland, *Khrushchev* (London, 1966).
[5] Harold Macmillan, *Riding the Storm* (London, 1971), p. 608.
[6] Arthur M. Schlesinger, Jr, *A Thousand Days* (New York and London, 1965), p. 332.
[7] N. S. Khrushchev, *Report of the Central Committee*, Soviet News Booklet No. 4 (London, Feb. 1956), pp. 11–12.

[8] ibid., p. 31. As Richard Lowenthal has pointed out ('Three Roads to Power', *Problems of Communism*, July–August 1956), this was a new departure revising Leninism.

[9] ibid., p. 29. Further, he conceded that there was much that was unique in socialist construction in China.

[10] ibid., p. 159.

[11] ibid., p. 64.

[12] ibid., p. 72.

[13] ibid., p. 87.

[14] ibid., p. 80.

[15] ibid., p. 78.

[16] The author has used the text put out by the *Manchester Guardian* (June 1956) under the title *The Dethronement of Stalin*.

[17] See the analysis of Myron Rush, *The Rise of Khrushchev* (Washington, 1958), pp. 59–65.

[18] See the interesting descriptions of them by Douglas Hyde (op. cit., chapter XIII), a former high-ranking British Communist journalist who became a Catholic. See also Copeman, op. cit. For a more scientific analysis see G. A. Almond, *The Appeals of Communism* (Princeton, 1954), p. 138 (on leaders); p. 145 (on Pollitt).

[19] *Daily Worker* (London), 7 March 1953.

[20] *The Times* (19 March 1956).

[21] From the *Nuovi Argomenti* interview of June 1956, as published in full in the British Communist Party journal *World News*, p. 7.

[22] ibid., p. 12.

[23] Dziewanowski, op. cit., p. 256.

[24] ibid., p. 274.

[25] Hansjakob Stehle, *The Independent Satellite*, translated from the German by D. J. S. Thompson (New York and London, 1965), p. 309.

[26] ibid., p. 33.

[27] This account is based substantially on Raymond L. Garthoff, 'The Tragedy of Hungary', in *Problems of Communism* (USIA), Jan.–Feb. 1957; and P. E. Zinner, *Revolution in Hungary* (New York, 1962). For a pro-Moscow version of events, see Louis Aragon, *A History of the USSR* (London, 1962), pp. 581–90. For the revolution see also: George Urban, *The Nineteen Days* (London, 1957); David Pryce-Jones, *The Hungarian Revolution* (London, 1969); Paul Ignotus, *Hungary* (London and New York, 1972), chapters 11–13.

[28] Garthoff, op. cit., pp. 6–7.

[29] ibid., p. 7.

[30] François Fejtő, 'Hungarian Communism', in William E. Griffith (ed.), *Communism in Europe*, I (Oxford, 1963), 196.

[31] Fejtő, ibid., p. 250, believes this was due to Chinese pressure, but it could have been a warning to other leading Communists not to 'betray' the Soviet Union.

[32] *Der Spiegel* (7 Nov. 1956).

[33] Lewis J. Edinger, *Kurt Schumacher* (Cologne, 1967) gives a convincing picture of Schumacher.

[34] Arnulf Baring, *Der 17. Juni 1953* (Bonn, 1957), p. 38.

[35] ibid., p. 56.

[36] ibid., p. 38; also Heinz Brandt, *Ein Traum der nicht entführbar ist* (Munich, 1967), p. 242.

[37] Baring, op. cit., p. 58; see also *Manchester Guardian* (22 June 1953).

[38] See David Childs, *East Germany* (London and New York, 1969), pp. 36–40.

[39] Auty, op. cit., p. 170.

[40] Fitzroy Maclean, 'Tito at Seventy', in the *Sunday Times* (London), 27 May 1962. See also his *The Heretic: The Life and Times of Josip Broz-Tito* (New York, 1957). Vladimir Dedijer wrote the official biography, *Tito* (New York, 1953), but it is a generally convincing study.

[41] *Basic Law on the administration of public undertakings and associations of undertakings by the staffs employed therein.* Dated 2 July 1950, published by International Labour Office, Legislative Series, 1950 – Yug. 2.

[42] *Workers' Management in Yugoslavia* (ILO, Geneva, 1962), p. 79.

[43] ibid., p. 33.

[44] ibid., Appendix 1. In 1953, 24.4 per cent of people over ten were illiterate.

[45] ibid., p. 247.

[46] ibid., p. 295.

[47] Hoffman and Neal, op. cit., p. 181.

[48] See, for instance, the review in *The Times* (28 April 1961) of the exhibition of contemporary Yugoslav paintings and sculpture at the Tate Gallery. See also 'The Artist's Lot in Yugoslavia', *The Times* (30 Nov. 1961).

[49] See Hugh Seton-Watson, 'The Soviet Ruling Class', *Problems of Communism* (May–June 1956).

[50] *The Programme of the League of Yugoslav Communists*, edited by Kurt Dowson (International Society for Socialist Studies, London, 1959), p. ix.

[51] ibid., p. 175.

[52] ibid., p. 59.

[53] ibid., p. 85.

# IX

## *Mao's Marxism*

THE Chinese Communists took over in 1949 a land which was far more backward than Russia had been in 1917, more backward in many respects even than India.[1] At the start of her first Five-Year Plan in 1928 Russia produced 4.3 million tons of steel (roughly the same as in 1913) against China's 1.3 million tons at the start of the First Plan in 1952. At the beginning of her Five-Year Plan in 1951, India produced slightly less steel than China in absolute terms, but more *per capita*. In 1952 China also produces less coal, cement, cotton, and electricity *per capita* than Russia or India at the start of their plans (in 1928 and 1951 respectively).[2] She had less rail track than they did *per capita*. The populations of India and Russia were better educated than the Chinese and when India became independent, she possessed a trained civil service and a fairly effective state machine. The Chinese Communists started virtually from scratch.

Most Chinese lived from farming and again the overall picture was one of extreme backwardness. In 1951 even India had relatively six times more tractors than China. An American study in the 1920s (and the position in 1949 was probably worse) estimated that the great majority of Chinese farms had no draught animals at all, under half had pigs, only 7 per cent had sheep, and only 1 per cent cattle.[3]

In 1949, then, 'by far the greater part of the country carried on, as for the last 2,000 years, an early-iron-age economy'.[4] Disease and illiteracy, concubinage and footbinding of females, were widespread; drought, flood, and famine were common. Banditry was a major problem. The country had endured insurrection, war, and chaos since 1911, and the whole of the last hundred years seemed to have been a steady march into the abyss. Yet American geographers in the 1920s believed:

> The two principal factors working against the rapid industrialization of China, quite apart from lack of capital or credit

organization, are the dishonesty of the officials, who prey on the developments of all kinds, and the lack of cooperation on the part of the people. Remove these disabilities and there is no reason why China should not be the greatest industrial nation in the world.[5]

Broadly speaking, one can say that this was Mao Tse-tung's view as well, though he would have added interference by foreigners to the list of disabilities.

True to their ideology, the Communists sought to transform China in the shortest possible time from her backward state into a modern industrial nation. It is only natural that the Chinese looked to the only country which claimed to have achieved such a revolution, a country with which they had ideological affinities – the Soviet Union. However, even in 1949 the Chinese did not copy the Soviets *in toto*. They introduced 'New Democracy', which was an alliance of 'the working class, the peasantry, the petty bourgeoisie and the national bourgeoisie'.[6] Of the national bourgeoisie Mao said in 1949:

> In the present stage a great deal of suitable educational work can be done among them. When the time comes to realise Socialism, that is, to nationalise private enterprise, we will go a step further in our work of educating and reforming them. The people have a strong state apparatus in their hands, and they do not fear rebellion on the part of the national bourgeoisie.[7]

Mao clearly recognized that China was so desperately short of managerial and entrepreneurial skill that capitalists, provided they acted under orders from the party, were necessary at that stage of the revolution. He thus avoided the pitfalls of 'war communism' in Soviet Russia. This was in some ways similar to Lenin's New Economic Policy, but it was conceived in a different atmosphere, not as a forced concession, and with an apparently more positive attitude to the 'national bourgeoisie', a category which Lenin did not identify in Russia.

Under the 'People's Democratic Dictatorship', as this stage was called, there was a mixed economy with nationalized undertakings, private firms, mixed enterprises, co-operatives, and the private farms of the peasants. As in Lenin's Russia, land reform had been carried through to break the large landowners and secure the support of the mass of the peasants for the new regime.

In 1952 the state owned all the railways, 80 per cent of heavy industry, 60 per cent of the shipping, and 50 per cent of light industry.[8] This was not so dramatic a turn to socialism, since during the war against Japan the Nationalist government had come to dominate many sectors of the Chinese economy.[9] Expropriation of foreign concerns was also a factor in boosting state ownership. It was between autumn 1955 and January 1956 that virtually all private and semi-private undertakings were nationalized, but even then many of the former owners were kept on as managers.[10] Most of this occurred in the space of about ten days. It was about the same time that there was a rapid transition to collective farming. Originally roughly 20 per cent of all peasant households were to become part of collectives by 1957 – that is by the end of the first Five-Year Plan. Yet by that date virtually all the farms had been collectivized.[11] It is impossible to be sure just how much, or how little, opposition there was to this vast transformation, but some Western observers believe there was 'remarkably little active unrest among the peasants', though considerable discontent came later.[12] The same experts believe the Chinese Communists avoided the calamitous effects which followed collectivization in Russia. They avoided violence and attempted to integrate the 'rich' peasant into the new system.[13]

Foreign experts seem agreed that in the period 1952 to 1959 the People's Republic did achieve a remarkable expansion of industry. This was made possible by an even greater concentration on investment in industry than Stalin dared attempt in his first plans.[14] It must have caused corresponding hardship to the Chinese masses. This expansion was also greatly expedited by Soviet aid[15] and possibly too by forced labour (see below, p. 241). If anything, this development was greater than that achieved by the Russians during their first seven years of industrialization from 1928 onwards.[16]

At the political level China's 'mixed economy' was reflected in the four-class alliance as defined above. For this reason the People's Republic was not officially a single-party state on the Soviet model. 'National' industrialists and merchants were represented in the China Democratic National Reconstruction Association; petty bourgeois intelligentsia, particularly educationists, were enrolled in the China Democratic League; and even remnants of the Nationalists were mobilized in the Revolutionary Committee of the Kuomintang.[17] And there were other small groups as well. In this respect the People's Republic was similar to East Germany: the alliance parties were subservient to the Marxist-Leninist party. And the reasons for maintaining the minor parties were the same: democratic window-dressing; additional groups of bourgeois could be mobilized for the regime without them officially becoming Communists; such groups could appeal to their fellow-countrymen in the non-Communist part of the country and, particularly important in China's case, abroad; such groups were useful in establishing contacts abroad at a time when the regime was not completely accepted.

In most other respects the People's Republic followed the Soviet pattern, with single-list elections, Communist-controlled mass organizations, the Communist Party itself subject to 'democratic centralism', totally controlled mass media, severe restrictions on contacts with abroad, indoctrination, and forced labour. The People's Republic moved faster along the road to a 'totalitarian' system than Russia had done. No doubt this was attributable to the availability of the Soviet example and to the Korean War.[18]

One feature of the Communist takeover which impressed foreigners who witnessed it was the discipline and order of the People's Liberation Army, qualities which made it quite different from any other Chinese army.[19] The way the Communists treated many former opponents who went over to them also gave grounds for hope that the worst excesses of a long and bitter civil war would be avoided. Yet in 1955 a United Nations report on forced labour spotlighted the appalling conditions of millions of Chinese forced labourers – 'counter revolutionaries', 'deviationists', and others.

The Chinese, like the Soviets before them, boasted of the way they reformed, through work, former enemies and common criminals. In fact the Chinese copied Soviet methods in this sphere. In September 1949 Article Seven of the so-called Common Programme of the Chinese Communist Party and its allies, prescribed 'corrective labour' for 'counter-revolutionary elements, feudal landlords and bureaucratic capitalists in general'. The Chinese Communists had, however, resorted to this measure on a small scale in the period before 1945. We need not dwell on the horrors of the system here, except to say that the conditions described by ex-prisoners were, at the very least, grim. It is nevertheless useful to recall one unusual witness who

caught a glimpse of the system. The British trade union leader
H. Earnshaw was a member of the Labour Party delegation which
went to China in August 1954. At Peking prison he was told how
prisoners under suspended death sentences attempted to redeem
themselves through labour. If they did not give satisfaction, they
paid with their lives. 'In fact we had never seen human beings
working at such a pace', he commented.[20] In addition to those
sentenced to terms of corrective labour, millions of others were
mobilized, military-style, into labour gangs mainly on construction projects. This, it could be argued, was a traditional Chinese
practice. This system of forced labour must be remembered when
appraising China's industrial achievements and contrasting them
with those of, say, neighbouring India.

## 1. FROM KOREA TO THE 'FIVE PRINCIPLES'

In its foreign relations the People's Republic sought in its early
years to increase its security through its alliance with the USSR
and through its wide recognition by non-Communist states as
China's sole government. Something has already been said above
about Peking's relations with Moscow; let us turn, therefore, to
its relations with the non-Communist world.

Within a few months of its coming into existence the People's
Republic was recognized by all the Communist states, and by
Burma, India, Pakistan, Afghanistan, Ceylon, Indonesia, Israel,
all the Scandinavian countries, by the United Kingdom, the
Netherlands, and Switzerland. The People's Republic did not
reciprocate in every case. It did not establish relations with Israel,
and delayed establishing relations with Britain and Yugoslavia.[21]
In all likelihood for reasons of trade, Peking did not attempt to
drive the British from Hong Kong, but it did seize British and
other foreign assets after Chinese intervention in Korea. It started
to orientate its trade with the Soviet bloc; it restricted intellectual
contacts with the non-Communist states, including contacts
between Chinese Christians and their brothers abroad.[22]

Communist China's relations with the non-Communist states
were not improved by the Korean War. The Chinese had no part
in North Korea's original attack on the South. They intervened
only when forces under General MacArthur were advancing on
the Yalu River frontier where the key power-stations for Manchurian industry were located. As an American expert on the

subject has commented, Chinese entry into the war 'was motivated overwhelmingly by concern for its own security, and only very secondarily by concern for North Korean survival'.[23] At least the timing of the invasion of Tibet by Chinese Communist troops in October 1950 seems to have been dominated by defensive considerations.[24]

If the Chinese were ever in any doubt, the Korean experience seems to have convinced them that, for the time being at least, they could more safely extend their influence by diplomatic, rather than military, means. This conviction opened up the so-called Bandung phase of Chinese foreign policy which lasted from about 1954 to 1959.

In April 1954 an agreement was concluded by the People's Republic and India in which Delhi recognized Peking's claim to Tibet and both states agreed to abide by the 'Five Principles' – mutual respect for territorial integrity and sovereignty; non-aggression; non-interference in each other's internal affairs; equality and mutual benefit; and peaceful co-existence – in their mutual relations. Chou En-lai, the Chinese Prime Minister, later visited Burma and again both sides accepted that the 'Five Principles' should govern relations between the two nations. No frontier agreements were concluded, which was to be significant in the case of India later on. The Asian-African conference held at Bandung, Java, in April 1955 gave Chou En-lai a platform from which he could explain the People's Republic's policies and increase its influence. The Chinese Prime Minister came in for some criticism because of some of China's internal policies, and because of fears about the position of Chinese nationals in the states of South-East Asia. But the conference helped to bolster Peking's image as a peace-loving state, and Chou En-lai made contact with President Nasser of Egypt. This opened a door for China to the Middle East after diplomatic relations were established between Peking and Cairo in 1956. Another sign that Peking was pursuing a conciliatory path was the Geneva Agreement of 1954 on Indo-China. On that occasion Chou En-lai joined Molotov, the Soviet Foreign Minister, in pressing the North Vietnamese of Ho Chi Minh to accept a compromise settlement. This involved dividing Vietnam at the 17th parallel, with unification of the country by means of a general election within two years, neutrality for Laos and Cambodia, and a UN truce commission to supervise the arrangements. The French had been prepared to negotiate as a result of their weak military situation; the Soviet and Chinese Communists as a result of certain bellicose statements from America. But the Communists assumed that elections would produce a majority for Ho Chi Minh.[25] The conference greatly improved the image of the People's Republic in western Europe and in the Asian neutral states.[26] However, the Chinese were angry that the United States did not sign the agreement, nor did the Americans modify their position regarding their defence of the Chiang regime on Taiwan or Peking's membership of the United Nations.

Although Chou went on improving the People's Republic's image with its neighbours, he had to turn his attention to another problem – the Twentieth Congress of the CPSU and its after-math.

## II. THE HUNDRED FLOWERS

The Chinese took up a special position on de-Stalinization which was rather different from Khrushchev, on the one hand, and Togliatti, on the other. The Chinese reaction to Khrushchev's anti-Stalin speech was contained in an article which appeared in the *People's Daily* (Peking) on 5 April 1956. The paper called 'combating the cult of the individual' this 'courageous self-criticism of its past errors' by the Soviet party, and saw it as a sign of strength, not weakness. It praised Stalin's early role in socialist construction, as Khrushchev had done, but went on:

. . . having won such high honour among the people, both at home and abroad, by his correct application of the Leninist line, Stalin erroneously exaggerated his own role and counter-posed his individual authority to the collective leadership, and as a result certain of his actions were opposed to certain funda-mental Marxist-Leninist concepts which he himself had propagated. On the one hand, he recognized that the masses were the makers of history, that the Party must keep in constant touch with the people and that inner-Party democracy and self-criticism and criticism from below must be developed. On the other hand, he accepted and fostered the cult of the individual, and indulged in arbitrary individual actions. Thus Stalin found himself in a contradiction on this question during the latter part of his life, with a discrepancy between his theory and practice.[27]

The Chinese accepted Khrushchev's list of Stalin's crimes:

> . . . he broadened the scope of the suppression of counter-revolution; he lacked the necessary vigilance on the eve of the anti-fascist war; he failed to pay proper attention to the further development of agriculture and the material welfare of the peasantry; he gave certain wrong advice on the international communist movement, and, in particular, made a wrong decision on the question of Yugoslavia.[28]

What made the Peking view of Stalin different from Khrushchev's was that it was less emotional in tone, and it attempted, albeit on a very limited scale, to give some Marxist analysis of how the Stalinist situation had arisen in Russia. The Chinese offered two reasons for the cult of the individual. Firstly, 'certain rotten, poisonous ideological survivals of the old society may still remain in people's minds for a very long time'.[29] Among these ideological survivals was the habit of depending too much on leaders. Secondly, the Chinese believed that because the Marxist movement was still young, 'experience in many fields of revolutionary work is still inadequate'.[30]

To sum up the Chinese attitude to the Stalin controversy at this time: they accepted Khrushchev's criticisms, but put much more emphasis on his achievements than the Soviet leader had done. Their less emotional tone can be attributed to the fact that they were less involved than the Soviet leaders. They called for an 'analytical attitude' to the 'errors made in the communist movement' and made a beginning in this direction. Finally, unlike Togliatti, they recognized the Soviet Union as the head of the socialist camp.[31]

Before the big repercussions of the Twentieth Congress – Gomułka's return to power and the Hungarian Revolution – there opened the 'Hundred Flowers' campaign and the Eighth Congress of the Chinese Communist Party. The Congress was held in Peking in September 1956. It is a sign of how the party functioned when one remembers that the Seventh Congress had been held in 1945! The leadership were in breach of the 1945 constitution which laid down that a national congress was to be convened once every three years.[32]

The mood of the congress was 'at once self-congratulatory and self-critical'.[33] With so many reasons for self-congratulation the leaders of the then 10.7 million-strong party could afford a measure of self-criticism. Mao Tse-tung attacked some comrades for their 'subjectivism', 'bureaucracy', and 'sectarianism'. It would be surprising if there had not been some political weaknesses in the party members, for 90 per cent of them had joined since 1945 and 60 per cent since 1949.[34] More serious were the admissions of Lo Jui ch'ing, Minister of Public Security, that innocent persons had been arrested, prisoners maltreated, confessions extorted by force, individuals exected without sufficient reason, and other serious errors committed.[35] On the economic front the congress agreed on a Second Five-Year Plan (1958–62) which would mean 'more of the same'.[36] Most of the old Politburo were re-elected, together with six newcomers. The new standing committee of the Politburo consisted of Mao Tse-tung, Liu Shao-ch'i, Chou En-lai, Chu Teh, Chen Yun, and Teng Hsiao-p'ing, who retained the post of Secretary-General. Mao was re-elected Chairman of the Central Committee and of the Politburo. The congress was given a pat on the back by Soviet representative Mikoyan who paid tribute to Mao as a creative adapter and developer of Leninism.[37] This contrasted somewhat to the attitude of the Chinese, who appeared to have taken a hint from the Twentieth Congress in that they emphasized the collective leadership.

The Chinese backed the new Polish leadership in their desire to find a Polish road to socialism in September-October of 1956 (see above, p. 221). However, in the case of Hungary the Chinese were fully behind the Russians in their invasion of that country. They regarded the Hungarian Revolution as 'the gravest attack launched by [the imperialists] against the socialist camp since the war of aggression they had carried on in Korea'.[38] The Chinese analysis of the debate about de-Stalinization and its consequences, up to the end of 1956, was again published in the *People's Daily* (29 December 1956). In this article the Chinese set out what they considered to be the fundamental lessons of the Russian Revolution which had universal application. These were:

1. The advanced members of the proletariat form a Marxist-Leninist party, built on democratic centralism and with close ties to the masses;
2. Led by this party the proletariat, in alliance with all labouring people, takes power from the bourgeoisie by means of a revolutionary struggle;

3. The dictatorship of the proletariat is established under the leadership of the Marxist-Leninist party, resistance is crushed, nationalization of industry and step-by-step collectivization of agriculture is carried through;

4. The state, led by the proletariat and the Communist Party, leads the people in the planned development of socialist economy and culture, and on this basis gradually raises the people's living standards and prepares the transition to communism;

5. The state opposes imperialist aggression, recognizes the equality of all nations and defends world peace; firmly adheres to the principles of proletarian internationalism, strives to win the help of the labouring people of all countries, and at the same time strives to help them and all oppressed nations.[39]

It did not matter then, according to this analysis, if the Poles went more slowly on collectivization, or if the Yugoslavs or some other socialist states developed some specific institutions which differed from those of the USSR.[40] For the Chinese there were, at this time, two dangers in the socialist camp – and this was the origin of their quarrel with the Yugoslavs – exaggerating Stalin's and Soviet 'mistakes', and chauvinism. The attitude of Tito and other 'leading comrades' in Yugoslavia could not be regarded as 'well balanced or objective'. It was understandable that the Yugoslavs felt a particular resentment against Stalin's mistakes. The Yugoslavs had, in the past, 'made worthy efforts to stick to socialism under difficult conditions. Their experiments in the democratic management of economic enterprises and other social organizations have also attracted attention'. But the Chinese were 'amazed' by a speech of Tito's (11 November) in which he attached '. . . those hard-bitten Stalinist elements who in various Parties have managed still to maintain themselves in their posts and who would again wish to consolidate their rule and impose those Stalinist tendencies upon their people, and even others . . .'.[41] Though in some part their criticisms were 'reasonable', the 'basic stand and the method they have adopted infringed the principles of comradely discussion'. The struggle against 'doctrinarism' was entirely necessary; 'But by adopting a negative attitude towards everything connected with Stalin, and by putting up the erroneous slogan of "de-Stalinization", some

Communists have helped to foster a revisionist trend against Marxism-Leninism'.[42] In another part of the same article the Chinese warned the Yugoslavs, without naming them, of the dangers of nationalist tendencies, admitting that Stalin and the Russians had been guilty here.[43] For the Chinese the maintenance of unity was the overriding concern. This did not mean they believed the Soviets could do as they liked in other socialist countries.

The 'Hundred Flowers' campaign appears to have been in response to the Twentieth Congress. It opened a month after the *People's Daily* article of 5 April. Mao called upon the artists and writers to 'let a hundred flowers bloom' and upon scientists to 'let a hundred schools of thought contend'. Understandably there was some reluctance to get involved in this fruitful controversy which the party proclaimed. The Eighth Congress in September was another step in this direction with its critique of the narrow outlook of many party workers. In February 1957, in a speech 'On the Correct Handling of the Contradictions Among the People', Mao tried to put new life into the campaign. But as the speech was only published in amended form in June, its impact was limited. There was only a brief period of outspoken criticism in May during the Rectification Campaign. Many criticisms were not unsimilar to those heard in Poland and Hungary. The party leaders were apparently taken by surprise by the volume and intensity of the outcry, for by the time Mao's amended speech was published in June, an 'anti-rightist' campaign was in swing against outspoken intellectuals.[44]

The Chinese Communist Party suddenly swung 'left' in the second half of 1957. In many respects this left-turn was a resumption of the Five Antis Campaign (against bribery, tax evasion, theft of state assets, cheating, and theft of state economic secrets) of 1952, the excesses of which had just been denounced. It was aimed at so-called Rightists. Many of those denounced were members of the China Democratic League, the party banned by Chiang Kai-shek in 1947 after it had attempted to take a middle position between the Nationalists and the Communists. Many of them had been educated in the Anglo-Saxon countries and were somewhat sceptical of the heavy emphasis on Soviet methods and achievements. They did not get on well with the poorly educated party bureaucrats, were opposed to dogmatism in economics and science, and were appalled by the treatment of alleged oppositionists. Their fate was 'reform through labour'. The Left Campaign gradually spread both outside and inside the Communist Party, in both town and country.[45]


## III. THE GREAT LEAP FORWARD AND THE COMMUNES

The turn left in the second half of 1957 was designed to retrieve a desperate situation.[46] The economy seemed to be in danger of seizing up. The industrial progress of the First Five-Year Plan had been gained at a price. The heavy concentration on basic industry brought about bottlenecks, disproportions, and shortages. The rapid collectivization of agriculture did not produce the anticipated surpluses. Moreover, the Soviet Union was not so forthcoming with aid as before. The Chinese came to the conclusion that they would have to go one of two ways: either the way of the moderates, with slower growth, more careful selection of projects, some compromise in the countryside; or the 'left' way, with even more rapid development of their resources – taking, in fact, a 'great leap forward'. They decided for the second road. The extreme shortage of capital and the abundance of labour led them to emphasize labour-intensive processes. Why modernize a labour-intensive factory when the capital could be used instead to build another factory? But they were not just leaving existing labour-intensive enterprises; they were constructing new ones. This in itself was not necessarily a bad thing in a country suffering from chronic underemployment. Another aspect of the Great Leap was the decentralization of control over much of light industry. This again was not necessarily a step backward in such a vast country. It might even have something to be said for it in defence terms.

The Chinese Great Leap did not achieve the desired results. As so often in Communist countries, the sudden campaign led to disruption of existing capacities. There was, for instance, an excessive withdrawal of farm labour for various projects which led to a decline in agricultural production. The removal of many citizens from the towns brought with it dissatisfaction and disruption. Much of the production from rural industries was worthless. The best-known example of this was that of the backyard blast furnaces which produced iron of sub-standard and often entirely unusable quality.[47] Perhaps, too, capital was switched from modern projects to the less useful traditional ones.

At any rate, by 1960 China was once again in a deep economic crisis.

Part and parcel of the Great Leap Forward was the establishment of communes. Indeed the commune was the organizational form of the Great Leap campaign. As larger labour-intensive projects were introduced throughout the land it became necessary to find a mechanism to organize and control the labour supply. This was probably the single most important factor leading to the commune.[48] In August 1958 the Politburo called for the adoption of the commune system throughout the country. By 1959 there were about 24,000 communes with an average of 5,000 households per commune, accounting altogether for the bulk of the People's Republic's peasants.[49] This writer does not pretend to know exactly what the commune system meant in practice. The extreme ideal was of the peasant becoming a rural worker, organized on military lines, spending much of his free time – especially his meals and recreation – with his fellow-workers. But it is doubtful whether this extreme form ever spread right across the country. Certainly it was later abandoned. One Western writer summed up the situation in 1963 like this: 'Conditions today vary from one Commune to another, but for the most part they now amount to little more than groups of farms and villages under an overall central administration and sometimes including one or more minor industrial projects'.[50] As early as December 1958 the party leaders were curbing the more extreme communizers. The party cadres were told that it was mistaken to attempt to collectivize homes, small tools, chickens, and personal belongings.

By the beginning of 1961 the Great Leap Forward was being called off and although the rural communes remained, they did so more as an administrative unit than as a way of life. The Chinese leader identified in the West as the champion of the moderate line, Chou En-lai, was once again in the ascendant, but the advocates of the Great Leap Forward – Liu Shao-ch'i, Teng Hsiao-p'ing, and Mao himself – clung on to their positions.[51]

## IV. MOSCOW VERSUS PEKING

An astonished press looked on at the congress of the Italian Communist Party in December 1962 as Giancarlo Pajetta, one of the Secretaries of the Party, denounced the Chinese. Turning to

Peking's representative at the congress Pajetta urbanely remarked
that what the quarrel was really about was China's attitude (to
world problems), not Albania's: 'When we mean China, we have
no need to say Albania'. Thus Pajetta brought into the open a
dispute which had been going on for years between Moscow and
Peking, a dispute thinly disguised as one between the Yugoslavs
and the Albanians.

We saw above how the Chinese had been unhappy about the
Soviet de-Stalinization campaign in 1956, and about the attitude
of the Yugoslavs to the problem of Communist unity. These
differences grew over the next five or six years despite efforts to
paper them over. One of the crucial turning-points in this direction was the Moscow conference of Communist parties in
November 1957.

Officially the conference was held to celebrate the fortieth
anniversary of the October Revolution. In fact it attempted to
iron out differences of opinion. It was attended by most of the top
brass of the world Communist movement – Khrushchev, Mao
Tse-tung, Gomułka, Togliatti, Ulbricht among them. Tito did
not attend, but he sent his trusted lieutenant Kardelj. About
sixty-four parties were represented.[52] The conference ended with
a Peace Manifesto and a Declaration. Only the Yugoslavs
decided not to be associated with the conference documents.
Ideologically, the conference marked a hardening of attitudes on
the part of the Soviet Union and the Chinese. Perhaps the
atmosphere of the post-Twentieth Congress period – troubles in
Poland and Hungary, the Suez crisis, outbursts from Soviet
intellectuals, and his own struggle with the 'anti-party group'
(Malenkov, Molotov, and Kaganovich) – made Khrushchev feel
there was every need for a firmer hand.[53] But if Khrushchev and
his colleagues were in any doubts about this the Chinese seem to
have persuaded them.[54] Later the Chinese were to claim to have
done this.[55] Another factor which influenced the Sino-Soviet
leaders was the launching of the first two Soviet earth satellites in
October and November of 1957, putting the Russians ahead of
the United States in the Space/arms race.

The Declaration of 1957 did not repudiate the decisions and
formulations of the Twentieth Congress, but at least there was a
significant shift of emphasis.[56] The possibilities of peaceful
change to socialism were made to appear less likely, and there
seemed to be greater expectation of war between the West and

the socialist states. In a word, the Declaration was 'a fighting and uncompromising statement of militant Communist intentions and of the necessity for strict discipline within the Communist world'.[57] This is certainly how the Chinese saw it: the Declaration 'corrected the erroneous views which the CPSU leadership had put forward at the 20th Congress on such questions as imperialism and war and peace, and it added many important points on a number of questions of principle'.[58]

It was at the Moscow meeting that Mao Tse-tung made certain statements which were later distorted, or at least oversimplified, in the West and in the Soviet bloc. These oversimplifications about Mao's views on 'paper tigers' gave the Chinese leader the image of a reckless adventurer indifferent to the colossal suffering which would result from a nuclear war, or even welcoming such a conflict as a necessary prelude to the final triumph of communism. Mao Tse-tung first referred to imperialists as paper tigers when discussing with the pro-Communist American writer Anna Louise Strong in 1946. At the 1957 Moscow meeting Chairman Mao expounded the same proposition. He said:

> All the reputedly powerful reactionaries were merely paper tigers. . . . For struggle against the enemy, we formed over a long period the concept that strategically we should despise all our enemies, but that tactically we should take them all seriously . . . Marx and Engels were only two persons. Yet in those early days they declared that capitalism would be overthrown all over the world.[59]

The Chinese later claimed that their leader's analysis was completely in accord with Lenin's view of 1919 in which he compared Anglo-French imperialism to a 'colossus with feet of clay'. Lenin had said that 'all these seemingly huge and invincible forces of international imperialism are unreliable, and hold no terrors for us'.[60] In 1946, during the Strong interview, Mao had mentioned the atom bomb:

> The atom bomb is a paper tiger which the US reactionaries use to scare people. It looks terrible, but in fact it isn't. Of course, the atom bomb is a weapon of mass slaughter, but the outcome of a war is decided by the people, not by one or two new types of weapon.[61]

Did this than mean Mao was not worried about nuclear war? It did not, claimed the Chinese. And in the next year the Russians did not accuse the Chinese leader of having a reckless attitude to nuclear war. On the contrary, during this time the Moscow-Peking alliance seemed, on the surface, stronger than it had done for some time. As we saw above (p. 234), the Chinese and the Soviets attacked the 1958 Programme of the Yugoslav Communists, with its emphasis on non-alignment, the Yugoslav road, and so on. The Chinese critique of Tito was tougher than the Soviet. Peking even claimed that the 1948 Cominform resolution was still valid.[62] On 3 June Khrushchev, speaking at the Seventh Congress of the Bulgarian Communist Party, endorsed this Chinese claim, accusing the Yugoslavs of spreading revisionism and acting like a Trojan horse in the socialist camp.[63] The Soviet party leader returned to the attack at the Fifth Congress of the East German Socialist Unity Party in July. His anti-Yugoslav tirade took up a major part of his speech.[64] On neither occasion, however, did the Soviet leader go as far in his attacks as his Chinese colleagues. They were once again calling Tito a traitor.[65]

There was evidence that the Russians and Chinese did not see eye to eye on international policy during the Middle East crisis of summer 1958. The overthrow of the pro-Western government in Iraq resulted in the landing of American and British forces in neighbouring Lebanon. Khrushchev demonstrated a more conciliatory attitude than the Chinese. The crisis was resolved by Soviet-American negotiations and Western withdrawal from Lebanon.[66]

In 1959 Sino-Soviet relations took another sharp turn for the worse. The diplomatic highlight of the year was undoubtedly the visit of Khrushchev to the United States. The Soviet leader praised President Eisenhower as a man of peace who could be relied upon to keep the professional warmongers of the Pentagon well under control.[67] The Soviets made a special film of the visit which was given wide distribution outside the Union and a lot of illustrated material was produced for world-wide distribution. The Chinese found this in 'complete disregard of the common conclusion of the 1957 Declaration that US imperialism is the enemy of all the people of the world'.[68] The Chinese later accused the Russians of unilaterally tearing up an agreement of 1957 under which the Soviet Union was to provide the People's Republic with a sample atomic bomb and technical data concerning its manufacture. Another cause of difficulty between the Soviet Union and the People's Republic was China's border dispute with India.

It is impossible even to outline here the changes in the Chinese frontiers over the last 130 or so years. It must be sufficient to say that the old Chinese Empire was dismembered by the Imperial powers after 1840, and that by no means all the states which emerged from that process were populated by Chinese. Thirdly, since coming to power the Communists have never clearly stated their position on their frontiers. However, certain maps published in China would have been enough by themselves to frighten the People's Republic's neighbours.[69] We have seen that Peking took control of Tibet, an area also regarded by Chiang's Nationalists as belonging to China; accepted the independence of the Mongolian People's Republic and Korea; and came to an agreement with Burma. With India there had been no agreement over the frontier. Chinese maps indicated a total of roughly 50,000 square miles of disputed territory with India,[70] much of it barren, empty, and worthless. In addition, the Chinese attitude to the frontier states of Bhutan, Nepal, and Sikkim was not unambiguous. In 1959 a rising took place in Tibet against the Chinese. Thousands of Tibetan refugees, including the Dalai Lama, their leader, fled to India. In its way the revolt was as big a setback for China as the Hungarian Revolution was for the Soviet Union. The Chinese alleged Indian, as well as American and Chinese Nationalist, interference. Angry notes were exchanged between the two countries and a series of frontier clashes occurred on the Indian-Chinese frontier. The Soviets did not support the Chinese. In public they made neutral statements, in private they believed the Chinese were deliberately increasing tension to make Soviet-American *détente* more difficult.[71]

The next round of the Sino-Soviet debate was carried on in June 1960 at the Third Congress of the Romanian Communist Party at Bucharest. Though avoiding naming each other, a bitter exchange took place between Khrushchev and P'eng Chen, a Politburo member, mayor of Peking, and the head Chinese representative at the conference. Khrushchev attacked the 'mechanical repeaters of what Lenin had said about imperialism', and denounced those who could not see that war, 'under present circumstances', was not inevitable. P'eng exploited the shooting-down by the Soviets of the American U2 spy plane over the USSR which led to the break-up of the May Summit conference in Paris. He celebrated the guerrilla fighters in Algeria and Cuba, claiming that the best way to avert war was to help the national liberation movements everywhere. 'Most strikingly of all, he got through his whole speech without once referring to peaceful co-existence'.[72] Both the Soviet and Chinese delegations carried on behind the scenes canvassing to try to persuade the representatives of the other parties of their point of view.

Shortly after the Bucharest meeting the Soviet Union withdrew her specialists from China, thus doing great harm to the Chinese economy.

The meeting of Communist parties in Moscow in November 1960 was the most representative conference of such parties ever held. In all, eighty-one parties sent delegations. It was claimed that at that time there were eighty-seven Communist parties. The conference was the last major attempt to present a united front of World Communism. It ended after much acrimony in a longwinded compromise Declaration. Compromise though it was, the Declaration owed more to the Soviet point of view than to the Chinese. It identified the United States as the main bulwark of world reaction and the Soviet Union as the opposite. The USSR was also called the 'universally recognized vanguard' of the world Communist movement. She was not, as in 1957, recognized as the 'head' of the movement. The Chinese contribution was summed up as follows:

> The people's revolution in China delivered a crushing blow to imperialism in Asia and contributed to a significant degree to changing the international power relationship to the advantage of socialism. To the extent that it gave the national liberation movements a mighty boost, it exercised a powerful influence on the peoples, especially in Asia, Africa and Latin America.

No mention here of the Chinese adapting Marxism to the special conditions of Asia or producing interesting experiments in socialist development! However, later on there is a concession to the Chinese in the admission that the practical building of socialism in all countries has contributed to the treasury of socialist experience. There is also a warning not to neglect the national characteristics of a particular country when building socialism. But in the same paragraph there is even more emphasis on the damage which can result from overstressing such characteristics. In line with recent Soviet policy, the Declaration put a great deal of emphasis on peaceful co-existence and the horror of nuclear war. But it was stressed that because of the firm line of the USSR and the growth of real forces which can frustrate the plans of the aggressors, wars were no longer inevitable. Elsewhere in the Declaration the Chinese were reminded of the value of the Five Principles which they and the Indians had composed. On the question of the socialist revolution the Declaration stated that revolution could not be imported or forced from outside. As for the form of the transition, this would depend on the concrete relationship of class forces in each country, on the degree of organization and maturity of the working class, on the amount of opposition from the ruling class. A lengthy paragraph was taken up to criticize the Yugoslav leaders. Their 1958 programme was attacked as 'anti-Leninist and revisionist', they were accused of endangering their country's socialist achievements by taking aid from the United States, and of undermining the unity of the socialist camp under the guise of so-called non-alignment. Dogmatism and sectarianism, allegedly the deviations of the Chinese, were also accorded a paragraph of condemnation. Finally, the decision of the Twentieth Congress of the CPSU were praised and there was a call for unity of all the Communist forces.[73]

The period between the Moscow conference and Pajetta's open attack on the Chinese in 1963 witnessed two international crises which particularly concerned the two major Communist powers. These were the renewed clashes between China and India, and the Cuban crisis.

Between 1960 and 1963 the People's Republic concluded border treaties with Burma, Nepal, Mongolia, Pakistan, and Afghanistan. The frontier dispute with India remained. Diplomatic exchanges failed to produce results and the Indians talked of clearing the Chinese out of the disputed area by force. On 12 October Premier Nehru of India made a statement that Indian troops had been ordered to launch an offensive to drive the Chinese out. India had

precipitated war with a stronger enemy, on whose dispositions it had no adequate intelligence, and who had evidently made considerable efforts from the autumn of 1959 to the spring of 1962 to avoid hostilities, but who had watched the steady advance of Indian troops in the western sector with growing concern.[74]

Local Chinese successes brought more exchanges of notes which again failed to produce agreement. The Chinese then launched a stronger attack which humiliated the Indians (some 3,000 of their troops were taken prisoner, for instance). The Chinese then withdrew from most of the territory they had overrun. Were the Chinese satisfied that they had taught the Indians a lesson and destroyed any Indian illusions about favourable revisions of the frontier? At any rate, Anglo-American aid, sympathy for India in the Afro-Asian bloc, as well as in the West, and worries about extending their supply lines, must have made the Chinese think hard. The Soviet attitude, moving from one of neutrality to a pro-Indian stance, must also have given the Chinese cause for concern. It certainly made them angry. They denounced Soviet military aid to India and claimed:

> The stand and policy of the Soviet leaders on the Sino-Indian boundary question amply prove that they have betrayed the Chinese people, the Soviet people, the people of all the countries in the socialist camp, the Indian people and all the oppressed peoples and nations. It is becoming clearer and clearer that the Soviet leaders no longer consider the imperialists, headed by the United States . . . to be their enemy. It is the Marxist-Leninists, the revolutionary people and China in particular who are their enemy.[75]

Naturally, the Soviets saw things differently:

> The border conflict in the Himalayas has given rise to serious concern in the young Afro-Asian states, which know from their own experience that the weakening of unity of the young independent states and that friction and dissent between them play into the hands of none other but the imperialists and colonialists.[76]

The Cuban crisis coincided with the Sino-Indian clash. Fidel Castro had gained power in Cuba in 1959. Though the nature of the new Cuban regime was not yet clear the Central Intelligence Agency started to train exiles. Early in 1961 anti-Castro rebels with American backing and air support unsuccessfully attempted to invade Cuba. In the summer of 1962 the Russians started to install nuclear missiles on Cuba, only some 90 miles from the Florida coast. Why the Soviets did this, and why the Cubans allowed them to, we do not know. It is even doubtful that the missiles would have made much difference to the relative American-Soviet military positions.[77] But the fact of those missiles so close to Florida, and with the United States still licking her wounds from her earlier attempt to overthrow Castro, caused President Kennedy to act. Nuclear war looked a distinct possibility until 28 October 1962 when Khrushchev announced his willingness to withdraw the missiles. As the Chinese saw the Cuban crisis, 'the leadership of the CPSU committed the error of capitulationism by submitting to the nuclear blackmail of the US imperialists'.[78] In 1963 the Soviet Union signed a partial nuclear test-ban treaty with the United States and the United Kingdom. 'The treaty appeared to the Chinese as final confirmation, if any were needed, of the Soviet determination to appease the United States at the expense of China and the entire Soviet bloc'.[79] The treaty kept the United States ahead of the Soviet Union in nuclear weapons[80] and the Chinese felt that if they agreed to it, they would be in a permanently inferior position regarding their own security.

Finally, one other cause of friction between the Chinese and the Soviets during this period, which is discussed below was the new Soviet party programme of 1962. This the Chinese regarded as revisionist.

And so we come back to Pajetta's statement at the Italian Communist Party Congress in 1962. Later in London he defined his party's differences with the Chinese:

> First, we have stressed the importance we attach to the policy of a co-existence for the development of the workers' movement for liberation. Then we have declared our complete support for the peace policy of the Soviet Union as it showed itself in the Cuban crisis. Thirdly, we do not understand the motives behind Chinese solidarity for the Albanian leaders in their actions against the Communist Party in every country and in the Soviet Union. We believe in the individual national roads, but the roads of slander and the sabotaging of the international movement are unacceptable to us.[81]

At the same time another leading Italian Communist, Giorgio Amendola, added:

We Italian Communists do not believe that imperialism is a paper tiger; in order to defeat the enemy the power of imperialism must be precisely estimated and in spite of the blows received in the last forty years, it still represents a danger one must estimate. A thousand million men live in Socialist states; the colonial system has crumbled but imperialism is a tiger which has atomic teeth and if it cannot defeat socialism it can cause a catastrophe. This can be avoided with a struggle for peace, with a struggle for peaceful co-existence.

The Chinese saw it differently. As was pointed out above, Mao's concept of imperialism as a paper tiger was to be understood in the sense that it was a historically doomed system. This was clearly in accord with Marxist thought. Basically the Russians would go along with the proposition that imperialism is a doomed system, but they put more emphasis on the horror of nuclear war than the Chinese. They were therefore more anxious for agreement with the United States. Mao, on the other hand, while he did not advocate nuclear war, believed that 'if the worst came to the worst and half of mankind died, the other half would remain while imperialism would be razed to the ground and the whole world would become socialist'.[82] Mao also argued that post-war developments had indicated that American nuclear bombs were not the 'ultimate weapon': 'Even while the US imperialists still retained their nuclear superiority they were unable to prevent the defeat of their war of aggression in Korea'.[83] The same was true, he argued, in Vietnam, Algeria, and Cuba. And he could have argued that in these cases it was not the Soviet Union's help which brought these revolutionary regimes into existence.

## NOTES

[1] Nai-Ruenn Chen and Walter Galenson, *The Chinese Economy under Communism* (Edinburgh, 1969), p. 35.
[2] ibid.
[3] Ygael Gluckstein, *Mao's China* (London, 1957), p. 20.
[4] T. J. Hughes and D. E. T. Luard, *The Economic Development of Communist China 1949–1960* (London, 1961), p. 16.
[5] Walter H. Mallory, *China, Land of Famine* (American Geographical Society, New York, 1926), p. 188.
[6] Mao Tse-tung, *On People's Democratic Dictatorship* (Peking, 1950), p. 33.
[7] ibid., pp. 18–19.
[8] Hughes and Luard, op. cit., p. 30.

[9] Chen and Galenson, op. cit., p. 17.

[10] Schram, op. cit., p. 279.

[11] Hughes and Luard, op. cit., pp. 151, 156.

[12] ibid., p. 167.

[13] ibid.

[14] Chen and Galenson, op. cit., p. 50; also Gluckstein, op. cit., p. 51.

[15] ibid.

[16] Chen and Galenson, op. cit., p. 57.

[17] Lyman P. Van Slyke, *Enemies and Friends. The United Front in Chinese Communist Theory* (Stanford, 1967), pp. 208–19.

[18] Hugh Seton-Watson, 'The Russian and Chinese Revolutions', *China Quarterly* (April–June 1960), p. 46.

[19] Derk Bodde, *Peking Diary*, as quoted in Schurmann and Schell, op. cit., p. 21.

[20] *Forced Labor* (UN/ILO, 15 Dec. 1955), pp. 264–5.

[21] Harold C. Hinton, *Communist China in World Politics* (London, 1966), p. 24.

[22] For the position of the Christians in the People's Republic, see C. Bush, *Religion in Communist China* (New York, 1970).

[23] Hinton, op. cit., p. 214. See also Francis Watson, *The Frontiers of China* (London, 1966), p. 65.

[24] ibid.

[25] Hinton, op. cit., pp. 248–54.

[26] ibid., p. 254.

[27] *The Historical Experience of the Dictatorship of the Proletariat* (English version, Peking, 1960), pp. 7–8.

[28] ibid., pp. 8–9.

[29] ibid., p. 9.

[30] ibid., p. 18.

[31] ibid., p. 20.

[32] Conrad Brandt, Benjamin Schwartz, and John K. Fairbank, *A Documentary History of Chinese Communism* (London, 1952), p. 420.

[33] Robert C. North, 'Peking on the March: The Eighth Congress of the CCP', *Problems of Communism* (Jan.–Feb. 1957), p. 18.

[34] Moseley, op. cit., p. 125.

[35] North, 'Peking on the March', p. 22.

[36] Moseley, op. cit., p. 126.

[37] North, 'Pcking on the March', p. 22.

[38] *The Historical Experience*, p. 22.

[39] ibid., pp. 29–30.

[40] The emphasis on 'revolutionary struggle' under (2) seemed to contrast with Khrushchev's emphasis at the Twentieth Congress on the possibility of a parliamentary road to socialism in certain countries.

[41] *The Historical Experience*, p. 12.

[42] ibid., p. 44.

[43] ibid., p. 59.

[44] Roderick MacFarquhar, *The Hundred Flowers Campaign and the Chinese Intellectual* (New York, 1960).

[45] Moseley, op. cit., pp. 133–4.

[46] Zagoria, op. cit., p. 67. Another explanation of the 'turn left' is Mao's disillusionment with the behaviour of the Western-trained intellectuals during the weeks of free criticism in May 1957. If he could not rely on them, he had better construct an economy which did not need their services.

[47] Chen and Galenson, op. cit., p. 47.

[48] Zagoria, op. cit., p. 88.

[49] Moseley, op. cit., p. 145.

[50] Fitzroy Maclean, 'Eye-witness in China', *Sunday Times* (London), 6 Oct. 1963.
[51] See Roderick MacFarquhar, 'China Takes a Step Backwards', *Daily Telegraph* (1 May 1962).
[52] *GDAB*, VIII, 100.
[53] Edward Crankshaw, *The New Cold War: Moscow v. Pekin* (London, 1963), p. 64.
[54] Zagoria, op. cit., p. 150.
[55] *The Origin and Development of the Differences between the Leadership of the CPSU and Ourselves* (English version, Peking, 1963), p. 20.
[56] Crankshaw, *The New Cold War*, p. 64.
[57] ibid., p. 65.
[58] *The Origin and Development*, p. 22.
[59] *Workers of all Countries Unite, Oppose our Common Enemy!* (English version, Peking, 1963), p. 39.
[60] ibid., p. 40.
[61] ibid., p. 43.
[62] Zagoria, op. cit., p. 181.
[63] ibid., p. 183.
[64] *Protokoll des V. Parteitages der SED*, I, 304.
[65] Zagoria, op. cit., p. 183.
[66] Crankshaw, *The New Cold War*, pp. 80–2.
[67] ibid., p. 86.
[68] *The Origin and Development*, p. 24. A visit by Khrushchev to Peking *after* his American tour did nothing to improve his relations with Peking.
[69] Watson, op. cit., p. 26.
[70] ibid., p. 108.
[71] ibid., p. 119.
[72] Crankshaw, *The New Cold War*, p. 98.
[73] The author has used the German (SED) text in *GDAB*, VIII.
[74] Hinton, op. cit., p. 299.
[75] *The Truth about how the Leaders of the CPSU have allied themselves with India against China* (English version, Peking, 1963), p. 34.
[76] ibid., p. 41.
[77] Brian Beedham, 'Cuba and the Balance of Power', *The World Today* (Jan. 1963).
[78] *The Origin and Development*, p. 48.
[79] Moseley, op. cit., p. 178.
[80] See Robert MacNamara's remarks before the Senate Foreign Relations Committee as reported in the *Guardian* (Manchester), 14 August 1963.
[81] The writer spent two days with Pajetta and Amendola when preparing a TV programme with them about the Sino-Soviet dispute. Most of their remarks were published in the Italian left-wing paper *Paese Sera* (11 Jan. 1963).
[82] *People of the World, Unite, for the Complete, Thorough, Total and Resolute Prohibition and Destruction of Nuclear Weapons!* (English version, Peking, 1963), p. 42.
[83] ibid., p. 48.

# X

## *East European Communism in the Sixties*

THE 1960s opened with the biggest ever gathering of Communist parties in Moscow.[1] The Soviet bloc and its friends seemed in a strong position. In Poland and Hungary the situation had been stabilized. All was quiet in Bulgaria, Czechoslovakia, and Romania. East Germany had just had a good year. In China Mao had successfully concluded a decade of power and looked stronger than ever. And the socialist camp had just gained a new member – Castro's Cuba. In western Europe communism had failed to make any significant progress, but in France the party had started to recover from the reverses suffered after de Gaulle took power in 1958, and in Italy the PCI maintained its strength. Within the Soviet Union conditions of life appeared to be improving – so much so, that Western experts were arguing about the extent of, and the significance of, the Soviet 'welfare state'. Alec Nove could point to improvements in social welfare under Khrushchev, in housing, pensions, the health service, and to a reduction in the hours of labour.[2] Spectacular space achievements – in April 1960 Yuri Gagarin became the first person to orbit in space – reinforced this impression of strength. However, the position of the Communists was not nearly so strong as it appeared.

As we have seen, the two colossi of the camp were soon to be calling each other names, relations between Moscow and Tirana were rapidly deteriorating; the crisis which led to the Berlin Wall was looming; Romania would soon be causing Moscow concern by her more independent posture; and within the Kremlin itself Khrushchev was heading for compulsory retirement.

### I. 'KHRUSHCHEV'S CUBA'

Albania has been called the 'Tibet of Europe'; she has also been labelled 'Khrushchev's Cuba'. The term 'Tibet of Europe' refers

to the fact that little is known about contemporary Albania. Even
before the war, few foreigners spoke the language and few had
cause to visit this mountainous, backward country, where roads
were few and railways non-existent. Her capital, Tirana, was a
'wretched, overgrown village'[3] of only 30,000 inhabitants and
most of her other 'towns' were correspondingly shabbier. Albania's primitive economy was subject to the 'lira imperialism' of
Italy, her small army Italian-trained. Surprisingly, the top police
officers were British. Clan, national, and religious differences
divided the million or so Albanians. Seventy per cent of the
population were Muslim, 20 per cent Orthodox Christians, and
10 per cent Catholics. After being independent from 1912 Albania was overrun by Italian forces in 1949. Ironically, the Albanians, under the autocratic King Zog, had been relying on the
Italians for protection against their neighbours Yugoslavia and
Greece.

Communist groups had existed in Albania before the war, but
they had little influence. It was in November 1941 that the
Albanian Communist Party was constituted with the help and
advice of Yugoslav Communist emissaries. Enver Hoxha was
nominated Secretary-General.

At the time of his elevation to the post of Secretary-General
the thirty-four-year-old Hoxha was running a cigar store in
Tirana. The store was a cover for his Communist activities. From
1939 until then he had been working as a teacher in a French
school in a provincial Albanian town. Hoxha was born into a
middle-class Muslim family and, after secondary schooling, was
sent on a state scholarship to university in France. He spent the
next six years in western Europe and devoted more time to studying communism than studying science. He did not complete his
official studies. When Communist partisan units were formed in
1942 he was made commander of them. The Communists went
over to the offensive and the Italians were soon forced to abandon
large areas of the country to them. King Zog was abroad with
some of his closest advisers. Some of the other pre-war politicians
had compromised themselves by working with the Italians. The
growing Communist movement influenced others to do so. A
non-Communist partisan movement did exist, but this was outmanoeuvred and outfought by the Communists. The war ended
with Hoxha's Yugoslav-backed guerrillas in control of most of
the country. Hoxha himself was already the Stalin of Albania.[4]

In the years 1944–48 Albania followed closely the lead given by Belgrade. No other choice seemed open. The country was small, poor, and isolated. It needed outside help to modernize. Moreover, the new regime was from 1946 until 1952 under constant pressure from Britain and America. Sabotage groups and anti-Communist partisans were infiltrated into the country in an attempt to bring down the regime.[5] When the Moscow-Belgrade struggle began, Hoxha backed the Russians. Perhaps the Albanian leader resented his dependence on Tito. Perhaps he felt his position with his own countrymen would be strengthened by an anti-Yugoslav line. (The Albanians were aggrieved that Yugoslavia held on to an area which was traditionally Albanian and is populated by Albanians.) A third possible reason for his sudden hostility to Yugoslavia was the assumption that Tito could not hold out against Stalin. This course was not without danger. Albania forfeited her aid and trade from Belgrade, and she was surrounded by hostile neighbours. When in 1954 Yugoslavia, Greece, and Turkey signed the Balkan Pact, Albania's position seemed extremely precarious. Given the geopolitical situation, it would have been difficult for the Russians directly to aid the Albanians had hostilities broken out.

Economic and military aid did arrive from the Soviet bloc throughout the 1950s. Considerable economic and social progress was made. Politically Enver Hoxha held a firm grip on things. Potential rivals for power were dealt with as alleged Titoites – Kochi Xoxe, Minister of Interior in 1949; three Central Committee members in 1950; General Vincani, Chief of the General Staff in 1952; Tuka Jakova, President of the Trade Unions; and General Berri Spahiu, President of the Albanian–Soviet Friendship Society, in 1955. According to Vladimir Dedijer, 'in no eastern country had the terror been so effective. Tribalism added its weight to the purges à la Stalin'.[6] Another expert has written: 'Communism in Albania today means simply the absolute personal rule of Enver Hoxha. He is in the true line of succession from such colourful Balkan rulers as the late King Zog and Ali Pasha of Janina'.[7] Yet under Hoxha: 'Tall, athletic, upright. . . . Even in civilian clothes . . . a "fine figure" of a man',[8] Albania has achieved more progress than under the earlier colourful figures.

Given that Hoxha's 'Stalinism' was increasingly in contradiction to Khrushchev's 'de-Stalinization', Albania needed a powerful ally to help her withstand Soviet pressure. That pressure mounted after the summer of 1960. Apparently Khrushchev told a left-wing Greek politician that the Soviet Union would support Greek claims to what the Greeks call Northern Epirus, which happens to be in Albania! This was the last straw for Hoxha: as David Floyd has commented: 'Every Albanian, Communist and non-Communist alike, is united on the question of Albania's inalienable right to this territory. No one who wishes to rule Albania, of whatever party or creed, can relinquish this right'.[9] At the Moscow Conference of Communist parties in November 1960, Albania stood by China and has continued to do so. In 1961 the Soviet Union and her allies meted out the same treatment to the Albanians that they had earlier reserved for the Yugoslavs – total economic blockade. Albania was in the same situation Yugoslavia had been in in 1948. Luckily for the Albanians, the Chinese stepped into the breach. Some help was also forthcoming from their old enemy, Italy.

By the end of the 1960s Tirana had become the meeting-place for Maoist splinter-groups from all over Europe. The regime even had confidence enough in its own people to start admitting a few genuine Western tourists (whose movements were, however, restricted). Hoxha seemed as firmly in the saddle as ever before. Only Tito and Ulbricht of the European Communist leaders had exercised power anything like as long. By 1971 Ulbricht, too, was gone.

## II. THE BERLIN WALL

Having overcome the de-Stalinization crisis without too much difficulty, Ulbricht and his colleagues in the Politburo of the Socialist Unity Party became more confident. In 1958 they held their Fifth Party Congress at which they showed themselves infected with Khrushchev's enthusiasm for overtaking the West in peaceful competition. Ulbricht promised that by 1961 his German Democratic Republic would overtake West Germany in *per capita* consumption of consumer goods and foodstuffs.[10] The East Germans followed their Soviet colleagues in condemning the Yugoslavs and proposing education reforms in the GDR similar to those introduced in the USSR. The congress proclaimed the aim of the SED in the next period the 'completion of Socialism'.

The year following the Fifth Congress was a relatively good

one for the SED leaders. A measure of this is the fact that fewer East Germans left for the West than in any previous year – 'only' 143,917 deserted the Democratic Republic. Perhaps the Unity Party leaders overestimated their own strength, for they swung 'left'. Measures were introduced to force through the collectivization of the remaining private farms – that is about half East Germany's farms – and to nationalize private businesses. The latter were mainly smaller firms and they were transformed into joint state-private undertakings, a form of enterprise introduced into the GDR in 1956, possibly under influence from China. The result was some economic dislocation, shortages, and so on. The numbers going West increased once again. Also of great importance in helping to explain why the stream of refugees became a flood in 1961, were the demands of Khrushchev and Ulbricht regarding West Berlin. In effect the Soviet and East German leaders, backed up in August 1961 by their Warsaw Pact colleagues, sought to sever the ties between West Berlin and West Germany and turn the Western sectors of the old capital into an 'independent political unit on the territory of the GDR'. This would have undermined the position of the Western powers in Berlin and put the two million or so West Berliners at the mercy of the GDR's goodwill. It would have also undermined the credibility of the Western powers in the eyes of the world. Even more than this, the Communists sought by pressure on West Berlin to secure recognition of the GDR by the Western powers. The feeling of insecurity about the future brought on by the Soviet leader's demands helped to swell the numbers of East Germans 'voting with their feet' to 155,402 between January and August 1961.[11] Clearly, the GDR authorities had to do something to stop the outflow of population through the open Berlin frontier.

When East Berlin was sealed off in the night of 12–13 August some who had observed the East German scene, including the author, were only surprised that this had not happened much sooner. But by erecting their 'anti-fascist defence wall' the East German leaders had struck the biggest propaganda blow *against* communism since the revolution in Hungary and, possibly, since the purge trials of the 1930s. Unlike past Communist crimes and blunders the Berlin Wall goes on, degraded to the level of a macabre tourist spectacle. The East German people accepted the Wall in a mood of resignation, many of the SED cadre were dismayed. The leaders had to work hard to justify their measures.

They rightly, from their point of view, emphasized that West Berlin was a spy centre.[12] They also mentioned *Menschenraub* – their claim that West German firms and organizations were attempting to recruit their workers and technicians for jobs in the West, thus 'robbing' them of people. There is some limited evidence that Western firms, in a booming economy, were doing this to a certain extent.[13] It is also true that most of the East Germans going West were not refugees as one usually pictures them. These were not the downtrodden, shabby, outcasts of earlier twentieth-century tragedies. As one British journalist described East Germans waiting outside a West Berlin camp: 'It is like a holiday crowd trudging from Brighton station to the sea front . . . some have cameras slung over their shoulders, teenagers in gay slacks, carrying blaring portable radios, tired babies sleep in their push chairs'.[14] And as official West Germans investigations of those leaving the GDR in July 1961 indicated, many were concerned with higher living standards, many wanted to join relations already in the West, many others were sick and tired of being pushed into 'voluntary' political and social activities. In other words, though some would have left anyway, the methods of the SED were a major factor in causing many to turn their backs on 'socialism'.

Well over two million East Germans had left the Soviet Zone/ GDR since about 1948, or a number of people roughly equal to the population of a country like Albania or Ireland or Paraguay. Throughout the 1960s people were killed trying to 'jump' the Wall, altogether sixty-four of them.[15] Others died attempting to break through the East–West German frontiers.

Faced with the Wall and with the inability of the West to do anything about it, most East Germans feared the worst. And to be sure the SED leaders took advantage of the new situation. Conscription was introduced in January 1962, the housing programme was cut, and there was a general tightening-up of labour discipline. Nevertheless, the GDR experienced a mild 'thaw' which lasted for most of the decade. This 'thaw' was in keeping with the Twenty-second Congress of the CPSU (described below, p. 278) held in October 1961.

It was Ulbricht who proclaimed the message in an interview in *Neues Deutschland*, his party's organ, on 1 January 1962. In the future, Ulbricht assured his readers, the SED would try to convince, rather than coerce, people and that honest differences of opinion would be tolerated. Once again Walter Ulbricht had shown his remarkable talent for political survival. The Berlin Wall had hurt Chancellor Adenauer's reputation. It had exposed his policy of negotiating with the Soviets from a position of military strength over German reunification as an empty slogan. Walter Ulbricht, on the contrary, seemed to prosper with the Wall. Politically Ulbricht took up a more centre position in his party than his stock image in the West suggested. As one Western writer on the GDR has commented:

> his longevity doubtless attests his basic acceptability to all factions, reformist as well as reactionary. There is also the question of competence. Here too Ulbricht has been grossly underrated. Of all the European Communist heads of state, only Ulbricht must contend with a divided nation longing to be reunited – and his portion of that nation is scarcely the largest, the richest, or the most productive.[16]

From a poor, working-class Social Democratic family in Leipzig, it was natural enough for any young Ulbricht either to join the Social Democrats or emigrate. These seemed to be just about the only ways for a worker in pre-1914 Germany to better himself. Walter chose the SPD, his brother the United States. Apprentice cabinet-maker Ulbricht deserted from the Kaiser's army in protest against the World War. He was among the foundation members of the KPD. In 1923 he was briefly a member of the party's Central Committee, but he was demoted in the factional struggles of those days. By 1927 he was once again on the Central Committee and from then on kept on rising. A year later he was elected to the German Reichstag. He evaded arrest by the Gestapo in 1933, and after working in the Communist underground in Germany was sent on various Comintern assignments around Europe. The war years he spent in the USSR doing propaganda work among German prisoners and at the front. The Russians sent him back at the head of a group of key functionaries to their Zone of Germany in 1945. His second wife, Lotte, whom he met in Russia, went with him. Though Wilhelm Pieck was nominally senior to him on the Communist side of the Socialist Unity Party in 1946, Ulbricht appeared to be the key man. In 1950 he became the First Secretary. In 1960, on the death of his colleague Pieck, he took over the chairmanship of the newly created Council of State, thus becoming official

Head of State. This showed his ambition, his need for personal recognition, and his readiness to promote his own cult of personality. Though East Germany in the 1960s did not retain all the worst features of Stalinism, as is commonly supposed, it did suffer from the cult of Ulbricht. No speech, article, or book was complete without the appropriate quote, however obscure. This servile adulation reached a new low in honour of the First Secretary's seventy-fifth birthday in 1968. The director of the Dresden *Staatstheater* said that Ulbricht was 'one of the most active, information-hungry, knowledgeable theatre-goers in the GDR.' Professor Lea Grundig thanked him for his tips on painting, and many other members of the academic and literary establishment, including the famous Jewish writer Arnold Zweig, contributed their hosannas.[17] Not content with all this lavish praise of his political and intellectual talents, the East German leader pushed his private life as an example to all. The image was of a modest-living, family man – he and Lotte have an adopted daughter – with a passion for sport.

The three most significant members of the SED Politburo, other than Ulbricht, in the 1960s, were Erich Honecker (b. 1912), Willi Stoph (b. 1914), and Günter Mittag (b. 1926). Ulbricht's protégé Honecker was born into the Communist movement in the Saar, and spent ten years in Nazi jails as a result of his activities on behalf of the Communist youth movement. Amid the ruins of Berlin he was lucky enough to impress Soviet talent scout Ulbricht who arranged for Honecker to lead the Communist-controlled Free German Youth in 1946. This office he held until 1955. He was a candidate member of the Politburo from 1950 until he became a full member in 1958. He had made his way by his loyalty to Ulbricht; he emerged as a Russophile and a hardliner. In view of his early background, bitter youth, and limited experience, this is hardly surprising. Honecker's second wife, Margot, fifteen years his junior, became Minister of Education in 1963. She started her career in the Free German Youth and worked for many years in the Ministry of Education.

Stoph has a more popular image than Honecker. He too was a Communist before 1933 and, although he claims anti-Fascist activities after that date, he avoided the attention of the Gestapo. During the war he was a driver in the *Wehrmacht*. By trade a bricklayer, he started his career after the war as a high functionary in the building materials industry. He held a variety of state and party posts in the fifties and early sixties, including Minister of Interior and Minister of Defence. In 1964 he became Chairman of the Council of Ministers on the death of Otto Grotewohl. By that time he had been a member of the Politburo for eleven years. From 1964 onwards he was also a deputy Head of State.

Dr Günter Mittag was born in Stettin, the son of a worker. He served his time as a railwayman and worked at various party, state, and trade union posts after 1945. He rose rapidly, becoming a candidate member of the Politburo in 1963 and a full member in 1966. His formula for success seems to have been staying clear of factional huddles and gaining technical expertise. He represents the coming generation of academically-trained experts who were given increasing scope after the Sixth Congress of the SED in 1963.[18]

It was at the Sixth Congress that the Unity Party announced its New Economic System which Mittag, together with Dr Erich Apel, a candidate member of the Politburo who took his own life in December 1965, helped to design. The New System followed economic reforms in the USSR and was meant to rationalize the GDR's economy. In the following years the lot of the East German people certainly improved. Whether this was a result of the New Economic System, the Wall, the maturing of earlier investments, or all three, it is difficult to say. By the end of the decade most East German homes had television, about half had refrigerators and washing machines. Most other goods were easier to get than they had been. A statutory five-day working-week was in force in industry. Yet when Ulbricht retired in 1971, he had not redeemed his pledge to overtake West German living standards. People grumbled about the lack of private motoring, the impossibility of travelling outside the Warsaw Pact states – even though the GDR had at last been recognized by several Afro-Asian states, Cuba, and Chile – the difficulties of getting things repaired, delivered, cleaned, or maintained. and the generally high level of prices. Occasionally too there have been famines of particular goods. In December 1970 Paul Verner reported to the SED's Central Committee that there were shortages of warm underwear, overalls, winter-shoes, slippers, ovens, batteries, certain types of furniture, electric irons, ball-point pens, and toothbrushes. He blamed the shortages on what he called 'a superficial and irresponsible way of working' by factory managements and state organs.[19] How often had the East German people heard such excuses! Housing remained a pressing problem in the GDR. The lamentable conditions which exist were mentioned in 1967 in the leading East German journal *Die Wirtschaft* (31 August). Then only 27 per cent of dwellings had baths, only 37 per cent had w.c.s, and 32 per cent even lacked running water. The journal admitted that in these respects East Germans were worse off than many other Europeans. Though wartime damage was a factor, neglect has been a more important one. Housing programmes have been consistently low, compared to other states and proportionate to population, and actual achievements lower still.

Ulbricht had often referred to the special problems of the GDR, pointing out that one of these was the fact that East Germany was the first industrialized state to attempt to build socialism. But granted her special difficulties and her real achievements, her living standards were not likely to impress workers from Sweden, Britain, West Germany – one of the reasons for the failure of communism there – or even from France or Italy. On intellectuals they would make possibly even less impression.

Like the Soviet Union the German Democratic Republic had achieved much in the fields of education, sport, and women's rights. In the 1960s better-informed West Germans came to recognize that the GDR's achievements in these spheres were worthy of study. In the GDR many from underprivileged backgrounds were given the chance to study and certain archaic aspects of the old system were swept aside. Of course, as elsewhere in the Soviet bloc, the reforms were bought at a price. Education from nursery to university was subjected to Communist ideology, centralization, dogmatism about methods, and heavy emphasis on vocational courses.

In the sixties, no less than in the fifties, the Democratic Republic was no place for any intellectual who had his own thoughts and wished to communicate them to others. This was underlined once again by the eleventh session of the Central Committee at the end of 1965. At that meeting Honecker attacked the youth movement, mass media, and certain intellectuals in the GDR for their alleged ideological failings. In particular he attacked Wolf Biermann, the poet, for his 'doubt everything, doubt all authority' attitude.[20] Biermann, it should be pointed out, regards himself as completely loyal to the GDR and her system.[21] Christa Wolf, a successful writer, who supported Biermann paid for her courage by being removed from the SED's Central Committee. Since 1965 the thirty-four-year-old Biermann has not been allowed to publish or appear before any audience in the GDR.

Of at least equal significance is the case of Professor Robert Havemann. Born in Munich in 1910, he joined the Communist Party in 1932. Later the Nazis sentenced him to death for his anti-state activities, allowing him a stay of execution to carry on research for the army – by training he is a chemist. In 1950 he was sacked as head of a research institute in West Berlin for criticizing the development of the American hydrogen bomb. This led to his appointment to a chair at the East Berlin Humboldt University. Later he was honoured with a GDR National Prize and elected to the Academy of Sciences. But lectures given by him in the autumn and winter of 1963–64 got him into trouble once again, this time with his political friends. In effect he called for democracy in the GDR: 'What is necessary, what is a condition of life for Socialism, and what was lost during the period of Stalinism, is Democracy. Socialism cannot be achieved without Democracy'.[22] Havemann claimed to be speaking, doubtfully in this writer's opinion, as a good Leninist. He showed even less caution when he attacked academic colleagues who, without any knowledge of the natural sciences, rejected 'Western' scientific theories because they did not fit in with their own dogmatic view of Dialectical Materialism. Such people had discredited Dialectical Materialism in the GDR. They were still at work, were still getting their views widely publicized in the republic even though they were regarded as obsolete in the USSR. Havemann further attacked what he regarded as the mechanical interpretation of the Hegelian–Marxist concept that Freedom is understanding Necessity (and acting appropriately). He believed we could only have true freedom when we had a wide range of possibilities. This is all very well, but he did not really square this view with the traditional Marxist idea that 'Freiheit ist Einsicht in die Notwendigkeit'. Havemann's heretical ideas earned him expulsion from the SED, the university, and the Academy of Sciences. His treatment brought protests from outside the GDR, the most impressive of which was from the American Nobel Prizewinner, McCarthy victim, peacemonger, and former honoured guest of the Humboldt University, Professor Linus Pauling. Havemann was not reinstated, as demanded by the American, but Pauling's interest no doubt did some good. Since that time Havemann has given a number of interviews to Western publications and his memoirs were published in Munich.[23]

Despite the bans, expulsions, and harassment of some East German intellectuals, they have fared better than their colleagues in the Soviet Union.

The SED congresses of 1967 and 1971 proved to be little more than routine affairs. With greater prosperity at home and increasing recognition abroad, the GDR's leaders could be fairly content with themselves. At its last examination, in 1970, of members' activities the 1.9 million-strong party found it necessary to expel only 8,706 comrades.[24]

By the end of the Ulbricht era the GDR certainly seemed one of the most stable of the Communist regimes.[25] Events in Czechoslovakia (1968) and Poland (1968–70) made little or no impact. Why this should be so it is not easy to say. True, East Germany enjoyed the highest living standards in the Soviet bloc, but, as the writer found in the summer of 1970, there was a good deal of grumbling. The East Germans will only be satisfied with standards of living equal to those of the Federal Republic. As the Communists claim, the SED had certainly mobilized the remnants of the old middle classes, through the bloc parties, for the regime. It readily accepted the services of bourgeois scientists, doctors, technologists, businessmen, even journalists and teachers. Their children too had 'perspectives'. But these people are not usually the stuff of revolutionary upheavals. It can also be admitted that many East Germans were developing some kind of GDR pride, consciousness, even patriotism. They were sick and tired of being patronized as poor relations by West German visitors. And though many young people were indifferent to the regime,[26] some admired its identification with Castro, Ho, and the Arabs. Yet even though well over 9 million East Germans out of a total of 17 million were under forty years of age and have therefore not really known any other system, interest in West Germany remained widespread (as Brandt's meeting with Stoph at Erfurt in 1970 revealed). If these factors have, nevertheless, contributed to stability, so have a feeling of resignation and the many Soviet army divisions known to be in the country. Ulbricht's retirement by instalments in 1971, starting with Honecker replacing him as First Secretary of the SED, was also no doubt calculated with the maintenance of stability. Certainly Ulbricht's transformation into a pensioner, whether voluntary or with a slight push, was more dignified and less dramatic than those of his colleagues in the other 'socialist' states.

### III. KHRUSHCHEV FALLS

Khrushchev's fall in October 1964 was the most dramatic of the decade, for it was potentially the most important and was the most unexpected. Unexpected though it was, and mysterious though the circumstances were, the failings which undermined Khrushchev's position were well known. First of all, there was the dangerous rift with China. This may well have occurred anyway, but there must have been those who felt that they or some other leader would have managed the situation better. If this worried the military leaders, so did his conduct of relations with the United States. It seemed too erratic, too unsure, too improvised to say the least. Such uncertainty could lead to nuclear war. Thirdly, his de-Stalinization policy was judged by many party officials to be misguided. There were those who opposed it outright both because they felt themselves threatened by it and for ideological reasons. There were those who felt that reforms could have been initiated quietly, without fuss and preserving the fiction of continuity. Again some feared that Khrushchev's leadership was becoming all too like Stalin's. It was too personal: he was both party boss and Chairman of the Council of Ministers. Was he suffering from megalomania?[27] Whether or not, some felt that the Soviet Union, with all her achievements and her great Russian heritage, needed a more dignified and restrained leader than this ungainly little man with his displays of temper (banging his shoe on the table at the United Nations) and his barnyard humour. Finally, the failure of his economic plans must be reckoned another cause of his downfall, and his nepotism a minor one.

Here no attempt will be made to identify and follow the shifting coalitions which intrigued to bring down Khrushchev. That task would require a volume to itself.[28] But on the manner of the First Secretary's removal the author will allow himself some comments. The tactics employed (a plot in the Politburo while

Khrushchev was on holiday and the mobilization of the Central Committee against him to confront him on his return) revealed once again the total lack of anything approaching democratic practices in the USSR. If the USSR had really built a system superior to other states, one would have expected her practices to be at least as good as bourgeois states, especially after fifty-odd years of trying. As it was, when Khrushchev's removal was announced, Western Communists could only wince again with embarrassment. John Gollan, General Secretary of the British Communist Party, was forced to ask: 'Would it not be better for the prestige and authority of the Soviet Union if the major facts were made public and clear?' His plea was to go unheard. Rightly he advised his Soviet colleagues: 'We need reasoned and friendly argument in place of bitter and personalised polemic'.[29] Still, it must be admitted that the Soviet leaders had made some progress in their way of doing things since Stalin's time. After all, Khrushchev was allowed to retire on pension and in comfort even if he became almost an 'unperson', prevented from having intercourse with the outside world, and even if, when he died in 1971, his passing received only about three lines in *Pravda*. This was a more civilized way of doing things and Khrushchev could be thankful that he had helped to set the pattern with his handling of Molotov and his friends. This was certainly a great achievement, of concern for the ruling few. What about the ruled? What achievements had he left them?

The boasts of Khrushchev that the USSR would overtake the United States in living standards in the 1960s proved to be hollow indeed. It is doubtful whether the gap between the two even narrowed. However, as mentioned above (p. 261), the Soviet standard of living did improve in certain respects under Khrushchev. To give a very rough impression, according to official Soviet figures in 1950 only 12,000 TV sets were manufactured in the USSR. Fifteen years later the number had risen to 3,338,000. In the same period, the numbers of refrigerators produced rose from a mere 1,200 to 1,458,000. The Soviet Union managed to turn out a ludicrous 300 washing machines in 1950, but in 1965 she reached the more respectable total of 3,141,000.[30] These and other consumer goods were also imported in greater, though still modest, numbers than before. Of course, proportionate to population, the USSR's production of consumer goods in 1965 was still relatively low when measured against that of other industrial nations. The variety and quality of Soviet goods often left much to be desired. Nevertheless, for a great many Soviet citizens, with no idea of life beyond the frontiers of the Union, life must have seemed a good deal better in this respect.

In another respect life did not get much better. The food supply did not improve much. In the period 1959–65 gross farm output increased by only 14 per cent instead of 70 per cent as planned, just about keeping ahead of population growth.[31] Whether this was the result of the collective-farm system, as many Western observers believe, or just the general backwardness of Soviet agriculture, is difficult to say.[32]

Under Khrushchev housing was recognized as a great social problem and considerable efforts were made to solve it. By the end of the 1960s no solution was in sight. Although between 1961 and 1965, 54.6 million Soviet citizens, out of a total of 230 million or so, are said to have moved to new or better homes,[33] housing conditions for many remained appalling. The Soviet journal *Literaturnaya Gazeta* (25 December 1968) reported the case of a married couple with a baby having only half a room to themselves, with only a partition separating them from their 'neighbours'. The paper remarked that there were 'many, very many' families living in similar conditions. An American expert, Timothy Sosnovy, using Soviet material, has calculated that even in 1965 Soviet citizens in urban areas had slightly less space than in 1923.[34] Moreover, the new dwellings are usually small, poorly appointed, with few amenities, and monotonously uniform in their exteriors. Rents are low for both old and new dwellings; most people live in rented accommodation; but this confers a privilege on those lucky enough to live in new homes. Even today a high proportion of Soviet citizens (in 1966, 107.1 million[35]) still live in rural areas. One does not have to travel very far through the Soviet countryside to realize how primitive are the conditions of the majority – no running water or modern sanitation. From 1957 to 1966 only 5 million homes were built in rural areas;[36] many of these were below Western standards.[37]

Despite the progress, the Soviet consumer still faces very many frustrations in the 1970s. Many services taken for granted in other industrial nations are few and far between; shopping involves much time wasted in queues; and many elementary things remain either desperately short or non-existent – ball-point pens, safety pins, ladies' tights, sanitary towels, contraceptive devices, disposable nappies, toilet paper and tissues, plastic goods of all kinds, for instance. These are not goods which would cost so much, even with imported know-how (the East Germans could provide that), as to endanger the arms programme. Naturally these acute shortages of goods and services encourage a thriving black market leading to degradation, corruption, and blackmail. It is sad indeed to see decent citizens of a nation which produced the sputniks pestering foreign tourists to sell their 'hard' Western currency to them, or even their used clothing.

The scarcity of so many goods, their low priority, is perhaps a sign of the indifference of the Soviet ruling class to the needs of their subjects. Perhaps they are so remote in their closed housing settlements, clubs, and private transport from the lives of ordinary people, that they are not fully aware there is any problem. After all, most articles are available at the special shops reserved for the privileged, and they are likely to be able to travel abroad where they can make purchases.

Notwithstanding this state of affairs, we still hear from Western Communist leaders, in the words of Dr Tony Chater, Chairman of the British Communist Party, that 'Socialism is no longer a theory but a living reality' in the USSR.[38] Clearly, the high level of material prosperity, traditionally thought necessary by Marxists for socialism, is still lacking in the Soviet Union. And a brief examination of just two differences between the 'few' and the 'many' in Soviet society indicates that fundamentally the situation is still the same as when Trotsky wrote his critique in *The Revolution Betrayed*.

If we take a few salaries, we notice great differences. In 1963 a Soviet textile-worker earned the equivalent of 679 U.S. dollars per annum. A steel-worker earned $872, and a coalminer $1,092. A high-school teacher received $824 and a physician $1,260. A qualified engineer in the oil industry was paid $4,238 and a factory manager $6,240. A minister in one of the fifteen republican governments drew over $9,000.[39] These do not include the lowest incomes, collective farmers among them, or the highest – top scientists, generals, members of the cultural and academic élite, and the men in the Kremlin. Moreover, the differences are even greater than gross earnings indicate. Little income tax is paid in the USSR and the top people enjoy many other privileges. Obviously, the strictures of Marx and Lenin about officials receiving workmen's wages have gone completely by the board.

Secondly, let us look at education, something about which many claims have been made. We saw above (p. 215) that Khrushchev recognized the inequalities in this field. In 1958 he introduced measures ostensibly aimed at reducing privileges, bringing the future élite closer to the people, and improving education in general. Fees were abolished, would-be students were supposed to get their hands dirty by production work before commencing their studies, and courses were to become more vocation-orientated. Right from the start, exceptions were allowed to the work rule for 'bright' students. In any case, experience shows that working-class children are more likely to give up their education if it is interrupted than are middle-class children. Opposition to the reforms from vested interests meant they were largely abandoned under the new management of Brezhnev and Kosygin. Today the offspring of the well-to-do, educated, city-dwellers in the USSR have the maximum chances to climb the educational ladder. The sons and daughters of collective farmers have the least chances. The best schools and universities are in the large towns, the better-off have more spacious accommodation, and the use of personal friendship and monetary bribery to secure university places is by no means unknown. Once at university the same factors prove advantageous; grants are available but they are modest.

The tremendous progress made in education in the Soviet Union in her fifty-odd years of existence cannot be denied, and is greatly to her credit. But equality of opportunity has not been achieved, nor is it in sight.[40]

The writer will join the late Isaac Deutscher in hesitating to try to answer the question as to whether the upper echelons of the Soviet Union merely represent Trotsky's privileged bureaucracy or have developed into Djilas's New Class. He will merely bring to the reader's attention Deutscher's comment that

What these groups have in common with any exploiting class – I am using the term in the Marxist sense – is that their incomes are at least partly derived from the 'surplus value' produced by the workers. Moreover, they dominate Soviet society economically, politically, and culturally.[41]

And: 'In truth, Soviet bureaucracy has exercised power greater than that wielded by any possessing class in modern times'.[42]

In view of Dr Chater's claim on behalf of the 'living reality' of socialism in the USSR one other aspect of her failure as a socialist example will be mentioned here. This is the total lack of pioneering work, of advanced thinking, in the Soviet Union in a wide variety of fields in which Marxists, socialists, progressives, in Russia in the past and in other countries today, have had novel ideas – educational methods,[43] sex education,[44] architecture and design, town planning and penology.[45]

In the six years since Khrushchev's removal we have seen, on the whole, a reversal of his policies in a more 'conservative' direction. Firstly, Stalin's role has been more generously interpreted, though the blood purges remain condemned. Secondly, there has been a general tightening-up of intellectual life. Here we can only mention Khrushchev's personal intervention, after the Twenty-second Party Congress which removed Stalin's body from the Red Square mausoleum, to get Solzhenitsyn's *One Day in the Life of Ivan Denisovich* published. This book dealt with life in Stalin's camps. Its publication was symbolic of the more liberal atmosphere between 1954 and 1964. It contrasted with what followed. The trial and imprisonment of the writers Daniel and Siniavsky in 1966 for allegedly slandering the Soviet Union is equally symbolic of the post-Khrushchev period.[46]

A third change since the Brezhnev-Kosygin team took over has been a return to greater centralization of the economy. In 1957 Khrushchev abolished the industrial ministries which controlled individual industries from Moscow, and divided the country into 105 economic regions. This experiment later came under fire because it was felt that the regions were going their separate ways and putting regional interests before national. At the end of 1962 another reorganization was introduced amalgamating many of the regions and setting up a new supervisory apparatus at the centre. In 1965 yet another change was carried through which involved a partial return to the traditional Soviet system of managing the economy. Once again ministries were set up to run particular branches of the economy – the automobile industry, the merchant marine, electronics, etc. But there was devolution within this framework of a kind which did not exist before 1957. From October 1965 state enterprises were given more initiative in carrying through the plans set for them. Their success is no longer measured by total gross output, but by the sale of output and the resulting profit calculated as a percentage of their fixed capital. This reform is associated with Professor Evsei Liberman of Kharkov University who, it should be noted, opened this debate on profit in 1962 with Krushhchev's blessing.[47] At the Twenty-fourth Congress of the CPSU in 1971 this system of central control and profit was confirmed.[48] But stress was put on the use of computers to aid central decision-making. As the Soviet economy continues to face many difficulties, despite a relatively high but in recent years declining growth-rate, the argument about economic organization is likely to go on.

Finally, another characteristic of the Soviet development since 1964 has been the maintenance of an uneasy form of collective leadership. The key figures in this leadership have been CPSU Secretary Leonid Brezhnev, and Premier Alexei Kosygin,[49] with N. V. Podgorny, officially Head of State, much less prominent than either, though placed ahead of Kosygin in the list of Politburo members at the CPSU Twenty-fourth Congress in April 1971.

Brezhnev, a Russian born in the Ukraine in 1906, joined the party in 1931. After five years at the Metallurgical Institute in Dneprodzerzhinsk, he made his way up the party ladder. Until 1964 his career was 'purely and solely a history of dependence on Khrushchev'.[50] He is said to be a conservative, but not a neo-Stalinist.[51] It is generally agreed that this football fan, who likes to cook for his guests,[52] strengthened his position at the Twenty-fourth Congress,[53]

Kosygin (born in 1904) has a reputation for being on the 'liberal' wing of the CPSU. He is a civil war veteran, former factory director, and former mayor of Leningrad. Only since 1960 has he held continuous full membership of the Praesidium-Politburo,[54] though he was a Politburo member under Stalin. Now Chairman of the Council of Ministers of the USSR, he was Chairman of the Russian Republic from 1943 to 1946. He slipped slightly at the Twenty-fourth Congress, being placed third on the list of Politburo members instead of second.

What of the future? Whither Russia? Will the members of the Politburo finally come to accept 'internal debate as a legitimate factor in decision making' and 'institutionalise opposition within the Politburo'?[55] Will they gradually draw into the debates the 240-odd Central Committee members until they become a kind of parliament for the competing élite groups of the Union – the party secretaries, the managers, the government officials, the cultural and technical intelligentsia, and the military? Will they be able to maintain the relative calm and stability of the USSR by delivering high living standards, granting the intelligentsia a modicum of freedom, and the minority nations enough autonomy to still their frustrations? Will they, in other words, develop a kind of 'muddling evolution' as predicted by Arthur Schlesinger?[56] Or is Giorgio Galli's view more likely? That the 'superannuated bureaucracy' of the CPSU is so beset by difficulties, with China, in eastern Europe, with its own intelligentsia and economy, that it has 'neither the time nor the perspicacity to realize that the society it governs is undergoing ineluctable changes',[57] and will, therefore, succumb to crisis. Galli's view is of course shared by some Soviet dissenters, in particular by Andrei Amalrik. He believes that:

> . . . at least some of the conditions that led to the first and second Russian revolutions probably exist again: a caste-ridden and immobile society, a rigid governmental system which openly clashes with the need for economic development, general bureaucratization and the existence of a privileged bureaucratic class, and national animosities within a multi-national state in which certain nations enjoy privileged status.[58]

Whatever the future of the Soviet Union may be, Robert Conquest's advice to us is sound: 'We should be prepared for surprises over the next decade and should not fall into the temptation of believing the status quo to be as stable as it may appear to the superficial glance'.[59]

## IV. ROMANIA'S NEW INDEPENDENCE

'Socialism' developed rather differently in a number of East European states in the 1960s than seemed likely in the 1950s. About Albania and the GDR we need say no more. As for Bulgaria, it was the most consistently orthodox of the Warsaw Pact states. Led by Todor Zhivkov, premier and party First Secretary, there was something of a zigzag course in economic reform, starting in 1965 in a more 'liberal' direction, and turning more 'conservative' in 1968.[60] To the thousands of Western tourists who flocked to the cheap holidays of Bulgaria's Black Sea resorts, the country seemed to be at least on the move, in economic terms. Yet what life was like for the workers and intellectuals was, surprisingly enough, hinted at by a prominent British Communist visitor, Sam Russell, Foreign Editor of the *Morning Star*. In the paper's issue of 14 May 1971, after praising Bulgaria's economic social, and educational progress, he admitted that 'Bulgarian unions must pull their socks up'. Among trade union and Communist Party officials in the plants that he visited he found 'an almost unbelievable spirit of smug self-satisfaction'. As for the nation's intellectual life: 'It came as rather a disappointment to learn of the very dogmatic attitude still prevailing in the arts and literature'. In party terms Bulgaria showed stability of leadership in the 1960s, but only just. Two attempted *coups*, one in 1961, the second in 1965, were put down. The precise nature of these mini-revolts is not known, though they seem to have been aimed at establishing a leadership less dependent on the Soviet Union. In that respect they had something in common with the new leadership in Romania. They they were led by military men and former Communist partisans gave them affinity to a similar group in Poland.

The Poles were not able to retain most of the gains they made in 1956. True, the peasants retained their land. In 1968 85 per cent of the arable land remained privately owned.[61] The state has confined itself to encouraging agrarian circles in which the machinery is held in common but the land remains privately owned. It also increased subsidies. Despite improvements, the peasants still use less fertilizer and fewer machines than in north-western European countries. Output per acre in the 1960s was higher than in the collectivized USSR, but lower than in East Germany where the land was also fully collectivized. Polish agriculture suffers from too many uneconomical units and too many hands. It is unable to feed the country; grain is regularly imported. Yet, as a West German expert found in 1965, 'Polish peasants have never had it so good materially as today'.[62]

After 1956 much was done to industrialize the country further, but an appropriate system of management of the economy was not worked out and, after being a leader in economic reform, Poland in 1970 'must now be counted among the most persistent laggards'.[63] The standard of living remained low and unemployment was officially admitted. The workers' councils, regarded as of great significance in 1956, had long ago been robbed of their importance.

The ordinary citizens of Poland found life in the 1960s a little less regulated than previously. There were more Western films at the local cinema, more translations from modern Western literature in the local bookshop. There was also greater personal contact with the West, including relatives living abroad. If he cared, the Polish citizen could be proud that his parliament remained unique among those of the Warsaw Pact states in that it did have more than mere formal duties and did even sport a small Catholic independent group!

In general, in political and cultural matters, however, there was a tightening-up in the 1960s which increased as time went on. This was partly in line with what was happening in Moscow, and partly the result of the power struggle in the ruling Polish United Workers' Party. Particularly affected were intellectuals and Jews. Having tasted freedom, and living in a country calling itself socialist yet faced with so many economic, social, and political problems, it was only to be expected that some intellectuals should want to air their concern and impatience. Gomułka was either unable or unwilling to allow this. Dissident intellectuals had to reckon with dismissal, harassment, and possible imprisonment. The case which attracted the most attention was that of the Warsaw academics Karol Modzelewski and Jacek Kuron. They were arrested in 1965 for having circulated pamphlets accusing the party of having betrayed Communist ideals. They were demanding a system of competitive workers' and peasants' parties, workers' control in industry, abolition of censorship, abolition of the state security service, academic and intellectual freedom, a people's militia to replace the armed forces, and a socialist market economy.[64] Both were expelled from the party and sentenced to three years' imprisonment. They got remission for good conduct, but were soon in trouble again.

Soviet bloc support for the Arab cause had increased the difficulties of Jews in the Soviet Union and Poland. In the Soviet Union this was more understandable, though still unjust, as there the number of Jews is fairly large, the Jewish religion persists on a significant scale, and a considerable number of Jews would like to emigrate to Israel. In Poland, on the other hand, most Jews had been exterminated by the Nazis, and many of those who remained were 'non-Jewish' Jews and good Communists. Indeed many ordinary non-Communist Poles tended to equate the Jews with the rule of the 'alien' Communist Party.

In June 1967, in the wake of the Middle East war, Secretary Gomułka warned, in a speech to the trade union congress, of the danger of a 'fifth column' of pro-Israeli Polish Jews. Remarkably, Gomułka's wife is Jewish, and his comments were probably a diplomatic move to still Soviet fears in view of the known sympathy of many Poles, and not just Jews, for Israel at that time. Perhaps his remarks were also a tribute to the 'Partisans' to bolster his precarious position. Led by General Mieczsław Moczar, the Partisans were former wartime Communist resistance workers. After the war they had resented the fact that they had been pushed aside by the Communists (a fair number of them Jews) who had spent the war years in Moscow. After 1956, with the 'Muscovites' discredited, the Partisans had pressed their claims increasingly. They were authoritarian as well as nationalist and to some extent succeeded in playing on the patriotism, frustration, and ambition of young party men looking for careers. They also joined forces with the remnants of the former (non-Communist) Home Army, and various other people. The June War and the rise of Czech reform communism at the beginning of 1968 gave the Partisans the chance to clamour for a purge of Jews and liberals. Of great importance to the success of this campaign was the student revolt which started at Warsaw University in March 1968. The explosion was sparked off by the banning of a nineteenth-century anti-Tsarist play which had provoked the wrong (from the authorities' point of view) audience reactions. Students at other universities demonstrated their solidarity with their Warsaw colleagues. The party's reaction was to dismiss a number of academics and jail or conscript many more students.[65]

Despite the campaign against liberals, revisionists, and 'Zionists', the Partisans suffered a setback at the Fifth Party Congress in November 1968. Moczar failed to gain full membership of the Politburo. The likely reason for this is that the Poles, always with one eye on Moscow, decided that they could not afford so prominent a nationalist so soon after Czech 'nationalism' had been destroyed on Soviet orders. So Gomułka kept his job, and his Jewish wife, but lost most of his Jewish comrades. About half of Poland's 25,000 Jews had left the country, including many leading intellectuals. Poland's problems, too, remained and erupted again in December 1970.

Faced with a dangerous economic situation, the leaders of the world's tenth largest industrial nation[66] voted to raise prices to mop up some of the workers' inflationary earnings. Strikes followed in the northern coastal area. Demonstrations, and some looting, were dispersed by gunfire. According to the official version, 45 people were killed or died of wounds, and 1,165 were injured, including 564 civilians, 531 police, and 70 soldiers.[67] In a deteriorating situation, Gomułka was shown the door. Thus, at sixty-six, ended the long political career of the former mechanic, wartime underground worker, and one-time hero of Poland's reform-hungry youth. Of Gomułka, his successor, Edward Gierek, said: 'more time is needed to assess fully the policy of the former leadership'.

Gierek, until taking over the leadership, was Party Secretary in the key industrial province of Silesia where he was born, the son of a miner in 1913. After his father was killed in an accident in 1923, he went with his mother to live in northern France. At eighteen, already a miner himself, he joined the French Communist Party. His political activities led to his expulsion from France. After military service in Poland, he worked in Belgium and took part in the wartime resistance there. He returned to Poland in 1948 and remarkably, in view of his late return and his Western contacts, rose rapidly in the party. Western experts have seen him as the spokesman for the younger 'technocrats'. His personal style contrasts with that of the austere and simple-living Gomułka.

On assuming office, Gierek's message to the Polish people was what by now is the traditional Communist speech in such circumstances, he admitted mistakes had been made, but the genuine grievances of the workers had been exploited by antisocial elements. He made vague promises of more democracy, more housing, and more consumer goods.

Whereas Poland was a disappointment for those hoping for reforms in eastern Europe, Hungary produced some pleasant surprises. In terms of economic reform Hungary went further than any other Warsaw Pact state. She did so in six ways. Firstly, her reforms were administered throughout the economy at one stroke rather than cautiously, sector by sector, or in a few selected plants, Secondly, there was greater decentralization of investment decisions than in the neighbouring states. Thirdly, numerous large enterprises were permitted to make their own export contracts with foreign firms. A further difference was that in Hungary small-scale private enterprise was encouraged. A more rapid and extensive movement to prices based on supply and demand was another difference. Finally, greater emphasis was placed on managerial expertise rather than political background in selecting managers. As for the general political and cultural atmosphere in Hungary, it must suffice here to say that under János Kádár, there was in Hungary probably the most relaxed atmosphere in the Soviet bloc (with the very brief exception of Czechoslovakia). The Hungarians prudently toed the Soviet line in foreign policy and did not trumpet their reforms too loudly.[68]

Romania's development in the 1960s was no less surprising than Hungary's. The Romanian Communists were able to assert their independence of Moscow to a far greater extent than any of their comrades in the Warsaw Pact, except the Albanians.

To understand how this came about we must briefly refer to the early post-war struggles among the Romanian Communists. As in the other East European parties, the Muscovites in the party were in a very strong position. Yet Gheorghe Gheorghiu-Dej (1901–65), the former railway electrician who spent the war years in prison in Romania, was made Secretary-General. In 1952 the Muscovites were defeated by Gheorghiu-Dej. This was only possible because the leading Muscovite was a rabbi's daughter, Ana Pauker, and Stalin was going through a strongly anti-semitic phase.[69] He was therefore prepared to acquiesce in her removal.

By the time the Twentieth Congress tremors had passed, in 1957, the Romanians had solved their leadership problems. Gheorghiu-Dej went on unchallenged as Party Secretary and, from 1961, Head of State as well. The Romanians exploited to the full Moscow's declining authority in the Communist world. They were determined to pursue the all-round industrialization of their country in contradiction to the Soviet policy of specialization and integration of the socialist states into the Warsaw Pact's version of the Common Market. They came to terms with Britain, France, and the United States regarding compensation for these countries' nationalized assets, thus opening the way for trade and aid. But they still needed trade with, and aid from,

Moscow. Skilfully they negotiated a trade and aid agreement with the Russians which was signed, significantly, on 10 November 1960, the day on which the world's Communist leaders went into conclave at Moscow to debate the growing Sino-Soviet rift. In the following years the Romanians steered a middle course in the jungle of Communist politics, cultivating relations with Moscow *and* Peking, Belgrade and Tirana. They refused to participate in the invasion of Czechoslovakia, indeed condemned it, and called for a reform of the Warsaw Pact.

The Romanians have also looked beyond the Communist world. They broke ranks and exchanged ambassadors with Bonn in 1967. More dramatic still was the tremendous welcome given by the Romanians to President Nixon in 1969. The united Romanian leadership could do all this knowing they had the backing of their people. As any visitor to Romania could easily find out, even before the invasion of Czechoslovakia, the Russians were not very popular. The Romanians have always felt that culturally as well as ethnically they belong to non-Slav Europe. They had developed their ties with France, Germany, and to a lesser extent Britain. Stalin's harsh treatment of them at the end of the war did the USSR no good. Resentment remains too about Bessarabia, the Romanian-speaking area which first the Tsars, and then Stalin, took from Romania. The relatively good treatment of two of Romania's minority peoples, the Germans and Serbs, ensured their loyalty in any crisis with the Soviets.

Romania's internal policy caused the Russians far less worry. Under Gheorghiu-Dej the tight controls remained, only relaxing a little towards the end. Nicolae Ceauşescu (b. 1918), the former shoemaker, political prisoner, and Communist youth leader, and party chief since 1965, has been a little more liberal. However, there has never been any question of undermining the party's monopoly of power. As Ceauşescu defined the position in 1966:

> Life proves that nobody can be better acquainted with the economic realities, the balance and disposition of the class forces in one country or another, the internal and international political situation and its evolution, than the Communist Party, the revolutionary and patriotic forces in the respective country. That is why they have the exclusive right to elaborate the political line, the revolutionary strategy and tactics of the

working class. . . . This right cannot be the object of any dispute . . . .[70]

At the same time he did seem to be offering a more relaxed intellectual climate, admitting that progress required 'a free exchange of opinions, investigations and searchings and not qualifications and labelling against any new opinion', but all in order to advance 'the communist and working-class movement'.

Yugoslavia's relatively free-and-easy communism brought no diminution of her problems, which, in 1971, appear as great as ever. One could almost say that despite the great development of industry under the Tito regime, despite the spread of education, the social progress, and so on, Yugoslavia's problems today seem very similar to those of pre-war Yugoslavia. Then as now there were economic problems caused by the backwardness of agriculture, overpopulation, and the difficulties facing exports. In the mid-sixties there was a surplus of 1.4 million workers on the land. In 1938 about 69,150 persons – 10 per cent of the insured population – were registered as unemployed. In 1966 450,000 persons (7.1 per cent) were so registered.[71] The numbers had been increased in the 1960s. Towards the end of the 1960s the Yugoslavs were confronted with debts to Western countries of almost one billion dollars and a pressing repayment schedule.[72] There were smaller debts to the Soviet bloc. To make Yugoslav exports more competitive and to curtail the consumption of foreign goods the dinar was devalued by 66 per cent. Much more than in the past, individual enterprises were forced to stand on their own feet without the benefit of subsidies from the federal authorities. At the same time the banks were given a more dynamic role. Private enterprise has also been permitted in the important tourist industry. In the last years of the 1960s, though, the Yugoslav economy still faced severe problems. If its deficit on foreign trade was reduced, stagnation resulted at home. If there was expansion of the economy at home, inflation and huge imports followed.[73] The economy also faced, not withstanding the system of workers' control, the growing problem of strikes.[74] Great progress in industrialization there had been, but in 1971 the economy was still desperately dependent on remittances from the half-million or so Yugoslavs working in Western (mainly West Germany) countries. It is therefore valid to ask, given Yugoslavia's heavy dependence on the West, if she can really protect herself to any fundamental extent from Western economic, social, and political ideas and influences? Can she for long remain outside the economic blocs? Does the backward and dependent state of her economy not greatly reduce her significance as a socialist model?

In another important respect Yugoslavia is still beset with the problems of the past: strong national rivalries reappeared in the 1960s. Alexander Rankovich, the Serbian head of the secret police, was dismissed in 1966, and with him went his organization. He had been seen as Tito's successor, but wanted to ensure his position by building his organization into 'a state within the state'. It is alleged that he represented those elements in the party who wanted centralization, and Serbs who felt that the Serbian Republic should be dominant in the Yugoslav Federation.[75] His removal opened the way for the individual republics to voice their grievances and their claims. In short, the more advanced republics, Croatia and Slovenia, resented the burdens placed on them to help the more backward republics in the south. They also resented any kind of dominance from Belgrade. Increasingly in the 1960s, politicians in Yugoslavia spoke as Croats or Serbs, Slovenes or Macedonians, Bosnians or Montenegrins. Rumours of secret Soviet collaboration with *émigré* Croat nationalists did not help matters. In this tense situation President Tito, seventy-nine in 1971, dared not retire.

## v. AUGUST 1968

Politically Czechoslovakia remained unmoved by Khrushchev's de-Stalinization. Under bricklayer's son and former Nazi concentration camp inmate, Antonín Novotný (b. 1904), the Czechs 'acquired a reputation for a perverse, inhuman kind of stability'.[76] In Prague the biggest statue of Stalin anywhere in the world appeared to survey the scene with grim satisfaction. Attempts to oust Novotný, who had modelled himself on Stalin and then, after Khrushchev's rise, 'made a few comic attempts at being folksy',[77] failed. His advancement, after the death of Gottwald in 1953, he owed to 'dedicated administrative work and always toeing the party line. . . . He possessed dull qualities at a time when they were at a premium'.[78] This quality of dullness, to which must be added callousness, had got him the posts of party boss, from 1953, and President of the Republic, from 1957.

It can rightly be asked how it was that the Stalinist leadership of the Czech party were able to resist de-Stalinization for so long. The writer knows of no definitive answer. But one expert has suggested[79] that the relatively good economic situation in the second half of the 1950s was an important factor, together with the lack of traditional anti-Russian feeling – a factor in both Poland and Hungary – and: 'The Czech-Slovak conflict often set at odds, and thereby fragmented, the potential opposition forces within the party'. It also seems likely that the change from Gottwald, the Stalinist responsible for the 1949–53 purges, to Novotný, also a Stalinist, must have rather confused the issue. The changeover was due merely to the sudden death of Gottwald, but coming in 1953 shortly after Stalin's death, it must have strengthened the 'wait-and-see' faction. After 1956 Khrushchev was probably glad of Novotný as a man who could keep order. Finally, in the period 1963–67, Novotný carried on a policy of limited concessions which must have aided his retention of power.

These concessions were the result of pressure from below and without. In the 1960s the Czechoslovak economy went downhill. It suffered from 'the accumulated problems of a distorted industrial structure, an adverse trade situation, an ageing or obsolete production base, relatively low labor productivity, and wasteful utilization of production resources'.[80] The growing crisis 'culminated in an absolute decline in Czechoslovak national income and in the real wages of the Czechoslovak worker in 1963. There was palpable dissatisfaction among the working people, and a number of progressive economists openly and courageously began to criticize the existing economic model'.[81] The Twenty-second Congress of the CPSU in 1961, which came out in favour of economic reform and further doses of limited de-Stalinization, provided the external stimulus. The Central Committee of the Czechoslovak party set up a commission to work out economic reform proposals. The head of this commission, Dr Ota Šik, came to the conclusion that 'the structural deformations which plagued the Czechoslovak economy were inextricably linked with the centralized, bureaucratic system of economic control'.[82] In 1965 the party Central Committee voted for reform.

From 1962 onwards there had also been reviews of the purge trials, with rehabilitations. Some of those still able to benefit from rehabilitation found their way back to political life. The reform movement among the intellectuals and students grew. The workers were less certain. Despite the dissatisfaction of many, some felt that a more market-orientated economy could harm their enterprises and therefore their livelihoods. Novotný dragged his feet on the implementation of the reforms. He also had dissident writers, who spoke out at the congress of the Writers' Union in June 1967, slapped down. His political end was close, however.

It was Alexander Dubček, forty-six-year-old First Secretary of the Slovak section of the party, a man of impeccable political background with thirteen years in the Soviet Union behind him, who fired the first shot of the last battle against Novotný. Speaking in the Central Committee in October, he openly accused Novotný of 'behaving like a dictator' and neglecting Slovakia.[83]

Ever since the setting-up of the Czechoslovak Republic after the First World War relations between Czechs and Slovaks have been subject to suspicion and rivalry. The Czech lands were more industrialized even in the inter-war periods, their people more Westernized and less Catholic. The role of the Nazi-dominated puppet state of Slovakia in the period 1939–45 caused much bitterness. After 1945 the Prague government pressed ahead with the industrialization of Slovakia. But Slovak doubts about being ruled from Prague lingered on. Novotný's way with outspoken Slovaks was to purge them as 'bourgeois nationalists'. In December 1967 this was no longer possible. Debate continued in the party Praesidium and the Central Committee – this in itself a new departure – until Novotný was forced to resign as Secretary in January 1968. By the end of March he lost his position as Head of State as well.

The Soviet leaders were naturally worried about the changes in Prague, but Brezhnev called in on Dubček and probably concluded he was fairly safe. The East Germans and the Poles had a special interest in what was going on in Prague and kept a sharp and critical eye on the new leadership. Any doubts they had were reinforced when the Czechoslovak party published its Action Programme in April.

The first thing which strikes anyone familiar with East European Communist documents is the almost total lack of reference to Leninism in the Programme. There are none of the usually obligatory quotes from the Marxist classics. The Programme seeks to justify the main lines of party policy and after 1945, including the Communist *coup* in 1948. It is careful to praise the part played by the Soviet forces in the liberation of the country. It goes on to admit that due to lack of experience, lack of knowledge, dogmatism, subjectivism, the Cold War, and the influence of the cult of the individual, customs and political conceptions which were at variance with Czechoslovak conditions and traditions were introduced. This then hardened into a bureaucratic system.[84] The time had come to change all this. But it was the party itself which had recognized this; this fact, and its earlier victories over capitalism, proved that it was capable of making the necessary changes. There was to be no compromise therefore on the crucial issue of the leading role of the Communist Party. But this concept was to be reinterpreted. The party's aim was not to be the universal administrator of society, to bind all organizations and every step in the life of society to its directives. The party must achieve its objectives by convincing people, and by the personal example of Communists. This is reminiscent of Yugoslav pronouncements on the subject. There is much emphasis on democratic principles, all sections of the National Front participating in formulating policy and so on. Much of this does not contradict what is said by other Communist regimes in this respect. It is also emphasized that the Marxist-Leninist concept would be the leading political principle in the National Front. There is no mention of other parties being allowed, but the minor satellite parties in the National Front are offered a more creative role, and it is envisaged that voluntary organizations of an interest-group type should be permitted. Czechoslovakia's allies were worried about this. They felt that this would open the way to anti-socialist groups.

On the rights of the citizens the Programme calls for thorough and speedy rehabilitation of those wrongly condemned in the past, freedom to travel abroad, even to live abroad, freedom of speech, etc. The Slovaks are promised a really effective socialist federal system giving them full equality; the cultural workers are promised artistic freedom; and the educationists are promised greater recognition. A reformed security service is also on the agenda.[85]

The Programme reiterated the conclusions of the Thirteenth Party Congress of June 1966 regarding the introduction of the New Economic Model in Czechoslovakia, stating:

The improvement of our economy and the transition to intensive economic development cannot be achieved by traditional approaches or by partial improvements in the directive system of management and planning, but only by a basic change in the socialist economic mechanism . . . an economic reform based on a new economic system, revival of the positive functions of the socialist market, necessary structural changes in the economy, and a profound change in the role of the economic plan, which would cease to be an instrument for issuing orders and would instead become an instrument enabling society to determine the most suitable long-range lines of development by scientific methods . . .[86]

One curious section of the Programme deals with eliminating equalitarianism. Levelling had developed to an unheard-of extent and was now hindering the further development of the economy. The talented, better-qualified, expert, diligent must be better paid than the poorly qualified, idle, and irresponsible.

The final section of the Programme deals with foreign policy. In it the party clearly states its intention of standing by the country's alliances. At the same time it talks rather vaguely, advancing its own views on international problems. In the past this had not been done.

By this time it was not just the Communist Party which was in a state of excited debate. The journalists had thrown out the 'conservative' leadership of their union and many conservative editors had been forced out of office. Thus the press and television helped to mobilize the nation in a great debate, about its past and its future. On 26 June censorship was formally abolished. One organization with growing influence was very much concerned with the past. This was the K231. The 'K' means 'club' and 231 is the number of the 1948 law under which widespread arrests were made. The club was extremely active in documenting cases of wrongful imprisonment for alleged political offences. In July it claimed to have registered 48,000 former political prisoners out of a probable total of 100,000.[87] This could have proved embarrassing to the Russians as well as to the Czechoslovak Stalinists.

As the pace of change quickened in Czechoslovakia, Prague's relations with its allies deteriorated. There was a great deal of diplomatic activity. On 17 July a letter to the Czechoslovak party criticizing their reforms and signed by the Soviets, East Germans, Poles, Hungarians, and Bulgarians was published. There followed meetings between the Prague and Moscow leaders at Cierna in Czechoslovakia at the end of the month. Further talks followed between the Czechoslovak leaders and the signatories of the July 'Warsaw letter' at Bratislava on 3 August. Relations seemed to be improving, for Soviet troops, on manoeuvres in Czechoslovakia under the Warsaw Pact and taking rather a long time over them, withdrew. On 9 August President Tito visited Prague to lend his authority to the Dubček regime. Two days later Ulbricht followed him. He got a cool reception, but the East German press seemed to conclude all was well and published a photograph of Ulbricht and Dubček smiling broadly and shaking hands. The London *Times* (14 August) also concluded that the East German leader's visit had ended on a friendly note. But on that same day the Soviet press was violently attacking the Czech reforms. One day later Nicolae Ceauşescu arrived from Romania to an enthusiastic reception.

The Warsaw Pact blow fell five days later on 20 August when armies from the Soviet Union, East Germany, Poland, Hungary, and Bulgaria poured over the frontiers. On the orders of the Czechoslovak authorities, they met with no resistance from the relatively strong Czechoslovak forces. The latter were not prepared for such a blow and were in a hopeless position. To cover their aggression with a fig leaf the Soviets claimed they had been invited in by 'a group of personalities of the Party and State in Czechoslovakia' to defend socialism from counter-revolution. Thinking Communists must have reflected that such a group, if it existed, were acting in an anti-Leninist way by forming a faction. Some of them would ponder Lenin's, and Marx's and Engel's, words:

'No nation can be free if it oppresses other nations,' said the greatest representatives of consistent democracy of the nineteenth century, Marx and Engels, who became the teachers of the revolutionary proletariat. And we Great-Russian workers, filled with a sense of national pride, want at all costs a free and independent, democratic, republican, proud Great Russia, which shall base its relations with its neighbours on the human principle of equality, and not on the feudal principle of privilege, which is degrading to a great nation.[88]

Later the Russians and their friends attempted to justify their action by using the pseudo-Marxist argument that the sovereignty of individual socialist states was limited by the needs of the socialist community of states as a whole.[89]

By the morning of 21 August all key towns, including the capital, were under the control of the Warsaw Pact forces. The Czechoslovak people showed their anger but also their impotence in face of this overwhelming force. The parliament and the organs of the Communist Party stood firm, but their leaders were sought out and hustled off to Moscow. On 27 August a communiqué was issued, claiming that an agreement had been reached between the Prague leaders and the Soviets. The Russians claimed understanding and support for the Czechoslovak party's January and May decisions. The occupation, it was claimed, would not interfere in the internal affairs of Czechoslovakia, and would be of temporary duration.[90] Here we need not record in detail the sad and sorry story of what in fact followed: how the Dubček leadership were squeezed out; how thousands of party members were either expelled or resigned; how the Czechoslovak party was eventually forced at its 1971 congress to thank the Russians for the invasion. Dubček's successor, from April 1969, has been his fellow-Slovak Gustav Husak, who himself had been jailed by Novotný as a 'bourgeois nationalist'. Dubček himself was pursued into obscurity, but at least he was spared a show trial and imprisonment.

One is left with two questions connected with the 'Prague spring'. Why did the Soviets stamp it out? And what were the reactions of Communists outside the Soviet bloc to the invasion? To the first question no final answer can be given. But it is unlikely that the Russians had made an early and firm decision to act. It is more likely that the Politburo debated the issue almost to the end. The men in the Kremlin had acquiesced in Hungary's quiet relaxation and Romania's independent road. To intervene in Czechoslovakia meant worldwide criticism and gave substance to the arguments of those people in the West calling for the strengthening of NATO. Yet the Soviet leaders were prepared to accept this. It is quite conceivable that they were swayed by their generals. Perhaps the new Defence Minister in Prague was unable to convince them of his reliability. No doubt they were urged to regard Czechoslovakia as of great strategic importance, and her importance as a supplier of uranium and key industrial goods was not lost on them. They had always been suspicious of West Germany and that state had been increasing its influence in eastern Europe of late. Bonn had established diplomatic relations with Bucharest in 1967, and was seeking to tempt other states. In August 1967 Prague signed a trade and payments agreement with Bonn. The two states agreed to set up trade missions in Prague and Frankfurt. The question of the agreement's applicability to West Berlin – so important because East Germany claims West Berlin is a separate entity, and not part of the Bonn republic – was settled in an exchange of letters which were not published. Bonn already had similar agreements with most other East European states. Yet these other states continued to behave themselves. Prague, on the other hand, was kicking over the traces. This brings us to the question of East German influence.

This writer is in no doubt that the East German leaders viewed with suspicion both Prague's external and internal policies. If things went wrong in Prague, it was so easy for the rot to spread to East Germany. Many thousands of East Germans went for their holidays to Czechoslovakia by 1968 and there were few frontier controls. It is likely that Ulbricht urged the Soviet leaders at least to keep a very close watch on developments. And he could speak as a very experienced Communist politician who had, from the Soviet point of view, delivered the goods. Yet it is doubtful that the Soviet leadership were goaded into action by Ulbricht. This would be allowing him too much influence in the Kremlin. The Soviet leaders would have had their suspicions of any German politician urging on them such a dramatic solution. And they would surely have reflected that they had had to secure Ulbricht in 1953 and 1961. It is more likely that a majority of the men in the Soviet Politburo themselves were deeply worried about the growth of any new model of socialism so close to home, a model in a (in some ways) more modern country than their own, and in a country in which some of their fellow-countrymen (and some Poles and Hungarians as well) had relations. Whatever and whoever influenced the Soviet Politburo in the direction of intervention it was certainly not the West European Communists.

Khrushchev's Twentieth Congress speech, with its talk of peaceful and different roads to socialism, and co-operation between socialists and Communists, had given the non-ruling Communist parties the ideological justification for pursuing reformist tactics. Moscow's admission that it had been wrong at the time of Stalin, that Yugoslavia was socialist after all, and the emergence of Peking as a rival centre of Communist orthodoxy – all made it possible for them to dissociate themselves from specific Soviet policies. While claiming to be Leninist, the West European parties came to deny that they sought to set up monolithic states on the lines of the 'People's Democracies'. The Dubček regime had been welcomed by them as a possible model for socialism in an industrialized country. They watched sympathetically Dubček's efforts, as Luigi Longo, the Italian Party Secretary put it, to give 'to socialist society its true face of liberty, humanity, and democracy'.[91] It is not surprising, then, that they should condemn the invasion of Czechoslovakia. In the words of the British Communist Party Executive's statement, it

> deeply deplores the military intervention in Czechoslovakia. ... The military intervention which took place had no support from any leading body in the Czechoslovak Communist Party or state and is opposed by them. No grounds have been brought forward that can justify this violation of the national sovereignty of the Czechoslovak people and Government. Equally deplorable is the interference from outside the country to remove some of the leaders of the Czechoslovak Communist Party and to prevent them carrying out their duties, less than three weeks before the Party Congress was due to open on September 9. This is a gross violation of the democratic rights of the Czechoslovak Communists.[92]

Only the totally insignificant KPD (of West Germany), the almost equally insignificant SEW of West Berlin, the 400–500-strong Luxembourg Communist Party, the illegal Greek and Portuguese parties, and the Cypriot party, backed the invasion. Against these were the mighty French and Italian parties, the important Finnish party, the Swedish, British, Belgian, and Icelandic parties; the Swiss, Norwegians, Danes, and Austrians. They all condemned the invasion in varying degrees. They were joined by the Chinese, Romanian, Yugoslav, and Albanian parties. On the other hand, the Cubans and North Vietnamese supported the Warsaw Pact action.

August 1968, then, provoked widespread discussion in the parties in which discussion was possible. Some felt the criticism of the Soviets should have been stronger, others deplored any criticism of the 'Socialist Homeland'. Later events indicated, however, that the parties not in power were still not able to face up to the lessons of the invasion. They still could not bring themselves to engage in dispassionate analysis of Soviet society. and Soviet policies and draw the necessary conclusions from this. Indeed, some critics such as Ernst Fischer, leading theorist of the Austrian party, and Roger Garaudy, theorist of the French Party, who were heading in this direction, were expelled for their efforts. No wonder, then, that many young people – and some not so young – seeking Marxist solutions to their countries' problems, should look to other models of socialism and to new prophets of the Marxist millennium.

## NOTES

1 See above, p. 254.
2 See *Problems of Communism* (USIA), 4/1958.
3 V. Robinson, *Albania's Road to Freedom* (London, 1941).
4 Harry Hamm, *Albania – China's Beachhead in Europe* (London, 1963), pp 78–94.
5 Page, Leitch, and Knightley, op. cit., pp. 207–16.
6 Vladimir Dedijer, 'Enver Hoxha Fights for Survival', *The Times* (22 Feb. 1962).
7 David Floyd, 'Khrushchev's Cuba in the Balkans', *Daily Telegraph* (20 June 1961).
8 Hamm, op. cit., p. 80.
9 Floyd, op. cit.
10 *Protokoll des V. Parteitages*, I, 23.
11 *SBZ von A bis Z* (Bonn, 1966), p. 144. For the Berlin Problem see Philip Windsor, *German Reunification* (London, 1969). See also his 'The Berlin Crises', *History Today* (June 1962). See further H. Siegler, *Wiedervereinigung und Sicherheitz Deutschlands*, I (Bonn, 1967).
12 See *Der Spiegel* (2 July 1958). See also series in *Der Spiegel* (April–June 1971).
13 Industrial editor, *Financial Times* (25 July 1961); *Daily Mirror* (London), 24 July 1961.
14 *Daily Mirror* (24 July 1961).
15 *Bulletin* (information journal of Federal Republic of Germany).
16 Jean Edward Smith, in *International Journal* (Toronto), spring 1967, pp. 232–3.
17 Childs, op. cit., p. 63. For a biography of Ulbricht, see Carola Stern, *Ulbricht: A Political Biography* (London, 1965).
18 The significance of this group is discussed by Peter Christian Ludz, *Parteielite im Wandel* (Cologne, 1968). See also his contribution to *Problems of Communism* (May/June 1970).
19 *Die Wirtschaft* (22 Dec. 1970), Beilage 38, 5–6.
20 Erich Honecker, *Bericht des Politbüros an die 11. Tagung des Zentralkomitees der SED 15–18 Dezember 1965* (East Berlin, 1966).
21 See, for instance, his interview in *Der Spiegel* (1 March 1971).
22 Robert Havemann, *Dialektik ohne Dogma* (Hamburg, 1964), p. 155.

[23] See series in *Der Spiegel* (Oct. 1970).

[24] *Der Spiegel* (12 April 1971).

[25] For books on the GDR in the 1960s see John Dornberg, *The Other Germany* (Garden City, 1968); Arthur M. Harnhardt, Jr, *The German Democratic Republic* (Baltimore, 1968); Jean Edward Smith, *Germany beyond the Wall* (Boston, 1969); Joachim Nawrocki, *Das geplante Wunder* (Hamburg, 1967); Ernst Richert, *Das zweite Deutschland* (Frankfurt/M, 1966); Hans Werner Schwarze, *Die DDR ist keine Zone mehr* (Cologne, 1969); Fritz Schenk, *Das rote Wirtschaftswunder* (Stuttgart, 1969).

[26] See Schapiro, op. cit., pp. 573–8.

[27] This was Macmillan's view of Khrushchev; op. cit., p. 557.

[28] Done with great skill by Michel Tatu, *Power in the Kremlin* (London, 1969).

[29] *Daily Worker* (*Morning Star*), 24 Oct. 1964 – 'Soviet Policy after Khrushchev Change'.

[30] *UdSSR Fragen und Anworten*, by Presseagentur Nowasti, Moscow (East Berlin, 1967), p. 377. Five years later the number of refrigerators had only risen to 4.1 million. See L. Brezhnev, *Report of the Central Committee of the CPSU* (Moscow, 1971), p. 41.

[31] Elisabeth Koutaissoff, *The Soviet Union* (London and New York, 1971), p. 107.

[32] According to Koutaissoff, for instance, in 1960 Soviet agriculture needed at least another 2.9 million tractors 'to approach anywhere near the area/tractor ratio prevalent in the USA' (ibid., p. 108).

[33] *UdSSR Fragen und Anworten*, p. 382.

[34] D. D. Barry, 'Housing in the USSR', *Problems of Communism* (May–June 1969). See also I. Deutscher, *The Soviet 7-Year Plan* (London, n.d.).

[35] *UdSSR Fragen und Anworten*, p. 10.

[36] ibid., p. 386.

[37] At the Twenty-fourth Congress of the CPSU in 1971 Chairman Kosygin admitted that housing will remain one of the most serious problems in the years to come.

[38] *Morning Star* (7 Nov. 1969).

[39] J. P. Nettl, *The Soviet Achievement* (London, 1967); figures taken from Soviet sources (p. 254). See also David Granick, *The Red Executive* (London, 1960). He concludes (p. 127) that salary differences between manager and worker are similar to those in the United States. Occasionally, Western Communists admit these differences are worrying; see Giuseppe Boffa, an Italian Communist journalist, *Inside the Khrushchev Era* (London, 1960), p. 180 on salaries, p. 212 on education.

[40] For an interesting review of Soviet education in the 1960s see Jeremy Azrael, 'Bringing up the Soviet Man: Dilemmas and Progress', *Problems of Communism* (USIA), May–June 1968. Regarding monetary bribes, Roger Bernheim, *Die sozialistischen Errungenschaften der Sowjetsunion* (Zürich, 1971), quotes *Pravda* (19 May 1970), *Trud* (24 June 1970), and other Soviet sources.

[41] Isaac Deutscher, *The Unfinished Revolution* (London, 1967), pp. 54–5.

[42] ibid., p. 57.

[43] Nigel Grant, *Soviet Education* (London, 1964), p. 103, calls Soviet educational techniques 'formal and old-fashioned in the extreme'. See also *A Firsthand Report on Soviet Schools* (National Educational Association of the United States, Washington, 1960), esp. pp. 19–20, 21. In fairness it must be mentioned that a British report praised Soviet work on backward children – E. J. Arnold, *Backward Children in the USSR* (London, 1966).

[44] *Morning Star* (28 Nov. 1968) reported only one sex clinic in the USSR. Youth depended on an East German sex manual.

[45] The wide use of the death penalty in the USSR hardly constitutes a modern approach to penology.

[46] The trial provoked a flood of protests around the world, including some from Communists such as the French writer Louis Aragon. For a full survey of the trials and tribulations of Soviet intellectuals and minorities see Abraham Bromberg (ed.), *In Quest of Justice* (New York and London, 1970).

[47] The *Economist* (London), 26 Feb. 1966, printed an article by Liberman. The journal commented that his aim was to work out 'a system of centrally planned profit that will act as an incentive to efficient use of capital in Russian industry'. He sought to 'measure profit against the amount of capital ("social production assets" or "materialised labour") used, whereas in traditional Soviet practice profit was measured only against the "living labour" input, because, according to Marx, it is from labour alone that surplus value (profit) arises'.

[48] Brezhnev, op. cit., p. 81.

[49] For two interesting contributions on the post-Khrushchev period, see Sidney I. Ploss, 'Politics in the Kremlin', *Problems of Communism* (USIA), May–June 1970; and Boris Meissner, 'Herrschaftssystem und Staatsapparat der Sowjetunion zwischen dem XXIII. und XXIV. Parteitag', *Das Parlament* (Bonn), 22 May 1971.

[50] Robert Conquest, *Russia after Khrushchev* (London, 1965), p. 136.

[51] Dev Murarka, in *Die Zeit* (Hamburg), 2 April 1971.

[52] *Der Spiegel* (4 May 1971).

[53] See Walter Osten, in *Vorwärts* (Bonn), 15 April 1971, for an interesting analysis.

[54] In 1966 the top organ of the CPSU, the Praesidium, reverted to its pre-1952 title of Politburo; at the same time, 'First Secretary' reverted to 'General Secretary'.

[55] Victor Zorza, in the *Guardian* (4 April 1971).

[56] Zbigniew Brzezinski (ed.), *Dilemmas of Change in Soviet Politics* (New York, 1969), a slender but most interesting volume on the USSR's future.

[57] ibid., p. 64.

[58] Andrei Amalrik, *Will the Soviet Union Survive until 1984?* (London, 1970), p. 41.

[59] Brzezinski, op. cit., p. 72.

[60] L. A. D. Dallin, 'Bulgaria's Economic Reform', *Problems of Communism* (Sept.–Oct. 1970).

[61] V. L. Beneš and N. J. G. Pounds, *Poland* (London and New York, 1970), p. 313.

[62] Stehle, op. cit., p. 124.

[63] Michael Gamarnikow, 'The Polish Economy in Transition', *Problems of Communism* (Jan.–Feb. 1970), p. 40.

[64] Günter Bartsch, 'Revolution und Gegenrevolution in Osteuropa seit 1948 (IV)', *Das Parlament* (28 Feb. 1970), p. 9 (Beilage).

[65] A. Ross Johnson, 'Poland: End of an Era', *Problems of Communism* (Jan.–Feb. 1970), p. 37.

[66] *Der Spiegel* (28 Dec. 1970).

[67] *Morning Star* (9 Feb. 1971); *Der Morgen* (East Berlin), 9 Feb. 1971.

[68] On Hungarian economic reform, see Harry G. Shaffer, 'Progress in Hungary', *Problems of Communism* (Jan.–Feb. 1970); and Ignotus, op. cit., pp. 276ff.

[69] David Floyd, *Rumania: Russia's Dissident Ally* (London, 1965), pp. 50–2. Pauker was not killed, but there were other Gheorghiu-Dej victims. See also Stephen Fischer-Galati, *The New Rumania* (Cambridge, Mass., 1967).

[70] Nicolae Ceaușescu, *The Romanian Communist Party – Continuer of the Romanian People's Revolutionary and Democratic Struggle, of the Traditions of*

the *Working-Class and Socialist Movement in Romania* (Bucharest, 1966), pp. 91–2.

[71] F. E. Ian Hamilton, *Yugoslavia: Pattern of Economic Activity* (New York and London, 1968), pp. 128–9.

[72] A. Z. Rubinstein, 'Yugoslavia: Reforms, Nonalignment, and Pluralism', *Problems of Communism* (March–April 1968).

[73] F. B. Singleton, *The Times* (14 April 1970). This is a special supplement on Yugoslavia.

[74] *Vorwärts* (1 April 1971).

[75] See St. K. Pavlowitch, *Yugoslavia* (London, 1971), p. 310.

[76] Z. A. B. Zeman, *Prague Spring* (London, 1969), p. 13.

[77] ibid., p. 32.

[78] ibid., pp. 32–3.

[79] Galia Golan, 'The Road to Reform', *Problems of Communism* (May–June, 1971).

[80] Ota Šik, 'The Impact of Stalinism', *Problems of Communism* (May–June 1971), p. 8.

[81] ibid., p. 9.

[82] ibid., p. 8.

[83] Kenneth Ames, 'Reform and Reaction', *Problems of Communism* (Nov.–Dec. 1968), p. 39.

[84] Paul Ello, *Czechoslovakia's Blueprint for 'Freedom'* (Washington, 1968), gives an official Czech translation of the Programme with a commentary by Ello.

[85] Christian Fenner, 'Liberalisierung und Demokratisierung des Sozialismus in der CSSR', *Das Parlament* (7 Nov. 1970) (Beilage) contains an analysis of the Programme.

[86] Ello, op. cit., p. 136.

[87] *The Observer* (London), 28 July 1968.

[88] V. I. Lenin, *The National Pride of the Great Russians* (English version, Moscow, 1951), p. 9.

[89] This unholy doctrine, later known as the 'Brezhnev doctrine', first appeared in *Pravda* (26 Sept. 1968).

[90] R. R. James (ed.), *The Czechoslovak Crisis 1968* (London, n.d.), pp. 183–4.

[91] *L'Unità* (27 March 1968).

[92] *Marxism Today* (London), Oct. 1968.

# XI

# New Prophets and Old Ones

THE Twentieth Congress of the CPSU and the Hungarian Revolution of 1956 had a devastating effect on the Soviet-orientated Communists. No non-ruling party was without its crop of defections. Most of those who resigned still regarded themselves as Marxists and revolutionary socialists, so it was inevitable that they should want to remain politically active. Britain was one of the few places where such ex-Communists had much impact at that time. Leaving aside the high intellectual quality of some of the defectors and their organizational talents, the reasons for this were threefold. Firstly, there was the feeling that the Labour Party had somehow failed because, after its great victory of 1945, its government had not lived up entirely to its promise, and it had been once again replaced by the Conservatives. Secondly, because the Labour Party is a relatively tolerant organization (compared with most other socialist and non-socialist parties), it was possible for the ex-Communists either to join Labour, or carry on a dialogue with its members from the outside. Thirdly, there was a deep feeling of unease, even guilt, among the more 'liberal-minded' in Britain about the Anglo-French-Israel invasion of Egypt (the Suez Operation) of 1956. With liberals worrying about Suez, and Communists about Hungary, there was the basis for a discussion.

The former Communists started to publish two journals: *The New Reasoner*, 'a quarterly journal of socialist humanism', and the *Universities and Left Review*. Among the leading contributors to the first-named journal were the social historian E. P. Thompson and the Marxist interpreter of the English novel Arnold Kettle. *The New Reasoner* was mainly concerned with raking over the ashes of Stalin's victims to find clues to explain the catastrophe, and in a fairly straightforward Marxist analysis of various problems. The *Universities and Left Review* saw its task as 'to try to make some principled critique of the quality of contemporary life, and to take a perspective on the socialist and humanist transformation of our society'. Although its most powerful single personality was the former Communist Oxford student Ralph Samuel, the *Review* was younger, broader-based, and more popular than the *Reasoner*. After a short time the two journals merged to form the *New Left Review*.

The 'New Left' movement associated with the *NLR* could claim considerable success. In 1960 it had forty clubs up and down the country carrying on a regular programme of political discussion and education – something totally lacking in the Labour Party. It could attract hundreds of people to pay to attend meetings in London's West End at a time when the major parties were moaning about television having killed off public meetings. The enthusiasts heard Isaac Deutscher, Doris Lessing the novelist, Clive Jenkins, the white-collar union leader, Stuart Hall, *NLR* editor, and Ralph Miliband, the London School of Economics political scientist, and many others – sometimes all in one evening! The New Left played a role, how important it is difficult to estimate, with the Campaign for Nuclear Disarmament and in the defence debate of the Labour Party, helping to defeat the party leader, Hugh Gaitskell. Even in 1964 the *NLR* could still persuade Barbara Castle, prominent colleague of Harold Wilson, and only a few months away from being a Cabinet Minister, to contribute on 'The Lessons of French Planning'. But it was in the cultural field that the British New Left was most successful. Richard Hoggart in his *The Uses of Literacy* examined the uses of the printed mass media to condition ordinary people to accept the values of the 'candy-floss world' and reflected upon the working-class world and culture of his youth. Raymond Williams's *Culture and Society 1780–1950*, as its title suggests, is a volume of social history. These books rendered the New Left 'more critically aware of the quality and texture of the individual lives and concrete relationships of people within our society than was the old left, and more distrustful of easy solutions to problems'.[1] Another volume which had immediate, but necessarily short-lived, success, was Clive Jenkins's examination of the ownership of commercial television in *The Power behind the Screen*. Though a competent piece of of research, it tended to overestimate the influence of the key shareholders on the policy of the programme companies. Richard Hoggart was appointed to the Pilkington Commission investigating commercial television, which reported in 1962, and undoubtedly exercised a great deal of influence. The *NLR* presented evidence independently and part of this found its way into the Report.[2] As the writer knows from personal experience in television at that time, the Commission helped to improve the quality of commercial television programmes even before it reported.

The obituary of the *NLR* was being written by journalists in 1962,[3] yet it is still in existence in 1971! Nevertheless, the New Left movement of 1957 could not maintain itself. Its clubs disappeared, and many of its leading personalities abandoned direct political activities for 'reform work' in the social or academic fields. Some retreated into the more rigorously Marxist sects. In its long-term goal, 'Public ownership, social priorities, civic democracy, workers' control, a liberated culture',[4] the New Left of 1957 did not succeed in making a breakthrough. It had no clear strategy. It was not clear whether it wanted to convert the the Labour Party to its version of socialism or establish itself as an alternative to Labour. As it was, the enthusiasm displayed for the New Left was drained away into the Labour Party in the years 1962–64. The death of Gaitskell and the emergence of Harold Wilson as the Labour leader, flanked by Barbara Castle, Anthony Greenwood, and Richard Crossman, and endorsed by Michael Foot and his *Tribune* group, appeared to offer a genuinely radical, though not Marxian, alternative to the politics of the *status quo*. Even before the election of 1964, the *NLR* was not entirely happy:

> In many ways, it has been a creative response, which has made the Labour Party into the dynamic left-wing of European Social-Democracy. But it also bears the ominous hallmarks of its lineage, traditional Labourism.[5]

The same editorial warned: 'the Left will have to maintain an unremitting vigilance'. Considering what was to come under Wilson between 1964 and 1970, the *NLR* comment was, from the left-wing standpoint, not too alarmist.

In the late fifties and early sixties other New Left movements started to surface in Europe and America. But unlike the British New Left of 1957, they looked less to nineteenth-century Marxism and traditional radicalism, and increasingly inscribed on their banners the names of Fidel Castro, Che Guevara, Mao Tse-tung, and Herbert Marcuse. It is therefore proper to say something about these alternative brands of 'Marxian' thought before looking at the movements they inspired

## 1. CASTRO AND CHE

Before the First World War what left-wing movements there were in Latin America were more likely to be anarchist- or syndicalist-orientated than Marxist. This reflected the pattern of European immigration into those countries rather than any natural sympathy for such ideas on the part of the indigenous population. Marx had not been very interested in the area and 'even when he was not being openly opposed by the anarchist groups, long remained an impressive though vague and unfamiliar figure in Latin America'.[6] Only in Argentina did a Marxist-influenced socialist party create a viable organization before 1914.

Influenced by the example of the Bolshevik Revolution on 1917, Communist parties were established in the 1920s in Argentina, Brazil, Chile, Mexico, Uruguay, and, in 1925, if Cuba. These parties remained without much influence until after 1935. Like their European comrades, the Communists of Latin America were caught up in the factional disputes which originated in Moscow, and were saddled with analyses which did not reflect their individual countries' differing historical developments.[7]

The Popular-Front line brought great gains for the Latin American parties. During this period the parties of Chile, Cuba, and Mexico started to count for something in the politics of their respective countries.

In Cuba the Communists went into alliance with Fulgencio Batista. Batista, an army N.C.O. of Afro-Chinese peasant stock, had come to power as a result of the Sergeants' Revolt of 1933. Dissatisfied with their pay and conditions these American-trained N.C.O.s cut down their officers and promoted themselves to power. Having no political or economic programme, and no political organization, their chief found it necessary to seek accommodation with various groups, especially organized labour. In 1939 he permitted the establishment of the Cuban Confederation of Labour with a Communist as secretary-general. Other concessions to labour followed: minimum wages, an eight-hour working day, a month's paid annual holiday, guarantees against dismissal. As regards its labour legislation the Batista regime was 'among the most advanced in Latin America'.[8] Allied with the Communists and other groups, Batista was able to win a genuine electoral victory in July 1950. At its Second National Conference in 1914 the *Partido Socialista Popular*, as the Communist Party was by this time called, reaffirmed its loyalty to the principles of Browder, Batista, and Marx![9] But in the election of that year the Communist-supported Batista candidate failed in his Presidential bid. The new President needed parliamentary allies and the Communists were willing to help. In the elections two years later the Communists gained an impressive 10 per cent of the total votes cast. However, as President Grau's friends had also improved their position and no longer needed Communist support, they broke their ties with the PSP. In any case, the international climate was turning against Latin America's Communists.

After some hesitation, Blas Roca, Secretary-General of the PSP, was forced to get in line with the harder Kremlin policy which put heavy emphasis on attacking 'US imperialism'. The United States was, for her part, presiding over an offensive against Communist influence in Latin America. Several states broke off relations with the Soviet Union, Communist parties were outlawed, the allegedly pro-Communist government of Jacobo Arbenz in Guatemala was overthrown in 1954. In Cuba the Communists lost their leadership of the unions, but held on to most of their support. When Batista returned to power after a successful *coup* in 1952, the Communists once again made conciliatory grunts. A few minor Communist leaders actually went over to Batista. The party was, however, outlawed in 1953, as much out of deference to the United States as out of genuine conviction; but the ban was only formal. Batista did not persecute the Communists with the harshness he used against some of his other opponents. Among these other opponents were Fidel Castro and his friends.

Fidel Castro's father was a self-made estate-owner who had emigrated to Cuba from Spain and made his fortune in sugar and timber. Fidel's mother was his father's former cook. It was an unhappy, uncultivated family that Fidel Castro was born into in 1926. But Castro senior was evidently concerned about his son's future, for he sent him first to a boarding school and then to a Jesuit college. During his stay with the Jesuits he became known as 'an athlete, a debater and a rebel'.[10] Like so many other young men of his social class, he continued his education by studying Law at Havana University. Of his student days he is reported as saying: '[I] never went to class, never opened a book other than on the eve of examinations'.[11] He did what many of his contemporaries did, and what their kind had done before them – he argued politics. This he must have done rather well, for he was elected to the vice-presidency of the student governing body. He had at least one other interest. In October 1948 he married a philosophy student and fathered a son. The marriage ended in divorce seven years later. On graduation in 1950 Fidel Castro practised law. If we are to believe his admirers, he had 'a busy practice, with most of his time spent in defending workers, farmers, and political prisoners'.[12] Castro at this time supported the 'Party of the Cuban People', the *Ortodoxos* of Eduardo Chibás. This group had broken away from the ruling party and its only platform was a campaign against corruption. Castro himself would probably have been elected to the Congress had not Batista's *coup* prevented the elections from taking place. Having been thwarted in his parliamentary plans, Fidel Castro turned to revolutionary violence.

In July 1953, at the head of a group of some two hundred, mainly students or young graduates like himself, he attempted to storm Fort Moncada, the country's second largest military installation. It was 'a mad adventure'[13] which ended with many of the rebels being killed on the spot, or captured and blinded or castrated before being killed.[14] Castro himself was luckier. He was only captured sometime later and after a secret trial was sentenced to fifteen years' imprisonment.

It is necessary to pause here and consider what kind of revolutionary Fidel Castro was. Both Castro in recent years, and his enemies, have claimed that he was already a Marxist and treading the Leninist road. Though one cannot be sure at this stage what Castro was in 1953, it seems doubtful that he was a Marxist, in the Moscow-Peking sense. A speech written in prison, *History Will Absolve Me*, which is regarded as a basic document of Castroism, is not Marxist in content. Though it called for the nationalization of some public utilities, it did not advocate the abolition of private property. On the contrary, it sought to create more owners through land reform. It also called for profit-sharing in large firms, something frowned upon by Marxists as a deception of the workers. Of course, as we have seen, particularly since 1945 Communist movements have presented programmes which did not hint of their long-term objectives. But there is other evidence that Castro was not a Communist in 1953. After the attack on the Moncada fort the PSP dissociated itself completely from the Castro rebels:

> We repudiate the putschist methods, peculiar to bourgeois political factions. . . . The heroism displayed by the participants in this action is false and sterile, as it is guided by mistaken bourgeois ideas.

In truth we can say that Castro's military adventure at this time was not in keeping with the conceptions common to Marx and Engels. From the Marxist point of view Castro's efforts were petty bourgeois radicalism in the classic Latin American tradition. Three years or so later when Batista accused Castro of being a Communist, Fidel brought up the earlier alliance between Batista and the PSP, thus indirectly attacking the Communists. As Theodore Draper has commented, it is 'hard to imagine a Communist, open or concealed, defending himself in this way'.[15]

Castro was released from prison under an amnesty in 1955. He emigrated to the United States to think out his plans, and gather funds and supporters for his next assault on Batista. This came in December 1956. It very nearly ended in disaster. Some eighty-two Castroites set out from Mexico on board the yacht *Granma*. Insurgents were to land in the remote, rugged, and sparsely inhabited province of Oriente where a popular rising was supposed to be under way. The boat did not arrive on time, the rising failed. Of the 'invaders' only twelve evaded Batista's forces. But the fact of their survival marked the beginning of the end for the 'self-enriching and corrupt dictator'.[16] That Batista with all the forces at his disposal was not able to destroy them undermined his authority. A regime so opportunist and corrupt has few real supporters when it does not appear to be in complete control, and fewer still when it is seriously threatened.

The Castro party were able to publicize themselves in the United States in the press and on television, which made them appear more significant than perhaps they were at the time. This seems to have been of considerable importance for their victory. In February 1957 Herbert L. Matthews interviewed Castro for the *New York Times*. The interview caused a 'tremendous sensation'.[17] Matthews had witnessed many wars and revolutions in his time and could claim to know what he was talking about. Castro impressed him:

> The personality of the man is overpowering. It was easy to see that his men adored him and also to see why he has caught the imagination of the youth of Cuba all over the island. Here was an educated, dedicated fanatic, a man of ideals, of courage, and of remarkable qualities of leadership.[18]

The result was that Matthews's story made Castro 'a hero and a symbol for the resistance'.[19] This was at a time when the Cuban regime was claiming that Castro was dead! Other journalists, both television and press, followed Matthews. In fact, 'the mountains became a Mecca' for them. Such publicity found its way back to Cuba and affected popular attitudes there. Other anti-Batista groups organized opposition in the towns, including an unsuccessful assassination attempt in March 1957. The dictatorship responded with indiscriminate violence which in turn antagonized more people both inside and outside Cuba.

The publicity and the repression led many young people to take to the hills with Castro. In May 1958 Batista launched a combined air, sea, and land operation against the rebels, but failed. Whether this failure was because his forces had already been undermined by, or whether it can be attributed to, Castro's 'military leadership of a high order',[20] this writer cannot claim to know. By January of the following year Castro was in Havana.

On 16 February 1959 Fidel Castro took over as Prime Minister. He did so with a great deal of popular support behind him. His considerable charm and manly bearing, the advance publicity, the relatively peaceful and orderly manner of the change-over, and the widespread contempt for the outgoing regime ensured this. At this time Castro still claimed he stood for a 'humanist revolution'. It would be unlike Western capitalism which provided freedom but no bread, and unlike Eastern communism, which gave the people bread at the expense of their freedom. His revolution would give the people both. But his political attitudes were still 'probably not quite clear even to himself'.[21] He was, however, optimistic. He even promised his TV audience: 'in a few years we will raise the Cuban standard of living above that of the United States and Russia, because these countries invest the

greater part of their economic resources in making war material'.[22]
Action followed the words: measures designed to have an immediate positive effect on many people's living standards were
introduced. Rents were cut along with many prices; wages were
raised; land reform was carried through; Batista supporters had
their property confiscated; public works schemes were started to
provide parks, sports grounds, bathing facilities, and housing
for the people. Some people both inside and outside Cuba were
impressed by the 'clean-up' of Havana's bars, brothels, and
beggars. Even at this stage the revolution had another side. If
corruption was gone, chaos had arrived. The untrained and incompetent took over; people were no longer sure who was in
authority. The new men soon found it was easier to issue decrees
than implement them. And even in those early months the first
shadow of retribution crossed over Cuba. Some 600 Batista supporters faced the firing squad. They were the victims of what
a pro-Castro writer called 'rough, swift justice that violated every
Anglo-Saxon idea of fair trial'.[23] But, as an anti-Castro commen-
tator admitted, most of the executed 'had undoubtedly been
guilty of murder and torture'.[24]

At the invitation of the American press Castro visited the
United States in April 1959. President Eisenhower was 'more
than irritated' by the invitation and 'refused to see him'.[25] However, the Cuban did meet Vice-President Nixon and other top
officials. Apparently he rejected American aid.[26] Yet at the
Economic Conference of American states at Buenos Aires in the
same year he invited the United States to loan Latin America
some 30,000 million dollars over ten years to aid stable freedom-
*and*-bread regimes.[27] This, and the very fact of his visit to the
United States, and his willingness to meet 'top people' there,
would lead one to conclude that, at this stage, he had not
definitely decided on cold-war relations with her.

Obviously the United States was concerned about any fundamental change of regime within 90 miles of her shores. Some
highly-placed Americans had greatly admired Batista, others had
detested him: all agreed he posed no threat to the United States.
When the Batista regime started to tremble, the United States
had imposed an arms embargo, though her military mission
remained. Opinions differ about the importance of this embargo
to Castro's victory. After Castro's conquest of power Washington had not hesitated to accord the new regime recognition.

As late as November 1959 General C. P. Cabell, Deputy Director of the American Central Intelligence Agency, in a much-quoted testimony had pronounced that 'Castro is not a member of the Communist Party, and does not consider himself a Communist'. The Communists, the general believed, regarded Castro as a representative of the bourgeoisie.[28] Nevertheless, many of those around President Eisenhower did not like Castro. Vice-President Nixon 'distrusted him from the start'.[29] As the months went by, there was much for this distrust to feed on. Firstly, there was the expropriation of American property. Secondly, there was the Communization of the revolution. Thirdly, the development of Cuba's relations with the Communist world. Fourthly, the provocative speeches of Fidel Castro excited American opinion.

Some United States property was nationalized in 1959 because of the support its owners had given to Batista. Land reform resulted in the loss of more American property. This land reform was 'the first important issue to divide Cuba and the United States'.[30] In June 1960 the three big American and British oil companies were taken over for refusing to refine Soviet oil. In July Eisenhower cut back Cuba's assigned share of the American sugar market. On the same day, the Cuban government authorized the nationalization of all American property on the island. By the end of the year American assets valued at between $800 and $900 million had been seized.[31] In December the American President responded by cutting off completely the American market to Cuban sugar.

The second cause for concern in the United States about the developments in Cuba was the early and rapid trend towards a totalitarian state. The free political life, free trade unions, and free elections promised in the guerrilla days failed to materialize. The free press was soon to disappear, together with academic freedom and the independence of the judicary. In most respects it was very similar to what had happened in eastern Europe: it is therefore unnecessary to go into all the details here. Although some Americans thought otherwise, all this, and the socialization of the economy, was achieved *without* the Communists taking the lead.

It was as late as November 1958, a matter of weeks before Batista's fall, that the Communist PSP concluded an agreement with Castro.[32] And even after the seizure of power, the Castroites and the Communists made open or veiled attacks on each other. The Communists were worried by Castro's extreme left policies, his lack of discipline, and personality cult. It was in the summer of 1961 that Castro formally went into close alliance with the Communists. This was with the setting-up of the ORI, which comprised the Castro '26 July Movement', the 'Directorio Revolucionario', another non-Marxist anti-Batista group which had been in alliance with Castro since 1957, and the Communist PSP. It was out of this that the *Partido Unido de la Revolución Socialista* (PURS), the ruling, officially Marxist-Leninist, party, was to emerge after June 1962. In December 1961 Fidel Castro declared that he was a dedicated Marxist-Leninist, and had been since 1953, But he probably felt himself converted to Marxism about the end of 1959.[33] This conversion was as much the result of seeing the need for trained and disciplined cadres at all levels, which only the PSP could provide, and a uniting ideology, as belief in, or knowledge of, Marxism-Leninism. It was also the outcome of growing dependence on the Soviet bloc.

The most significant of these East bloc ties was the development of relations with the Soviet Union. On 4 February 1960, Anastas Mikoyan, Soviet Politburo member and Deputy Chairman of the Council of Ministers, visited Cuba and signed a five-year trade agreement which included provision for Soviet arms. Over the next year and a half Cuba established relations with all the Communist states, including China. Meanwhile Castro kept up a war of words against the United States, as hostile as much of the American press was hostile to him. For if the United States had cause to be apprehensive about developments in Cuba, many Cubans felt Washington had much to answer for in its relations with Cuba.

None other than John F. Kennedy admitted that in the pre-Castro period the United States had declined to help the island meet its desperate need for economic progress, and had employed 'the influence of our Government to advance the interests and increase the profits of the private American companies, which dominated the island's economy'. He further admitted that the United States had given 'stature and support to one of the most bloody and repressive dictatorships in the long history of Latin America'.[34] The American record in the years before Batista was no better. Others defending the American position could claim that Cuba's close ties with North America had resulted in the island having *per capita*, more radios, TVs, and automobiles than the other Latin American states. It ranked fourth in *per capita* income, and was near the top in education, literacy, social services, and urbanization. Yet such facts 'concealed shocking disparities in the distribution of wealth, especially as between city and countryside and between white and Negro'.[35] Nor did they take account of the way some Americans treated Cubans in their own country. The large United States base at Guantanamo, there since 1903, emphasized the inequality between the neighbours. It was these unequal relations over half a century which helped to produce the Cuban leader whose political ambition it became 'to leave behind in history a picture of himself as a Cuban David before an American Goliath'.[36] Castro was impetuous. Had he not been so he would never have gained power. But once in power he needed wisdom rather than impetuosity; this he had not got.

One can rightly ask whether the Americans showed much wisdom in their response to Castro. This writer still has nagging doubts that if the United States had been prepared to take a few more slaps in the face from Castro, things might have turned out differently.

In March 1960 President Eisenhower authorized the CIA to prepare a force of Cubans for a possible attempt to overthrow Castro. This possibility became reality in April 1961 when 1,400 exiles landed in the Bay of Pigs, and American B-26 bombers, some piloted by Americans, made strikes against Cuban targets. The operation was a fiasco. Those who did not die fell into Castro's hands. The Americans had underestimated the amount of support Castro had, the efficiency of his military and security systems, and the man himself.[37] American prestige suffered and Kennedy dissipated much of the hope placed in him by liberals around the world. Later he was to wonder: 'How a rational and responsible government could ever have become involved in so ill-starred an adventure'.[38] Needless to say Castro emerged from the encounter strengthened.

Since 1961 Fidel Castro has survived other attempts to remove him. What have been his other achievements? He has not solved his country's economic problems or raised living standards. After early attempts at crash industrialization between 1959 and 1963, Cuba reverted to her traditional reliance on sugar which still accounts for about 85 per cent of exports.[39] Virtually everything, including sugar, has been severely rationed for years. Life is long hours of work, followed by more long hours of 'voluntary', unpaid labour or militia duty. Virtually everything is socialized, to an extent which is unknown in the Soviet bloc, down to every last Havana hot-dog stand. That everybody is not happy with this state of affairs is indicated by the round 700,000 Cubans, out of a population of under 8 million, either in exile or waiting to go in 1969.[40] The law against loafers introduced in 1971 is another indication. Under it, it is an offence, punishable by a year's forced labour, to be out of work or to be absent from one's job for more than fifteen days without a doctor's certificate.[41] However, very many are the students of the Cuban scene, who record the progress in education, in welfare, in improving life in the villages, in giving Cuba's black minority a better deal, in creating full employment, and in giving Cubans a new sense of national dignity.[42]

Some would present Castro's main achievement as offering a new strategy for revolution, and a new style of leadership in refreshing contrast to East European and Soviet methods. Once Castro had officially declared his revolution socialist and himself a Marxist-Leninist, and started to merge his movement with the Communists, it seemed likely that Cuba would soon fall into line with Soviet bloc practices, real power passing to the old Muscovites. This did not happen.

The Communists had seen Castro's guerrilla tactics against Batista as 'Left adventurism' but had been prepared to share his success. For a short time he was ready to play softly the armed insurrection theme in order to improve his relations with them and Moscow. Starting in 1962, he began to retrace his steps, removing old-guard Communists for alleged sectarianism and factionalism, taking over as Party Secretary himself, and promoting guerrilla groups in other Latin American states – a policy frowned on by Moscow. But:

The decisive factors that impelled the Latin American Communist parties to reject Castro's ideology as articulated in the period 1962–67 were that he assigned leadership of the revolutionary struggle to the guerrilla fighters rather than to Communist cadres, that he extolled the virtues of the peasants as the army of the popular revolution instead of the industrial proletariat, and that he downgraded political movements in the cities – where the Communists' strength was concentrated – to an auxiliary role subordinate to that of the guerrilla forces in the countryside. In short, Castro's 'guerrilla formula' denied to the Communists their self-assigned role of vanguard of the revolution in Latin America and arrogated it to his own guerrilla followers. [43]

Before going on to outline the relations between Castro and the Communists after 1962, it is necessary to say something about the theory of the guerrilla road to revolution. This theory, as applied to Latin America, has become associated with two names – Ernesto 'Che' Guevara and Régis Debray.

Guevara (1928–67) was a good-looking Argentine doctor from a radical middle-class background. Precocious as a child, restless as a youth, he was as courageous in his early fight against personal difficulty (severe asthma) as he was in his later fight against oppression. After medical studies he went off to work for the Arbenz regime in Guatemala. When this fell victim of an American-organized *coup* in 1954, he left for Mexico where he lived 'as poorly as a sparrow in winter' [44] and studied Marxism. In 1955 he met Fidel Castro there and took little persuading to join Castro's revolutionary group. 'The price was his first marriage'. [45] He took a decisive part in the struggle which brought down Batista and was suitably honoured with high office in Castro's administration – as President of the National Bank, Minister of Industry, etc. He gave up the comfort and relative security of office to launch a guerrilla movement in Bolivia in late 1966. He was killed in the attempt. He was already a legend. He has been described as 'the Garibaldi of his age', [46] as a man who was prepared to take risks because he did not feel indispensable. Or was it simply that he had 'become obsessed with the idea of death in action and, indeed, the sheer thrill of war'? [47] Whatever the truth, he was primarily a doer, and for this reason the best account of his ideas comes from his friend Régis Debray.

Debray was born in France in 1941, the son of middle-class parents. He went to Cuba in 1961 as a young Marxist student of Latin American revolutionary movements. His studies took him to various parts of the continent until arrested and sentenced to thirty years' imprisonment in Bolivia in 1967. It was alleged that he had been helping the rebels. His friends and admirers claim that his imprisonment was punishment for publishing his work on Castro-Guevara revolutionary tactics, *Revolution in the Revolution?* This appeared in Havana in January 1967.

The basic Castro-Guevara thesis as expounded by Debray was that the Cuban example offered a model for the Latin American countries, the key element of which was 'by means of the more or less slow building up, through guerilla warfare carried out in suitably chosen rural zones, of a *mobile strategic force*, nucleus of a people's army and a future socialist state'.[48] While praising the achievements of Mao and General Giap, it consciously rejects important tenets of their theories as unsuitable for Latin America. One of the most important of these is control by the Marxist-Leninist party of the guerrilla movement. 'Fidel Castro says simply that there is no revolution without a vanguard; that this vanguard is not necessarily the Marxist-Leninist party; and that those who want to make the revolution have the right and the duty to constitute themselves a vanguard, independently of these parties'.[49] The reason for this is that the urban party leaders are to some extent tarnished by the decadence of life in Latin America's cities: 'those big Yankee branch offices in the Caribbean'.[50] In them, 'even a comrade, who spends his life in a city is unwittingly bourgeois in comparison with a *guerrillero*'. Within the guerrilla movement there could be no democracy, military discipline was essential. Another important difference from China and Vietnam was that in Latin America the guerrillas could not be 'like fish in water', mingling with the teeming peasant masses so that their enemies could not identify them. Firstly, in Latin America, where the guerrilla areas were sparsely populated, any stranger could not remain unknown for long. Secondly, the guerrillas would be met with suspicion on the part of the peasants; for many of them were Indians and as such sceptical of white men's promises. For this reason military action preceded propaganda. The peasants had been oppressed for so long that they respected the recognized uniforms of their oppressors. It was, therefore, necessary to prove to them the military effectiveness of the guerrillas before seeking to educate them, get their help and participation. In this situation the guerrilla war would become a race between the 'experienced forces of repression', with their helicopters and paratroops, and the inexperienced guerrillas.[51] The army must seek a short campaign 'to destroy the *foco* in its embryonic stage, without giving it time to adapt itself to the terrain or link itself closely to the local population or acquire a minimum of experience'.[52] Once that experience had been gained, once a link had been forged with the local population, the tide would slowly turn in the guerrillas' favour.

This strategy was put into operation by Castroite guerrillas from 1963 on. Until about 1965 the Soviets and their client parties in Latin America gave reluctant support to guerrilla action, though never accepting Castro's theories.[53] Increasingly, after 1965 Brezhnev and Kosygin opted for the development of diplomatic and trade relations with Brazil, Chile, Colombia, and Venezuela, even though the governments of these states were under attack from Castroite guerrillas. Moscow-orientated parties withdrew from the guerrilla struggle. In the case of Venezuela, this led to an open break between Havana and the Communist Party of Venezuela in March 1967. In 1968 the Guatemalan party dropped out. Both parties felt the loss of support was too high a price to pay for this kind of militancy. But pro-Castroites, and here and there insignificant groups of Maoists, continued the struggle. They were mainly from the middle and upper-middle classes, with no roots among the peasants or workers, and drawn from non-Communist left-wing parties – Socialist, Democratic, even Christian Democratic. They were not successful. Their biggest reverse was in Bolivia.

This is not the place to detail the sad, sordid, little tale of the last months of Che Guevara. He did not win the race with the Bolivian helicopters and paras. Some of the virtues he himself preached – vigilance, mistrust, mobility – he neglected. In his urge to act he forgot that Bolivia in 1967 was not Cuba in 1957. There was no revolutionary situation in Bolivia. Her regime, unlike Batista's, was not tottering on the brink. Her regime, too, was American-backed, whereas the Americans had indicated at least some indifference to Batista towards the end. In any case, the Americans and the regimes they support have learned from the Cuban experience. As for the guerrillas themselves, unlike the Castroites of 1957, they had proclaimed themselves Marxist-Leninists and thus lessened their appeal. And Fidel and his comrades had been on native soil; Guevara and most of his band were foreigners.

Towards the end of the 1960s Castro's relations with Moscow and its friends in Latin America and elsewhere seemed to improve. Castro put less emphasis on supporting foreign guerrillas and more on developments at home. But he probably remained sceptical of the USSR's brand of Marxism. He felt that the Soviets were not doing enough in Vietnam, had not done enough to aid the Arabs in the June War of 1967. He welcomed their intervention in Czechoslovakia and they were very gratified by this. The biggest difference between the two was Cuba's continued rejection of 'material incentives' – the use of profit, salary differentials, and payment by results – to produce a socialist version of the 'affluent society'. His regime continues to denounce bureaucracy; only time will tell whether it really has any practical answer.

Moscow and Havana are tied together in a marriage of convenience; but, like so many other such marriages, it might well last. Castro needs Soviet help. The Soviet Union alone absorbed more than $1.1 billion in Cuban trade deficits between 1961 and 1967.[54] The Soviets also provided massive arms aid. Moscow must go on helping unruly younger brother, otherwise its credibility as a world revolutionary power would slump badly.

One wonders after twelve years of Castroism whether the regime will retain the interest of Left circles as a distinctive model of Marxian socialism. In addition to failure at home and abroad, Castro faces new competition. This is from the Communist-socialist coalition experiment in Chile, and anti-imperialist generals in Peru and Bolivia.

In September 1970 the veteran socialist, and self-proclaimed Marxist, Salvador Allende emerged with the highest number of votes in Chile's Presidential election. He was the candidate of a left-wing alliance which included, in addition to his own Socialist Party, the Communists, the left-wing Christian Democrats (MAPU), the Radicals, and another small left-wing group, API. This socialist physician had stood several times before. On the previous occasion, in 1964, his only rival was Christian Democrat Eduardo Frei, the candidate favoured by the United States. Then Frei had narrowly defeated his Communist-backed rival by advocating reform as an alternative to revolution. Many of the propertied classes, as well as the masses, had opted for this recipe. This time a right-wing candidate, Jorge Alessandri, had drawn votes away from Frei's Christian Democratic successor, Radomiro Tomic, Tomic's electoral platform was broadly the same as Allende's. Despite his slight victory at the polls (he got fewer than the other two candidates combined), Allende still had to convince the majority of Congress that he was their man. As it turned out, this 'pragmatic and crafty politician'[55] did convince enough Christian Democrats to get himself elected as President. They got him to promise to uphold a Statute of Democratic Guarantees including civil liberties, freedom of the press, of unions, and parties, and neutrality of the armed forces. The new government assured everyone that it believed in 'political and ideological pluralism'.[56] The Christian Democrats did not fear Allende, who had always been 'a relative moderate in that curious, ill-organized, rhetoric-rich, ever-disputing movement, the Chilean Socialist Party'.[57] Some on the Right pointed to his friendship with Castro and Che. But as the sixty-two-year-old recently elected President Allende told the thirty-year-old recently released writer Debray, Che had recognized that he aimed at the same thing 'by other means'.[58] For some Castro-style guerrillas, as well as some on the Right, such statements failed to satisfy, and they continued their illegal activities.

In its first year Allende's regime showed itself as a government of radical reform rather than Red revolution. It used legislation introduced by its predecessors to further land reform, control business, and give the unions more say in the factories.[59] The Christian Democrats had been somewhat independent in foreign affairs and had established diplomatic relations with the USSR. Allende took up relations with Peking, Havana, and East Berlin. For the East Germans, and even more so for the Cubans, this new link was of considerable moral importance.

It would be foolish to speculate about the Chilean experiment after so short a period. Allende is no charismatic leader like Fidel; his coalition is made up of disparate elements often at loggerheads with each other in the past; the constitutional and the unconstitutional oppositions remain – so do Chile's daunting problems of inflation, rural backwardness, securing growth, and abolishing gross inequality.

## II. MAO'S CULTURAL REVOLUTION

It is the writer's impression that after initial left-wing enthusiasm for Mao's China, interest fell back as Peking adopted Soviet methods. Yet in the 'Year of Revolutions', 1968, Mao's prestige ran high among the young revolutionaries. This was because of the so-called Great Proletarian Cultural Revolution. This 'Revolution' remains something of a mystery and recent developments in China could rob it of much of its significance.

It appears that the Cultural Revolution started quietly in January 1965 when Mao set up a five-man 'cultural revolution group' led by P'eng Chen, the boss of the Peking party organization.[60] Chen's task was to expose revisionism among the intellectuals. In June Mao moved against bourgeois degeneration in the armed forces, the People's Liberation Army, and returned to the earlier tradition of a rankless, guerrilla force. At an enlarged meeting of the standing committee of the Politburo in September, Mao called for a struggle against 'bourgeois reactionary thinking', and specifically hit out at a play by the deputy mayor of Peking, Wu Han. Chen apparently tried to keep the attacks on his subordinate, Wu Han, in low key. He drafted a 'pussyfooting report'[61] which was repudiated by the Central Committee of the party in May 1966. In the same month P'eng Chen was dismissed as Peking Party Secretary and mayor; his cultural revolution group was dissolved and another put in its place. The announcement of the fall of the 'smiling Mayor', one of the six most powerful men in China, was the signal for other attacks. The next to fall were the President of Peking University and the university's Party Secretary. This was on 3 June. A day later the purge spread to other parts of the country. During the following two months hundreds of educators and party officials lost their jobs.[62] The nation's educational establishments closed. The next dramatic move was Mao's reappearance after some time off-stage. On 16 July he made his celebrated nine-mile swim in the Yangtze, thus dispelling rumours about his health. He also took over direction of the Cultural Revolution from President Liu Shao-ch'i and Party General Secretary Teng Hsiao-p'ing. He put out his own poster, on which he attacked 'some leading comrades' for having adopted 'the reactionary stand of the bourgeoisie' towards the Cultural Revolution. Under his influence the Central Committee issued a sixteen-point document which attempted to lay down the ground rules for the revolution – or was it just window dressing?

The sixteen-point document called the Cultural Revolution 'a new stage of development of the Socialist revolution'. It accused the bourgeoisie of attempting a comeback by corrupting the minds of the masses. Therefore:

At present, our objective is to struggle against and overthrow those persons in authority who are taking the capitalist road, to criticize and repudiate the reactionary bourgeois academic 'authorities' and the ideology of the bourgeoisie and all other exploiting classes and to transform education, literature and art and all other parts of the superstructure not in correspondence with the socialist economic base, so as to facilitate the consolidation and development of the socialist system.

The main forces of the new revolution were the workers, peasants, soldiers, revolutionary intellectuals, and revolutionary cadres, and 'large numbers of revolutionary young people, previously unknown'. The party leaders were urged to put daring above everything else and boldly arouse the masses. The authors of the document were convinced that unity could be achieved with more than 95 per cent of the cadres and more than 95 per cent of the masses. The strictest care should be taken to distinguish between 'the anti-Party, anti-socialist Rightists', and those who in general supported the party but had written some bad work or made some other mistakes. Special care should be taken of 'those scientists and scientific and technical personnel who have made contributions. Efforts should be made to help them gradually transform their world outlook and their style of work'. The vehicles of the Cultural Revolution were to be cultural revolutionary groups, committees, and congresses. These should be 'under the leadership of the Communist Party'. They should be elected and, like those of the Paris Commune, delegates should be subject to immediate recall if the electors lost confidence in them. Educational reform was stressed. The period of schooling should be shortened and combined with manual labour, with cultural revolutionary groups, committees, and congresses in the institutions consisting mainly of representatives of the revolutionary students. Point fifteen protected the People's Liberation Army from too much youthful enthusiasm. In the armed forces the Cultural Revolution was to be carried out in accordance with the instructions of the Military Commission of the Central Committee and the forces' Political Department. Finally, study of Mao's thought was urged as a guide to action.[63]

On 18 August 1966 a million-strong rally was held in Peking. It indicated the biggest party shake-up for thirty-one years.[64] Lui Shao-ch'i dropped from second to eighth place in the party hierarchy, Defence Minister Lin Piao taking his place. Chou En-lai retained his third place, but there were other important changes below him.

A second important feature of the 18 August rally was the unveiling of the Red Guard movement. It is difficult to be completely sure about all aspects of the Red Guards. The first group was set up at Peking University with official blessing. To what extent they were made up of members of the official Communist youth movement is not clear. It is believed that there was much dissatisfaction among the youth which Mao sought to mobilize. First, the Communist youth body embraced only about 20 per cent of China's youth. The children of peasants and unskilled workers were badly represented both in this organization and in the nation's schools and universities.[65] They found it difficult to get apprenticeships and access to training.[66] Many of these must have been Red Guard material. But if their dissatisfaction was spontaneous, their mobilization appears to have been, in the circumstances, well organized. In Peking the Red Guards had a centre with over 200 officials, with finance and technical services provided by the city administration.[67] The army provided over 100,000 'commanders and fighters' who stayed with the revolutionary youth the whole time, looking after them, eating and studying with them.[68] Free transport was provided for the Guards. The mass media, both ancient and modern, were behind them.[69]

In the days after the 18 August rally Peking's Red Guards turned demonstrations into riots as they attacked all remaining manifestations of revisionism and bourgeois values – street names, shops with Western fashions, churches, mosques, Buddhist temples, and private homes. This type of activity spread to other cities and towns. By the end of the year Mao decided to draw in restless workers from the great industrial centres and the peasants. Strikes, demonstrations, and a good deal of industrial chaos followed. Officials gave in to workers' wage demands and there was a run on what consumer goods were in the shops. The Red Guards got out of hand as rival factions were formed and fought it out in the streets. The army was first called in to dampen things down and then forbidden from taking sides or even intervening. In the first half of 1967 violent clashes took place in several centres with casualties running into hundreds of thousands.[11] Party officials and foreign diplomats were attacked, the

British mission being burned down. Mao's China was rapidly dissipating the considerable goodwill she had around the world; only small groups of self-styled Red Guards and other Maoists in the West were applauding. In the second half of the year Mao started to put the brakes on, whether out of a sense of fear or satisfaction is not clear.

Early estimates at the end of the Cultural Revolution indicated that the licensed rebels' attacks on the party and state machines had inevitably increased the influence of the People's Liberation Army. Evidence indicated that some nineteen of the twenty-nine Revolutionary Committees – created in 1967 to replace the party committees as the ruling authorities in the provinces – were chaired by PLA military or political officers. Many ministries were headed by military men. Higher up, of the twenty-one members of the Politburo in 1969, ten were military men. Just below them, on the Central Committee, at least 58 of the 170 full members of the Central Committee were important military figures. However, at the very top, on the five-member standing committee of the Politburo, there was only one soldier, Defence Minister Lin Piao.[71]

Many of the nation's élite had fallen.[72] Of those elected to the Central Committee at the Eighth Congress in 1956, 69 per cent did not find their way on to the new Central Committee elected at the Ninth Congress in 1969.[73] Of the six members of the Politburo's standing committee elected in 1956 only two, Mao and Chou, were re-elected in 1969. The other 'victors' at the end of the Cultural Revolution on the standing committee were Lin Piao, designated Mao's successor by the Ninth Congress, Ch'en Po-ta, and K'ang Sheng. Chiang Ch'ing was a member of the Politburo, but not of its standing committee; yet the fourth Madame Mao was regarded as very influential in promoting the Cultural Revolution.

Lin Piao, sixty-two in 1969, was said to have 'a quiet and modest manner'.[74] The son of a Hupeh factory-owner, and a professional military man trained at the Whampoa Military Academy at Canton, he had been associated with Mao in every political battle since the 1930s. But from early October 1971 his name ceased to be mentioned by the media. His fate is unknown.

Apart from Mao, and evidently Lin, Chou En-lai has been the most successful leader in Communist China. Aged seventy in

1969, this mandarin's son helped to set up a Chinese Communist Party in France in 1921. He was elected to the Politburo of the party in 1927 and has remained a member of that body ever since. Also a graduate of Whampoa, he directed the Military Affairs section of the Central Committee between 1928 and 1935. He has been the Chinese Prime Minister since 1949, and although associated with Mao since the 1930s, this man of charm and diplomatic and organizational ability is regarded as being on the side of moderation and orderly progress.[75]

Even by Communist standards the Chinese Communist Party has an abysmal record so far as keeping to its constitution is concerned. Since the Seventh Congress in 1945 it has held but two congresses. The ninth was at least eight years overdue. Its Chairman seems not to have even bothered with the electoral charade customary in the socialist camp. Of course, his supporters would argue that the whole point of the Cultural Revolution was to go over the heads of the party, state, and industrial bureaucracies to appeal to the people direct, indeed to institute direct democracy. However, there is no evidence that this has happened. Mao was always concerned with the triumph of the General Will rather than with merely the Will of All. How could any meaningful exercise be carried on anyway in a country where there is no open, free confrontation of competing philosophies, ideas, and claims? How could any version of socialist democracy prevail when officially only Marxist categories were admitted, and even then, not the Marxism of Marx but only that of Mao?

At the time of writing even more mystery than usual hangs over the People's Republic of China. There has been a massive effort to rebuild the diplomatic bridges smashed up during the Cultural Revolution. The Chinese have gone further than ever before in their efforts to normalize their relations with the outside world. Three examples will be enough to demonstrate the dramatic shift of emphasis. First, the great improvement in Sino-Yugoslav relations helped by mutual fear of the Soviet Union. Secondly, the cordial relations between China and Iran – a regime long despised by left-wing militants the world over. Thirdly, and most incredible of all, the visit of President Nixon to the People's Republic. This very welcome move in international relations must surely have given Maoist purists outside China food for thought about the regime they admire. These and other moves have led to much speculation about the post-Mao leadership of the republic. It appears likely that a collective leadership will take over from Mao rather than a leadership based on the pre-eminence of one man. Western analysts believe that the military leaders will add their weight to that of the non-radicals like Chou En-lai to promote stability, discipline, and material progress at home, and normal diplomatic relations abroad.

Whether Mao's Marxism, especially as practised in the last decade or so, will be subject to the drastic downgrading that Stalin's was, is difficult to say. But even if it is, as long as China regards herself as a Marxian socialist state, her version of the credo must continue to exercise considerable influence. The sheer size of her developing economic and military potential, and her exciting, colourful, and courageous revolutionary past, of which the younger Mao was so much a part, will ensure that.

### III. HERBERT MARCUSE

It is impossible to estimate just how much influence Herbert Marcuse has exercised on the Left in the 1960s. On the old Marxist movements he has remained without influence. Indeed, he has often met with hostility from the Communists when they have felt he was too dangerous to ignore. Marcuse's following has been largely confined to the revolutionary students, especially those of the United States, West Germany, and France.

Born in Germany in 1898, Marcuse must have been greatly influenced by a number of sad experiences in that country – the 1914–18 War, the failure of the German Revolution of 1918, the failure of the German Left in the early 1930s. These events, and his later life in the United States, caused him to modify, some would say abandon, his Marxism. If he can still be classed as a Marxist, his Marxism is that of the affluent society, of the era of the Wastemakers, the Hidden Persuaders, and the Warfare State.[76] Its clearest exposition is found in his *One-Dimensional Man: the Ideology of Industrial Society* published in the early 1960s.

The basic thesis of *One-Dimensional Man* is that 'a comfortable, smooth, reasonable, democratic unfreedom prevails in advanced industrial civilization'.[77] The tremendous productive capacities of the 'late industrial society' have made it possible to give widespread concessions to the working class. Automation and other technological advances were also changing the nature of the labour force from manual to white-collar employees. In addition, the growth of welfare, propaganda, indoctrination, advertising and public relations, all ensure the disappearance of widespread radicalism. This society tends to be totalitarian.

> For 'totalitarian' is not only a terroristic political coordination of society, but also a non-terroristic economic-technical co-ordination which operates through the manipulation of needs by vested interests. It thus precludes the emergence of an effective opposition against the whole. Not only a specific form of government or party rule makes for totalitarianism, but also a specific system of production and distribution which may well be compatible with a 'pluralism' of parties, newspapers, 'countervailing powers', etc.[78]

In this situation 'Western freedom' is an illusion:

> Free election of masters does not abolish the masters or the slaves. Free choice among a wide variety of goods and services does not signify freedom if these goods and services sustain social controls over a life of toil and fear – that is, if they sustain alienation.[79]

If this view of American society should give comfort to the Communists, they will get none from Marcuse's equally negative view of Soviet reality:

> The situation of hostile coexistence may explain the terroristic features of Stalinist industrialization, but it also set in motion the forces which tend to perpetuate technical progress as the instrument of domination; the means prejudice the end.[80]

The Soviet economy would be able to exploit the productivity of labour and capital without structural resistance, but by delivering more of the goods, it would wed the masses more firmly to the ruling bureaucracy. Alas! the transformation of such a system into a truly socialist one 'is a revolutionary rather than evolutionary process'.[81] The same is true in the West, for 'the totalitarian tendencies of the one-dimensional society render the traditional ways and means of protest ineffective – perhaps even dangerous because they preserve the illusion of popular sovereignty'.[82] Unfortunately,

Nothing indicates that it will be a good end. The economic and technical capabilities of the established societies are sufficiently vast to allow for adjustments and concessions to the underdog, and their armed forces sufficiently trained and equipped to take care of emergency situations. [83]

Marcuse's essay *A Critique of Pure Tolerance* could be said to be even more pessimistic than his earlier work. In it he takes up the theme that the new totalitarianism renders traditional opposition methods ineffective. Further, 'within a repressive society even progressive movements can have a reactionary effect if they accept the rules of the game'. [84] He denounces the indiscriminate tolerance of liberalism. In a society attempting to free itself from totalitarian democracy it would probably be necessary to withdraw toleration of speech and assembly 'from groups and movements which promote aggressive policies, armament, chauvinism, discrimination on the grounds of race and religion, or which oppose the extension of public services, social security, medical care, etc.'. Worse still, 'the restoration of freedom of thought may necessitate new and rigid restrictions on teachings and practices in the educational institutions'. [85]

If one is kind, one can say that Marcuse's intolerance is in part the result of his experience of Nazism in Germany, McCarthyism in America. The East Germans, going far beyond what he advocated, claim that their laws reflect the Nazi experience, and even West Germany, not going as far as he would apparently go, has restrictions on extremist parties, anti-semitism, and so on. But other victims of Nazism, Willy Brandt for instance, have drawn the opposite conclusion: that wholesale restrictions on the traditional liberal freedoms lead, if not to Auschwitz, then at least to the secret police interrogation centre and the political prison. Marcuse has already admitted the folly of his argument, in the sentence quoted above, 'the means prejudice the end'. As to Marcuse's more fundamental ideas of the totalitarian nature of Western, particularly American, society, it is difficult to counter them by citing examples of victories by opposition groups because these could always be shrugged off as sops, part and parcel of the 'repressive freedom'. The pessimism of Marcuse regarding the 'manipulated masses' does not at any rate appeal to this writer. To take just one example, his contention that the gradual transformation of a manual labour force into a white-collar one will lead to greater docility and conformity is not borne out by British experience. Teachers, technicians, and local government officers, among others, have shown greater militancy in the last decade and a half. And even though they do not completely reflect the views of the average member, left-wing socialist leaders have maintained themselves in the Draughtsmen's Association and certain other white-collar unions. Some European Marxists are aware of such potentialities and have modified their concept of the proletariat accordingly.

However much influenced by Marx Marcuse is, this American academic's pessimism and lack of faith in the masses are profoundly un-Marxist.

## IV. 1968 – THE YEAR OF 'REVOLUTIONS'

The British New Left struggled on through the late 1950s and early 1960s, mainly as part and parcel of the much wider Campaign for Nuclear Disarmament, a largely non-Marxist affair. Meanwhile, other New Lefts were being born.

Even before Herbert Marcuse's *One-Dimensional Man* other American academic and non-academic writers were preparing the way. The most notable of these was the late C. Wright Mills with his notion of *The Power Elite*:

> The men of the higher circles are not representative men; their high position is not a result of moral virtue; their fabulous success is not firmly connected with meritorious ability. Those who sit in the seats of the high and the mighty are selected and formed by the means of power, the sources of wealth, the mechanics of celebrity, which prevail in their society. They are not men selected and formed by a civil service that is linked with the world of knowledge and sensibility. They are not men shaped by nationally responsible parties that debate openly and clearly the issues this nation now so unintelligently confronts. They are not men held in responsible check by a plurality of voluntary associations which connect debating publics with the pinnacles of decision. Commanders of power unequaled in human history, they have succeeded within the American system of organized irresponsibility.[86]

American films – *Dr Strangelove, Five Days In May, The*

*Apartment* – critical of the military and business also made their contribution.

After a period of comfort and conformism which was 'pre-eminently the era of the motel, of the drive-in movie', of bingo, 3-D movies, TV quiz-shows, newer and gaudier automobiles, and Eisenhower,[87] there was 'one affront to America's dignity and calm after another'.[88] Within the space of a month there came the school-integration crisis in Little Rock, caused by opposition to seventeen Negro students being admitted to the hitherto all-White High School, and the launching of the first Soviet sputnik. In the following year Vice-President Nixon had a rough time on a tour of Latin America. 1959 saw agitation against compulsory military service. In the following year, the year of the election of John F. Kennedy to the White House, an election itself stimulating much discussion, the pilgrimage to Cuba commenced. In 1961 there was the Bay of Pigs; in 1962 the Missile Crisis; the year after, the Negro March on Washington and the assassination of the President. The year 1964 witnessed the riots in the Black ghetto of Harlem and the rebellion of the students at the huge, impersonal University of Berkeley (California). More devastating urban riots took place in the next three years and in 1968 the Black, pacifist, Civil Rights leader, Martin Luther King, and, in a separate incident, Senator Robert Kennedy, were shot down. From 1964 there was increasing agitation against the Vietnam War as the toll of dead mounted. The dispatch of American troops to the Dominican Republic in 1965 to save her from an alleged Communist plot only served to aggravate the mood of opposition. If the radicals disliked Johnson, they felt they could stomach Nixon, elected President in 1968, even less. The agitation and anger continued to erupt. To what extent was all this agitation the work of Marxist, or even just left-wing, movements? Only in the most superficial sense, says one expert, could they be described as left-wing.[89] The Communist Party and the other old, left-wing groups had little influence on them. Most of the young revolutionaries – for most of them were young – knew little of Lenin or Trotsky, and even less of Marx and Engels. And many of their older admirers encouraged them to retain such ignorance:

> Lenin was great. So was Trotsky. So were Eugene Debbs and Thomas Paine, and so are Mao and Fidel, but they have

nothing to teach you except guts and perseverance because your situation is different. Honor them for their courage and their example, but most of all, for their ability to let go of sacred texts and do what was necessary in their given society even when it contradicted received doctrine.[90]

In Europe the situation was different. The young revolutionaries who came into prominence in 1968 were influenced by events in America and by the tactics of the young American oppositionists, their sit-ins and teach-ins, but they were the products of the domestic situations of their own countries. They were also more clearly Marxist-orientated.

The rise of the student Left in West Germany is to a considerable extent linked with developments in the German Social Democratic Party (SPD). That party had not disavowed Marxism during the Weimar Republic, nor did it do so in the dark days of underground and exile. In 1946, when it was still battling with the Communists, its leader, Kurt Schumacher, reaffirmed its Marxism:

We as Social Democrats have no intention whatsoever of damning Marxism wholesale and throwing it overboard . . . the Eastern degenerate form of Marxism has nothing to do with what German Social Democracy derives from Marx. Marxism in its two most important forms – the economic conception of history and the class struggle – is not obsolete. . . . It is no ballast . . . no catechism . . . it is the method . . . we must thank for more strength, more knowledge and more weapons than all other scientific and sociological methods.[91]

Even at that time, though, many Social Democrats wanted a clear rejection of the SPD's traditional ideology. The Nazi experience had profoundly shaken their belief in the inevitability of socialism. Nazism and communism alike had convinced them that any dictatorship, whatever its declared aims, was bad. And the experience of Social Democratic emigrants in Scandinavia and Britain led them to the conclusion that they could learn much from the welfare, non-Marxist, socialism of those countries. Schumacher had spent the Nazi years in a concentration camp; his successor, Erich Ollenhauer, was an immigrant in Britain. Brandt, who in turn succeeded Ollenhauer, had lived in Norway and Sweden. The apparent success of the 'economic miracle' chaired by Chancellor Adenauer, his brilliant electoral success of

1957, the association in the public mind of socialism and Marxism with communism, and the hostility of the powerful Catholic Church, all undermined the SPD's 'Marxism'. The official break came in 1959 when the party adopted its Godesberg Programme in which it dissociated itself from widespread nationalization and Marxism, and associated itself with private property, the armed forces, and a 'free partnership' with the Churches.

Though never officially and explicitly pacifist, the SPD had opposed first German rearmament, and then the introduction of nuclear weapons into Germany. This had given the Left in the party something to get their teeth into. In 1960, however, it gave up such opposition and announced its intention to join forces with the governing Christian Democrats on national and defence matters. The SPD seemed to be destroying itself as a radical alternative to the Establishment Christians. Its electoral campaigns of 1961 and 1965 were largely indistinguishable from those of its opponents. Willy Brandt, who was projected as the Kennedy of West Germany, recognized the party's weakness on policy after his defeat in 1965. A partial readjustment was made in the following years. But not until after a spell in office with the Christian Democrats led by ex-Nazi Kurt Georg Kiesinger. This marriage of convenience, which caused widespread disapproval in the party, helped the Social Democrats in the campaign of 1969 by giving them a better chance to get known as ministers. Over a considerable period the party's Marxists had either been silenced, left the party, or been driven from it.

It was the SDS, or *Sozialistischer Deutscher Studentenbund*, which became known as the standard-bearer of Marxism in West Germany. For years this organization had been the SPD's official student body and had given the party little cause for concern. However, in 1959 the SPD broke with the SDS, largely as a result of a congress organized by the students in Frankfurt which took up a strongly anti-military and pro-Marxist line. Remarkably, the SDS was able to hold its own with the SPD-financed SHB in the coming years. It gained financial and other help from a number of academics and trade unionists, the most prominent of whom was Professor Wolfgang Abendroth (b. 1906) of Marburg University. Abendroth is a Marxist of the Rosa Luxemburg variety.

The SDS might have remained a small, relatively unknown, force in German politics had not 'the objective situation' altered in its favour. One incident in this changing situation was the arrest of the editorial staff of the liberal weekly *Der Spiegel* in 1962, on the instigation of Defence Minister Strauss, for allegedly publishing a defence secret. The incident profoundly shocked West German opinion and led to Strauss's resignation. A whole series of cases involving ex-Nazis in high places had the same effect. Proposed emergency powers legislation, designed to replace Allied reserve powers, provoked hard and bitter discussion for several years. And the relative success of the extreme nationalist National Democratic Party (NPD) between 1966 and 1969 caused extreme reactions far beyond the small groups of SDS supporters. SDS groups joined forces with trade unionists to oppose NPD meetings and rallies; violence often followed.

The Berlin SDS became the vanguard of the militant students. With only about 250 members out of a student body of roughly 29,000, they managed to produce the maximum effect. They launched a series of successful demonstrations. The first of these was in December 1964, when several hundred students demonstrated against the then Congolese Prime Minister Moise Tshombe. In February 1966, 1,500 students demonstrated against the Vietnam War in a march authorized by the police. In December of the same year a thousand students defied the police to make a similar protest. In April 1967, 2,000 turned out against American Vice-President Hubert Humphrey. In between there were several demonstrations, including a sit-in (involving 3,000) against the university authorities for preventing the use of official buildings for political meetings. The climax came when students met the Shah of Iran with slogans and tomatoes on 2 June, and a student was shot in the back by a plain-clothes policeman. A protest against the shooting attracted 4,000. Silent marches throughout West Germany on the day of the funeral brought 100,000 students into the streets.

The young man who came into prominence as the leader of the Berlin SDS was a clergyman's son, a refugee from East Germany who had come to the West because he did not wish to serve in Ulbricht's army. His name was Rudi Dutschke. Before the building of the Berlin Wall, the Free University of West Berlin had attracted dissatisfied East German students who were often almost as critical of the West as they were of the East. It also attracted West German students impressed by its high reputation for social-science teaching and the fact that West German military service laws were not operative in the former German capital.

Dutschke dismissed the 'false alternative in the East–West conflict' and claimed: 'Now the world-wide alternative is very clear: anti-authoritarianism, world-wide revolution, and authoritarian imperialistic counter-revolution'. He admitted he was attracted to the Cuban regime and the Cultural Revolution in China. His critique of West German society was basically the same as that of Marcuse. But where Marcuse had used the term totalitarian, he substituted fascist.[92]

In the case of the West German SDS after 1968, decline set in. This was the result of several factors. Firstly, they were deprived of Rudi Dutschke who was severely wounded by shots fired by a young NPD fanatic in 1968. Dutschke later left West Germany for treatment and study in Britain. Secondly, the Cultural Revolution in China was fading. Thirdly, the Left started to disintegrate. At the beginning of 1969 there were thirty-eight SDS groups with about 2,500 members.[93] But these varied from anarchist and hippy groups to old-style Marxist and new-style Maoist cells. The anti-authoritarian structure of the SDS was partly to blame for this. Fourthly, the victory of the Social Democrats and their coalition with the liberal Free Democrats in September 1969, emphasizing a new approach to eastern Europe, reduced the impact of some of the Left's arguments. It is worth noting that at that election the Moscow-orientated Communists were allowed to compete for the first time since 1953.[94] They were in alliance with a pro-Communist neutralist party, the DFU, and did worse than the latter, standing alone, had done in 1965. Finally, the decline of the NPD since 1969 also reduced the impact of SDS charges of official Fascism. Late in March 1970 the SDS decided to dissolve itself.

Throughout 1968 the 'silent majority' watched on their TV screens demonstrations and scenes of violence from Germany, the United States, Italy, Japan, Mexico, Yugoslavia, Sweden, and even Britain. But the most dramatic film came from France.

It was again the students who in France, Germany, and other countries were the vanguard in 1968, and if the French had learned something from SDS emissaries, they soon felt they had much to teach their German comrades. Why should this be?

In French and West German universities, at Berkeley, and at the London School of Economics, at the time Britain's most turbulent academic institution, the same material conditions were apparent. Unlike most British universities, there is gross overcrowding in these places. There is not the same relatively close relationship between staff and students. And, excluding the LSE, there is not the same careful selection of would-be students. In France and West Germany, unlike Britain, students are not under the same pressure to pass examinations and finish their studies. And at continental universities there are more older students on hand to lead the younger ones. In Britain most students get grants from public funds. In West Germany and France they do not. A far higher proportion of British students come from the working class and these 'tend to be more practical and less high-flown'.[95] In France, on the other hand, there is a powerful revolutionary tradition, a tradition accepted by the majority of the middle classes. In France there is a powerful Communist Party attracting considerable middle-class support, and there are other left-wing groups which also draw support from the middle class. In West Germany feelings of guilt about Nazi crimes among the young cause extreme reactions to domestic neo-Nazism and foreign war crimes. Perhaps to some extent this plays the same role as French revolutionary tradition.

In the new, unfinished, University of Nanterre, the main centre of the French student revolt, conditions were just that bit worse than elsewhere. Ironically, this university is about the most bourgeois in France:

> For most of the students at Nanterre, education was not a necessary stepladder to social promotion: their status was already secure. It was the planting of revolutionary ideas in a context of arrogant social confidence which was perhaps most responsible for creating the peculiar Nanterre climate of daredevilry, contempt for authority, and a sort of idle openness to reckless suggestions.[96]

The students of Nanterre were dissatisfied about the irksome restrictions on them, including the complete segregation of the sexes. In 1967 and early 1968 clashes between the authorities and the students of Nanterre increased. The leaders of the small groups of left-wing students were active in promoting such clashes. Among these leaders we were to hear most from Daniel Cohn-Bendit.

Cohn-Bendit, the 'dynamic teddy-bear',[97] was born in France of German, Jewish, middle-class parents. He was educated in France, Germany, and Britain, and opted for German nationality at eighteen. Short, with red hair and a podgy face, 'with a clown-ish manner which makes him fascinating to watch',[98] Cohn-Bendit was a twenty-three-year-old sociology student in 1968. He had already imbibed the SDS gospel and thought out a few refinements of his own.[99]

Less well known, but more substantial politically, was Alain Krivine. The twenty-seven-year-old son of a well-to-do Russian-Jewish dentist, Krivine was a student of history at the Sorbonne and a Trotskyite. It was his organization, the JCR, which was to give the May revolt many of its disciplined cadre. The JCR had been set up in 1966, mainly by young people expelled from the official Communist youth organization. Their heroes were Marx and Engels, Luxemburg, Lenin, and Trotsky. Subsequently, the *Jeunesse Communiste Revolutionnaire* was to be banned and then to re-emerge in 1969 under the new title of Communist League of France. It was to be recognized by the Trotskyite Fourth International as its French affiliate.[100]

The JCR became Cohn-Bendit's principal ally, 'stiffening his anarchism with Leninist political intelligence'.[101] It joined his 22 March movement. This had been set up to protest against the arrest of students who had carried their hatred of the Vietnam War to the point of bombing American property in Paris. Later they were joined by a pro-Peking group, the UJC (M-L) and the *Mouvement d'action universitaire* (MAU). The MAU was made up of postgraduates and research workers of a Marxist orienta-tion, many of them veterans of earlier campaigns against the Algerian War.

On 29 March the MAU seized Richelieu Amphitheatre at the Sorbonne to hold an unauthorized meeting. At Nanterre a boy-cott of examinations was organized and at Toulouse University police had to intervene on 25 April to stop brawling between left- and right-wing students. The incidents multiplied and it was not only the Left who initiated them. It was on 3 May that France's mini-revolution got under way. Cohn-Bendit and some others had been summoned to appear at the Sorbonne[102] before the university disciplinary council to explain their activities. Their political friends gathered in the courtyard to show their solidarity. The authorities feared a clash between them and right-wing students. After unsuccessfully appealing to them to disperse, they called in the police. Apparently police attempts to arrest students led to violence. This united the mass of un-committed students behind the Cohn-Bendit group: 'In a few minutes a mass movement was created'.[103] By the end of the day hundreds were wounded and nearly six hundred students were under lock and key.

During the next days cobblestones flew, tear-gas bombs exploded, cars were burned, truncheons and water cannon were brought into action. Paris was becoming a battlefield. Students at many provincial universities came out in support of their Paris colleagues. The students presented three immediate demands: withdrawal of the police from the Latin Quarter, the student quarter; the release and pardoning of students under arrest; the reopening of the university. Only if these demands were met would the students negotiate their other grievances. Various attempts at compromise were made, but the authorities refused to budge on the second demand. Even if they had, it is by no means certain that the Marxist student leaders would have become more conciliatory. Cohn-Bendit and the others sought to escalate the crisis into a revolution, using the students as the detonator with which to bring about a working-class insurrection. Premier Pompidou had been abroad during the first phase of the troubles. On his return he decided that concessions were called for. These he could make because he had not been responsible for the earlier, tougher policy. He arrived on 11 May after a night of extreme confrontation between students and authorities. The students were 'acting out the "colonial revolution" in the heart of'[104] Paris. Pompidou released the students, withdrew the police, and opened the Sorbonne – too late! New demands were being made: the resignation of the Minister of the Interior and Prefect of Police.

The attempt to turn a student revolt into a working-class revolution looked as though it was about to succeed on 13 May. On that day 800,000 students and workers demonstrated in Paris. The workers were on strike, led by their unions, the Communist CGT and the Christian CFDT. The main federation of teachers' unions had also joined in. The occasion of the demonstration was the tenth anniversary of the Algiers settlers' revolt which brought de Gaulle back into power. The strike was to last 24 hours, but the following day the workers occupied an aircraft factory at Nantes just as the students the day before had occupied the

Sorbonne. Strikes and occupations spread like wildfire throughout the country. The reason for this amazing development was
the seething discontent of wide sections of the people.

General de Gaulle had saved France from civil war in 1958,
turned against his right-wing supporters and given Algeria her
independence, and given France more stature in international
affairs. But he had done no better than his predecessors in home
affairs. France was experiencing substantial unemployment for
the first time in fifteen years. Consumer prices had risen by
45 per cent since 1958. Basic wages remained low, industrial
relations archaic. There was a chronic housing shortage. And
though more people had TV sets and cars, 'there is a strong
impression that inequalities have grown between various
categories of people, between economic sectors, and between
regions'.[105]

The strikes were largely spontaneous. The union bosses had
been taken by surprise. By 22 May over 9 million were on strike
from car-workers to merchant seamen, from undertakers to
weather forecasters. Pompidou's answer was to defuse the situation by granting the union leaders' demands. However, both
government and union leaders were shocked when the strikers
were not appeased by the terms. De Gaulle had helped to secure
this by making a TV speech which offered the strikers a referen-
dum rather than reforms. It served only to lead the student
leaders to attempt more militancy which resulted in even greater
violence.

The French Communists under Maurice Waldeck-Rochet
would have nothing to do with such militancy. They had been
laboriously recasting their image as a popular reform party
which, though still inspired by Marx, was dedicated to France's
republican institutions. They had moved out of their earlier
isolation and had reached electoral agreements with the Socialists
at the 1965 Presidential elections and the general election of
March 1967. Their electoral fortunes had slumped somewhat
after de Gaulle's return to power in 1958 when they attracted
19 per cent of the vote. This rose to 22 per cent in 1962 and 1967,
or 3.8 million votes in 1958 and 5 million in 1967. In 1967 support for de Gaulle's political friends had slumped. The Communists' association with the USSR had not been too much of a
disadvantage because the general had for years pursued a policy
friendly to Moscow. The Communists could therefore legiti-

mately hope that at the next elections, in alliance with the Socialists, they could at least further erode support for Gaullism and at best topple the general's government. For the Communists, the student revolutionaries were playing the general's game by scaring off the silent majority. This was de Gaulle's view, too. He cunningly united all the Right behind his banner by ordering the release of OAS officers imprisoned since 1962 for using terrorism to sabotage his Algerian policy. And, confident of army backing, he broadcast a fiercely anti-Communist speech and promised new elections. Meanwhile, on the same day, 30 May, his organization men were launching a demonstration of his supporters in Paris. Over a million neatly-dressed, tricolour-waving, anti-Communists marched for the President – a decisive psychological blow against the Left from which it did not quickly recover.

The elections were then fought on a militantly anti-Communist ticket. Further student disturbances in the pre-election period assured a landslide victory for the Right. The workers had made economic gains, some of which were later lost in higher prices, but they had not won anything like 'participation' in the factories. Their political representatives were in disarray.

Cohn-Bendit, already banned from France, slipped into the shadows. De Gaulle resigned. Pompidou, after a brief spell in the wilderness, made scapegoat for his master's failures, became President. The French Communist Party, under a new leader, Georges Marchais, has continued its old reform alliance policy. With an estimated 300,000 members and control of the CGT, it remains the main force on the French Left.

## V. HAS MARXISM A FUTURE?

In the autumn of 1971 the campuses are relatively peaceful. China, Cuba, and the Soviet Union give young and old revolutionaries like little comfort. And Brandt and Nixon push in the direction of *détente*. Yet the small groups of revolutionaries still peddle their wares and significant Marxist parties remain in several non-Communist countries. It is appropriate to ask whether such Marxist movements have a future. So much depends on the power and policy of Moscow and Peking. But whatever happens there, or in the other Marxist capitals, Marxism will, in the foreseeable future, continue to attract some. It is possible that new versions of the old gospel will appear. The Moscow archives are said to be full of unpublished material written by the original prophets. This could lead to some reinterpretations, revisions, or shifts in emphasis. Secondly, there could well develop other neo-Marxisms outside Europe – in Black Africa or Japan, for instance. Thirdly, even without these, Marxism will continue to serve some men's needs. At least some of the million or so British workers spending the winter of 1971 on the dole will wonder whether they are part of the 'reserve army of labour'. Perhaps Jimmy Reid, the Communist trade union leader on the Clyde, who has led the fight to save the shipyards, will re-read with bitter satisfaction: 'The bourgeoisie has through its exploitation of the world market given a cosmopolitan character to production and consumption in every country. . . . All old-established national industries have been destroyed or are daily being destroyed'.[106] And some of the white-collar militants and intellectuals will agree with Marx's view that 'the bourgeoisie has stripped of its halo every occupation hitherto honoured and looked up to with reverent awe. It has converted the physician, the lawyer, the priest, the poet, the man of science, into its paid wage-labourers'.[107] Again, despite all the undoubted social and economic progress in the advanced countries made in the last twenty-six years, the maldistribution of property, with its actual and potential evils, remains. The Marxists can still argue,

> You are horrified at our intending to do away with private property. But in your existing society, private property is already done away with for nine-tenths of the population; its existence for the few is solely due to its non-existence in the hands of those nine-tenths.[108]

The challenge of these and some other problems raised by Marx remain. It would be folly to ignore them.

Another attraction of Marxism remains. Many, especially the young, seek a short-cut to understanding society and its problems. For a time Marxism provides that short-cut. 'The dialectic is a sort of social X-ray apparatus, enabling us to see the very bones of human society; and to see how they move',[109] wrote John Strachey in 1932. Experience later taught him otherwise.

Finally, George Bernard Shaw once commented:

Marx's Capital is not a treatise on Socialism: it is a jeremiad against the bourgeoisie, supported by a mass of official evidence and a relentless Jewish genius for denunciation. It was addressed to the working classes; but the working man respects the bourgeoisie, and wants to be a bourgeois. It was the revolting sons of the bourgeoisie itself: Lassalle, Marx, Liebknecht, Morris, Hyndman: all, like myself, bourgeois, who painted the flag red.[110]

Future generations are likely to go on producing those who paint the flag red. And so long as society is less than a utopia, how can such sons, often among the best of their generation, be expected to resist the seductive call

'The philosophers have only *interpreted* the world differently, the point is, to *change* it'.?

## NOTES

[1] J. M. Cameron, 'The New Left in Britain' (II), *The Listener* (London), 15 Sept. 1960.

[2] See the analysis of Stephen Fay, 'The Late New Left', in the *Spectator* (21 Sept. 1962).

[3] ibid.

[4] Perry Anderson, 'Critique of Wilsonism', *New Left Review*, 27 (Sept.–Oct. 1964), p. 27.

[5] ibid., p. 4.

[6] Luis E. Aguilar, *Marxism in Latin America* (New York, 1968), p. 5.

[7] See Robert J. Alexander, *Communism in Latin America* (New Brunswick, 1957).

[8] Robin Blackburn, 'Prologue to the Cuban Revolution', *NLR* (Oct. 1963), p. 72.

[9] For Browder, see above, p. 206.

[10] Boris Goldenberg, *The Cuban Revolution and Latin America* (London, 1965), p. 148.

[11] Theodore Draper, *Castroism: Theory and Practice* (London, 1965), p. 114.

[12] Leo Huberman and Paul M. Sweezy, *Cuba: Anatomy of a Revolution* (London, 1960), p. 27.

[13] Goldenberg, op cit., p. 150.

[14] ibid.

[15] Draper, op. cit., p. 28.

[16] As Eisenhower was to call Batista. See his *Waging Peace 1956–61* (London, 1965), p. 520.

[17] Goldenberg, op. cit., p. 156.

[18] Herbert L. Matthews, *Castro* (London, 1969), p. 108.

[19] ibid., p. 106.

[20] ibid., p. 125.

[21] Hugh Thomas, *Cuba or the Pursuit of Freedom* (London, 1971), p. 1051.

[22] Matthews, op. cit., p. 134.

[23] ibid., p. 142.

[24] Goldenberg, op. cit., p. 179.

[25] Eisenhower, op. cit., p. 523.

[26] Goldenberg, op. cit., p. 181.

[27] ibid., p. 182.

[28] Matthews, op. cit., p. 165.

[29] Schlesinger, op. cit., p. 200.

[30] James O'Connor, *The Origins of Socialism in Cuba* (Ithaca, 1970), p. 91.

[31] Matthews, op. cit., p. 159.

[32] Goldenberg, op. cit., p. 162.

[33] ibid., p. 244.

[34] Schlesinger, op. cit., p. 203.

[35] ibid., p. 195.

[36] Hugh Thomas, letter to editor of the *New Statesman* (21 Dec. 1961), p. 899.

[37] For an account of the operation, see Haynes Johnson, *The Bay of Pigs* (London, 1965). Schlesinger, op. cit., p. 265, calls Castro's performance 'impressive'. See his comments on the operation, ibid., pp. 265–8.

[38] ibid., p. 265.

[39] There was much talk of producing 10 million tons of sugar by 1970. Unhappily this target was not reached.

[40] Michael Frayn, in the *Observer* (19 Jan. 1969).

[41] Richard Evans, in the *Guardian* (11 June 1971).

[42] Both Frayn and Evans make these points. See also Richard Wigg in *The Times* (16 July 1968); Edward Gonzalez, 'Castro: The Limits of Charisma', *Problems of Communism* (July 1971).

[43] Luis E. Aguilar, 'Fragmentation of the Marxist Left', in *Problems of Communism* (USIA), July–Aug. 1970, p. 6.

[44] Andrew Sinclair, *Guevara* (London, 1970), p. 15.

[45] ibid., p. 16.

[46] ibid., p. 92; and John Gerassi, *Venceremos! The Speeches and Writings of Ernesto Che Guevara* (London, 1968), p. 21: 'the Garibaldi of social revolutions'.

[47] Hugh Thomas, 'Romantic hero of our time', the *Observer* (23 June 1968).

[48] Régis Debray, *Revolution in the Revolution?* (London, 1968), p. 25.

[49] ibid., pp. 96–7.

[50] ibid., p. 68.

[51] ibid., p. 62.

[52] ibid., p. 61.

[53] For Castro's relations with these Communist parties, see Bruce Jackson, *Castro, the Kremlin, and Communism in Latin America* (Baltimore, 1969).

[54] Gonzalez, op. cit., p. 14.

[55] Leon Gouré and Jaime Suchlicki, 'The Allende Regime: Actions and Reactions', *Problems of Communism* (USIA), May–June 1971, p. 52.

[56] Sergio Voskovic, 'Political Pluralism', *Marxism Today* (July 1971).

[57] Alan Angell, 'Chile: From Christian Democracy to Marxism?', *The World Today* (Nov. 1970), p. 495.

[58] 'Wir Schlagen Hundertfach Zurueck', *Der Spiegel* (15 March 1971), p. 126.

[59] 'Der Doktor, das ist unser Genosse', *Der Spiegel* (9 Aug. 1971), p. 72.

[60] Emily MacFarquhar, *China: Mao's Last Leap*, the *Economist* Brief 6 (London, 1968), p. 5.

[61] Joan Robinson, *The Cultural Revolution in China* (London, 1970), p. 18.

[62] This is Emily MacFarquhar's estimate, op. cit., p. 8.

[63] Robinson, op. cit., gives the 16 points in full.

[64] MacFarquhar, op. cit., p. 10.

[65] Dietmar Albrecht, 'Die Roten Garden', *Das Parlament* (Beilage 46/69), p. 7.

[66] ibid., p. 7.

[67] ibid., p. 21.

[68] ibid., p. 20.

[69] See Oskar Weggel, 'Massenkommunikation in der Volksrepublik China', *Das Parlament* (Beilage 13/71).

[70] MacFarquhar, op. cit., p. 18.

[71] These facts are from Stephen A. Sims, 'The New Role of the Military', *Problems of Communism* (Nov.–Dec. 1969).

[72] The exact fate of many of them is unknown.

[73] Donald W. Klein and Lois B. Hager, 'The Ninth Central Committee', *China Quarterly* (Jan.–March 1971).

[74] The quoted comments are from Dennis Bloodworth, in the *Observer* (20 April 1969).

[75] Kai-Yu Hsu, *Chou En-lai: China's Gray Eminence* (New York, 1968).

[76] Herbert Marcuse, *One-Dimensional Man: The Ideology of Industrial Society* (London, 1968), p. 14; here he freely acknowledges indebtedness to Vance Packard and others on this genre.

[77] ibid., p. 19.

[78] ibid., p. 20.

[79] ibid., p. 23.

[80] ibid., p. 48.

[81] ibid., p. 49.

[82] ibid., p. 200.

[83] ibid., p. 201.

[84] Quoted Maurice Cranston, 'Marcuse', in Cranston (ed.), *The New Left* (London, 1970), p. 107.

[85] ibid., pp. 109–10. For another interesting essay on Marcuse, see Alasdair MacIntyre, *Marcuse* (London, 1970). Marcuse's views on the USSR are set forth in his *Soviet Marxism* (London, 1958).

[86] C. Wright Mills, *The Power Elite* (New York, 1959), p. 361. For his relationship to Marxism, see his *The Marxists*.

[87] Daniel Snowman, *USA: The Twenties to Vietnam* (London, 1968), pp. 126–7.

[88] ibid., p. 128.

[89] ibid., p. 149.

[90] Massimo Teodori, *The New Left* (London, 1970), pp. 452–3. The words are William Domhoff's.

[91] David Childs, *From Schumacher to Brandt* (Oxford, 1966), p. 37.

[92] Rudi Dutschke, *The Students and the Revolution*, Spokesman Pamphlet no. 15 (Nottingham, 1970).

[93] *Zum Thema Hier: Verfassungsschutz 1968* (Bundesministerium Des Innern, Bonn, 1969).

[94] The KPD was banned in 1956. It now exists under another name – DKP.

[95] Anthony Sampson, *The New Europeans* (London, 1968), p. 450.

[96] Patrick Seale and Maureen McConville, *French Revolution 1968* (London, 1968), p. 27.

[97] ibid., p. 22.

[98] Sampson, op. cit., p. 445.

[99] See his *Obsolete Communism: The Left-wing Alternative* (London, 1969).

[100] I. Grieg, *Today's Revolutionaries* (London, 1970), p. 51.

[101] Seale and McConville, op. cit., p. 60.

[102] Technically Nanterre was an annexe of the Sorbonne.

[103] Seale and McConville, op. cit., p. 69.

[104] ibid., p. 89.
[105] Pierre Uri, in *The Times* (21 May 1968).
[106] Marx and Engels, *Manifesto*, pp. 58–9.
[107] ibid., p. 57.
[108] ibid., p. 83.
[109] Strachey, *The Coming Struggle*, p. 224.
[110] *Karl Marx* (Inter Nationes, Bad Godesberg, 1968), p. 25.

# Bibliography

As this book was written for the English-speaking reader, only English texts are listed as a guide to further reading. Obviously some of the books are useful for more than one topic or period but, for reasons of space, individual titles are only given once. No articles are listed. Ironically, the best magazine on Communist/Marxist affairs is *Problems of Communism* published by the United States Information Agency in Washington. Other key English-language magazines in the field are *Survey* (London), *China Quarterly* (London), and *World Today* (Chatham House, London). *New Left Review* (London) and *Science and Society* (New York) give the views of sophisticated Marxists.

CHAPTERS I and II

Adams, H. P., *Karl Marx in his Earlier Writings*, London, 1965

Althusser, L., *For Marx*, London, 1970

Avineri, S., *The Social and Political Thought of Karl Marx*, Cambridge, 1968

Berlin, I., *Karl Marx*, London, 1963

Bottomore, T. B., *Classes in Modern Society*, London, 1965

Briggs, A. (ed.), *Chartist Studies*, London, 1959

Cliff, T., *Rosa Luxemburg*, London, 1959

Cole, G. D. H., *The Meaning of Marxism*, Ann Arbor, 1964

Cole, G. D. H., *The Second International 1889–1914*, London, 1956

Curtis, M. (ed.), *Marxism*, New York, 1970

Delfgaauw, B., *The Young Marx*, London, 1967

Dobb, M., *Wages*, Cambridge, 1948

Dobb, M., *On Economic Theory and Socialism*, London, 1955

Drachkovitch, M. M. (ed.), *The Revolutionary Internationals, 1864–1943*, new ed., Stanford, 1968

Engels, F., *Anti-Dühring*, London, 1943

Engels, F., *The Housing Question*, London, 1943

Engels, F., *The Condition of the Working Class in England*, introduced by E. J. Hobsbawm, London, 1969

Fischer, E., *Marx in his own Words*, London, 1970

Freedman, R. (ed.), *Marx on Economics*, London, 1971

Garaudy, R., *Karl Marx: The Evolution of his Thought*, London, 1967

Gay, P., *The Dilemma of Democratic Socialism*, New York, 1962

Henderson, W. O. (ed.), *Engels: Selected Writings*, London, 1967

Hook, S., *From Hegel to Marx*, Ann Arbor, 1962

Hunt, R. N. C., *Marxism Past and Present*, London, 1954

Hunt, R. N. C., *Theory and Practice of Communism*, London, 1971

Inter Nationes, *Karl Marx 1818/1968*, Bad Godesberg, 1968

Joll, J., *The Second International 1889–1914*, London, 1968

Jordan, Z. A., *The Evolution of Dialectical Materialism*, New York, 1967

Koren, H. J., *Marx and the Authentic Man*, Pittsburgh, 1967

Lichtheim, G., *Marxism: an Historical and Critical Study*, London, 1961

Lidtke, V. L., *The Outlawed Party: Social Democracy in Germany 1878–1890*, Princeton, 1966

MacIntyre, A., *Marxism and Christianity*, New York, 1968

Mandel, E., *The Genesis of Marx's Economic Thought*, New York, 1971

Marx, Karl, *Capital*, Chicago, 1919

Marx, Karl, *Early Writings*, edited by T. B. Bottomore, London, 1963

Marx, Karl, *The Class Struggle in France 1848 to 1850*, Moscow, 1952

Marx, Karl and Engels, F., *Manifesto of the Communist Party*, Moscow, 1955

Marx, Karl and Engels, F., *Manifesto of the Communist Party*, London, 1948, introduced by Harold J. Laski

Marx, Karl and Engels, F., *Manifesto of the Communist Party*, London, 1970, introduced by A. J. P. Taylor

Marx, Karl and Engels, F., *Selected Works* (2 vols.), Moscow, 1951

Mayer, G., *Friedrich Engels*, New York, 1969

McLellan, D., *The Thought of Karl Marx*, London, 1971

McLellan, D., *Marx before Marxism*, London, 1972

McLellan, D., *Karl Marx: The Early Texts*, London, 1971

McLellan, D., *Marx's Grundrisse*, London, 1971

Mehring, F., *Karl Marx*, London, 1951

Meyer, A. G., *Marxism, the Unity of Theory and Practice*, Cambridge, Mass., 1954

Mills, C. W., *The Marxists*, New York, 1962

Morgan, R. P., *The German Social Democrats 1864–72*, Cambridge, 1965

Ollman, B., *Alienation: Marx's Critique of Man in Capitalist Society*, Cambridge, 1971

Page, R., *Marx*, London, 1968

Plamenatz, J., *German Marxism and Russian Communism*, London, 1954

Rotenstreich, N., *Basic Principles of Marx's Philosophy*, New York, 1965

Sanderson, J. B., *An Interpretation of the Political Ideas of Marx and Engels*, London, 1969

Schumpeter, J. A., *Ten Great Economists from Marx to Keynes*, London, 1951

Stolper, G., *The German Economy: 1870 to the Present*, New York, 1967

Strachey, J., *Contemporary Capitalism*, London, 1956
Tucker, R., *Philosophy and Myth in Karl Marx*, Cambridge, 1961
Tucker, R., *The Marxian Revolutionary Idea*, London, 1970
Venable, V., *Human Nature: The Marxian View*, London, 1946
Wolfe, B., *Marxism: 100 Years in the Life of a Doctrine*, London, 1967


CHAPTER III
Charques, R., *The Twilight of Imperial Russia*, London, 1959
Deutscher, I., *Stalin*, London, 1966
Deutscher, I., *The Prophet Armed: Trotsky 1879–1921*, London, 1954
Harrison, L. H., *The Russian Marxists and the Origins of Bolshevism*,
    Cambridge, Mass., 1955
Keep, J. H. L., *The Rise of Social Democracy in Russia*, Oxford, 1963
Krupskaya, N. K., *Reminiscences of Lenin*, Moscow, 1959
Mavor, J., *An Economic History of Russia*, London, 1925
Miller, M., *Economic Development of Russia 1905–1914*, London, 1967
Pares, B., *The Fall of the Russian Monarchy*, London, 1939
Plekhanov, G. V., *Fundamental Problems of Marxism*, London, 1969
Schapiro, L. and Reddaway, P., *Lenin, the Man, the Theorist, the Leader*,
    London, 1967
Schwarz, S. M., *The Russian Revolution of 1905*, Chicago, 1967
Seton-Watson, H., *The Russian Empire, 1801–1917*, Oxford, 1967
Shub, D., *Lenin*, London, 1969
Stalin, J. V., *Marxism and the National Question*, Moscow, 1950
Treadgold, D. W., *Lenin and his Rivals, The Struggle for Russia's Future,
    1898–1906*, London, 1955
Walkin, J., *The Rise of Democracy in Pre-Revolutionary Russia*, London,
    1962
Wilson, E., *To the Finland Station*, London, 1970
Wildman, A. K., *The Making of a Workers' Revolution: Russian Social
    Democracy 1891–1903*, London, 1967
Wolfe, B. D., *Three who Made a Revolution*, London, 1966.


CHAPTER IV
Beale, H. K., *Theodore Roosevelt and the Rise of America to World
    Power*, Baltimore, 1956
Bell, D., *Marxian Socialism in the United States*, Princeton, 1967
Berlau, A. J., *The German Social Democratic Party 1914–21*, New York,
    1949
Braunthal, J., *History of the International, 1914–1943*, London, 1967
Browder, R. P. and Kerensky, A. F. (ed.), *The Russian Provisional
    Government: Documents* (3 vols.), Stanford, 1961
Carsten, F. L., *The Reichswehr and Politics*, London, 1966

Cole, G. D. H., *Communism and Social Democracy, 1914–1931*, London, 1958

Coper, R., *Failure of a Revolution*, Cambridge, 1955

Chamberlain, M. E., *The New Imperialism*, London, 1970

Chamberlin, W. H., *The Russian Revolution*, New York, 1935

Eyck, E., *A History of the Weimar Republic* (2 vols.), Cambridge, Mass., 1962–64

Footman, D., *Civil War in Russia*, London, 1961

Gooch, G. P., *Recent Revelations of European Diplomacy*, New York, 1967

Katkov, G., *Russia 1917: the February Revolution*, London, 1967

Kautsky, K., *The Dictatorship of the Proletariat*, Ann Arbor, 1964

Kendall, W., *The Revolutionary Movement in Britain 1900–21*, London, 1969

Kennan, G., *Russia Leaves the War*, London, n.d.

Kerensky, A. F., *The Prelude to Bolshevism*, London, 1919

Kerensky, A. F., *The Crucifixion of Liberty*, London, 1934

Lee, D. E. (ed.), *The Outbreak of the First World War*, Boston, 1958

Lenin, V. I., *Socialism and War*, London, 1940

Lenin, V. I., *Imperialism the Highest Stage of Capitalism*, London, 1948

Moorehead, A., *The Russian Revolution*, London, 1958

Mowry, G. E., *The Era of Theodore Roosevelt*, New York, 1958

Nettl, J. P., *Rosa Luxemburg* (2 vols.), London, 1966

Northedge, F. S., *The Troubled Giant*, London, 1966

Page, S. W. (ed.), *Lenin: Dedicated Marxist or Revolutionary Pragmatist?*, Lexington, Mass., 1970

Reed, J., *Ten Days that Shook the World*, London, 1928

Ryder, A. J., *The German Revolution of 1919*, Cambridge, 1967

Schorske, C., *German Social Democracy: 1905–1917*, Cambridge, Mass., 1955

Stansky, P. (ed.), *The Left and the War: The British Labour Party and World War I*, Stanford, 1969

Sukhanov, N. N., *The Russian Revolution 1917*, Oxford, 1955

Swettenham, J., *Allied Intervention in Russia 1918–1919*, London, 1967

Tökés, R. L., *Béla Kun and the Hungarian Soviet Republic*, Stanford, 1967

Trotsky, L. *The History of the Russian Revolution* (3 vols.), London, 1932

Trotsky, L., *Terrorism and Communism*, Ann Arbor, 1963

Tuchman, B. W., *August 1914*, London, 1962

Ullman, R. H., *Intervention and the War*, Princeton, 1961

Watt, R. W., *The Kings Depart*, London, 1969

Wheeler-Bennett, J. W., *Brest-Litovsk: The Forgotten Peace*, London, 1956

Wright, H. M. (ed.), *The New Imperialism*, Boston, 1961

Chapter V

Alliluyeva, S., *Twenty Letters to a Friend*, London, 1967

Avrich, P., *Kronstadt 1921*, Princeton, 1970

Beck, F. and Godin, W., *Russian Purge*, London, 1951

Carr, E. H., *The Bolshevik Revolution 1917-1923* (3 vols.), London, 1966

Carr, E. H., *German-Soviet Relations between the Two World Wars 1919-1939*, Oxford, 1952

Conquest, R., *The Great Terror*, London, 1968

Crankshaw, E., *Khrushchev's Russia*, London, 1959

Daniels, R. V. (ed.), *The Stalin Revolution*, Cambridge, Mass., 1965

Deutscher, I., *Stalin*, London, 1966

Djilas, M., *Conversations with Stalin*, London, 1962

Dobb, M., *Soviet Economic Development since 1917*, London, 1966

Dobb, M., *USSR - Her Life and Her People*, London, 1945

Edelman, M., *How Russia Prepared*, London, 1942

Erlich, A., *The Soviet Industrialization Debate, 1924-1928*, Cambridge, Mass., 1960

Fainsod, M., *How Russia is Ruled*, Cambridge, Mass., 1954

Foreign Languages Publishing House, *History of the Communist Party of the Soviet Union (Bolsheviks)*, Moscow, 1948

Gorbatov, A. V., *Years off my Life*, London, 1964

Karpinsky, V., *The Social and State Structure of the USSR*, Moscow, 1950

Jasny, N., *Soviet Industrialization 1928-1952*, Chicago, 1961

Joravsky, D., *The Lysenko Affair*, Cambridge, Mass., 1970

Katkov, G., *The Trial of Bukharin*, London, 1969

Kolarz, W., *Religion in the Soviet Union*, London, 1961

Kopp, A., *Town and Revolution - Soviet Architecture and City Planning 1917-1935*, New York, 1970

Lenin, V. I., *Collected Works*, Moscow and London, 1966

Lewin, M., *Russian Peasants and Soviet Power*, London, 1968

Marcuse, H., *Soviet Marxism*, London, 1968

Nove, A., *Was Stalin Really Necessary?*, London, 1964

Nove, A., *An Economic History of the USSR*, London, 1969

Nutter, G. W., *Growth of Industrial Production in the Soviet Union*, Princeton, 1962

Russell, B., *The Practice and Theory of Bolshevism*, London, 1962

Sutton, A. C., *Western Technology and Soviet Economic Development 1917 to 1930*, Stanford, 1968

Schapiro, L., *The Communist Party of the Soviet Union*, London, 1970

Sloan, P., *Soviet Democracy*, London, 1937

Solzhenitsyn, A., *One Day in the Life of Ivan Denisovich*, London, 1963

Souvarine, B., *Stalin*, London, no date

Stalin, J. V., *The Foundations of Leninism on the Problems of Leninism*, Moscow, 1950

Trotsky, L., *My Life*, New York, 1960

Trotsky, L., *On the Suppressed Testament of Lenin*, New York, 1970

Trotsky, L., *The Revolution Betrayed*, London, 1967

Webb, S. and B., *Soviet Communism: A New Civilization?*, London, 1944

Wolfe, B. D., *An Ideology in Power*, New York, 1969


CHAPTER VI

Benson, F. R., *Writers in Arms*, London, 1968

Bolloten, B., *The Grand Camouflage*, London, 1961

Bracher, K. D., *The German Dictatorship*, London, 1971

Brandt, C., *et al.*, *A Documentary History of Chinese Communism*, London, 1952; Cambridge, Mass., 1959

Brandt, C., *Stalin's Failure in China 1924–1927*, Cambridge, Mass., 1958

Calder, A., *The People's War: Britain 1939–1945*, London, 1969

Carroll, E. M., *Soviet Communism and Western Opinion, 1919–1921*, Chapel Hill, 1965

Cattell, D. T., *Communism and the Spanish Civil War*, New York, 1965

Chabod, F., *A History of Italian Fascism*, London, 1963

Ch'ên, J., *Mao and the Chinese Revolution*, London, 1965

Chesneaux, J., *The Chinese Labour Movement 1919–1927*, Stanford, 1968

Cole, G. D. H., *The People's Front*, London, 1937

Conquest, R., *The Nation Killers*, London, 1970

Crossman, R. H. S. (ed.), *The God that Failed*, London, 1950

Dallin, A., *German Rule in Russia*, London, 1957

Drachkovitch, M. M. and Lazitch, B. M. (ed.), *The Comintern: Historical Highlights*, New York, 1966

Draper, T., *American Communism and Soviet Russia*, London, 1960

Fischer, R., *Stalin and German Communism*, New York, 1948

Gilbert, M., *Britain and Germany between the Wars*, London, 1964

Gollancz, V., Strachey, J., and Orwell, G., *The Betrayal of the Left*, London, 1941

Jackson, G., *The Spanish Republic and the Civil War 1931–1939*, Princeton, 1968

Johnson, C. A., *Peasant Nationalism and Communist Power*, Stanford, 1962

Klugmann, J., *History of the Communist Party of Great Britain*, I, London, 1968

MacFarlane, L. J., *The British Communist Party*, London, 1966

McKenzie, K. E., *Comintern and World Revolution*, New York and London, 1964

Orwell, G., *Homage to Catalonia*, 2nd edn., London, 1968
Seaton, A., *The Russo-German War of 1941–45*, London, 1971
Shirer, W. L., *The Rise and Fall of the Third Reich*, London, 1960
Shulman, M. D., *Stalin's Foreign Policy Reappraised*, Cambridge, Mass., 1963
Smith, D. M., *Italy: A Modern History*, Ann Arbor and London, 1959
Snow, E., *Red Star over China*, London, 1938
Strachey, J., *The Coming Struggle for Power*, London, 1932
Thomas, H., *The Spanish Civil War*, London, 1965
Toynbee, A. J. (ed.), *The Impact of the Russian Revolution*, London, 1967
Weber, E., *Varieties of Fascism*, New York, 1964
Weinstein, J., *The Decline of Socialism in America, 1912–1925*, New York, 1967
Weintraub, S., *The Last Great Cause*, London, 1968
Werth, A., *Russia at War 1941–1945*, London, 1964
Wheeler, G., *The Peoples of Soviet Central Asia*, London, 1966

CHAPTER VII
Armine, M., *The Great Decision*, London, 1960
Churchill, W. S., *The Second World War. VI: Triumph and Tragedy*, London, 1954
Communist Party of Great Britain, *The British Road to Socialism*, London, 1951
Dedijer, V., *Tito Speaks*, New York, 1953
Dziewanowski, M. K., *The Communist Party of Poland*, Cambridge, Mass., 1959
Finkelstein, S., *How Music Expresses Ideas*, London, 1952
Fitzgerald, C. P., *The Birth of Communist China*, London, 1964
Flemming, D. F., *Cold War and its Origins*, London, 1960
Gallacher, W., *Rise Like Lions*, London, 1951
Gittings, J., *The Role of the Chinese Army*, Oxford, 1967
Hertz, M. F., *Beginnings of the Cold War*, Bloomington, 1966
Hoffman, G. W., and Neal, F., *Yugoslavia and the New Communism*, New York, 1962
Howe, I. and Coser, L., *The American Communist Party*, New York, 1958
Ingram, K., *History of the Cold War*, London, 1955
Ionescu, G., *Communism in Rumania*, London, 1964
Klugmann, J., *From Trotsky to Tito*, London, 1951
Kohler, H., *Economic Integration in the Soviet Bloc with an East German Case Study*, New York, 1965
Leonhard, W., *Children of the Revolution*, London, 1957
Loebl, E., *Sentenced and Tried*, London, 1969

London, A., *On Trial*, London, 1970
Luard, E. (ed.), *The Cold War: A Reappraisal*, London, 1964
Mao Tse-tung, *On People's Democratic Dictatorship*, Peking, 1950
Mao Tse-tung, *Selected Works* (3 vols.), London, 1954
North, R. C., *Moscow and the Chinese Communists*, Stanford, 1963
Page, B., Leitch, D., and Knightley, P., *Philby: The Spy who Betrayed a Generation*, London, 1969
Seton-Watson, H., *The East European Revolution*, London, 1956
Shannon, D. A., *The Decline of American Communism*, London, 1959
Stalin, J. V., *Economic Problems of Socialism in the USSR*, Moscow, 1952
Werth, A., *Musical Uproar in Moscow*, London, 1949
Yindrich, J., *Tito v. Stalin*, London, 1950
Zagoria, D. S., *The Sino-Soviet Conflict 1956-61*, Princeton, 1962
Zhdanov, A. A., *Essays on Literature, Philosophy and Music*, New York, 1950

CHAPTER VIII

Almond, G. A., *The Appeals of Communism*, Princeton, 1954
Aragon, L., *A History of the USSR*, London, 1962
Copeman, F., *Reason in Revolt*, London, 1948
Crankshaw, E., *Russia without Stalin*, London, 1956
Dedijer, V., *Tito*, New York, 1953
Dedijer, V., *The Battle Stalin Lost: Memoirs of Yugoslavia 1948-1953*, New York, 1971
Frankland, M., *Khrushchev*, London, 1966
Granick, D., *Management of the Industrial Firm in the USSR*, New York, 1954
Griffith, W. E. (ed.), *Communism in Europe* (2 vols.), Oxford, 1964
Hyde, D., *I Believed*, London, 1960
ILO, *Basic Law on the administration of public undertakings and associations of undertakings by the staffs employed therein*, Geneva, 1950
International Labour Office (ILO), *Workers' Management in Yugoslavia*, Geneva, 1961
Ionescu, G., *The Break-up of the Soviet Empire in Eastern Europe*, London, 1965
Kardelj, E., *Problems of Socialist Policy in the Countryside*, London, 1962
Khrushchev, N. S., *Report of the Central Committee*, London, 1956
Korbonski, A., *Politics of Socialist Agriculture in Poland, 1945-1960*, New York, 1965
Pethybridge, R., *A Key to Soviet Politics*, London, 1962
Ripka, H., *Eastern Europe in the Post-War World*, London, 1961
Schwartz, H., *Russia's Soviet Economy*, London, 1951
Seton-Watson, H., *The East European Revolution*, London, 1956

Shaffer, H. G. (ed.), *The Soviet Economy*, London, 1964
Ulam, A. B., *The New Face of Soviet Totalitarianism*, London, 1963
Zinner, P. E., *Revolution in Hungary*, New York, 1962

CHAPTER IX

Bush, C., *Religion in Communist China*, New York, 1970
Carrere, D., Encausse, H., and Schram, S. R., *Marxism and Asia*, London, 1969
Chen, N. and Galenson, W., *The Chinese Economy under Communism*, Edinburgh, 1969
Cohen, J. A. (ed.), *The Dynamics of China's Foreign Relations*, Cambridge, Mass., 1970
Crankshaw, E., *The New Cold War: Moscow v. Pekin*, London, 1963
Dawson, O. L., *Communist China's Agriculture*, New York, 1970
Donnithorne, A., *China's Economic System*, London, 1967
Eckstein, A., Galenson, W., and Liu, T., *Economic Trends in Communist China*, Edinburgh, 1968.
Fairbank, J. K., *The United States and China*, Cambridge, Mass., 1971
Fraser, S. E. (ed.), *Education and Communism in China*, Hong Kong, 1969
Gluckstein, Y., *Mao's China*, London, 1957
Hinton, H. C., *China's Turbulent Quest: An Analysis of China's Foreign Relations since 1945*, New York, 1970
Hinton, H. C., *Communist China in World Politics*, London, 1966
Hughes, T. J. and Luard, D. E. T., *The Economic Development of Communist China 1949–1960*, London, 1961
Lowenthal, R. (ed.), *Issues in the Future of Asia: Communist and Non-Communist Alternatives*, New York, 1969
MacFarquhar, R., *The Hundred Flowers Campaign and the Chinese Intellectual*, New York, 1960
Moseley, G., *China – Empire to People's Republic*, London, 1968
Pan, S. and de Jaegher, J., *Peking's Red Guard: The Great Proletarian Cultural Revolution*, New York, 1968
Price, R. F., *Education in Communist China*, New York, 1970
Robinson, J., *Cultural Revolution in China*, London, 1970
Scalapino, R. A. (ed.), *The Communist Revolution in Asia*, Englewood Cliffs, 1969
Schram, S., *Mao Tse-tung*, London, 1966
Schurmann, F. and Schell, O. (ed.), *China Readings, 3: Communist China*, London, 1968
Simmonds, J. D., *China's World: The Foreign Policy of a Developing State*, New York, 1970
Vogel, E., *Canton under Communism: Programs and Politics in a Provincial Capital, 1949–1968*, Cambridge, Mass., 1969

CHAPTER X

Amalrik, A., *Will the Soviet Union Survive until 1984?*, London, 1970

Andrews, W. G. (ed.), *Soviet Institutions and Policies: Inside Views*, New York, 1966

Barghoorn, F. C., *Politics in the USSR*, Boston, 1966

Beneš, V. L. and Pounds, N. J. G., *Poland*, London and New York, 1970

Bernard, P., *Planning in the Soviet Union*, Oxford, 1966

Boffa, G., *Inside the Khrushchev Era*, London, 1960

Brezhnev, L., *Report of the Central Committee of the Communist Party of the Soviet Union*, Novosti Press Agency, Moscow, 1971

Brown, D. R., *The Role and Status of Women in the Soviet Union*, New York, 1965

Brown, J. F., *Bulgaria under Communist Rule*, New York and London, 1970

Brumberg, A. (ed.), *In Quest of Justice: Protest and Dissent in the Soviet Union Today*, New York and London, 1970

Brzezinski, Z. (ed.), *Dilemmas of Change in Soviet Politics*, New York, 1969

Childs, D., *East Germany*, London, 1969

Conquest, R., *Russia after Khrushchev*, London, 1965

Cornell, R. (ed.), *The Soviet Political System: A Book of Readings*, Englewood Cliffs, 1970

Crozier, B., *Since Stalin*, New York, 1970

Deutscher, I., *The Unfinished Revolution*, London, 1967

Dornberg, J., *The Other Germany*, Garden City, 1968

Drachkovitch, M. M. (ed.), *Fifty Years of Communism in Russia*, University Park, 1969

Ello, P., *Czechoslovakia's Blueprint for 'Freedom'*, Washington, 1968

Fejtő, F., *A History of the People's Democracies*, London, 1971

Fischer-Galati, S. (ed.), *Eastern Europe in the Sixties*, New York, 1963

Floyd, D., *Rumania: Russia's Dissident Ally*, London, 1965

Gamarnikow, M., *Economic Reforms in Eastern Europe*, Detroit, 1968

Gehlen, M. P., *The Communist Party of the Soviet Union*, Bloomington, 1969

Granick, D., *The Red Executive*, London, 1960

Grant, N., *Soviet Education*, London, 1964

Hamilton, F. E. I., *Yugoslavia: Pattern of Economic Activity*, New York and London, 1968

Hamm, H., *Albania – China's Beachhead in Europe*, London, 1963

Harnhardt, A. M., *The German Democratic Republic*, Baltimore, 1968

Ionescu, G., *The Politics of the European Communist States*, New York, 1967

James, R. R. (ed.), *The Czechoslovak Crisis 1968*, London, no date

Kaser, M. and Zielinski, J. G., *Planning in Eastern Europe*, London, 1970
Koutaissoff, E., *The Soviet Union*, London and New York, 1971
Lendvai, P., *Eagles in Cobwebs: Nationalism and Communism in the Balkans*, New York, 1968
Madison, B., *Social Welfare in the Soviet Union*, Stanford, 1968
McCauley, M., *Labour Disputes in Soviet Russia 1957–65*, London, 1969
Miller, M., *The Rise of the Russian Consumer*, London, 1965
Nettl, J. P., *The Soviet Achievement*, London, 1967
Nove, A. and Newth, J. A., *The Soviet Middle East*, London, 1967
Robinson, V., *Albania's Road to Freedom*, London, 1941
Rush, M., *Political Succession in the USSR*, New York, 1968
Schapiro, L., *The Government and Politics of the Soviet Union*, London, 1967
Scott, D. J. R., *Russian Political Institutions*, London, 1965
Shub, A., *An Empire Loses Hope*, New York, 1970
Šik, O., *Plan and Market under Socialism*, New York, 1967
Smith, J. E., *Germany beyond the Wall*, Boston, 1969
Stehle, H., *The Independent Satellite*, New York and London, 1965
Stern, C., *Ulbricht: A Political Biography*, London, 1965
Svitak, I., *The Czechoslovak Experiment*, New York, 1971
Tatu, M., *Power in the Kremlin*, London, 1969
Vucinich, W. S. (ed.), *Contemporary Yugoslavia: Twenty Years of Socialist Experiment*, Berkeley, 1969
Werth, A., *Russia: Hopes and Fears*, London, 1969
Zartman, W. (ed.), *Czechoslovakia – Intervention and Impact*, New York, 1970
Zeman, Z. A. B., *Prague Spring*, London, 1969

CHAPTER XI

Aguilar, L. E., *Marxism in Latin America*, New York, 1968
Barcata, L., *China in the Throes of the Cultural Revolution*, New York, 1968
Childs, D., *From Schumacher to Brandt: The Story of German Socialism 1945–1965*, Oxford, 1966
Chalmers, D. A., *The Social Democratic Party of Germany*, New Haven, 1964
Cranston, M., *The New Left*, London, 1970
Debray, R., *Revolution in the Revolution?*, London, 1968
Draper, T., *Castroism: Theory and Practice*, London, 1965
Dutschke, R., *The Students and the Revolution*, Nottingham, 1970
Eisenhower, D., *Waging Peace 1956–61*, London, 1965
Fagen, R. R., *The Transformation of Political Culture in Cuba*, Stanford, 1969

Gerassi, J., *Venceremos! The Speeches and Writings of Ernesto Che Guevara*, London, 1968

Goldenberg, B., *The Cuban Revolution and Latin America*, London, 1965

Gott, R., *Guerrilla Movements in Latin America*, London, 1970

Gray, J. and Cavendish, P., *Chinese Communism in Crisis*, New York, 1968

Greig, I., *Today's Revolutionaries*, London, 1970

Hall, S., Williams, R., and Thompson, E., *1967 New Left May Day Manifesto*, London, 1967

Hsu, K., *Chou En-lai: China's Gray Eminence*, New York, 1968

Huberman, L. and Sweezy, P. M., *Cuba: Anatomy of a Revolution*, London, 1960

Hudson, G. F., *Fifty Years of Communism*, London, 1971

Jackson, B., *Castro, the Kremlin and Communism in Latin America*, Baltimore, 1969

Johnson, H., *The Bay of Pigs*, London, 1965

Lichtheim, G., *Lukács*, London, 1970

Macaulay, N., *A Rebel in Cuba: An American's Memoir*, Chicago, 1970

MacIntyre, A., *Marcuse*, London, 1970

Marcuse, H., *One-Dimensional Man: The Ideology of Industrial Society*, London, 1968

Matthews, H. L., *Castro*, London, 1969

Mehnert, K., *Peking and the New Left: At Home and Abroad*, Berkeley, 1969

Mills, C. W., *The Power Elite*, New York, 1959

O'Connor, J., *The Origins of Socialism in Cuba*, Ithaca, 1970

Oswald, J. G. and Strover, A. J., *The Soviet Union and Latin America*, New York, 1970

Petras, J., *Politics and Social Forces in Chilean Development*, Berkeley, 1969

Ruiz, R. E., *Cuba, the Making of a Revolution*, Amherst, 1968

Schlesinger, A. M., *A Thousand Days*, London, 1965

Seale, P. and McConville, M., *French Revolution 1968*, London, 1968

Sinclair, A., *Guevara*, London, 1970

Snowman, D., *USA: The Twenties to Vietnam*, London, 1968

Teodori, M., *The New Left*, London, 1970

Thomas, H., *Cuba or the Pursuit of Freedom*, London, 1971

Trumbull, R., *This is Communist China*, New York, 1968

Vega, L. M., *Roads to Power in Latin America*, New York, 1969

# Index

*Printed in Great Britain by*
*Western Printing Services Ltd.*
*Bristol*